Nell

NELL MCCAFFERTY

PENGUIN
IRELAND

PENGUIN IRELAND

Published by the Penguin Group
Penguin Ireland Ltd, 25 St Stephen's Green, Dublin 2, Ireland
Penguin Books Ltd, 80 Strand, London WC2R ORL, England
Penguin Group (USA) Inc., 375 Hudson Street, New York, New York 10014, USA
Penguin Books Australia Ltd, 250 Camberwell Road, Camberwell, Victoria 3124, Australia
Penguin Books Canada Ltd, 10 Alcorn Avenue, Toronto, Ontario, Canada M4V 3B2
Penguin Books India (P) Ltd, 11 Community Centre, Panchsheel Park, New Delhi – 110 017, India
Penguin Group (NZ), cnr Airborne and Rosedale Roads, Albany, Auckland 1310, New Zealand
Penguin Books (South Africa) (Pty) Ltd, 24 Sturdee Avenue, Rosebank 2196, South Africa

Penguin Books Ltd, Registered Offices: 80 Strand, London WC2R ORL, England

www.penguin.com

First published 2004
1

The lyrics of the Thornhill School song on page 55
reproduced with kind permission of Thornhill College.

All photos, unless otherwise acknowledged, are from
Nell McCafferty's private collection.

Set in 12/14.75 pt PostScript Monotype Bembo
Typeset by Rowland Phototypesetting Ltd, Bury St Edmunds, Suffolk
Printed in Great Britain by Clays Ltd, St Ives plc

A CIP catalogue record for this book is available from the British Library

ISBN 1–844–88012–5

To Sister Agatha and Mother Gertrude

Chapter One

When I went looking for help the head nun said, 'You might have to live with it for the rest of your life.' It was 1961. I was seventeen. I had gone first to my mother, but she, bewildered, had turned me over to my father. 'Do you use a dildo?' he asked. When he had fancied young women in his youth, he said, he exercised self-restraint, and prayed at morning mass for help in resisting temptation. One cripple to another. That's when I turned myself over to the nun I trusted, who turned me over to the head nun, who was not one bit bewildered. She did not try to convert me, did not say that I was a sinner, did not blink. She was calm and gentle and solemn. I was old enough to sense the subtlety. She could hardly say, 'Fair play to you.' She made it clear I was not to be condemned. For the rest of my life, I was to live with it. Honourably? Actively? As a martyred celibate? My parents were relieved I had been to see a holy person. They turned me over to silence and to God.

Nearly two decades later, in 1980, my father dead, I turned to my mother again. It was Christmas. I was heartbroken again. I had been living with a woman, in the home we had bought. I was about to lose my home.

'Just think of me as one of God's freaks,' I said to my mother. 'You're no freak,' she said fiercely. She was passionate about that, and full of love. She had been polishing the banisters. She sat on the stairs, exhausted. So why can't I tell the neighbours? I wanted to ask, but I didn't. The night before I had offered to go round the neighbours, and her reply was instantaneous. No, she had said. There was fear in her voice. Shame, maybe? That's how I came up with the freak thing. I was no freak, but I wasn't to talk about it either. I was thirty-six years old.

I often think of the night my mother bade me be silent. I had

I

only offered to go round the neighbours – who probably knew anyway, or had heard the rumours – because of the example that these same neighbours, and my mother, had already shown to a troubled woman who lived in our street. She was modest and burdened, so shy that she never joined the other women when they gathered round Ettie Deeney's door, in the evening, to gossip, taking a break before they tidied the house up for the night. This woman, in frail health, acted as if she hadn't done enough to deserve a break. She wasn't known for her baking or cooking; she had no scabrous tales to tell; she never gave out about her husband – and she did not even know enough to realize that she was sitting on a wonderful story about her cousin.

The cousin had married a man from Glasgow, spent a month over there and come home, tight-lipped, never to see him again. There was good-natured meat and drink in that, sneaking admir-ation, indeed, for a woman who walked smartly away from disaster, though she should have been glad that any man at all would have taken her in: the cousin was a sour, thin, shrill woman, no fun at all in her, and she ran a small shop, inherited from her parents. When officialdom arrived, she always gave her married name, though nobody else could remember the name of the man she married, it had been so long ago.

That was a story that could have borne a wondrous retelling; you'd never have tired of the angles to it. For instance, the day the man came from Glasgow to fetch her, she had run down the street, arms outstretched, calling out to him, 'Darling, darling,' as if she were in a movie. She told everybody he owned a newsagent's in Glasgow, but a fortnight after she went to Scotland they were both seen selling papers on a street corner over there, and she looked wretched. Our modest neighbour never told the story, not once in thirty years, though she went to the shop every day and lingered there to chat to the cousin. Really, it was an awful waste of a terrific tale.

On top of this woman's woes, a daughter became pregnant. She was only a schoolgirl. All the women knew about it. Sometimes, when they'd light their cigarettes, it became known that the younger females should take a walk. How we knew that, I no longer remember, but you'd just melt away while the older women turned serious. This time round, I was old enough to be allowed into their confidence, and I heard them gently mention the woman's trouble. There was nothing they felt they could do, though the odd one said, 'Jesus, I wish we could help her, the poor soul.'

Then one night, after dark, there was a knock at our front door, and it was the woman asking for my mother. She would not come in. They talked quietly on the doorstep. She was just going round all the doors, the woman said, to tell the neighbours that her daughter was pregnant. And sure what of it, and wasn't it God's will, and God love the wee girl, and if there was anything they could do, and dare anyone say a word, the neighbours said, protective and encircling. 'You hold your head up, Mary,' I heard my mother say. Then she came into the kitchen and said thank God that was over. Now that it was out in the open they could help the woman bear it, talk to her – no more of that awful silence when the woman bade people the time of day. The men nodded and took their instructions, and tipped their hats and foreheads warmly to the woman after that night. She was discreetly enveloped in affection and solidarity. The pregnant girl was to be mothered, soothed from neighbour to neighbour when she walked to school or went on an errand.

I was proud as punch of the street after that night: I lived among diplomats, people who took your cross as their own, stood with you because you were not different from them. The same would apply to me when I, too, would knock on their doors. Except that it would not.

One night a few years ago, my mother went mad, and her own secret came out of her. She had been ailing for some time, and I travelled regularly from Dublin, where I worked, to Derry, to be with her. This night, she saw malign people coming out of the wallpaper. There was also a black man seated at the foot of the bed, claiming to own her house; he had deeds to prove it, and he wanted to evict her. She suggested to me that we leave the house, go down to the bus shelter, spend the night there and leave at dawn on the first bus out to anywhere. She was so frightened that, although she could not walk unaided, she reared up in the bed and tried to force her body out of it. I had to hold her down. I soothed her, distracted her, sat by her bed for hours as night turned blacker and the hours of desolation set in.

Suddenly she asked where Brian was. Luckily, I knew who Brian was, though my mother had never uttered his name in the presence of her children. Always, in distress, she had called out loud the names of her sisters, and sometimes, albeit rarely, the names of her brothers, all of them long since dead, and heartbreakingly, she regularly asked for her mother and father. Her mother died in 1927, when she was seventeen; her father in 1935. She had been housekeeper and surrogate mother since 1927 to her father and those two brothers and one sister, all younger than her, who were still at home. The rest had emigrated or married. It had been her intention to follow Peggy to America, but her mother's death had changed all that. In her bedroom drawer, all her life, she kept – I keep it now myself – an application for a passport to America. Also included in her memorabilia is a copperplate copy of the letter from her father, a police sergeant (hence the careful copy of all documentation), to the American embassy declaring that her application was now defunct.

All her adult life, my mother was a full-time mother and home-maker, except for a brief job she had in the cinema, selling tickets. On her third day in that job, her brother Jim, aged seven, had come to the cinema looking for her. He was lonely. She went home immediately with him and never again had a paid job. Often, when her children were celebrating their latest modest progress, she would declare that she could have been somebody, too, had she emigrated to America, and not been saddled with rearing her three siblings.

'Where's Brian?' she now asked. Brian was one of her older brothers. She had written him out of history, and her brothers and sisters and her relatives and our neighbours had observed the edict. Brian did not exist. He had murdered a woman in America who

4

worked as a prostitute, been sent to jail there, and wiped out of memory.

This used to puzzle me, in the days when my mother argued with me against abortion, which I was espousing through the women's movement, through newspaper articles, and on radio and television. If all life were precious, how come Brian had been sacrificed? My mother defended most people – most Derry people, anyway. Hitler apart, all politics was local, and she would be hard pushed to condemn anyone totally. Men got swiped for domestic malfeasance; women would have had to be serial killers of their own children, and certifiably sane while they tortured those children, before she would bring herself to condemn them. During one row about abortion, she told me fiercely that she had once miscarried on the scullery floor. 'I put a newspaper down and the wain landed on it. It was a little thing, like one of those stick children in your man's paintings. The doctor said it was the most perfect specimen he had ever seen. Don't you tell me it was not a baby. It was my baby.' It was small enough that it fitted into a specimen jar in Edinburgh, where the doctor had donated it to medical science. Some days, she would laugh when I teased her about whether we had a baby sister or brother in a jar in Edinburgh.

My mother also said sometimes that if one of her grandchildren were raped and impregnated, she would go to the Pope, and she was sure he would make an exception and allow a termination. She changed my language on abortion. I never again thought of it, or talked about it, as anything less than something to do with motherhood.

Brian, though. Was he not a human being?

The night she mentioned his name, and anguished about him, he was fully human to her. There was love in her voice. She wanted to know her brother's fate. I told her that he had died in London, that I had visited his grave, that there was a headstone with his name on it and that I had placed flowers there. She fell back, relieved. He had received a decent burial, at least.

I was lying. I was delighted to bring her peace.

'How did you know about him?' she said, suddenly sane.

The letter from America, I said.

When I was about ten, a letter from America had come to the house. She had cried for days after receiving it. We had discussed this among ourselves, my three sisters, two brothers and I. Muireanna, the eldest of us, was fifteen; Nuala thirteen; Hugh eleven; Paddy eight; and Carmel, the youngest, was six and so didn't understand much. We knew a dreadful thing had happened in our house, and it was connected with the letter from America. My mother's brothers and sisters and their wives and husbands – those who still lived in Derry – came and went, and there was fear, and whispering and tears, and even my father could not bring peace to our mother.

We decided to read the letter, which was kept in a brown tin box. The box had originally held two pounds of loose tea leaves, evidence of the shabby gentility of our heritage. Most people in the 1920s bought tea by the ounce. The box of tea had been a gift from my mother's relatively wealthy Belfast Protestant relatives. Her mother, our granny, who died before we were born, had been a Belfast Protestant before she was forced to convert to Catholicism in order to marry my grandfather, the Catholic cop. He, too, died before we were born. They moved to Derry. The beautifully decorated brown tin box was part of my mother's inheritance. It contained all the important family papers – birth, death and marriage certificates, the rent book, debt books, black-and-white photographs and letters in brown envelopes. The American letter shone brightly, with its airmail logo and multicoloured stamps.

It was from a priest over there. Brian had been released from prison and was on his way 'home' to Derry. There were no details about his crime. It was a long enough letter, but none of us can remember what the rest was about. The most I knew about prison – apart from movies starring James Cagney, where the bad guy always repented before a loving Catholic priest – was that my father kept a paperback in the sitting room which none of us was allowed to read. It was the true story of a murderer called Caryl Chessman, and I think it was about sex crimes. My father always read forbidden stuff in the sitting room, which was not used except for visits from the priest, swanky guests, or private discussions between adults. In the 1950s, he retired there on Sunday afternoons to read an English newspaper called the *Empire News*. Once, I went in there and found him fast asleep in the leather armchair. The centre pages of the paper, which had fallen open on to the floor, carried headlines about a doctor and a nurse, and a cartoon showed the nurse half-undressed. The doctor had been sacked for bad behaviour. Perhaps it was in the *Empire News* that my father found out about dildos.

The American letter left us children much relieved – now at least we knew the distant cause of our mother's grief and fear. The night we were all sent to bed early, we guessed that matters were coming to a head. Silence and secrecy pervaded the house. My mother's brothers arrived, and they all convened in the sitting room. The door to the room was kept closed. We crept out of our bedrooms upstairs, put our heads through the banisters and listened. We heard nothing except the rise and fall of urgent voices. As the night wore on, we retired back to bed, weary and afraid of being caught. Next day, there was peace of a kind. Our mother's tears had stopped, anyway.

Seven years later, when I was seventeen, and still going out with the schoolgirl who had broken my heart – thus driving me to tell all to my parents and the nuns – her wealthy parents, who were businesspeople, took us for a run in their family car. Hardly anybody owned a car in 1961. Her father took golf clubs out of the boot and invited me to whack the ball about a field with him. As we knocked the ball into the far distance – I was quite good – he asked me how was my Uncle Brian? It was the first time I had ever heard Brian's name mentioned. I said that we were not supposed to know about him, but that I knew he had been released from prison. He nodded, and changed the conversation.

And that was all I knew about Brian, until I met my cousin Jimmy in America in 1972. He told me Brian had arrived in Derry, after release from prison in 1954, and been dispatched next day to London, where he spent a little time with Jimmy's parents, my mother's sister Aunt Sadie and her husband, Bill. Jimmy remembered little about it – he had been a teenager – but had the vague impression that Brian had found lodgings, and a labouring job. 'My father saw that he had a decent burial.' Jimmy knew that Brian had murdered a woman, and he vaguely thought that Brian's own father, Sergeant Duffy, had run his eldest son into exile in America in 1923 – Brian had been a policeman, too, and got into some trouble or other.

The night that my mother finally spoke Brian's name I could tell her no more than that I knew he had murdered a prostitute. A newspaper cutting about him being sent to jail had been sent to someone in Derry, in 1937, she said, and word had filtered back to her younger brother John. John had come to her in amazement. My mother was due to marry my father later that year, in July, and she suggested to him that they put off the wedding, such was the shame brought on her family throughout the town. My father would have none of it. That was the best thing I ever heard about my father, that he married the woman he loved in the midst of staggering scandal.

Brian had written several letters to my mother after going to prison. She had written and told him to stay out of their lives, which he did, until bursting back in, nearly twenty years later, via the letter from the priest. 'He thought he could just waltz back into Derry as if nothing had happened. Why couldn't he just have stayed in America?' she asked, anguished. 'He could have married somebody there.' Ah, marriage: the solution to all ills.

All her life, she said, she had worried that her children would hear about the murder. 'I worried yese would find something about the house; I cleared out everything about him,' she said. I remarked that the neighbours were great at keeping her secret, and marvelled at their generosity and compassion. She asked me again about his grave. A wonderful smile lit up her face. Her eyes, half-blind, shone in the glow coming from the streetlight. 'No more secrets,' she said. Her voice was heartfelt. She repeated the words that had finally brought her peace, at the age of ninety-one. 'No more secrets.' She was deeply happy.

I seized what I thought would be my last chance: 'Can I go and tell the neighbours now that I'm gay?' Her expression, when she turned to me, was sceptical. 'How do you know you are?' She was serious. How, indeed? The answer that flashed through my head, as I considered voicing it, brought my worst fears to the fore. Was I now to talk to my mother about sex? Not about her sex life, but my own? Was I now to talk about sexual relations with a woman? She had turned the tables on me. A lifetime flashed in front of me, of all the heterosexual friends who had never once asked me about sex between women. Had the lifetime of silence been my fault, or theirs?

I quailed and laughed nervously, and didn't answer her question. Next day, when the neighbours came in to enquire about her health, I told the older women, the ones around her age, that the story of Brian was now out in the open. I thought they would be glad that the terrible burden had been lifted off her and would feel free to speak about him. They just nodded and shrugged, and said, 'Ah, well, God love her.' They did not want to answer questions about him. I persisted. He was a good singer, one woman said. He was a trouble to his mother, another said, reluctantly. He had been working in Belfast before he went to America, another allowed. He was a good-looking fellow, tall like his father, lively . . . he was a trouble to his mother, they repeated. It occurred to me that they felt I was violating my mother's privacy and theirs; they thought she should be left in such peace as moments of clarity in her madness would allow.

That afternoon, we took her to the mental asylum. Six weeks later she was restored to full mental health. She never mentioned Brian again. Maybe the revelation died with the stroke to which, the doctors told us, the madness had been a precursor. I could not shake off or forget the refusal of the neighbours to talk about my Uncle Brian. Murdering a woman who worked as a prostitute was awful. It was the dark side of sex. Was that why my mother did not want me to tell people that I was gay? Was this, too, a dark secret?

Chapter Two

One day, a group of us children was spieling up the lampposts in the street. We often did this, imitating Tarzan, hauling ourselves up by the arms, and screwing our legs round the posts to get purchase. Then, we stopped spieling almost simultaneously, kept our unmoving arms wrapped round the posts, and continued, without climbing the posts, to move our legs up and down and in and against and around them. The sensation between my legs was soothing, and the rhythmic motion sent rivulets of pleasure through me. Every child on every post was silent, happily lost to the world. Suddenly, doors opened and our mothers came racing out, waving tea cloths with which they whipped us down to ground level. 'Get down . . . Go on away and play . . . Get down out of that.'

We knew never to screw the street lampposts again, but found another means of forbidden pleasure when a new playground was built on the field at the foot of our street, after the air-raid shelters from World War II were dismantled. Chief among the playground's delights was a giant curved 'banana' slide, standing high above the ground on thin metal stilts. You could use the metal staircase to get to the top, or spiel up the stilts. Either way, it was a dangerous enough climb for any child, but, after the amiable playground superintendent 'Big Dan' ruled that only boys should be allowed to spiel up, his eye fell on me and he said, 'Except you; you can climb anywhere you want.' The slide was far enough away that our parents could not easily spot us through the gate in the wall that separated the field from our street. As the mood took us, we spieled up faster than Tarzan, or lingered, screwing, pretending to pause for breath. This was not discussed among us. We knew not to linger when the 'big boys' – any male over ten – joined us at play.

I do not remember ever telling this at confession, which I had been attending since making my first Holy Communion in 1950, at the age of six. Sexual sin, as I understood it, consisted of impure thoughts. For instance, I was fascinated by the bulge in the crotch of Superman's tights in the comic cuts. I gazed at the hole in the bum of the tight shorts worn by a wrestler when my father took me to a wrestling match, and confessed that. Once, wandering away from the family at the seashore, I came across a fully dressed man whose leg was between the legs of a full-skirted woman beneath him. She groaned every time he flexed his leg. I hid behind rocks and watched them and listened for a long time. It was frightening and compelling, and it felt wrong to watch, and I was repulsed and fascinated by the woman's groans. The couple seemed old and ugly. Rejoining the family was a relief.

Going off to catch mackerel which leaped in their hundreds from the water round the pier, practically begging to be caught, was pure joy. There was no sin at all in that, or in most of the pastimes of our childhood. There was no fear at all in us, of people or places. Once, sunburned after a day at the beach, and unable to sleep, I got up and dressed before anyone was awake, and went walking round the city. I was slightly dazed. There were pints of milk on doorsteps and no one else about but a postman. He called me over, asked me where I lived, took me by the hand and walked me home. That was normal to us: if you were a child, people would mind you and take you home. They called you 'daughter' or 'son' or 'wee girl' or 'wee boy' or 'wain' (wee one). Decades later, two men in our area told me that they had been roundly raped as boys by two local men. So that was why, when we played, these two had often stood apart. I thought back to an occasion when one of them declined to go into the woods and kiss the girls waiting there. He had been a noticeably beautiful boy, with blond curls, and I had been glad to hang behind with him. Though I well knew by then what was different about me, I couldn't figure out what was different with him. He and the other boy had not been friends. 'We were raped together, so we stayed away from each other.'

There was a girl in our group who became increasingly nervy and high-pitched. She gradually drifted away. When she ended up a wino and street prostitute, I learned that her father used to send men over to the house to her, if they put up a drink for him in the bar. This began when she was fifteen. It was widely known among adults in our area. It was not the sort of thing you would report to a holy priest.

The lives of those of us who escaped those horrors were safely bound by the rituals of play, prayer and food, which changed with the two seasons – winter, when you went to school, and summer, when you did not. Summer was for fields, trees, street games, grottoes decorated with May flowers, new clothes for the annual religious retreats, swimming in the sea, and picking berries for jam. We roved for miles outside Derry, climbing hills and mountains, hitching lifts in tractors, and in the few cars that moved along the roads, and said hello to everyone we met. We visited places considered sacred or historical. There was a round fort called Grianan of Aileach, the oldest in Europe, which meant far less to us than the fact that its thick walls contained tunnels where animals and people were supposed to have sheltered when the fort was under attack. We scared ourselves to death crawling into them, in search of the wishing seat set far along inside its vast round bulk. Set atop a broomy hill, Grianan overlooked all of Lough Swilly, and looking backwards you could see Derry. It was a big stone cake, visible from miles around, but it was lonely. Why would anyone want to spend their lives on top of a windy mountain, keeping an eternal eye out for the enemy? It held none of the excitement of the forts into and out of which John Wayne led the cavalry. Anyway, we had our own walled city, also the oldest in Europe, and you could buy sweets in Derry, better by far after a day's play in the city than raw turnips from the fields around Grianan.

Summer was also the season for lettuce, bloody lettuce, for the salad every evening when the sun made its brief annual appearance. The only good thing about lettuce was being sent for it up to the plots, daydreaming along the green paths, actually noticing the fresh scented air, heading for Sergeant Burke's patch of tilled earth. He being a policeman like my grandfather, and having served under him, there was a feeling of privilege, a belief that he gave us the bigger, better lettuce, and a strong sense of extra protection. He lived near the top of our street. My mother always stressed that we had to buy from him. He had been taught by her father how to grow things in the garden that surrounded Sergeant Duffy's barracks.

It was comforting to be related to the police force, and not so bad to be related to the Catholic Church, which at least gave you a place where you could watch movies or do Irish dancing on becalmed, morbid Protestant Sundays when shops were ordered closed by civic ordinance. Also, the Church gave you loads of paintings, stained-glass windows and statues to look at. And, through confesssion, it gave you a clean start and a sense of purpose every Saturday morning: three Hail Marys and your soul was pure again; one round of the Stations of the Cross and you had saved hundreds of dead people from hell. An especially fervent religious retreat – two visits to church a day, by dawn and by night, for a whole week, with Jesuits roaring and everyone roused and applauding – and your special intentions would be granted. Jesus, give us a proper house, a job, a windfall of money, an exam pass, and good health to all the family. Throw in the incense, flowers, bells ringing, choir soaring, and it was the best show in town.

You look lovely, ladies, the Jesuits said, and they did, in their new frocks. You look great, men, they said, and the scrubbed men, in their suits and hats, did.

'God bless God,' said the banner strung across St Columb's Well. And so said all of us. God was our only hope in unionist Derry, and God was Catholic. Faith of our fathers, holy still, we will be true to thee till death.

Winter was for back lanes, cinema, Christmas presents, school competitions, dances, and a sight that always made my father smile: my mother standing with her back to the range, legs spread, skirt hitched up, warming her bum. From his eternal seat beside the fire, he would see the tops of her stockings and the bottom of her knickers. There was confession every Saturday, followed by mince, potatoes and baked beans, cinema in the afternoon and feet up on the sofa when we came home, while the kitchen lino which my mother had scrubbed dried under sheets of newspaper; mass and communion every Sunday, followed by roast meat; soup and potatoes on Monday; stew on Tuesday; mince and baked beans on Wednesday; spare ribs on Thursday; and fish on Friday. There were baked apples in the range when night came early and we came in cold; porridge on the glowing range when we shivered around it in the early morning chill.

From the beginning of December, choirs would come into the street to sing 'Silent Night', 'Away in a Manger' and 'Jingle Bells'. My father would bring home a fir tree, set it up in front of the sitting-room window on the wooden base made in the shipyard and stored in the attic, and drape it with fairy lights. Most houses in the street shone forth the good news. Spinster women and their bachelor brothers, of whom there were quite a few in the street, gave over their wardrobes for secret storage of toys for the children in the street. A job my father once had, delivering post around Donegal, came in handy as neighbours brought him gifts to wrap for relatives abroad. He could make up a parcel as neatly as a nurse could make up a hospital bed. The turkey, naked and raw, was an object of awe. 'You clean it out, Hughie,' my mother ordered my father. It was a horrible, fascinating operation. He pulled innards out of the bird and handed them to her. We averted our eyes. 'You stuff it, Hughie,' she said. Then, 'You sew it up.'

On Christmas morning my mother would light the range and make breakfast while my father started the day's play, setting out the boards for draughts, ludo, snakes and ladders, Monopoly. Santa always brought us exactly what we had written on the notes that we sent up the burning chimney the night before; our parents oversaw the writing. Off we'd go for first morning mass, 6 a.m. sharp, holstered and pushing prams. The baby Jesus had appeared overnight in the crib on the altar, and we tried piously to reflect that this kid had no bed and no presents, but – what would a baby know about presents? Exhausted and out of our minds with riches, we played all the way home.

There was always a linen cloth on the table for the feast; we always fought over the cauliflower in the jar of pickles. Afterwards my father sat in the sitting room, game boards at the ready, the once-a-year fire lit in the grate there, the lights of the tree winking in the mirror above the fire, a piney smell coming from its leaves. My father played to win. He once accused me of cheating, and walked out of the room. My mother called him a 'huffy jaws'. I am fairly sure I didn't cheat. I had been caught out once by Sister Agatha, and the shame never left me. I had been chosen to draw the letters on the big seasonal banners she strung about the classroom, while my lessers coloured them in. One banner read 'Chrisstmas'. I blamed the extra letter on a boy. 'Don't be stupid. You wrote the letters, not him,' she yelled at me. All that material, all that time, wasted; worst of all, her star pupil was telling a stupid lie. 'When you're wrong, you take your oil,' she said, a reference to the free, slimy cod liver oil that the British government was pouring down our throats in an effort to improve our health. 'I take my oil,' I reproached my father when he accused me of cheating. I felt strongly about this because he had always taught me that cheating proves nothing. 'Anybody can cheat. How many people have the brains to win by being the best?' he would recite like a mantra. Then again, how many fathers get tired on Christmas day coping with children who just want to play, play, play? Christmas night always ended with my father, a member of the local church choir, singing 'Jerusalem'.

Beechwood Street is a hilly terrace of twenty-six houses. At the top of the street is the Lone Moor Road, which forms the outer boundary of the Bogside. Cross the road, continue on up the hill and you'd be in Donegal, on the other side of the border, in fifteen minutes. Ireland was fine, but Beechwood Street was best, especially the day my father climbed the smooth high wooden telegraph pole at the foot of it – a death-defying feat – and hung a tricolour from it. It was 1951, and Eamon de Valera, whoever he was, was coming. All I knew was my father was the best climber in the world. In my whole life, I never attempted to climb that pole. There is a forty-foot drop from its height to the ground.

All the houses were faced with grey concrete, which gave the street a solid, unchanging feel. The houses were furnished in stone, iron, linoleum, brass and wood. We lived in number eight, fourth from the bottom of the hill. The brown varnish on our front door was renewed regularly by Mr Carlin from Elmwood Street, who also repapered the rooms. When he arrived to redecorate there was a feeling of luxury, of all being well in our world. Unlike the other houses, the hallway in ours was half wood-panelled, and there were brass stair rods, features of which my mother was inordinately proud. The piano in the sitting room spoke of refinement, as did the bookcase there, all of its shelves filled with hardback tomes on flora and fauna inherited from my grandparents, and paperback classics, and the novels we gradually accumulated from the school curriculum, as well as a dictionary. The leather suite of sofa and two armchairs was particularly luxurious.

The kitchen was where we lived. There was an armchair by the fire where my father always sat, a sofa, and a drop-leaf table and chairs, and a sewing machine. The black-leaded, brass-trimmed range, glowing day and night, was a massive, majestic source of power. A clothesline was strung over it. The portrait of the Holy Family, gentle and smiling, and hung above the holy-water font, established our priorities. My mother has always been fond of St Joseph. He was a carpenter. Sure, you couldn't go wrong if a husband had a trade and respect for his wife.

The 'master' bedroom was dominated, and still is, by a huge, beautiful, sombre print of Mary returning from Calvary. The frame of the picture is ornately wrought walnut. 'My father gave me that picture as a present for my twenty-first birthday. Why would he give me that for a present?' my mother said angrily when she was ninety-two and reviewing her life.

Of the twenty-six houses on the street, three were occupied by elderly unmarried sisters and their brothers, one by an unmarried aunt and her unmarried niece, and seven by some combination of grannies and granddads and their unmarried daughters and sons – and of those seven houses, three had many children, from wherever they came. Apart from the grandparents, we addressed all these single women and men by their first names. Anybody who was married was called 'Missus' or 'Mister'. The distinction between first name and titles meant nothing to us, though we knew to make them when addressing adults. There was a married woman in the next street, however, whom we always addressed by her first name, though her husband lived with her. I realize now that it was because she was dirt poor. We used her back yard with impunity for storing up rubbish for the annual August bonfire. Branches of trees, broken furniture, anything at all that could burn was shoved into it. That was one way for her children to acquire status: they took our rubbish once a year; we gave them respect once a year. I cheered as an adult when word sped around that the eldest son of the family had leaped over the wall, married a Protestant, and moved into the Protestant redoubt, the Fountain. He got a job to go with it.

In our own street were also families that were poor – because of the huge number of children. The boys of one house would collect leftover food, called 'brock', for pigs. They pushed their foul-smelling cart up and down the hilly streets of the neighbour-hood. One of them became a millionaire. In another household, the mother was fined for stealing food from a shop. It was reported in the newspaper. The street waited for the woman's husband to come home. He could read; she could not. Her children poured out the door as the battering started. We could all hear the screams. The women of the street never again greeted the man when he stood at his front door, though the men of the street continued to salute him.

Those women who had paid jobs worked in the shirt factories, returning home at dinnertime to prepare and cook the midday meal for their mothers, men or children. The men worked as shop assistants, postmen, labourers, in the bookies, in coal yards, the slaughterhouse, and as skilled factory hands. My father was one of the two males who had a clerical job: he was employed by the British admiralty as a storehouse clerk. The McBreartys, at the foot of the street, were the exception to all: not only was none of them married, but the brothers had a coal and coffin business, and the sisters were in the civil service or professional jobs. Most importantly, Nurse McBrearty was a midwife and delivered all the babies in the street. No child dared play ball games against their gable wall. Keeping themselves mostly to themselves, they seldom had any news to impart, though, having listened to neighbours take telephone calls in their kitchen, they did not hesitate to enquire what was going on; they had a phone years and years before anybody else. Nurse McBrearty's relative silence was considered to be discretion. She had a dead swanky, gentle voice. It was a great and reassuring thing, to have the next best thing to a doctor living in the street.

It was just as good having shirt-factory workers, who brought imperfect goods back to the street at a reduced price. 'Put that up against your chin, Hughie,' Annie used to say to my father, holding the checked shirt against his chin. She and my mother would grin and tease him about how well he looked. 'You wouldn't even notice it,' my mother would say about the invisible imperfection. 'Sure, blue is nice on you,' Sadie would chuckle, though blue shirts were rare in black-and-white-and-grey Derry.

Technicolor came to Beechwood Street in the 1950s in the form of Billy Browne, a thirteen-year-old American. He was borne around by his cousins like a trophy, but though he was actually staying in the next street, Tyrconnell Street, he opted to play in ours, and so we had our own Hollywood matinée idol. He wore multicoloured lumberjack shirts, blue jeans with turn-ups, and – we had never seen one before – a white T-shirt. All the Derry boys wore vests for warmth; leisure clothing was unknown then in the Bogside. Billy had height and muscle. He had tanned skin and big, blindingly white, perfect teeth. His accent was straight out of the movies. Surprisingly, he did not chase girls; he played with both boys and girls. He was as unthreatening as the houses in which we lived. When he lay on the pavement with us, reading comics, I would look up from the comics and gaze at him – he was the image of the very fellows we were reading about.

How glad they must have been, my parents, that their children liked to read. Well, not always actually read – on rainy days we would take down the great books that Sergeant Duffy had put in the bookcase, and pass the time colouring in the 'a's and 'o's and 'b's. On Thursdays, we were absorbed in the comic cuts that were ordered for us in Barr's shop, and were allowed to read them over dinner. One of the big thrills of my life was joining the library. It was situated in Brooke Park, a huge, sombre green place associated with Protestants, though on the edge of the Bogside. Nobody actually played in it. There was a man in charge to make sure we didn't disturb the enormous goldfish that flashed in the stark ornamental pond beside the library. If a thing wasn't fun, it was Protestant. Our own playground superintendent Big Dan never had to worry about greenery and goldfish, of course, because there weren't any in his concrete concourse.

The library was a place of wonderment. All them books and you could borrow three a week. The silence inside was a sacred thing. I used to hold my breath as I perused the titles. I remember snuggling into the leather sofa, in the sitting room – the most private room in our house – all alone, reading *The Secret Garden*, for which I had abandoned a summer afternoon's play, stupefied with pleasure and barely able to breathe. It was just getting to a good part when my mother came in from her after-dinner chat with the neighbours. 'You'll lose your eyesight reading so much. Get out and enjoy God's good fresh air.' She insisted upon it. I still read in the way I did then. Edna O'Brien looked at me in blank astonishment once when I babbled to her that I'd held my breath for three pages of her novel *In the Forest*. Not being a literary critic, it was the highest compliment I could think of.

Somewhere around the age of eight, when taking part in the city's annual Christmas pantomime, I developed a crush on the Principal Boy, who was of course a woman. If I feigned illness, she would take me on her knee and hold me to her bosom backstage, until a parent arrived to take me home. Being a 'delicate' child, suffering from rheumatic fever and occasional asthma, I sank every night, in her arms, into a miasma of happiness. Anyway, I was a star, wasn't I? The leader of a platoon of soldiers. It was my job to save the others by shooting a crocodile. 'Never smile at a crocodile,' I warbled, finishing off the song and the crocodile simultaneously by going down on one knee and shooting the beast with my rifle. A stagehand was supposed to fire a blank pistol offstage, to coincide with my gallant finale. One night, he forgot, and I had to shout, 'Bang-bang.' I knew this was idiotic. The Principal Boy was most consoling.

I was not generally drawn to females. My preferred companions were boys – usually boys who were outside the flock. Joe was my best pal. He lived across the street. He was an only child, and his father was not around. His mother was a ramshackle woman who lived in a ramshackle house and did not exercise authority. She had a booming laugh. She gave us big pieces of bread and jam. There was no home cooking in her house such as I was used to in mine, where there was always apple tart, or scone bread, or boil cake.

Joe did not have the playthings that the rest of us had. He had no father from whom to borrow a working-man's bicycle, no football bought for a whole tribe of sisters and brothers. When I was confined to bed with rheumatic fever, and he wandered up to keep me company in the bedroom, he played for hours with my toys. We did not need toys in the street, however, for Joe was inventive and daring. We hardly talked; he thought of something to do, and we went off and did it.

One day there was a tractor at the foot of the street, parked just round the corner, at the gable end of a house which had a barn in its back yard. The tractor was unusual; the barn was not. In my mother's youth, people kept pigs, some dairy cows, and chickens in the houses on the other side of our street, which had much bigger back yards. In my youth, farmers from Donegal drove their animals through our streets, en route to the great market in Rossville Street, which abutted the city centre, thence to Britain via the Scotch boats which steamed between Derry and Scotland, carrying animals for sale and Irish people for hire. There was hay in the barn outside which the tractor was parked. Joe climbed up and sat on the seat; I climbed up and stood beside him. The farmer had left the keys in the ignition. Joe switched the engine on, and we were away. The vehicle zigzagged in a semicircle, Joe pulled uselessly at the wheel, and we crashed into the wall of the barn. Hay came tumbling out. It was great. I don't remember the aftermath, except that we were forbidden to use the barn where we had sometimes hidden in the hay, high up above the road, using elastic bands to shoot paper pellets at passers-by.

When we removed the grating in the gutter, and used a weighted hook to fish for wealth, a passing fellow kicked me in head first, and Joe pulled me out. When we played marbles, we cleaned out everybody else, and drew with each other. We were really skilled at this game, and other children, when they were knocked out, with no money left to buy their marbles back from us, stood on to admire our contests. When gangs played cowboys and Indians, Joe roamed so far and wide, me following, that we often ended up in the city centre, the game forgotten, dashing into the cavernous loading bay of Stephenson's Bakery, where we found stray buns in emptied delivery vans. Men roared, but we were not caught, and the stolen meal was delicious.

Teeming tenements and slums, built directly beneath the city walls, attracted and frightened us. Hordes of people went in and out the same front door. The hallways were dark. There were low, deep arches leading into crammed courtyards. These people, we knew, were poorer than us. Beggar women walked about, wrapped in shawls. Men stood in the street, cap in hand, and sang, hoping for coins. Other men sold bundles of sticks, kites and newspapers. Smoke poured from chimneys. The children of these houses were skinnier than us, and had more sores about their mouths, and bigger snotters running down their faces.

I did not know then that my father's people grew up in the worst of these slums. His mother was a shirt-factory worker from Walker's Place; his father a tailor from Wapping Lane. They married in 1887, and prospered to the extent that they set up a second-hand clothes shop in Waterloo Street, the main Catholic shopping thoroughfare outside the Walls. The hilly top of Waterloo Street, which merged with the hilly top of Fahan Street, formed the apex of a triangle that led directly through Butcher's Gate into the walled city. This was the gate that the Protestant Apprentice Boys closed in 1690, to keep out the Catholic King James of England, who had made his camp in the Bogside. My father's people travelled out of the Bogside to Scotland for the clothing, going over by ship on the Scotch boat, bringing it back to the Bogside and tailoring it, if necessary, for resale. My father's mother, Mary McCafferty, was known for the beautiful quilts she made from rags. She died before I was born, as did all my grandparents. My father's sister Kathleen took over the shop, and her daughter Mona opened a second outlet across the street, while her other daughter Dola married a watchmaker and they set up a jeweller's shop next door to Aunt Kathleen. Having three rich relatives in Waterloo Street was handy for an escape should Joe and I feel threatened in Fahan Street. If my father's people were rich compared to us, my mother would quip, her side of the family was the shabby genteel, being related to police and Protestants. All the same, it was magic to enter my Aunt Kathleen's sitting room one Saturday afternoon to watch England play football on a black-and-white television, one of the few sets in Derry in the 1950s. We sat on the floor at my father's feet, entranced. She remained in the front downstairs room, which served as her shop. 'If there's a penny to be made in Waterloo Street, I'll make it,' she used to say.

For all his nerve, Joe did not climb the steps at Butcher's Gate and go up on to the wide walkway provided by Derry's Walls. We associated the gate's name with the fate of Catholics. James's Catholic troops had been butchered there, we believed. Everything inside the Walls comprised the city proper, owned by unionists, and everything outside comprised the Bogside, where Catholics lived. Once a year, Orangemen paraded round the Walls, looking down at us Catholics, sometimes throwing pennies, loudly celebrating the victory of Orange Protestant King William of Holland over Catholic King James.

For the rest of the year, the Walls, which are about a mile in circumference and afford magnificent views of Derry, were virtually deserted. On a Sunday, the city within the Walls being closed for the Protestant Sabbath, they were particularly lonely, with church bells clanging and mourning. A tour of the Walls would bring you past the inner sanctum of the Protestant ruling class: the courthouse, the huge Church of Ireland cathedral and its cemetery, the tiny Presbyterian church and cemetery, the Gothic Apprentice Boys' Hall, the Masons' Building, the City of London Gentlemen's Club, the Protestant Bishop's palace – and not a place for a cup of tea, or a bag of chips, or an ice cream or a bottle of lemonade. Sometimes, when I went to Aunt Nellie's crooked little house in Stable Lane, within the Walls, I'd venture down with her only child, Desmond, to the walkway at the foot of her street, and we'd scare the life out of ourselves. There was a Protestant children's primary school there, and we believed that if you bent down to the ground-level window, which gave on to its basement, and called out, a Protestant ghost would call back. Which it did, given the echo. There were cannon guns there, aimed right into the Bogside. If you kicked a football and it went over the Walls into the Bogside below, a drop of twenty feet, and went on rolling down the hill, you'd never get it back.

Within the walled city there was one place where we could relax. The name of my father's brother Joe was inscribed on a tablet of iron at the War Memorial in the Diamond, the crossroads of the four streets that bisect the inner city. He died at the Somme in World War I, aged sixteen. The memorial therefore belonged to us as naturally as the cinemas where Aunt Nellie and Uncle Jimmy worked – except on Remembrance Sunday, 11 November, when unionists gathered there to lay wreaths and play 'God Save the Queen' in honour of all those who laid down their lives for king and country, meaning Britain. That was not what Joe was doing, we knew. It was an exciting job in hard times, and he ran away with a group of pals to join the army and get into a battle with anyone at all. Above the panel bearing Uncle Joe's name is a cast-iron statue of a barefoot soldier, rifle and bayonet at the ready, teeth clenched in the face of adversity. We tickled the soldier's toes, ran our fingers over Joe's name and raced on to the cowboys-and-Indians movies.

On winter nights, Joe and I took to the back lanes, climbing walls in the dark, sitting there like cats, in silence, watching families move about their kitchens. Once we saw a man strike a woman. We took it upon ourselves to dismantle the remains of the World

War II air-raid shelter at the foot of our street, patiently using chisels to chip the concrete slabs away from the iron rods that bound them, and packing the rods into a flour sack to sell at the rag-and-bone merchants down on the Lecky Road. A week's work after school could earn you the price of the matinée on a Saturday afternoon. We were proud to save our parents the money. As I grew older, and my parents did not go to the movies together so often, I got into the movies for nothing, using the free weekly passes given as perks to my Uncle Jimmy, who worked as a doorman in the Strand cinema, and to my Aunt Nellie, who worked as assistant to the manager in the Rialto and sometimes in the box office.

There was one movie which assuaged any fears I might have had that, being a tomboy, I was other than a totally normal girl. When Doris Day played Calamity Jane, wearing buckskin trousers, toting a six-gun and singing love songs, I felt totally at ease in my skin. That was the year, 1953, when I was selected out of all the children in the area to ride a horse through the streets in the local carnival. Sam Campbell, who also kept the big pig in his barn, provided the mount. I had my own cowboy outfit, renewed every Christmas, and wore my father's broad-brimmed Sunday hat.

When Joe's mother died he was sent to live with his aunt in the next street. It was another country. We never played together again. I was around eleven then, and attending the girls' grammar school, absorbed in books and crushes on senior girls. Thirteen years later – I was a university graduate and had just returned from my world travels – there was a knock on my mother's front door. There stood Joe, who had left town as a sixteen-year-old. He had an album of classical music for me. He told me that he worked his way round fun fairs and holiday camps in England, drifting. When I asked how he knew I loved classical music, he just gazed at me. I never saw him again. My mother told me after Joe's last visit that his mother had become pregnant in World War II by an American serviceman. Her parents took her to the camp, seeking justice, and many soldiers claimed knowledge of her, and the camp commander shrugged his shoulders. This was deeply unfair, my mother said. Joe's mother had only ever been with one man, briefly, and there was 'a wee want in her', a gentle phrase that meant that she was educationally subnormal. She was an only child, and her parents died soon after, and she had little enough money to live on.

Jimbo succeeded Joe as my pal. His hair was much more tightly curled into his head than mine, and this, for some reason, marked him as a socially inferior sort. It did not help that he came from a huge family, and his parents were poor enough, and sometimes the police were called to the house to sort out rows. Jimbo could turn cartwheels and shared my love of comic cuts. We discovered a little shop where the man bought second-hand comic books for a halfpenny and another shop, even smaller, where the man sold second-hand comic cuts for a halfpenny. So Jimbo and I sold our comic cuts for a halfpenny to one man, and used the coin to buy another magazine from the other. The enterprise involved a certain amount of hard work. On Saturdays we went to Sam Campbell's field, adjoining nearby Limewood Street, to read our comics. When we had both finished reading, one of us used my father's bicycle to negotiate the ruts and bumps of the path across the field that had been made by the huge pig that lived there, ride up and down Derry's hilly streets, and sell and buy comics in the two shops we had discovered. The whole business of reading, cycling, selling and buying might take two hours from start to finish. The person left behind in the field would study the pig.

Jimbo left school early and went to England. While I was at university, I took a summer job in the English coastal resort of Great Yarmouth, where I ran a small lunch diner along with the cook. On the beachfront one afternoon I saw a sign which declared that a daredevil called Jimbo would dive off the pier every evening and defy the killer eel. I just knew it was him. After his performance, he was slightly embarrassed to see me. He was skinny and poorly dressed. His ambition was to become a stunt man in the movies, and Yarmouth had many show-biz connections. I gave him a free lunch every day for weeks, and he bought me an initialled tin cigarette case. We went to see a show starring a singer-cum-funny-man called Des O'Connor, planning an introduction for Jimbo, but our nerve failed at the backstage door. Jimbo did not return to the restaurant, and I knew not to seek him out again. Years later, his photograph was shown on a television programme which sought to reunite people with the relatives they had not contacted in ages. It was no use.

Every Tuesday night, my mother would visit Aunt Maureen, another full-time mother. Aunt Maureen made egg-and-onion sandwiches, and she always splashed out on store-bought pastries, a wildly extravagant gesture, to supplement my mother's apple cake. After the Rialto cinema closed, they would be joined by Aunt Nellie, who had only one child. Their three husbands, and their sons, never joined these gatherings. Just as age determined how much of the talk outside Ettie Deeney's door you were allowed to hear, so it determined if I and my sisters and my cousins were allowed to sit in on our mothers' conversation. If the gossip, elevated to an art form on these nights, was too hot or serious for the girls, we knew to leave the room. There was never an order to leave, just a curt direction to 'Go and get the tea ready', or 'Go and teach a new word to the budgie'; the budgie was kept in the sitting room. Over the years, we learned to intuit when each girl could ignore this and remain sitting in on the chat of the matriarchs.

We were at the hub of a social wheel that had many spokes. The women ranged widely on each topic: jobs, housing and health, the weekly budget, relationships within an astonishingly extended family. When Aunt Nellie arrived, we learned who sat with whom in the back seats of the cinema, whether they sat in the much more expensive balcony, and whether the male treated the female to ice cream, soft drinks or chocolates, or – ye gods – all three.

There was a woman in our town, famed for her terrifically good looks, dashing sense of fashion and devil-may-care attitude to men. Her husband was in England, her children with her, and she frequently took up with male consorts. One night, we heard, she had sat in the back row of the balcony with a young man under twenty years of age; she was over forty. He was a champion Irish dancer, though the sight of men in pleated skirts, flashing bare legs and battering the floor with their steel-tipped shoes, was not then considered a turn-on.

The matriarchs allowed themselves a grin at the sheer cheek, glamour and defiance of the Rita Hayworth of Derry; women were never condemned at our gatherings. The dancer surely did not earn enough to hand money up to his own mother for his keep and also keep Rita in the price of weekly balcony tickets and the full gamut of treats, but – hell rub it into him, if he wanted the glory of Rita's company, he should pay the expense of it. There was a distinct sense of two cheers for Rita. Her doings provided a defiantly happy spectacle in a town where divorce was unheard of, marital separation consisted of the man spending most of his time working in England, unremitting pregnancy was a nightmare and most women were in aprons, rather than skirts slit to the thigh. There was a definite affection for her. Her children never missed a day of school, and they were always well turned out, like their mother.

At this time all movies deemed racy were subject to a film censor, who was aided and abetted in his deliberations by elected members of the all-male town council. These pillars of public society, Catholic and Protestant, and their invited guests, turned up to a man to special late-night showings of movies of ill repute, and my mother and Aunt Maureen calmly took their seats among them, courtesy of Aunt Nellie. One night they all viewed a documentary about childbirth, which showed actual labour and delivery. The men's toilets, Aunt Nellie reported afterwards, were full of vomit. This was a cause of righteous satisfaction at our next Tuesday-night gathering.

Sometimes, before her husband, Jim, arrived home – 'I have to get to bed to get up for work in the morning,' he would talk up his male status – Aunt Maureen would sing a song. She had a fine high voice, and the looks of a flamenco dancer, all long, dark curls and make-up and earrings. 'Love's Old Sweet Song' and 'Silver Threads among the Gold' were her favourites. If Jim, my mother's youngest brother, whom she had raised since he was an orphaned boy, had quietly enjoyed himself too well at the pub while the women talked, my mother would assert her status and censor him with a glance. Uncle Jimmy, who never drank, arrived to escort Aunt Nellie home – she lived within the walled city among the Protestants, and it was usually deserted and gloomy, whereas my mother felt safe to saunter through the Bogside with her daughters.

One night passed into legend. Aunt Nellie had brought her dog, Pal, along, Jimmy not being available for escort duty. He always stayed in the kitchen, which Aunt Maureen hated, as Nellie made more of a fuss of him than was considered suitable for an animal. However, he was wont to pursue the budgie if let into the sitting room. The gossip that night must have been great because nobody missed Pal until it was time to go home. Nellie called out his name. There was no response. Maureen called out the budgie's name. He did not reply. Dawning horror filled the silence. Pal pranced in, yellow feathers hanging from his mouth. Aunt Nellie went home crying. After expressing due condolence my mother laughed all the way home, water streaming out of her eyes. She had no time for either the budgie, Joey, a useless pet, or Pal, a spoiled dog. 'I never knew Pal had it in him,' she chortled. 'Pal Joey.'

In the summer, my mother and Aunt Maureen communicated daily by means of sending a child from one house to the other with a written message, discussing the prospect of a day trip to the seaside. Everything depended on whether my mother's brother John, a bus conductor, was on the Derry–Buncrana run that day. If he was, we were sure he would turn a blind eye to the masses of ticketless children who accompanied my mother and Maureen. The written notes were always terse and to the point:

MOTHER: Will we go to Buncrana?
MAUREEN: Yes, but can you lend me a tanner . . . Shilling?. . . Yes, I'll make the egg-and-onion sandwiches . . . Yes, but I can't go till three o'clock.

These days were always tense to begin with. We would arrive at the bus stop, join the inevitably long queue and, if Uncle John did not lean out the door of the bus when it arrived, demur and usher others forward. When he was on board, the children – usually about twelve in number – were instructed to scatter themselves between the upper and lower decks, and cling to other people's mammies if an inspector came aboard. The lucky ones sat with our mothers, depending on how many tickets they could afford to buy.

In Buncrana, we were warned not to whinge, cry or look for things as we made our way to the shore past shops filled with buckets and spades and sweets. Our mothers parked themselves amid a nest of rocks at the foot of a cliff face. We swam within their eye-line, disappeared over to the pier to look at the boats and fishermen and mackerel shoals, if any had come in to feed, made sandcastles and moats, searched for crabs in rock pools, climbed the cliff, and tried to make ourselves scarce when it came time to go for hot water to make the tea. We had to carry an empty can up the cliff, knock on the door of a woman who charged sixpence for filling and heating the can of water, wait about, and bring it back down. The egg-and-onion sandwiches were strictly for the women; the rest of us gorged on jam and bread and biscuits and lemonade, and a sneaky slurp out of our mothers' cups if we were adjudged blue in the face from too much time spent in the Atlantic waters of Lough Swilly. Aunt Nellie and her son, Desmond, joined us on Sundays when she wasn't working. So did Aunt Mary, with her large brood; being John's wife, Mary could travel practically at will through Donegal on reduced-price tickets.

When my father and Uncle Jim sometimes joined us around sunset, their day's work done in Derry, there would be a shiver of apprehension. Two of the girls would be selected to take off their big navy-blue knickers and loan them to the men for a late-evening swim. When the men were finished, the victims would have to put on the damp underwear. 'Our daddies were the first cross-dressers,' cousin Geraldine remarked years later.

On a great day, if we had lingered late at the beach and the women were in funds, our mothers would bring us to the fish and chip shop, pack us into one booth and order several – but never sufficient unto our number – plates of chips. Once, when there were more forks than children, a head count showed that I was missing. A stranger had retrieved me from the beach and brought me to the police station, where I was found happily consuming biscuits and a glass of milk.

On an adventurous day, we would shamble to the back beach, over the arched stone bridge below which salmon leaped, past the ruined castle, along leafy lanes and down on to a more deserted shore. We were invariably dispatched – 'Go away and give us head peace' – to Father Hegarty's rock, which jutted in the distance. The way there lay through a path overhung with ferns and wild flowers. Legend had it that Father Hegarty was trapped on the rock by British soldiers, as he said a forbidden mass during penal times. He was beheaded and flung into the sea. There were holes on the rock's surface where his head had bounced, one, two, three – seven times in all – before falling into the sea. If you looked carefully you could find his footprint. Through such stories we came to understand that the Irish Catholics of old had a dreadful time under the British, before the Republic gained its independence.

Once, in my childhood, when my Aunt Peggy returned from New York, we had a 'Big Night'. She had not been home for thirty years. There was a gathering in my mother's house, which ended up out in the street with children, neighbours, friends and relatives banging saucepans, singing and dancing. She brought dollars, tales, tears and joy. Uncle Joe had lost a great deal of money when the movie he was showing at the cinema he ran was picketed and banned by the Catholic Church. She herself had been courted by Captain Van Houten, who had made a fortune out of chocolate-covered bars of coconut, and he bought rings for her toes, she told us children, but she loved for ever her Joe. We absolutely believed her. She dismantled and cleaned my mother's cooking oven, a great feat, for which she was much admired. She bought us a new sofa. She made her living shovelling coal on the railroad. She was tall and loud and wisecracking, and we adored her salty language that goddamned every son of a bitch who ever crossed her. My mother revelled in her company.

Nobody could compete with her dollars. I was well grown before I realized that she hadn't had the money to bring her husband and two sons with her. What the women left behind in Derry could offer her was an array of home-baked buns and cakes. Trays of these confections, covered in tea cloths, held proudly high in both hands, were borne through the streets. When they were spotted coming, we would abandon our games and rush home. Aunt Mena's tea cakes were covered in hard icing and dried fruit; Aunt Vera specialized in cream filling; Aunt Nellie (who couldn't bake) procured home-made toffee from a Protestant neighbour; and my mother countered with apple pies and scone bread.

The women always exchanged gifts of food, Aunt Peggy or no. This was deeply reassuring, given the notices posted in all the shops that war rationing would end in 1952. Tea and butter and sugar were officially scarce, and coupons had to be produced when buying them, but the problem was solved by simply walking across the border on Sunday mornings, an uphill distance of about four miles, which my father accomplished easily, and 'smuggling' the necessary goods back from a border trader who operated out of a structure known as the Black Hut. The habit persisted even after rationing was abolished because cigarettes were cheaper in the Republic, and as we grew big enough to slog along with him the entire family would make the excursion to the Hut. It became a Sunday-afternoon ritual for our family and others: the trek out of the city, the stop for a drink of fresh spring water at a dark bend in the road known as Hell's Kitchen and, before we went home, the ritual visit to the Stone Man, a mound of bricks atop the gorse-covered Hollywell Hill, overlooking the Hut. We were told that Eddie McAteer, our member of the provincial Stormont parliament, always placed a stone on the mound when he went up there, and prayed for a United Ireland. The higher the mound, the closer his chance of achieving this. It never seemed to grow much. The gorse scratched our legs. The mystery of the smallness of the Stone Man endures. Later, the IRA used the hill to bury its weapons, the British army sowed dragon's teeth to block the IRA's passage, and the path has long since been closed off by a farmer.

On the journey home, my father indulged his fondness for order, much to our chagrin. He liked military formations, and he wanted his children (and nephews and nieces, if they were there) to walk abreast, or in step, and always in front of him so that he could keep an eye on us. Once, when he ordered us not to jump on and off the low walls that divided gardens in the newly rising Creggan estate – the houses crept ever closer to the border as Catholic Derry expanded – my brother Hugh turned to me and said, 'What a miserable life. I hate me da. Do you?' On the other hand, he made walks interesting by asking us to memorize and spell the names of streets, and telling us the origins of their names. The names of the older streets were associated with the British Empire and its wars – Wellington Street, Nelson Street, Blucher Street – and those of the Creggan – Fanad, Leenan – with yearning for what we had lost through partition.

When our fathers were not present, our mothers took us on different excursions entirely, up to the nearby cemetery, which lay between the Bogside and Creggan. There, we learned to spell the names of people and heard their life stories. The cemetery was fairly evenly split in two: the Protestants on one side with their great tombs and high crosses, the Catholics on the other with engraved kneeling stones – or low tombstones if such could be afforded. In later years, the IRA used the Protestant tombs to store weapons. In my childhood, we could only marvel at the wealth these tombs represented, and the titles that preceded the names engraved on them, and the professional letters after the names, the meaning of which we could only guess at. The Catholic titles were easily deciphered. Everyone was RIP, including, Mrs Barber pointed out, a maid called 'Anno Domino', whom a family had kindly buried in their plot.

The cemetery was an outdoor garden for us who had none, in front or back of our houses, though my parents always had a small strip of soil opposite the coal house, in which they grew a rose bush and orange lilies. The lilies had been a present from one of my Aunt Nellie's Protestant neighbours, and my father had bought the rose bush, which was fertilized by manure dropped from the milkman's horse. My mother regularly snipped a cutting from the fabulous rose garden in the cemetery, smuggling it home under her coat – it gave her enormous satisfaction to steal something from the unionist-dominated local council, which refused to build houses for Catholics – but the cuttings never took, and her strip of earth often comprised more horseshite than soil. The cemetery is clothed in trees at its boundaries, and the tombscape is nobly pierced with yew trees, its crown surmounted by a weeping willow. It affords marvellous views of the river Foyle, the hills of Donegal, the great city walls, and Saturday-afternoon football matches in the Brandywell football ground directly beneath, if the police prevented us children climbing over the walls into the stadium. There was no gloom on this hill of death, as the women judiciously doled out sweets and stories, and looked with hope at the foundations of the new Creggan estate being laid on the hill above. One day there would be houses there, with indoor toilets and bathrooms. One day we'd raise engraved stones to our dead relatives. Meantime, we could gather under the weeping willow and sing Fats Domino's 'Blueberry Hill'. We, too, would find our thrills, we sang hopefully.

Chapter Three

Between the ages of six and ten, when I was not out playing with boys, I spent a lot of time ill with rheumatic fever, a murmur in the heart, and asthma. Usually, I had to spend six months a year in bed, 'resting', though I do not remember feeling ill at all. I do remember a period of going to the infirmary every week to stand in my knickers, wearing protective goggles, in front of a machine which glowed blue, but that was dead exciting. I felt like Superman. My mother tells me that I used to come in from playing, lie down on the sofa and gasp for breath – and yet I was always among the first picked to play in any team games. When I was abed, Joe came to visit every day, and we took turns using my father's good hat to play cowboys. The nurse came daily as well, to inject my bum, with what I do not know. This scarcely mattered, as she was gorgeous, with a heap of dark, curly hair.

I don't remember feeling sorry for myself, apart from that day once a year when we'd return from a check-up visit to the doctor and my mother would send me upstairs to bed. Sweets and books and games would follow, I knew, to entertain me through the incarceration. There were heaps of comic cuts from the American relatives to read. On Friday nights, while the other children had to make do with one supper of fish and chips between them, I was given a fish dipped in batter all to myself. It was a nice life, reading and eating and talking and learning games and being petted. Missing the first and third of five years at primary school affected my learning not one bit. I was always top of the class when I returned.

One night, the neighbours came in to hold a special party for me. They were solemn, which was puzzling, given the great time I was having as they crowded round the bed, pressing sweets and holy medals into my hands. A priest came, the newly ordained nephew of a relative, and blessed me. People spoke in hushed tones, and I revelled in the attention. I did not know that I was dying and that the priest was anointing, not blessing, me.

I became dead religious, using a special set of bright red beads to pray to St Philomena. The Catholic Church saw fit to delist her, in 1961, declaring that there had been a mistake and she was not a saint at all. Counting the beads through my fingers passed the time every morning, while my mother went about her work. It was my wont to stand up in bed before going to sleep, and bless the house by tracing a gigantic sign of the cross in the air.

My father cycled home every lunchtime, and after eating he came upstairs to teach me new games or test me on the ones he had already taught me. One game involved a circular board, made at his workplace, in which holes were punched. He filled all the holes with nails, leaving only the hole in the centre vacant, and the trick was to jump one nail over another, eliminating a nail each time, until you ended up with just one nail in the middle hole. Over time I worked out several methods of achieving this objective and became better than him. He was delighted with me.

There was a night when he was not. He had finished his day's work, and my mother sent him upstairs to toilet me. This involved him holding me over a tin bucket and waiting for my bowel or bladder to move. The main point of the exercise was to make sure my little legs did not rest on the rim of the bucket because it cut into my flesh. I remember him going downstairs, and my mother shouting at him because I had produced nothing. 'Could you not have held her a while longer?' There was a constant tension also about the leaving on of the hall light outside the bedroom because I was afraid of the dark. He wanted to switch it off; she wanted it left on. I did not tell them that I was sorely afraid of the large print of Christ on the cross on Calvary, hanging in the bedroom, which gave me waking nightmares. Nor did I tell them that the American comic cuts, which featured vampires, also frightened me. Torn between shame at knocking religion and a voracious appetite for the stories in the comic cuts, I kept silent.

I paid no attention at all to the fact that I was displacing my father from his marital bed for six months of every year. I slept with my mother, so that she could keep an eye on me. Every morning, as dawn lightened the dark outside, my father appeared at our bedside with a tray of tea and toast. He always smiled as he kissed my mother, she murmured sleepily to him, and he went off to work, leaving us to dip the toast in the tea, comfortable, at queenly ease, knowing there was time afterwards to snuggle back down for another sleep.

There again, I paid no attention to the fact that my mother never came to bed until well after the rest of the household had retired because her own work was not done.

Why, Daddy? Why did you hit her that night?

I never, ever, forgot the sight of my mother being in terror of my father. I never saw him hit her again. It didn't matter.

We knew that other women were beaten, or terrorized, or cowed by their husbands. Once, a woman, Patsy, managed to stumble into my mother's kitchen. My mother ran immediately to the man's house. 'Paddy, Paddy,' I heard her call him by his first name. 'For God's sake, now, that's enough.' She spoke on familiar and equal terms with him, cajoling and stern. He replied civilly to her, but was not for turning. Patsy spent the night at our house, she and my mother crouching over the dying fire. My father, risen for work, wished them good morning and knew not to talk. He and Paddy left for work at the same hour. Did they mention the assault? When the women heard the sound of Paddy closing his front door, Patsy returned home to get the children ready for school.

It was my father who first taught me the magic of words. I was back at school again and had to write an essay on the local postman, George. I read out to my father a sentence that declared that George wore 'a blue uniform'. It was a blue 'serge' uniform, my father informed me. Serge was the name of the material. You could have clothes made of silk, satin, leather, wool, linen, cotton, he said. I was enchanted. After he had checked my spelling and grammar, and congratulated me, my mother said there was more to be written about George. He had a wife and children, and he lived in a certain street, and his parents were so-and-so from this district, and his wife's parents were so-and-so from that district.

'I was just telling her about George's work,' my father said.

'And I was just telling her about George's life,' my mother replied.

Life was what you heard about when the women of the street gathered round Ettie Deeney's door for a break after dinner at midday and after tea in the evening. Tales were all the women had to barter during time off. If a person who did not live in the street chanced to walk up it, their seed, breed and generation would be known by the time they got to Ettie's house, number fourteen. My sister Muireanna's first words, uttered as she sat with my mother on a cushion at Ettie's feet, were, 'Who's that?' Ettie, who had a club foot, balanced herself against the doorjamb on her crutches. The others sat on cushions brought from their homes, or sprawled on the footpath. If the conversation was mighty, our mothers used to call us to go into the house and bring up another cigarette. As girls grew older they were allowed to bring their own cushion to Ettie's door, a precious rite of passage that signified that they were now old enough to hear what was really going on.

Ettie was considered educated because she could do crosswords. Sometimes she'd ask me to ask Sister Agatha the answer to number four across in the *Derry Journal*. Sister Agatha would send me back with a written reply, on the understanding that Ettie would divulge to her the answer to six down. With their encouragement, I did the annual children's Christmas crossword, also in the *Derry Journal*, and several times won the ten-shilling prize.

Ettie was always beautifully dressed, usually in pleated skirts and twinsets, and had her hair permed regularly. It helped that she never did housework and so didn't have to wear an apron. She was considered refined. It also helped that she had neither children nor husband at which to roar. Significantly, though, when a widowed woman in the area took in a male 'lodger' and others muttered, Ettie said, 'Isn't it better to see her come out of the house with a smile on her face than those awful tears tripping her?'

She lived with her two sisters, also unmarried. One of them died of untreated breast cancer, too modest to call in a doctor. My mother dressed her wounds one night, and they were raw and smelly. Reticence about the female body was widespread. An unmarried male neighbour came discreetly and in desperation to my mother, to enquire after his unmarried sister who had been rushed into hospital: 'Lily, will you tell me, for Christ's sake, what's wrong with Lorna?' She had been brought in for a hysterectomy. 'Just women's trouble,' my mother soothed him. One woman who found herself pregnant at the late age of forty was too affronted to step into the street, and would communicate by talking over her backyard wall to any woman who used the lane as a shortcut to get to the corner shop. When her time approached, she set off on foot into the countryside, heading for her mother's house, and miscarried by the wayside, in the snow.

Though nobody said anything in the church when it happened, there was sadness and seething anger around Ettie's door when the name of a local Catholic woman who had married a Protestant was 'read' off the altar, the priest declaring her excommunicated. It was accepted that priests could do this and that the Church had the power of life and death. There was a commotion in our street, early one Sunday morning, and men gathered outside a neighbour's door and commiserated with the man of the house. They shook his hand, patted his back and God blessed him. The hospital had sent for him, and the doctors wanted him to make a choice between saving the life of his wife, or the child she was delivering. He chose to save the life of the baby, struggling to get into the world. There was no choice, anyway. His wife would go to heaven, her soul already saved. It was his duty to save the baby and its soul. No baby, no soul. They had ten children already. When he came back from hospital – Oh, miracle. Oh, thanks be to the loving mother of God, – both mother and child had lived. 'Do you think this baby is blind?' the baby's mother asked my mother after some months. It was, and it died.

There was worry, not anger, when a young woman would go away to have her child and come back to have her mother rear it. We, who played with these children, never knew that their considerably older 'sisters' were in fact their mothers. This had been done for generations, with what consequences I do not know, but women who had the babies of my generation during World War II could lie to their children about soldier-fathers who had come, gone and perished on the battlefield. No such lies could be told to the generation born after World War II who came of age in the late 1970s and early 1980s, as they went off to get baptismal certificates for weddings or passports, and found out who their real mothers were. I was sent for once, to mediate between such a son and his mother, on the grounds that I had been to university and studied psychology. I advised the woman to phone the boy and say to him the word he wanted to hear. He wanted her to call him 'son'.

'And what if he asks about his father?' my mother sharply intervened.

She was right. It was his next question.

As I grew older, and probed further, my questions were invariably met, from my mother and older neighbours alike, with the retort, 'Ach, they were innocent.' Still innocent after four children? I enquired. 'Even the priest said she had a wee disease in her,' my mother replied fiercely. And the stainless-steel sink, the first in the neighbourhood, supplied by American soldiers in 1941, which the mother of four proudly invited the neighbours in to see? 'It was a lovely sink. We were all dying to get one,' my mother said. She had the stone Belfast jaw-box until 1961, when I bought her the coveted stainless-steel sink out of my first university grant.

The 1950s housewives boiled, washed, wrung and mangled, polished and swept, and even went down on their knees in the front street to scrub a perfect semicircle in front of their doors. My father erected a huge wooden cross against the wall of the back yard, with perfect steel cabling attached to the wall of the house, for a clothesline for my mother. He had smuggled the cabling out of the admiralty yard, and was deeply proud of his handiwork, not to mention the labour he saved her, for the cable ran smoothly through the runner wheels. His face fell when he came in from work and she told him the cable had broken. He rushed out to examine the disaster. 'April fool!' she called out the window to him.

If the women round Ettie's door showed us life, my father showed us work. When he couldn't come home for lunch, and one of us was chosen for the great privilege of bringing his sandwiches to his place of employment, a naval base at the bend of the river Foyle, on the outskirts of town, he always introduced whichever child cycled into the vast yard to whichever workmates were around. The introductions were always formal, and we always had to shake the hands of the other men, and my father would have a great proud smile on his face. He would make a point of telling me which man had made which board game or toy for me. Sometimes he would ask me questions which were designed to elicit answers which showed that I was a clever girl.

In the evenings, if he was on his bike that day, we would wait for him at the end of the big road. He would dismount, grinning, and pile us on to the handlebars, the crossbar, the saddle and the pillion. He would then push us home, doffing his work cap at the women. He loved to show off his growing brood. He kept photographs of us in his wallet. He loved it when we queued up at the table to get a spoonful of the egg my mother had boiled him for his tea. He never told us – and my mother, when I asked her to explain the trick in her old age, could not remember – how exactly he managed to divide one egg between so many children and still have plenty left for himself. She did recall, though, that, on the eve of the wedding to my father, her future mother-in-law had said to her, 'If there are three eggs in the house, Lily, give him one and eat the other two yourself.'

Another trick my father had, which annoyed and worried me all his working life, was to open his wage packet on a Friday night and give a certain amount to my mother, while concealing how much he kept back for himself. 'What I earn is for me to worry about. As long as there is enough for the family, don't you be annoying your brain.' The money he kept back was for savings and unexpected bills, my mother explained to me, but she, too, would rather have known. My father was not a mean fellow: he was trying to save us from any anxiety about debt and poverty. He always held two jobs, working at the bookmaker's at the weekend, and often going along to the dog track at night, as a bookie's clerk. But, Jesus Christ, the patriarchy has no idea what it's like to go through life not knowing if there are enough pennies to make ends meet.

All I knew was that my mother went round the shops every week paying down her hire-purchase debts in furniture, clothing and shoe stores. They were never fully cleared. As soon as the amount owed was negligible, she would order up more stuff. I used to go with her, holding the books and scrutinizing them. I could understand that growing children needed new shoes and clothes, but the day she ordered a whole heap of new furniture the heart moved sideways in me in despair. After that almighty expenditure, I pointed out, using the arithmetic skills my father had taught me, we would be in debt for another couple of years. She brought me to a swanky tea shop where some ladies wore hats and gloves, and ordered tea and hot sugared lemon pancakes for us both. More cash down the drain, but the dainty repast was delicious. 'You have to enjoy yourself once in a while,' she explained. I suggested we walk home to save the bus fare. She suggested I could do that when I was old enough to carry the heavy load of groceries slung about her person.

In the modernizing 1950s practically every woman in Derry decided to get rid of the heavy black ranges in their kitchens and replace them with tiled fireplaces. Gas-fired ovens had already been installed in the sculleries, so the range was no longer of practical value. It was a big broad black heavy iron object, decorated with brass knobs and handles, and fire glowed in its belly. The women stoked them day and night, like men on the *Titanic*, and polished them more lovingly than Humphrey Bogart polished his boiler on the *African Queen*. I went with my mother across the river – a more extended journey than I had ever undertaken with her – and together we chose a dinky little cream-and-white tiled fireplace.

When we got home, the range had been ripped out and a huge sooty hole, from floor to ceiling, defaced our lovely kitchen. When the tiled fireplace was installed, it seemed such a small, petty thing. My mother wept buckets. No more baked apples, we children wept. Where would we hang our socks to dry in winter? How would we burn rubbish? Plus the workmen had to be paid for ripping out the glorious range and installing its pathetic replacement. Plus the whole room had to be repapered, at more cost. That night, my mother retreated next door to Auntie Annie's, an elderly woman who still had her range. They took snuff, and Mammy sniffled.

At times of stress my father retreated to the back yard, walking past the water-barrel stand and into the shed adjoining the scullery – his workshop – which we called the 'Big Shed', which adjoined the outside toilet, which adjoined the 'Wee Shed' where we kept our sleighs, which adjoined the tin-roofed lean-to 'Coal Shed'. In his workshop he taught things I just could not learn. He and my older brother, Hugh, made a crystal radio; they dismantled and reassembled the bike; they worked with tins of paint, spanners, screwdrivers and nails, busy and deeply content with their compli-cated work.

What I could do was cut newspaper pages into squares, punch holes in them and thread them through a string, which was hung in the toilet for use as toilet paper. This saved money, and it also meant plenty of stuff to read in there. My father kept the toilet spotless, whitewashing it every year, painting the door and the skirting board, wiring it up himself with an electric light. If he did not flush the toilet after urinating, the sharp smell of his pee was horrible, and the yellowed water in the bowl was peppered with suppurating bubbles. Sometimes, on a Sunday, if he and Mammy had had a quarrel, he would lie late in bed, then appear at the dinner table unshaven, in his sleeveless white undervest. Sparse hair poked out from under his arms. I intuited his appearance to be a deliberate insult to my mother's work, and the underarm hair revolted me. Marlon Brando, my father was not.

When his job was shifted to a deep-water site many more miles downriver, on the other side of Lough Foyle, where the big ships could dock and refuel at the navy's new depot, his children could not cycle to see him any more. Part of his job was to determine how much fuel the ships took from the oil tanks in the depot. Every evening he came home smelling of oil, his clothes and face and hands darkened by the foul-smelling stuff. I no longer knew his workmates. I had no picture in the mind's eye of where he earned his money. One night he rang the doorbell – the key was not in the door – and pushed past me down the hall, silent, his face grim and grimy. He and my mother were not speaking, and he clearly felt that his children would not speak to him either, having taken sides in the row. I looked at his angry, lonely back. I felt awful sorry for him, though I'm sure that I was, as ever, on my mother's side, for my father had an awful quick temper, which was not helped by dangerously high blood pressure. I just wanted to indicate that I was still speaking to him. I said nothing. I felt lonely, for him and for myself. My father, the working man, was gone from me.

Perhaps I had left him when he and Hugh worked on the bicycle together, and I, unable to figure out the intricate workings of the machine, went off to construct a bicycle of my own. Or, rather, I found an abandoned machine somewhere. There had always been frustration about whose turn it was to ride my father's bike when he wasn't using it, and I arrived home one day with my own rusty contraption. It met the minimum requirements of a bike. There were pedals, but no chain; wheels, but no tyres; a seat, but no saddle; no brakes or light or bell. I pushed it off with one foot, jumped aboard, and steered until it stopped. Sometimes I didn't bother to mount, content to just push with one foot and stand on one pedal, making my rickety way around the neighbourhood. I braked by dragging my foot along the ground. A policeman arrived at the door and informed my mother that I faced prosecution unless I got off the road. Such was the level of crime and detection in the Bogside in the 1950s.

The police barracks was actually a great house set in an orchard – a relic of private Victorian grandeur – and the police grew vegetables for their families in its vast garden. It had an apple tree that never flourished like the others because my mother's brother Jim had shot it when he was a lad, and it had never recovered from

43

the bullet wound. As we grew up, we learned to love that tree, peeking at it through the wire fence. It was ours; Uncle Jim had shot it. He had discovered his father's revolver in a drawer and taken it outside for a practice shot. Wasn't our grandfather careless, leaving a gun lying around the place like that? My mother wouldn't hear of that. Your grandfather was a good cop. The mantra deepened as the civil rights struggle deepened, and the cops became the armed wing of the one-party, seemingly permanent, unionist state. Even as she made petrol bombs for us, her adult children, to throw at the cops in 1969, my mother rehearsed the contradiction to herself: 'Your grandfather was a good cop.'

His own father and grandfather had been cops, and his brother. When Britain ruled all of Ireland, they were members of the Royal Irish Constabulary, and the composition of the force reflected the Catholic majority on the island, though not at senior level, which was Protestant and Anglo-Irish. My grandfather served always in the North, where Protestants were in the majority. He worked first in Belfast, then in the rural outpost of Brookeborough, County Fermanagh. The village there was small, and named after the nearby vast estate of Lord Brookeborough. Constable Duffy was promoted to sergeant when he was transferred to Derry. The Lecky Road Barracks of which he was put in charge was in the heart of the Bogside. He went there in 1916, the year of the Easter uprising in Dublin against British rule. That year his father had written from Belfast: 'What do you think of this Home Rule bill? The Irish Party has put its foot in it to allow any separation of the Six Counties to take place.' The Bogside bristled with IRA volunteers, who helped fight, from a distance, the war of Irish independence, which took place mainly in the South. When the insurrection ended in 1921, with Britain pulling out of twenty-six of Ireland's thirty-two counties (which then became the sovereign Free State of Ireland), and retaining control of the six north-eastern counties, which became Northern Ireland, a part of the United Kingdom, my grandfather became overnight a member of the Royal Ulster Constabulary. He also became a British subject, against his will. It was that or lose his job on an island which had been plunged into turmoil.

44

The RUC reflected the religious balance of the new 'province'. As a Catholic, my grandfather, Sergeant Duffy, must have stuck out like a sore thumb. During the changeover, the IRA, the Black and Tans and the British army all shot at him. The fighting in Derry was of mercifully short duration. My mother, aged eleven in 1921, remembers only that one night, as her father was coming home, bullets whizzed by, penetrating the window of a house three streets away; the man inside was shot dead.

Sergeant Duffy knew everybody in the IRA. They were his neighbours. He was not known as a great fellow for bringing them to book. That was the work of the mainly Protestant police force in the senior Victoria barracks, in the city centre. Sergeant Duffy concentrated on becoming a scourge of poitín makers. He sometimes had to remonstrate with vexatious neighbours who emptied their night soil into the street instead of into the lime pits in their back yards. They threw the faeces into the street to get at a neighbour, or because they were just plain socially ignorant. Incidents turned into stories. 'The reddins [remains] of Darkie's shite' was about a man of swarthy complexion who threw his bucket of stuff over a neighbour. Even now, a hundred years later, if there is a quarrel with an ignorant neighbour, people will give the offended party a warning to watch out or 'you'll get the reddins of Darkie's shite.'

Sergeant Duffy's position in the community and the police force was further complicated by the fact that he had married a Belfast Protestant, my granny, Sarah McAleer, who immediately converted to Roman Catholicism. It was invariably Protestants who were forced to change religion in a mixed marriage; if they insisted on retaining the faith in which they were reared, it was on condition, sworn before a Catholic priest, that the children be raised as Catholics. The Catholic spouse was allowed a Roman Catholic Church wedding on that condition only, and promises of hell faced those who failed to live up to the RC rules. My grandmother, by all accounts, took her 'conversion' handily enough, was a devout practising Catholic, but when my grandfather had put on his uniform and gone out to work, she sang the old Protestant hymns, such as 'The Old Rugged Cross' and 'Abide with Me', to her children.

Every summer, she sent her children to Belfast to holiday with her mother, their Protestant granny, whose family ran a small pub in Agnes Street off the Shankill Road. Sometimes they spent a night in Belfast with their father's mother, their Catholic granny. My mother far preferred the Protestant granny. The Catholic granny lived in a large, gloomy, highly polished house in which silence reigned. She was austere and aloof. She was known as 'oul' piano legs', a nickname conferred by her Protestant daughter-in-law. The Protestant granny lived in a large, rambling house, packed with people. My mother and her sisters and brothers were cheerfully thrown into the streets to play. There were alleyways and tenements to explore, and singsongs and home baking and even Protestant Sunday school. There was a gregarious one-armed uncle who had lost his other limb at the Battle of the Somme. He was an Orangeman, and he wore his sash when he came to Derry to march in defence of the Protestant faith. He also wore it going to visit his sister and her husband, Sergeant Duffy, exchanging civil greetings with Bogsiders all the way. He brought boxes of tea and swathes of linen remnants, lifted off the floor of the great linen mills of Belfast.

Sergeant Duffy's wife died in childbirth, in 1927. My mother remembers that a neighbour came in to help with the birthing, that her dying mother asked for bacon and eggs, that the doctor forbade it, that the neighbour cooked it, that her mother ate it with great pleasure. She died in hospital some days later. 'You will have to be housekeeper now, Lily,' Sergeant Duffy said to his daughter, my mother. She was seventeen. She repeated the phrase all her life, in tones that varied from awe to despair. She had to rear John and Jim and Nellie, aged thirteen to six. Sadie, aged sixteen, was sent to London to take up a position with the civil service. Mena was married and living in Derry, but the three other older children – Brian, Leo and Peggy – had already emigrated to America.

Sergeant Duffy died in 1935 at the age of forty-seven. 'He died of a broken heart,' my mother insists. When his wife was alive, she played piano, he played the violin, and neighbours joined in

46

singalongs. The music ceased after her death. 'He sat in the chair by the fire, crying, every night.' My mother nursed him through death by cancer. He left a tiny amount of savings. A Protestant charity for boys in the city gave my mother £2. 10s. a month. The hungry 1930s laid waste around the Bogside. Sometimes, when my father was courting her, if my mother saw him wave from the foot of the street, she would send Nellie or John or Jim down to him to ask if he had a shilling that would allow her to buy food.

It was not until she was ninety-two that, under prodding from neighbours who had come in for a cup of tea after Saturday-night mass, she revealed to us what happened one evening during their courtship. 'Go on, Lily, what happened? When we got off the train, Hugh was waiting for you. You linked our arms, one on either side and said: "Now, girls, if Hughie asks, I was with the two of ye all evening." Come on, Lily, where were you that evening?'

My mother and Molly and Tessie had taken a train to Buncrana, fourteen miles across the border in Donegal. The summer train journey was known as the 'Tanner Special', a tanner being sixpence. The train left Derry at six in the evening and returned at 11 p.m., leaving three hours for entertainment. My mother went off by herself the minute the train hit Buncrana. For three years she had been meeting a Scottish man who came over for his summer fortnight. She had also been going out with my father for three years.

Jesus. Mammy?

'Ah, your mother had men flocking around her,' beamed Molly.

But – Jesus. Mammy?

'Well . . .' she said with a grin, tossing her head. 'Well . . .' was all she would say, pleased as punch with her ninety-two-year-old self.

And did you ask him for a shilling, too, Mammy?

I remembered then that just after her eightieth birthday, in 1990, when her eyesight was failing, she had given me the address of a man in Scotland and asked me if I would write and ask him how he was doing. He had courted her once, she said with a smile. I lost the address. At ninety-two she could no longer remember it.

47

All the same . . .

'Jesus, Mammy, now that it's all coming out, tell us about Mickey Quigley.'

The neighbours laughed in gleeful anticipation, and settled back for a good night's crack. Mickey had sent my mother a dozen red roses for her eightieth birthday. He waltzed with her that night in the ballroom we had hired. He was a beautiful dancer. 'When Mickey dances with you, you know you're danced,' she had said afterwards.

We had known that Mickey and my father were pals; that Mickey had bought a barrel of herring and asked my father if he wished to go into business with him by paying half the price of the herring; that my father declined, preferring the certainty of the little bookmaker's business he had just started. Mickey stood on a street corner, sold all the herring and went on to prosper as the city's main fishmonger. My father's bookmaking venture failed within weeks, and he took a clerical job by day, working for another bookie at the greyhound track by night.

So why had Mickey – the best man – come to see my mother the night before she got married?

'He wasn't the only one,' she announced. 'Father Conway called and begged me not to marry your father. He said, "Hughie's a doggy-man, Lily, a gambler. Don't do it."'

'And what did you say, Mammy?'

'I said, "Ah, Father, sure, I'll see in the morning what I'll do."'

'It was a busy night,' said Molly, slapping her two hands against her two knees. 'We were all young, too, just like youse were. Yese forget that we were young, too.'

'So what did Mickey say, Mammy?'

'He arrived after Father Conway left and asked me to marry him. I said no, and he said he'd pay for the car anyway, to take your father and me to our honeymoon in Bundoran. Then the next day, after the wedding breakfast, he and the bridesmaid said they may as well come along, too, and we all went to Bundoran, and Mickey danced with me all night.'

'And what did me daddy say, Mammy?'

48

'He just laughed at it. There was a pile of Scotsmen over for their summer holidays in Bundoran, and, sure, they danced with me, too.'

And the first baby, I swiftly, silently calculated, which was stillborn, was born forty weeks after the wedding night of 12 July 1937. What a night they must have had, my father proudly, confidently watching all the men queue to dance with the woman who had chosen him as her husband.

I made more tea for my mother and the neighbours, and the storytelling of their youth went on until midnight, and the stories were marvellous.

Mammy, Mammy, I thought as I made the tea, I was pursued by loads of women in the early days of the women's movement. Mammy, Mammy, I could tell tales of love and courtship and flirting before I settled down with my woman. Mammy, Mammy, I could tell such stories . . . and the neighbours would not slap their hands on their knees, and laugh at the telling, and you would not tease me, would not ask what happened next.

Chapter Four

One evening my father lined me up with my equally bare-chested brothers for the usual Friday competition. After we had bathed we flexed our muscles, puffed our chests out, and he decided who was champ. I won. Later that night, my mother told me to shift out of the bed where I slept with Hugh and Paddy, in the return bedroom, and go up to join Muireanna and Nuala in the back bedroom. Carmel, the youngest child, decamped gleefully down to the boys, where all was fun and pillow fights, and I trailed myself up to the back bedroom, where all was face powder, talcum powder and quarrels about clothes.

I was at the annual Feis, watching the Irish-dancing competitions, when I first noticed blood on my knickers. Other girls told me this was my 'period', and it would come every month. I hadn't a clue what they meant, and was anxious. When I got home and told my mother, she brought me upstairs to the front bedroom, sat me on an armchair beside the marital bed and told me in a hurried, anxious voice that this blood was a 'gift from the Blessed Virgin'. That meant nothing either. She wrote out a message and sent me with it to the pharmacist. The big man, Eugene O'Hare, also a city councillor, did not change his grave expression as he read the note, then made me up a package. I was troubled by the cost.

Back in the bedroom, my mother bade me take off my knickers and step into the strap and pouch. She placed a sanitary pad in the pouch, which hung by a belt from my waist. When I pulled the contraption up, then my knickers, the whole thing felt lumpy and bumpy. I did not like being strapped in. I could feel my mother's embarrassment as she murmured prayers and assured me I'd be grand. I should change the pad every night and every morning, she said, and place the soiled object under the mattress, and she would burn it in the range when everybody else had left the house for school and work. Soiled, strapped, expensive . . . I was not pleased. Later that night, though, as I rejoined my school friends, there was a mounting sense of excitement. I could get pregnant, they told me. I should avoid sex. One of them described a family in a street nearby which engaged in incest. Every night, she said, the wife, lying in bed with her husband, called down to her son, who was in bed with her daughter, 'Are you dipping your pen in the wee girl's ink? Your father's doing the same to me.'

It got worse – every month, when the supply of sanitary towels had to be renewed, I had to go to a local corner shop, which was usually staffed by a man. I had to ask him if his sister was in, code for what I wanted. He would nod, and go into the kitchen, the door of which was open – where she sat at the fire in full view of the shop. She would come out with a knowingly raised eyebrow, and I'd ask her for a packet of towels. Why, oh, why couldn't I just knock on her open door and deal with her directly? Etiquette dictated that she be left undisturbed when she wasn't officially working behind the counter.

Shortly after the onset of menarche, as I sat in the tin bath on the floor of our scullery, while my mother poured in pots of water that she had heated on the cooker, she decided that I would need a bra. I had no more noticed the need of this than I had noticed the reason for new sleeping arrangements a year before. The night I was fitted with Muireanna's hand-me-down bra was completely different from the night I was fitted with the sanitary towel. I was wearing a white knitted Aran sweater. I believed my breasts swelled beautifully underneath. When I came downstairs, my father gravely shook me by the hand and a smile broke his proud face. I looked just gorgeous, he told me. Then he brought me across the street to a neighbour, and told the man of the house, George, the great news. George shook my hand, said I was beautiful and gave me two shillings. Walking to the shop to spend it, chest thrust out, I lingered under lamplight and sang 'Blue Moon'. Alone, but not lonely, my mind cloudy with romance, I stood there, longing for love. I did not know, or think, to call this sex.

My hormones were, as they say, at me. There were what the

police called 'riots' the first night *Rock around the Clock* played at the City cinema, and one of the teenage boys in our street, Gerard Sharkey, was arrested and fined for dancing in the city centre after the movie closed. Muireanna and her boyfriend, Maurice, used to give jiving exhibitions at street corners while we sang and clapped our hands.

The jukebox in the fish and chip shop awaited us every weekend after our father gave us pocket money. Our gang would order a plate of chips between us, and sit in the booth playing Elvis, Buddy Holly, Brenda Lee, Fats Domino, Connie Francis, Little Richard and Jerry Lee Lewis. If the NATO fleet was in, and depending on the owners of the Italian cafés, you might be allowed just to hang around the jukebox, spending nothing. Being a girl, and as ever alone while other girls went out with boys, and, as always, self-trained to stand alone, I was allowed more than most to stand around the jukebox by myself, gladly lost in a world of my own.

I stepped outside that world dramatically and unexpectedly: my first ever truly sexual engagement with a fellow has marked me to this day. His name was Eamon Stitt. Aged twelve, slim and dark, he was far and away the most beautiful boy in the neighbourhood. Like Elvis, he wore his shirt collar up and slicked back his hair, which he continually combed. The whole gang, boy and girl alike, deferred to his smouldering sexuality. The other males had simply no chance when he was around. One summer day he cycled with my brother Hugh and me to the seaside. I was there, as always, because I was as adventurous as any boy. We lay in the sun, in our swimsuits, laughing at what had befallen us minutes before: all of us were taken short, and the only place to pee was in the sea. Each of us, without letting on to the other, had also used the occasion to evacuate our bowels. Suddenly, we were surrounded by floating turds. It felt like a really amusing gang thing, an initiation of some kind.

My brother wandered off later, and without warning Eamon rolled over and kissed me. His mouth tasted lovely, like crumbled biscuits. We fed off each other contentedly. When it was over, he said, 'Don't tell anybody about us kissing.' I accepted the insult;

was glad even that I had finally tasted his beautiful mouth. I didn't tell him that his girlfriend and I were also having a romance, though it was platonic. This girl and Eamon went further than anybody we knew of our age, and they advertised their intentions in advance: in the cinema, all of us had waited and watched with bated breath as he put his hand up her knickers. We were thrilled with the daring of it, but not remotely interested ourselves in going there – wherever 'there' was, whatever it contained. More often than not, kissing consisted of a boy and girl standing together in the back lane, in late-evening daylight, the rest of us watching and counting to see who could kiss, lips tightly closed, for the longest time. My favourite was a fellow called Neill, who had the good sense on a Friday night, when our parents had given us pocket money, to buy chocolate and eat it before each kiss. With him, a chocolate-starved girl could keep a kiss going until the magic figure of a hundred had been reached, or our mothers had called us in for the nightly family rosary.

The rosary doubled as an inventory of a family's well-being, or lack of it. It was the habit, after finishing the formal prayer session, to remain on our knees in the kitchen while saying extra Hail Marys for 'special intentions', which had to be named. We would pray for a relative to get a job, or a home, or recover health, or pass an exam, or be watched over in America or England. When the time taken to pray for special intentions exceeded the time taken to say five decades of the rosary, we children sensed that things were not well. You could learn, in that way, to dislike the extended family and all their lousy troubles, which kept us on our busted little knees on linoleum, or you could learn a sense of safety and security: somebody, somewhere, was also always praying for us. Our sense of religion depended on hormones, the amount of daylight left for another game in the streets, and whether or not the person being prayed for was a warm light in our lives. There was one special part, the Hail Holy Queen, always led by my mother, which haunted and soothed and frightened: 'And after this our exile, show unto us, the blessed fruit of thy womb, Jesus; O clement, O loving, O sweet virgin Mary . . .' Exile, exile, exile . . . we were

Derry Catholics, in an inhospitable political environment, and we were all destined to take the boat, but, for the moment, we were safe with our parents.

Before doing the Eleven-Plus examination in 1955, which would determine whether or not I went on to grammar school and thence, presumably, into teaching, I was sent to a Catholic secondary school, St Eugene's, for one year's special preparation. It was just a transition year: I was not planning to stay at secondary school, where the law obliged girls to put in time until they reached fourteen, the minimum age for leaving school, whence most went into the shirt factories or shops. The only thing I remember about education in the secondary school is the singing classes conducted by Mrs Boucher. It was a marvellous thing, an absolute luxury, to spend a half-hour singing songs such as 'Vermeo', 'Will Ye No Come Back Again' or 'Innisfree' – and learn how to harmonize. Everybody got to take part. (Years later, if the class I was teaching was unruly or restive, I would halt the lesson, get the students to sing, and exult in the peace that flowed from that.) The classes were full to overflowing, and I made a fortune in sweets doing exercises for other girls who just could not keep up.

We were all struck on the day we sat the Eleven-Plus in a state secondary school that pupils there – Protestants – got a delicious hot lunch which fabulously included custard and prunes. Protestant girls were fed by the state, we were not, was our conclusion. Martyred as ever, Catholics had to make do with jam sandwiches, prepared by our mothers, because our church needed the entire financial subsidy paid by the state to maintain an independent Catholic education.

In that year at secondary school I stood out from other children because of the way I skipped home. I would stand rigidly in the street, jerk my head, then run forward, leap into the air, and try to kick my own bum. I was diagnosed with St Vitus's dance. I did this routine terrifically well, though at times I got fed up with the compulsion, as jerking my head hurt my neck. I found it very calming when the compulsion came over me to pause at the abattoir on the way home and watch the men slaughter pigs. We were allowed to walk through the big gate into the yard, lean over the half-door and watch one of the men hit the pig on the nose with a mallet. This brought great gouts of blood from the animal's nose, and it ran in circles, squealing, until it lay down and died. Its stomach was then cut open, and huge piles of guts were pulled out, coiling on to the floor. Wonderful.

When my puppy, which I was training, would not sit or fetch or do anything at all which I asked, I dragged him along the ground by the leash while he squealed, scourging his bum ragged. He might as well have been in the slaughterhouse. I hoped somebody would stop me. Nobody did. I maltreated the dog for quite a while that day, tears running down my face. I knew I was doing wrong. I never did it again. I was brought to a priest known to have the power of 'curing', and the St Vitus's dance disappeared. Sometimes, albeit rarely these days, I jerk my neck under stress.

The day my mother took me across the river to the Waterside, to Morrison's shop, where she had to pay cash for the school uniform, and I put on the blazer, the badge blazed forth on its pocket. It was a shield, a proclamation, and an announcement that I was a step above the common cut. It marked us out from other Catholic girls in the town. We were given to understand, and knew it anyway, that we were the elite. The very word 'grammar' meant posh: we would speak proper English. While others took the walk through the streets to the factories, we 'grammar' girls took the bus out of town, to a green, vast place, set among trees. Thornhill was the former home of a merchant. It now belonged to the Catholic Church, and was run by the Sisters of Mercy, who had their own convent there.

Proudly waves the Mercy banner
Floating over old Thornhill.
It's the standard of our Master,
And our well-beloved Queen.
There's a starry Kingdom waiting
And a Royal Throne on high

For each victor in the contest
'Neath our banner's ancient sheen
For each victor in the contest
'Neath our banner's ancient sheen.

As long as the Foyle goes sailing to the sea
Dear Alma Mater, we'll be true to thee.
March we gaily down the golden years
All through life until the harbour nears.
Thy honour's in our keeping
Wheresoever we may wend
Adveniat Regnum Tuum
Our motto to the end
Adveniat Regnum Tuum
Our motto to the end.

I had to go to buy the year's books second-hand from a girl who had finished first year. She lived inside the walled city, in just the kind of tenement that Joe and I had feared to penetrate. The hall door was open, the hallway malodorous, and the stair up to her family's flat dark and damp. She brought me into the sitting room, which was also a kitchen. There was a low fire, high windows and children sitting about the place. Her mother swept them away, and I was alone with the girl. There was a bare light bulb. I had never been in such a dimly lit room. I had one shilling in my hand, and was to pay no more, my mother had warned me. The girl said her mother wanted one shilling and threepence. My mother just didn't have it, I said. She disappeared, came back, took the money and gave me the tattered books. She was sad. I felt rotten.

There were some books that I had to buy brand-new. Then there was the daily bus fare of sevenpence, which my mother counted out of her purse every morning. She always gave me the exact amount. There was no question of surplus, and bring back the change. She would have saved a good deal had she the cash to buy a monthly ticket in advance, but such a huge sum was out of the question. There was no question of buying a school scarf to complete my school outfit. I would inherit my sister Nuala's scarf when she should leave some years hence. Still, we had the navy-blue berets and the badge. I would have dusted the gold lettering of the badge if I could. I insisted on wearing the blazer to the launderette, which had just opened in William Street, enjoying the gleam of it under the pillow full of clothes over my shoulder. 'Make sure she gives you a full cup of powder,' my mother warned. 'Watch the suds, and make sure they come up halfway.' Watching the clothes roll round and the suds rise and fall was soothing. We watched them the way we would later watch television. Things that went in dirty came out clean. They saved our mothers a huge amount of labour. If the woman gave you enough powder, life was perfect. Clean and educated, our mothers at their ease – what more could a girl want?

Some of the teachers began each lesson with a request that we pray for a husband for them. They laughed while they said it, but you could feel the urgency, even though female teachers were then required by state law to resign from a permanent job upon marriage. The only married teacher in the school was a widowed Protestant who had converted to Catholicism. We could not see why any man would turn down some of our more attractive teachers, but the fact that they plainly had done so was a worry, even to me, for what did life offer but marriage and children, or the nunnery.

Then there was Miss McDevitt: ancient, single, tweedy, amused and aristocratic. From the start, I was drawn to Miss McDevitt, the new Sister Agatha in my life, albeit without the bad temper or the visits to my home. She lived in a great house by the river, outside the town. It was called Boom Hall, in commemoration of the fact that the siege of Derry was broken when a ship broke the boom laid across the river there. Winter or summer, I fetched tea from the staffroom for her because she was too old or too cold to make the journey herself. Sometimes she let me take the class while she rested her weary bones. She didn't bat an eyelid when the class intellectual, Mairead Fleming, pushed the boundaries of discussion by introducing, say, the Oedipus complex as a basis for understanding *Hamlet*. Mairead was our version of the Parisian Left Bank. She had a dark fringe, long legs and kooky ways. She read the *Observer*, and quoted its columnists, particularly Katherine Whitehorn. In Derry, we had never heard of a woman who wrote for a newspaper. Miss McDevitt let Mairead rip. That was the closest we ever came to peeping over the intellectual Catholic barricades behind which we led the sheltered life of convent school.

Love hit me in my first year at grammar school, aged eleven. I stood behind a senior girl, listening to the school's annual Gilbert and Sullivan operetta. I wanted to lean into her back. I did. Her coat smelled lovely; her back felt strong. She turned, and smiled down at me. I fell in love. Afterwards, in the rain, she let me stand under her umbrella. I wrote about our contacts in my diary. ' "A" let me sit beside her at the school pictures.' 'I gave "A" a holy picture.' ' "A" let me play tennis with her.' 'I sat behind "A" on the school bus.' The diary was decorated with hearts. I kept it under the mattress. Looking for soiled sanitary towels there, my mother found and read it. She was anxious, angry even. Her voice was soft. I was to stop this. I stopped the diary, but continued to follow 'A' home, for three years, often standing in the dark near her front door, hoping it would open and she would come out. Not once did she. Not once in three years. This is a thing I have noticed frequently in the decades since. On the street where she lives, in the neighbourhood even, you seldom spot the beloved. The best thing is to join an organization to which the beloved belongs. It makes socialism that much more attractive. It makes feminism irresistible. It made school a daily joy. Of course, you have to love these things in the first place. I would not recommend dance halls, where you could be stuck against the wall all night, or poker games where a straight flush outweighs all other considerations. 'A' was clearly middle class. Who else had an umbrella? I could tell from the cut of her uniform and the confident way she held herself, though the term 'middle class' had not then entered my consciousness. Her father was a schoolteacher. She could not make the teachers laugh like I did. Nobody could. Jesus, but I was confident among girls – in school.

I was worried, though. When I was thirteen I somehow acquired a copy of *The Well of Loneliness* by Radclyffe Hall. I hid it in the hot press in the kitchen, and got up late at night to read it there, pretending to study, when the family was asleep, or under lampposts in streets far from home. If what the novel revealed was true, I was in for an awful life. I was, according to Hall, an 'invert', who would lead a life of shame, secrecy, persecution, and I would find salvation only through joining the British army, which would accept any-body's services in time of need. Also, I would have to dress like a man, or find a woman dressed like a man and always wear a frock myself. I would have to emigrate after retiring from the army and live in a continental European city, and hang out with other inverts who succumbed to drugs, drink and orgies. If I ever formed a relationship with a woman, one of us would have to submit to sexual intercourse with the other woman's brother and produce a baby. I could not see myself having a baby, so that meant that I would have to dress like a man and let the other woman have sexual intercourse with one of my two brothers. I could not envisage either of my brothers obliging, so that meant, I concluded, that I would have to live alone all my life long, with neither female partner nor baby. Especially as, at five feet, I was too small to join an army, which was the only place I would meet another invert.

I did not reread *The Well of Loneliness* until I was fifty-nine and started writing this book. To my astonishment, Radclyffe Hall's heroine, Stephen, joined the British army only to be of service to her country as an ambulance driver during World War I. Although she had been warned by army chiefs about the crushes other women had on her, she met her lover in the army, and they subsequently settled in Paris. And, crucially, there was no episode involving impregnation of her partner by Stephen's brother. Stephen had no brothers at all.

Despite this awful intimation of my future, the dalliances with older girls at school remained blissful. When 'A' left Thornhill, her best friend, 'B', accepted the transfer of my affections. She had been encouraging me for some time. Both her parents were professionally employed. I was aware of moving up in the world, socially. This was very important to me. I saw it partly as a reward to my parents for all the hard work they had put into getting me educated. 'B' was exciting. She smoked, loved cycling into the countryside, had a boyfriend, spoke Irish, held my hand in the dark of the movies, brought me to her parents' home where I saw wealth beyond reach. There were two sitting rooms. They never sat in the kitchen other than for meals. Her parents engaged me in conversation. My parents were curious to hear what her home looked like. When she came into mine, my father extended his ritual courtly greeting. 'You are welcome to my home.' I loved bringing people into my house. I loved the way my parents spoke, putting people at their ease, curious always about who, what, where, telling more stories than they were told. If a friend was middle class, though, I always felt as if I was bringing home another trophy.

In 1960 President Kennedy was elected, despite being Catholic and Irish, which we intuited was a good thing. In the same year we were brought to a cinema to see an educational film that Protestant grammar school girls were also attending. As the lights went down, a photograph of the Queen appeared on-screen, and the British national anthem rolled out. The Protestant girls and their teacher rose to their feet. Our teacher, Miss McGeown, who taught Catholic apologetics and was a sister of the Thornhill principal Mother Aquinas, sat resolutely in her seat. Taking our cue, we also stayed seated. The silence that followed was thunderous, as we contemplated our own daring and wondered exactly what it meant. As ever, I thought it had to do with defying Northern Protestantism and the unionist government. Staying seated was more a statement that we children were Catholics than that we were Irish nationalists. For Miss McGeown, it was probably more: like my parents, she woke up one morning in 1921 to be told that the country had been partitioned and she was now British, not Irish. To us children, in the late 1950s, enjoying the benefits of free health and education under British rule, that was history. To Miss McGeown, it was yesterday. Either way, our gesture was thrilling. The Thornhill badge on my little chest glowed and thumped as I revelled in the dignified rebellion of it all – whatever it was.

Whatever it was had to be better than the night a group of us went to the circus which had rolled into town. There would be amusements as well, and, before we went, we counted out our money to see how many rides we could afford on the hobbyhorses, dodgems and wheelchairs. One girl had less than us. We groaned, and gave her sufficient pennies from our own stash to enable her to have as many rides as us – which would now be one fewer each than expected. Our distaste for her poverty was as lacerating that night as is the shame, now, of recalling how we treated her. The drive to get away from poverty could be cruel.

Chapter Five

In May 1960, my mother's brother Jim was woken by police knocking at his door to ask him to come to identify the body of a relative. It was that of young John Duffy, the sixteen-year-old son of John, brother of Jim and Lily. The police wanted to spare his parents the ordeal. My Uncle Jim went to the house in the heart of the Bogside where young John, eldest child of the family, lay dead of a bullet wound. He had been cleaning a revolver. He was, it seemed, a member of the IRA. He had been in the company of older men who had recruited him, including the manager of the bakery where he worked as an apprentice.

Our family was somewhat embarrassed by the thought of young John being involved in such a hare-brained outfit. The IRA commanded no respect whatsoever. Eejits, they were, running about with guns when Derry cried out for jobs and housing. The IRA's fitful campaign of the 1950s against the Northern unionist state had faded away. Most of the campaign had been directed from the South, and it was a surprise to hear that Derry men – or anybody at all – were still involved, as a stand-down had been declared around 1956.

The agony was that young John had been left to die without benefit of a priest. The men had fled across the border, then rung a priest in Derry. Perhaps he died at once and there was no point, and why should the men risk jail by lingering? As my mother had reared the boy's father, it was her place to be with him in this crisis. She decamped to his house, bringing all the children with her. As did Jim's wife, Maureen, with her children, and Mammy's sister Nellie with her only child. The body lay in a coffin in a large L-shaped living-room-cum-kitchen, which stretched the length of the downstairs quarters. Through the three days and two nights of the wake, we children and women hung about the coffin, and after the neighbours had gone we lay on the floor. Fifteen children and three women. Young John's mother, Aunt Mary, might have stayed with us, or gone upstairs to sleep with her husband. All the men, except Uncle John, had to work each day during the wake; there were bills to be paid.

My father, who did not drink, did not join the men in their consolation stout and whiskey when they came back to the wake. And when young John's body was removed to the church in Creggan the night before the funeral, my father was not there. Though nothing was said, his absence was noted. My mother asked me to go down home and talk to him.

I found him on the sofa in tears. She was always looking out for her brothers and sisters, he said. They had been in the house when he married, and they might as well never have left it. He was abandoned – no tea, no fire in the hearth, no nothing – despite working to bring in the money to feed and clothe my mother, us, her relatives . . . words to that effect. My memory is that I was sent to soothe him. My sorrow is that I hadn't a clue about a husband missing his wife. A man missing his woman. A lover wanting attention.

Fifteen months later, it was a broken heart that drove me to my parents seeking solace, salvation, any release at all from the pain. We had finished our last year at grammar school, and Maureen was the first female with whom I had had a relationship that went beyond kissing. I cut the pocket of my school gymslip so that she could slip her hand inside. I sat on her knee first thing in the morning on the always-overcrowded school bus, and again on the way home, and beside her during class, so that the day passed in an erotic haze. Her parents were rich, so she had a room all to herself, and we spent the Feast of Corpus Christi in her bed.

I went to confession afterwards, seriously worried and contrite. The priest, Father Mulvey, refused absolution unless I swore never to kiss Maureen again. 'I'll try not to,' I said.

'You must not,' he said.

'I need help not to.' I pleaded for absolution and God's grace.

He refused, again.

I argued that I could not absolutely promise to refrain from a thing that tempted me, that I could only promise to try not to do it, that it would be a lie to swear I'd never do it again. I argued the difference between trying not to do a thing and swearing absolutely that I would not. (I took religion seriously.)

He insisted there would be no absolution, no grace or help from God, unless I swore that I would not do it.

I insisted that I needed God's help through absolution of all my sins, particularly this one.

He refused. Confession ended, and I left the confessional and never confessed again in my life. I cannot explain the moral courage of that. If I had chosen a different confessor, all would have been well. But that would have been hypocritical. I'm dead proud of myself that I did this thing at seventeen.

The night I turned to my father after Maureen had dumped me I pleaded that I thought I could cure myself if he would just let me go to dances more often. No, he said. I wouldn't be doing anything – just dancing with boys and trying to cure myself, I said. He sent me to the nuns. Nuns would protect me against lesbianism; he would protect me against pregnancy.

My father would only allow his daughters to go to dances on condition that we were back at a time determined by him: usually ten minutes after closing, if the dance was in town; thirty minutes if the dance was across the border. He made no allowance for the desperate desire to hang on until the very last dance was announced, in hope of being asked out on to the floor; the length of time it took to queue for our coats; the way the bus driver in Donegal would wait until the bus was full.

When I'd come in the door, glad of the band, delirious if even one fellow had asked me up to dance, disgusted at the smell and stupid talk of the fellow, happy not to have been molested passing the dark laneways on the way home, my father would be waiting in the kitchen, or would get up out of bed to come down and argue the toss.

'What time is it?'

It is midnight, Daddy.

'Yes, but what time is it?'

It is midnight, Daddy.

'Yes, but what time is it? You know what I mean, so what time is it?'

It is midnight, Daddy, and thirty minutes after the last dance was called (in the city); or one hour after the last dance was called (across the border).

'So you're late, aren't you?'

Yes, Daddy, but that's because . . . the cloakroom was crowded, the bus was delayed.

'You're late, isn't that so?'

Yes, Daddy, by your deadline I'm late, but in the circumstances I'm not late.

'Never mind the circumstances, I asked you what time it was, and you lied.'

No, Daddy, I told you the exact time, literally; however, by your standards – the time by which you ordered me to be home – I gave the wrong time. I know I should have said that it was midnight by the clock, but in your time it is half an hour past the deadline you set, therefore I should have said it is midnight, half an hour past the deadline you set, and therefore I should have said the time is thirty minutes past the deadline I agreed with you, and that I have broken your trust, defied your authority, and showed you contempt . . .

My father danced, literally, on his toes when I surrendered to his mad logic and gave the answer he desired. Triumph eased his demeanour, and he went off to bed, a martyred Catholic patriarch, doing his best to protect his daughters. Though his fist was raised against me during the altercation, he never hit me. I was his intellectual equal, and he had won the argument. The eldest child, Muireanna, invariably got the fist, and worse – if she was late, he went out to the streets to find her, and she was often beaten home by a stick. All that was needed to complete the picture was a cheerleader like the old woman in John Ford's movie *The Quiet Man*, encouraging John Wayne, and he dragging his wife home: 'Here's a good stick to beat the lady home with, sir.' Except that no women cheered in Derry when fathers behaved this way.

My father's worries did not apply when we went to the céilí dances held in the local Lady of Lourdes parish hall. All things Irish, from newspapers to dances to summer-camp holidays away from home, in the Irish-speaking Gaeltacht areas of Donegal, were considered more than safe – they were sexually pure, and there was always a priest about the place, supervising our initiation into Irish culture.

The Gaeltacht holidays, for which I always won a scholarship, were in fact founts of sexual adventure, especially for someone of my sexual orientation. The houses in which we stayed in Rannafast were sexually segregated, which suited me very well. The landladies were at ease with our hormonal rages – and never knew of mine. We usually slept four to a room, two to a bed. We were discouraged from talking to local boys, the natives, who came home every summer from Scotland, having learned, presumably, a trick or three about life on the wild side, but there was also an element of class distinction. These boys had left school, usually at fourteen, and were therefore not suitable prospects or company for the educated elite such as us, from across the border in Northern Ireland. We should speak Irish, yes, but not imitate Irish ways, or we'd all end up picking potatoes.

There was a wild child who would sneak out the window every night to go dancing with the local boys, then wake me up when she came home and embrace me passionately. We kissed long into the night. It was lovely.

A wonderful landlady used to take me on forbidden excursions, to wakes and late-night chats with locals. She liked it that I used to sit beside her at the fire, listening to her, the way I sat and listened to my own mother. That habit, of listening to older women, did not come about simply because I was not interested in chasing fellows as other teenage girls did. It was just that I had an ear for a good story. She talked to me about her children, their job prospects, the price of things, and the relationships between neighbours in her area. One wonderful Sunday afternoon she brought me with her to a wake, in a house far away, that was best accessed by a shortcut through the fields. We took off our shoes, to save them from being scuffed, and went barefoot. In the wake house, she allowed me to have a glass of poitín, my first alcoholic drink, and we sang all the way home. The same thing happened with summer-school teachers in the Gaeltacht as had happened in school – they showered affection on me and praised my fluency, little realizing how I had acquired it. One revered teacher from the area christened me a *spéirbhean*, or fairy woman, a mystic.

In Rannafast also I had my first cigarette and my first French kiss – the latter from a desperately handsome Belfast fellow who had arrived on a visit to his teenage haunts, riding a motorcycle and wearing a leather jacket. I don't know why he favoured me, the least sophisticated of the girls I hung out with, but I presumed, as always when a fellow came after me, that it was because of what I fancied was my superior mind. I was always up for a conversation, which spared them, I suppose, from girlish chitchat or the need to talk sweet nothings. One lad was absolutely frank with me when we met for an alleged courtship down by the sea, a forbidden place. If he gave me a cigarette would I lend him my bra, to bring back to the other fellows as a trophy? Five cigarettes, and it was a deal. It wasn't my own bra anyway – as so often, it was a hand-me-down from one of my older sisters.

The Gaeltacht school had a rigorously enforced tradition, which I loved: everybody had to dance at the nightly céilí. The boys lined up on one side of the hall, the girls on another, and the master, or *cigire*, would insist that every male pair up with a female. As this was an obligatory part of the school curriculum, no girl was left feeling like a wallflower, and no boy had to face the cruel walk across a vast, empty floor with possible rejection staring him in the face. I was having a fabulous time – danced off my feet every night by a boy, and the face kissed off me later in bed, by a girl.

The scholarships I won every year to Rannafast, which paid for full bed and board for a fortnight, were a great saving to my parents, so there was no bother at all from my father when I went twice a week during winter to night classes in Gaelic in Derry. I was interested in improving my language skills, of course, but the added incentive of sex and romance every summer, as a reward, played a huge part. The night classes were extremely relaxed, and poorly attended because speaking Irish was not considered a means of advancement. At most, the night classes would mean that we had free, practically one-on-one private tuition in a subject which would allow us to gain sufficient extra marks to qualify for university, and thence a career over in England or Canada or America.

There was also a faint air of antisocial subversion about the night classes, which appealed to the socially enforced loner in me, the girl without a boyfriend who went round the city on her own. The classes were held in a romantically run-down wooden hall, situated down a short dark laneway, which was accessed by a rickety wooden stairway. I thought of them decades later, when I sat entranced in a wooden hall in New Orleans listening to blacks playing jazz. The fact that we were allowed to smoke openly, unbeknownst to our parents, gave the place the air of a speakeasy. And there was a further bonus in that, every Sunday night, the class closed with a lesson in English dancing – the waltz and the foxtrot. There being a shortage of females, I was always danced. It was in this place, known as the Craoibh, or branch, that I first noticed Eamonn McCann. He didn't speak much, but he was different from other schoolboys in the town. He wore sideboards, in honour of Elvis Presley. He came, like myself, from the Bogside. He arrived into the Craoibh one Sunday night, dressed for a date, in a new white raincoat borrowed from his father. I found this moving, but I was equally fearful for the girl he was meeting. Her interest in speaking Irish to anyone was as negligible as Eamonn's interest in speaking English to a female. There was a sense about him of not being as socialized as the more tame boys with whom she was used to stepping out. And I did not rate her intellectually. But in these matters, of boy meets girl, I was deeply ignorant.

I had had some narrow escapes in the pursuit of love. In the cinema one night, the woman seated behind us leaned forward and murmured to the senior girl whose fingers I was sucking that she ought to desist from encouraging me. A teacher to whom my romance with the rich girl was reported asked us not to sit together in her class. Luckily for us, this teacher was that most unusual specimen in a convent – a Protestant – and she took the matter no further.

For all that I was in love, I was lonely. The rich girl held on to her boyfriend. The other girls were also going out with boys. In my last year at school, aged sixteen, I had to go to the cinema alone, at night. My aunt and uncle worked in cinemas, so I always had a complimentary pass to the balcony, to the best seats, which were usually the preserve of heterosexual couples. It had to be a serious relationship if the fellow was prepared to pay such a fortune. I trained myself into the routine of sitting alone, sticking out like a sore thumb, assiduously reading movie magazines during lights up at the interval. I was training myself for the future. I might be alone, but I was damned if I was going to hide and not travel first class.

Because Maureen was rich, I saw my mother do a thing that burned into my brain: when I brought her home for tea, my mother ran out the back, down the lane, into the corner shop, and returned with a Swiss roll, bought on credit. This luxury cake was normally reserved for the entire family on a Sunday. I loved my mother for making the effort not to let me down, as she must have seen it, before the bourgeoisie – other friends would have been given a slice of home-made scone bread – and felt a flash of hatred for the system of rich and poor, which made my mother feel shame. At the same time, I knew that the friendship of this girl, Maureen, was a sign that my family and I were on the way up; that brains and education could take you anywhere.

A similar thing happened again, when I returned from my first meal in a hotel, to which Maureen and her unsuspecting boyfriend Edward had taken me. Ever curious about the world beyond home, my mother questioned me about what we had eaten and I told her: lemon sole. Next day, after school, my mother proudly served me up lemon sole. I nearly cried with pride in her, and sorrow for her. I knew enough to know that the grammar-school education was designed to encourage me to live above the station into which I was born. For instance, we pupils were encouraged not to link arms when walking through the town, like shirt-factory girls. The factory 'girls' were females aged fourteen to sixty-five, the economic back-bone of Derry, where male unemployment among Catholics seldom went below 25 per cent, and rose to 60 per cent in the working-class Bogside where I lived. Catholics, male and female alike, educated or uneducated, were reared for emigration, except for factory girls, who were always sure of employment. Their wages kept the town going; their high spirits were infectious; their habit of linking arms was interpreted as common, a sign of no ambition or prospects.

My own godmother, Sadie, who lived on the other side of our street – and who bought me a new pair of shoes every Christmas, which was a financial godsend, and who gave me pocket money – was in theory considered beneath me because she was a factory girl. A class system operated in the school itself: to be appointed head girl, you had to be the daughter of a schoolteacher or a doctor.

Maureen's sister, working in London, arranged jobs and a bedsitter there for us, in which we were to pass the summer before going to university back in Belfast. I had never been on an aeroplane before. The lights of London, looking down, were a stunning necklace. Maureen, standing behind me as we queued to disembark, held me close and kissed the top of my head.

There were two single beds in the flat; we used one. We had dinners out of tins and packets – steak pies, chips, Swiss roll with custard. We worked in Liberty's in the West End, selling luxury goods to fabulous women, had subsidized meals in the staff canteen, and hung around Carnaby Street before going home on the Tube, amazed that trains could run underground. We had little surplus cash, after paying for rent, food and utilities.

I switched to an office job where English ways continued to astonish me.

'Would you like to fetch the file?' the supervisor asked me.

'No, thanks. I'm busy,' I replied.

She explained that 'would you like' meant 'Do it now. I'm the boss.'

Luncheon vouchers were given as part of the wage system – a

marvel: people would pay me to eat – and I sometimes stood on the Strand and sang that indeed, Mary, this London was a wonderful sight.

Our life together, in love and in London, went horribly wrong when we started going out with our colleagues in the department stores. We moved into a flat in Earl's Court with young English-women, to save money on rent. They didn't read books. They invited us to dances. We could hardly refuse. One day I looked over the balcony of the flat, and there was Maureen walking down the street with Edward, who had come over to visit her. That Saturday night, making the ritual weekend telephone call to my parents, who stood in the shop waiting for it, I said to my father, 'I love you, Daddy.' I took strength from his delight. 'I love you, daughter,' he shouted down the line. I could hear the smile in his voice.

After eight weeks, Maureen and I travelled home in silence. She wore a beautiful new coat and brooch, bought from money her parents had sent to her. There was one final reunion at school, at a mass of thanksgiving and prayer for the future, as we all prepared to go our separate ways. A handful of us, including Maureen and myself, were destined for university. The British government had introduced free university education, complete with a scholarship that in some cases came close to the wages our fathers earned. Those of us who came from the working class were the first generation ever to reach such dizzy heights. Maureen and I arrived separately at the mass. I knelt behind her. She was at ease. I wept as the class sang 'Panis Angelicus'. That night, my mother passed me to my father, who passed me to Sister Agatha, who passed me to Mother Gertrude.

Chapter Six

By the time I set off for Queen's University in Belfast in October 1961, the vague outline of our family's future, and its attendant worries, was taking shape. School was giving way to work and marriage, but would there be a permanent job in a city with 25 per cent unemployment? And even if there were, would there be decent accommodation in Derry for the married couple? What would happen when children came along? Couples were already crowding in on top of parents in our street.

Muireanna, the eldest, had married that year, at twenty-one, and emigrated immediately to London with her husband, Maurice, a Teddy boy who earned his living laying tiles in his native Donegal. Muireanna had worked in shops and shirt factories after leaving Thornhill at sixteen. There is still a dispute about whether she left school to dance her rock'n'roll youth away – she was of the first generation to be known as teenagers – or whether our parents sent her out to work to supplement the family income. And was our father wrong when he refused her permission to play with the local dance band, which was interested in her considerable skills as a pianist?

Nuala, at nineteen, was at work as a secretary for the town's leading Catholic butcher, having completed her senior certificate at Thornhill and a spell at secretarial school. There is still a dispute as to whether my father was right to insist she work in Derry, instead of accepting a position in the civil service in Belfast.

Hugh, at eighteen, was a trainee butcher, also at Doherty's, a job he had held since leaving the Christian Brothers at fourteen. It obliged him to rise every morning at six while his sisters and brother slept on.

Paddy, aged fifteen, was at St Columb's College, the male equivalent of Thornhill.

Carmel, aged thirteen, was at secondary school.

When I left, my father, Nuala and Hugh were earning money,

and the almost simultaneous departure of myself and Muireanna meant that sleeping space in the three-bedroomed house was luxuriously decreased to two people per room. I had a scholarship worth £450 a year, nearly half my father's wages, and I was able to send thirty shillings home every week.

The grandeur of Queen's University left me stunned with delight. It had enclosed courtyards, gothic steeples, a library with shelves so high you had to use steps, cobbled walks, trees, lawns, a students' union with stained-glass windows under oak rafters – and we students could do what we liked and go where we liked, when we liked. Queen's was ours to treat as we pleased: attend lectures or no, eat at any hour we chose, spend money as we wished. I was a rich intellectual with my own castle at seventeen years of age.

Once outside the university gates, I reverted to convent-school status, living in Aquinas Hall, an all-female establishment run by nuns, sharing a room with three others, all of us in single beds. The erotic hothouse fever of Thornhill that burned in all-girl schools in the 1950s might never have existed; such was the change between school and university. I would go unkissed for the next six years.

Maureen, who was also going to Queen's, went straight into a flat in Belfast. A fellow I had met in Rannafast, quiet and rural and too shy to attempt a kiss, escorted me to the Freshers' Ball, and we sat in the balcony looking down at her as she waltzed with a new boyfriend from Derry who could scarcely rub two words together. I wept and told my escort that I was lesbian. He nodded, and said nothing. I asked him to dance anyway, and he said that he didn't know how. I left him to his solitary devices and went home, quickly. It didn't matter that I thought myself gorgeous in the blue satin ball gown, panelled and petalled like a flower, made for me, at great expense to my parents, by Maisie Curran, the local dressmaker. It was irrelevant that I had eyes more beautiful than those of Elizabeth Taylor. I wept myself to sleep under the smart tartan – and expensive – travelling rug that my parents had bought to keep me warm in Belfast. I was a heartbroken social misfit: a lesbian. Immediately, I wrote an epic prose poem about heartbreak for one of my tutors, who pointed out that she had asked for an essay, not the story of my life.

Scholastically, I went from hero to zero, failing two of three first-year exams, but I was entranced by reading books, writing poetry, attempting prose and dreaming of trains, and boats and planes. Mairead Fleming, the only schoolgirl I considered my equal, had a similar temporary nose dive.

Men ruled the roost. Some of them, consolingly, were exciting company. On Freshers' Day – when new students explored their new universe, examining the stalls of intellectual wares set out by student societies – a fresher with a beard had stood by himself waving a Bible and declaring himself an atheist. This was dead frightening. I had never met an atheist. His name was Michael Farrell. At Freshers' night in the premier debating society, the Literific, Eamonn McCann made what was, for the time, a risqué speech on the meaning of Aquinas Hall – a horse's ass was his loose translation. Austin Currie formed a New Ireland political party, with the stated object of fostering closer relations with the sundered Republic. This attracted the debating ire of a young unionist called John Taylor.

Writing was the only outlet for women, none of whom spoke in the Literific. We didn't dare; we feared the mockery of the men. The little known, sedate English Society, of which I became secretary early in first year, attracted no female speakers either, but it at least gave an entrée into the glamour of the male world. Seamus Heaney, then in his third year, had to accept that the poem I wrote for the society's magazine was better than his, which was rejected. He wrote about turf; I wrote about sex. There was no contest.

> I read the *News of the World* because,
> I am bound by stringent Catholic laws
> That say I must not have intercourse,
> Nor enjoy by any other source,
> Premarital sinful pleasure.
> And yet though were I to tell the truth,
> I might admit that I'm just loath
> To run the risk of pregnancy and so
> I sex myself through another girl's endeavours.

As English Society secretary, I attended dinners given in honour of visiting male lecturers, was waited on at table, just like the men, and drank wine and port. One such dinner gave rise to yet another poem, which was politically prophetic, however pathetic the verse:

Tittle tattle, table talk,
A toast now to the Queen,
While my glass remains unseen,
Still on the table.

I was not a nationalist. I was not an Irish rebel. My future career, such as I thought about it, would be in England. And yet, I was having none of this nonsense about subservience to the British throne. None of the Protestant students threw their weight about in any sectarian way: they didn't need to. The cinemas in Belfast played 'God Save the Queen' at the end of every evening, which never happened in Derry, and viewers of a Catholic background rushed to leave before the alleged 'national anthem' or chose to remain seated. It wasn't hard to remain seated after viewing Marlon Brando stand up for his trade union rights in *On the Waterfront*, or seeing Natalie Wood fight for ethnic freedom in *West Side Story*.

The most sustained political gesture I ever made in Queen's was pious attendance every Friday at bread-and-cheese lunches held in support of Oxfam's campaign against famine in Third World countries. Even then, I finished one bread-and-cheese sandwich early so that I could go next door to hear Phil Coulter, another student from Derry, make his first ever recording, 'Foolin' Time'. I ranked his provincial efforts along with those of the bog man Seamus Heaney. What chance had Coulter in the era of the Beatles? Still, one had to support the local boy, though I chastised him for not paying enough attention to his classical music course.

My sister Carmel was there for the Coulter recording. Determined to further her truncated education, I had brought her to Queen's for a week. She spent late nights in Smokey Joe's eating chips, had been hoisted on to the shoulders of Mairead Fleming's boyfriend Michael Morrison during a Beatles concert, slept through one lecture, and read magazines in the library – the compleat university experience, it seemed to me.

During this time I went on my first-ever trip to Dublin, capital of the Republic, as part of an Irish-language student drama group. I had been cast as a ghost, which obliged me to cover myself in a white sheet and wail 'Ooohhh' in Gaelic. The expenses-paid trip to Dublin revealed a world apart from anything I had ever intuited or been taught about the Free State. We gazed at the beautiful Georgian houses and spacious roads, and had coffee in late-night student haunts where we felt instantly provincial and dowdy. Our leader, who had a student cousin in Dublin, brought me to meet him on a Sunday morning in a brass, tiled and mirrored pub in the vast main thoroughfare of O'Connell Street. She ordered me something called an Irish coffee – whiskey, coffee and cream, dark and gold and hot in a glass – and pointed through the window at the bullet holes in the General Post Office where the fight for Irish freedom began in 1916. I was more impressed by the Irish coffee – booze at half-eleven on a Sunday morning? Belfast remained adamantly shut on the Protestant sabbath, and here I was drinking, then going on to see this confident young man's amazing flat, all high ceilings and French windows, and the world bustling past his front door. Something stirred in my intellectual undergrowth. Someone had not been giving me the full picture of Ireland, about which all I knew was that it had no native mineral wealth, and that the people were still not the better of the Famine, which had cut the population in two and forced a million survivors to emigrate to America and England.

I changed my mind again after Dominic Behan, brother of Brendan, came to Queen's as a guest at some debate or other. He lived in London, despised Dublin as a conservative backwater, and led us all at a party afterwards in singing an anti-Irish government song, dating from the Civil War, called 'Take It Down from the Mast'. As I understood it, he was telling us that the future lay in a left-wing alliance between Ireland and England, and taking up guns against the Dublin government.

But we stand with Enright and Larkin,
With Daly and Sullivan bold,
We will break down the English connection,
And bring forth the nation you sold.

At the end of my first year at Queen's, my parents had greeted with
equanimity the news that I had failed two of my three exams. I had
phoned Belfast from the corner shop to get the results, and the walk
up our street was a Calvary. I was shocked and crying. The women
were gathered round Ettie's door as I called up to them that I had
failed. 'You'll pass next time,' Ettie responded immediately. 'Never
mind them,' my mother snorted. I could not face standing with
them, though they all offered me cigarettes and novenas of prayer.
My father had no doubts at all that I would pass the resits after a
summer's study, using my student card to gain access to Magee
library. In the week before the resits, as I sat up late in the kitchen
revising, my mother played and replayed on the gramophone the
last movement of Tchaikovsky's 1812 Overture. 'That'll keep ye
awake,' she said, grinning at the sound of cannon booming, while
she ironed and mended and tended the fire. We would sometimes
still be there at dawn when my father came downstairs to start his
day. I failed one of the two exams, but was able to carry it into
second year.

The notion that education would make us somebodies was
reinforced, that year, by the publication by Brian Friel of his first
book of short stories, *A Saucer of Larks*. Though not officially from
Derry – he had been born elsewhere – he lived all his adult life in
the town and we basked in his reflected glory. It was the first book
I ever bought by choice, and my sister Nuala and I had to club our
money together to raise the price of it.

Later in 1962, Eamonn McCann wrote and staged a satirical
revue on Irish history called *No Man's Prayer*, the title taken from
what Terence MacSwiney had said while dying on hunger strike
during the War of Independence – 'He who dies for Ireland needs
no man's prayers.' The lead role was taken by a quiet, self-effacing
Protestant student of liberal bent, Stephen Rea. I agreed to lend

77

my talents and give the young lad support by my presence. No rehearsal was necessary, McCann pledged. None needed, I believed. My character walked onstage to praise the real uprising – of people who looted profitably while British soldiers' attention was on the IRA occupation of the General Post Office. The play was anti-IRA, and mocked its preoccupation with the Irish national flag while the poor went in rags: 'Jesus, I've just seen Maggie Muldoon with a pair of silk knickers down to her knees,' I said. The revue caused ructions.

Eamonn McCann was the Establishment's worst nightmare: a Fenian at Queen's, seducing the Prods. Some time after the play, I spotted him in the street, leaped off the bus, and asked him to accompany me to the Aquinas Hall formal dance. He agreed at once, but turned up dead drunk. He had accepted my invitation only because he thought I had spotted another Queen's leading light, Bowes Egan, kiss him goodbye outside the pub and feared that I had misinterpreted the gesture. Egan was the Brideshead Reduced figurehead of the university: tall, blond, slight, brilliant, rich and Catholic, always surrounded by men in a faintly homoerotic atmosphere. When I told Eamonn that he need not worry about proving his heterosexual credentials with me, me being lesbian and all, he nodded sympathetically and proceeded to drink even more. This saddened me; I longed to dance. Phil Coulter's student band was playing the hits, cha-cha numbers and Bobby Darin's 'Multiplication' about birds and bees, boys and girls. Eamonn soon left, and I took off the ball gown, never to wear one again.

Bowes Egan, helped by Eamonn McCann, became president of the Literific in an election marked by an extraordinary cruelty against the other contender, a mature student called John Duffy, who wore callipers as a result of childhood polio. Egan was going to win handily anyway, but cartoon posters appeared depicting the crippled man dismounting awkwardly from an aeroplane. Did we want such a fellow to represent the university? the posters asked. There was a frisson of horror about this, but no protest. We were afraid of an equally horrible riposte against our unlovely selves.

★

I sailed through second year and switched to psychology in the third year, where I exulted in the results of a test that showed me to have the highest marks for neurosis in the whole class. This was an indicator of genius, I thought.

As we came out of a dance in the university one night in November 1963 someone told us that President Kennedy had been killed. We agreed glumly to go on to another dance, at a Catholic teacher-training school, but when we got there it was no use. Nobody had a heart for it. I went home and sat up all night listening to short-wave radio broadcasts about the assassination. Next morning, I went out and bought all the newspapers, my first adult experience of trying to follow the news.

A student called Róisín McAuley from Cookstown, Co. Tyrone, actually hired a television set, a grainy black-and-white luxury in those days, and threw a party on the night the 1964 British election results were announced. We cheered when Labour's Harold Wilson was elected prime minister. We convinced ourselves that, if Wilson only knew what was going on in the North, he would extend proper British rights to us – a proper job and a house. Our Muireanna and Maurice could come back home; our Hugh would not have to live in a cold-water room with his new wife. Equality for all, under British rule. Up Labour and down with the Queen; at most we were anti-monarchy.

Graduation day, 1964, when I was twenty years old, was lonely. I had scraped an arts degree. All of the Derry graduates had boyfriends or girlfriends. All of us from a Catholic background feared a future of emigration, and joining the masses in working for a living. My mother had just undergone a hysterectomy and was in considerable pain, sitting through an interminable ceremony just to see me walk across a platform in five seconds. Afterwards came the moment I dreaded, when all the Derry parents agreed to repair to a hotel for a drink before going home. If any of the swanky ones should slight my parents . . . My father went straight up to the bar where the men were standing, ordered drinks for everyone, and started telling his stories. The women clucked around my mother, and they discussed hysterectomies and all things female. I was tearfully proud of both of them.

They called in on relatives of a Derry neighbour on the way back to the train, and I stayed the night in Belfast with a friend who was about to go to England to teach. No graduation balls for those of us who didn't have a boyfriend between us, and no regrets either. Far from it, we were aghast at the number who were planning to marry immediately; the vast majority of the Catholic graduates were bent on marriage and emigration. Their average age was twenty-one.

I returned to Queen's for another year, ostensibly to get a Diploma in Education that would allow me to teach in a grammar school, but the real aim was to have another lovely year on the generous scholarship. Bored, and with little else to do, I roused myself to support well-meaning, modest local boy, the Derry teacher John Hume, when he led a protest into Stormont, the seat of government, in February 1965. The Unionist government was refusing to locate a proposed second university for the North in Derry, despite our town's superior claim. Derry is the second city of the North, and it already had a third-level institution, Magee College, which fed students through to Trinity College in the Republic of Ireland. The local unionists who supported Hume and, in an unprecedented display of Derry unity, drove in cavalcade with him to Stormont, were later revealed to be working behind the scenes to divert the university to any place but Derry. They feared loss of local power to an educated Catholic majority, and the opening of closed Protestant minds. The second university went to Coleraine, a minor backwater, but with the crucial Protestant majority. It were ever thus, we glumly concluded, and the waters closed over the first real challenge to Unionist domination of Northern Ireland.

The most dramatic event to happen during my years in Queen's, a harbinger of the future, was the expulsion of Eamonn McCann from the university during his fourth year, 1965. By this time McCann was vice chair of the Queen's Labour group, and his presidency of the Literific had caused ripples straightaway when the English leftie playwright John Antrobus stood up on the debating table and dropped his trousers. This passed for sexual daring, and the men applauded their hero. Ostensibly, McCann was expelled for 'stealing' several bottles of champagne and some wine from the Botanic Inn bar, attached to a hotel. It was the night of a dinner held by the Literific. The bar was closed and he wanted more after-dinner champagne, so he had helped himself. We accepted Eamonn McCann's expulsion like lambs, fearing that we, too, might lose our precious chance at university education. We believed the university was keen to get rid of him: McCann had just starred in an unprecedented televised debate about the future of the North with Brian Faulkner, Minister for Home Affairs in the Stormont government. All of us at the debate knew that a seismic change had occurred: McCann wiped the floor with Faulkner. The most brilliant orator of his generation, Eamonn laid bare the sectarian, anti-Catholic, anti-Irish nature of the state-let. He was fearless, informed, young – just twenty-two – and breathtakingly beautiful.

The debate had sad, albeit secret, consequences for me. Television captured me seated in the front row, dressed, as I thought, to the nines, in the latest fashion: a sheepskin jacket, with black trousers stuffed into fur-lined knee-length leather boots, inspired by the movie *Doctor Zhivago*. Julie Christie I was not, and my legs did not comfortably reach the floor together when I sat on a chair, so I rested one foot on an ankle, using the leg on the floor to prop myself upright. A schoolboy in Derry, discussing the debate with his classmate, my brother Paddy, had asked, incidentally and scornfully, who the woman was in the front row who dressed like a man. Paddy punched him to the ground. When he gruffly informed me of how he had defended my honour, I burned inwardly with shame and horror, had nightmares about looking like Radclyffe Hall, put away the garments and wore frocks for the remainder of my student days.

McCann soon left for England, where he became a tree-pruner and trade union activist. I continued to go to the Literific, one of the few female regulars, and became known as a barracker: 'Rhubarb,' I would murmur loudly during boring speeches. This was thought quite daring for a woman. Most of the time, though, I haunted the second-hand book stalls in Smithfield Market, a downtown place, and the only venue, apart from cinemas, which would attract me away from the cosseted environment of Queen's. I began by reading every detective book written by Mickey Spillane, moved on through the James Bond novels, graduated up to John O'Hara, immersed myself in beatnik literature, and began buying classical records. A social low point occurred when I stirred myself to take part in a fundraising student Rag Week, put on a lumberjack shirt and a cowboy hat, and sat glumly on the back of an open-topped lorry which moved unnoticed through the streets of Belfast. It was freezing, I felt like an idiot and I was lonely.

I had left Aquinas Hall after two years and moved into a bedsitter on the top floor of a gloomy house, spending most of my days sleeping. The house was run by a dour sister and brother, Protestants, in a street that ran parallel to one which was later immortalized by Van Morrison's 'Cyprus Avenue'. While Madame George ran the brothel there (all unknown to us Catholics), a bunch of us got our kicks from playing poker practically every night, after a lingering supper in Smokey Joe's café of a plate of chips and a cup of tea. I had at last found a suitable milieu for whiling the nights away. The students who played poker, mainly male, did not waste time in trifling, irritating talk about romance, though one night one of them, a lovely character called Jimmy, gave us a glowing report on losing his virginity. Jimmy went to bed with a female whom he loved, while we played on steadily in the kitchen. He returned after a couple of hours, having left his girl home. 'Afterwards, we just pushed away from each other on the bed, wrecked. I just wanted to sleep. So did she. Honest to God, it was just beautiful.'

This was deeply encouraging, given the stories women were telling me. Because I lived alone, lit an extravagant fire in the grate every night, and had started buying the odd bottle of wine, and because I liked listening, a succession of females came to me with their woes. A gentle, reticent rural student, who occasionally had me round to her crowded flat for tea – shy girls often felt sorry for me, seemingly brainy, radical and totally alone – told me she didn't want to get married without having seen her fellow's body, and he felt likewise, but their Catholicism prevented them from physical intimacy. All the same, she wanted to get the thing over with that she dreaded: seeing his penis, that mighty baton which could not possibly fit into her little vagina and would draw blood. And he wanted to see her vagina – in case, à la Norman Mailer, there was a pair of teeth up there which would bite off the penis if a woman were displeased.

I told her to go to a priest in confession, say she just wanted to look, promise that she wouldn't touch, and ditto for her boyfriend. The priest gave her permission to so do; the pair disrobed beneath the waist, sitting on a sofa in her parents' house, and all was well. This was a great relief to me because the woman was of stout girth, and it is hard to look dispassionately enchanting when the stomach hangs over the nether regions. And, yes, she said, he had got down on his knees to look up there.

A rumour swept Queen's that a used condom had been found on the pavement outside the Catholic students' union club. Everyone heard of it; nobody saw it. The sale of contraceptives from under the chemist's counter was surreptitious (but legal), and even Protestants baulked at buying or using them.

An Englishwoman with a racy reputation collapsed one night in my room, blood pouring out of her. She had had an illegal abortion and was afraid to go to hospital. Her story fitted the stereotype on which we Irish Catholic virgins had been reared: she was English and Protestant, and had been sleeping with a black medical student whose bedside lamp boasted a red bulb. Relying on hearsay, I placed a towel under her as she lay on my bed – it was common then for new brides to bring a towel on honeymoon to staunch the blood which would flow after their groom had pierced them – and watched her drift into unconsciousness. Then I left the house, raced to the nearby hospital, asked to see a Catholic doctor, explained the dilemma, and was reassured by him that the woman would be treated with total discretion. The police would not be involved. Returning by taxi, I woke her, helped her downstairs and brought her straight to the nice doctor. She never came back to the university. (Years later, when I stayed with her for a couple of days in London, while looking hopelessly for a professional job, she and her new fellow mocked me for being such a provincial little Irish thing. I was astonished and hurt, and left immediately.)

A worldly fellow called Maurice set his cap at me, but gave up after a few weeks of listening to classical music. He switched his attention to an acquaintance of mine, Susan, who was more hetero-sexually daring and had learned by heart the sleeve notes of the albums he liked. The three of us worked in England over a summer, lodging with a divorced woman who worked on the buses. The landlady's twelve-year-old daughter wept one morning as I ordered her to go out and buy the bread for our breakfast, which her mother had neglected to do before going to work the early-morning shift. I watched from the window as the child dragged herself down the street, and was ashamed for treating her so. It was a far cry from my own childhood.

Susan came back pregnant. She and I went to a public phone and rang Maurice at home, where he had gone for the weekend. She wept with such fear that snotters ran from her nose. He declined to marry her and hung up. We rehearsed a threatening speech – we would go to his hometown and tell all to his parents – and rang again. They were married within weeks; both soberly suited, at a lonely, virtually secret ceremony, in a Catholic church in Belfast, after early-morning mass. Her brother was best man, I was her bridesmaid. The groom, used to swanning about as a prince of the universe, was for the first time in his life without a mutually congratulatory group of friends. Susan wept through the ceremony, and I had to dig her in the ribs when the biggest question in our universe was posed. 'She does,' I said to the priest, who had asked her if she would take this man in marriage. The priest waited. 'You do,' I urged her. 'I do,' she said, finally. The four of us took a taxi immediately afterwards to the airport: Maurice was to continue his postgraduate degree in Britain. I heard him whisper to her in the back seat of the car that his mother had bought him a new pair of pyjamas. He was smiling, and had his arm around her. They are still married.

The poker school had resumed, and took us into the summer of 1965, and all of us who played cards failed to get the diploma, which was quite a distinction, nobody having failed it before. That didn't mean I wouldn't be able to teach; only that not every school would take me. The references given by my professors were not entirely encouraging for someone who wanted a career in the Establishment. One wrote:

. . . she exasperated me at times . . . she would have achieved a higher competence if she had been more willing to conform . . . Undoubtedly Miss McCafferty's independence is her greatest asset, even if it has occasionally got in the way of performance . . . since she is not the sort of person one can possibly disregard, I imagine she has one of the basic qualifications of our profession – power to engage attention.

Another said:

. . . she has a straightforward manner, too direct, perhaps, for some refined tastes . . . Her work was uneven but not without promise, interesting and individual, but marked more by boisterous and intermittent insights than by conventional knowledge and careful judgement . . . Her sharpness of response and her disdain for mediocrity, when tempered with sensitivity and charity, led to unusual animation in class and to noteworthy activities.

Chapter Seven

A motley bunch of us, the only ones of our generation who were still unmarried and were still avoiding careers, took off to London for the summer of 1965, rented a flat and worked at anything that came our way. I went to see Marlene Dietrich in a one-woman show. She came onstage in a full-length white fur coat, let it slide off her shoulders to the floor, and allowed us to admire her bare-shouldered bosom-to-ankle silver-frocked splendid self, while the band struck the opening chords of 'Lily Marlene'. After we roared with hunger and admiration, she thrust a long leg through a slit in her garment, to show a foot clad in a high stiletto.

My friend Michael, from Derry, who was working in London, escorted me to a gay club. I explained to him that I had to see for myself what other gay people looked like. The club was located in a dingy basement in Soho. The first person I saw was a young black woman, still wearing her Post Office uniform of jacket, trousers and boots. She was fat. She was butch. She was awful. I clung to Michael's arm, saw through the dim light that the men were effeminate, the women aggressively unwomanly, and I fled the place in shame and despair. A woman with whom I had been having a passionate platonic relationship – books, music, worry about family preoccupied us – stayed the night with me before we embarked on our separate emigrant lives. We were in a single bed. I kissed her. She recoiled. It was over in seconds. The word 'lesbian' rang out. Our friendship endured. I never again made the first move on a female.

I went to Cannes in September, where I had been engaged at low pay with full board and lodging in a school that overlooked the sea front, as an *assistante anglaise*: my job was to engage secondary school girls in English conversation. It was a ruse to get yet another year away from the world of real work. The real aim was to attend the Cannes Film Festival the following May and look at all the stars. Before leaving, I dumped all my jeans and flat shoes, and I arrived at the school wearing an outrageously expensive white wool coat, trimmed with white llama fur, and stiletto heels. That night, an assistant teacher from Sicily, flirty and cheeky, invited me into her single-bed room to play cards. When I finally went back to my own room, I heard her out in the corridor gleefully telling the other assistant teachers, 'Elle est lesbienne.' So much for the frock and fur.

At weekends, I spent most of the time travelling about the South of France, with young British men who were teaching in a nearby boys school. One of them, Mario, a Glasgow-born Scot of Italian parentage, told me after our first meeting that his heart had sunk at my appearance when I came walking down the street towards him. Being Scottish, he had been hoping for an English rose, and instead 'this small, roly-poly Irish female came barrelling at me.' I pointed out that he was of pretty small stature himself, was less than an oil painting, and that I had felt relief upon seeing him because he clearly had not the wherewithal to push his luck with any female, and most certainly not with the statuesque English rose we found teaching in a school in the village of Grasse, up in the hills, where the film star Dirk Bogarde lived. All the same, I liked Mario's mind. He was biting, cynical and as worried as myself about what the future might hold. We sparred all year over the women we met, trying to seduce them with conversation, and I always won handily. Unlike yourself, Mario, I consoled him, no woman need fear that I'm going to jump her bones. That's because you don't dare, he said shrewdly.

We grumbled our way around Nice, Monte Carlo, Arles, Aix-en-Provence, sharing a double room, even a double bed, to save money. I read every English book in the local library, then *Gone with the Wind* in French, and once spent an entire week's wages buying a Chinese dinner for the English rose from up the hill – she wanted a change from French food. Mario was hugely gratified when I told him in despair that conversation between her and me had ground to a halt.

That was the year I discovered the works of Henry Miller, from the effects of which I am not yet recovered. One of his books opened up with a man inserting a candle into the woman's vagina. I had already been persuaded by the French girls to try a tampon, had not grasped that I was supposed to remove the cardboard tube, and had nearly caused myself serious injury. This was also the era of the Profumo scandal in England, and in general the Swinging Sixties seemed to consist of men in suits consorting with women who worked as high-class prostitutes, or male rock stars who hung about with female groupies. There was nowhere in this scenario in which I could fit. Once, on the beach, on a sad, lonely Saturday afternoon, while all the other teaching assistants had gone home to their parents, a swarthy man picked me up. I dutifully laid myself out on the rocks, like a fish on a slab; he bent over, kissed me, then uttered a dismissive snort. I did not blame him, and hated myself for even trying to accommodate him. Another night, I allowed myself to be picked up by an Algerian immigrant, the most despised of France's colonized people, and the poor bastard spent a fortune taking me to a nightclub. There was a handful of people there, staring dispassionately at an overweight woman who sat in a swim-suit in a foaming bathtub, listlessly passing a tubular sponge back and forth between her legs.

After that, I contented myself with evenings spent in the school reading, or going to cultural evenings of chamber music. On rare occasions I treated myself to a morning in a café, drinking coffee and inserting precious coins into a jukebox, which played the Byrds singing 'Hey, Mister Tambourine Man'. We were all wait-ing, waiting, in that small, windy, flyblown town, for the film festival.

I swam a lot to lose what I now realize were delicious curves. Once I reached a buoy far out in the sea. Grabbing it, I wrapped my legs round the thick chain that bound it to the ocean floor, and swayed there, looking back to shore. Eventually, the childhood sensation of clinging to a lamppost came back. It was pleasurable and shameful. Was this to be my life, screwing a life buoy? At least I wasn't kissing the rubber ball, I consoled myself. I swam disconsolately back to shore. My bikini bottom and upper thighs were covered in oil from the chain.

During that year, my sister Nuala went to Lourdes seeking solace and maybe a miracle for the cancer that had made her a guinea pig in the North's medical institutions. It was characteristically brave of her to strip in a lecture theatre before students. I hitched to Lourdes to join her, fighting off male drivers who thought me fair game, then succumbed to the entreaties of a little man who was out driving for the day. He was a bachelor farmer, he said, living alone, aware of how physically ugly he was, and he would consider it an honour if I would dine publicly with him in his neighbour-hood. The restaurant overhung a river from which trout were fished as we watched, and locals admired him as the fish was cooked at table. I was delighted for him, and thought it a fair exchange to accept his excited offer to drive the extra hundred miles to Lourdes, where I declined his offer of marriage and he gravely thanked me anyway for a great day in his life. I learned a lifelong lesson from that: it is easy to please.

Nuala beat the cancer, and we agreed to differ on how and why: she believed in the curative powers of the Mother of God, and I could see that religion was a great comfort to believers. Also, Lourdes is a place where people who are ill, maimed, crippled or dying are given respect, care, tenderness and wheelchair access. I was happy there. I could see the future and how it should work for people who are ill.

The festival finally opened. The first film star I ever saw in the flesh was a dreadful disappointment: Dirk Bogarde, standing on the platform at the railway station, was dressed in sports jacket and cavalry twill, and had legs as thin as pipe cleaners. I was too ignorant to appreciate that, looks aside, he was a great actor. Then Kirk Douglas came sauntering along the beachfront. He paused, and grinned while I took his photograph. 'Do you want to put your finger into my dimple?' he asked, and stuck out his famous chin. I noticed that he had the gnarled hands of a labourer, and was moved and duly obliged. Sammy Davis Jr came along. 'Do you want to see my glass eye?' He popped it into his hand. In the hotel, in an armchair in the foyer, James Garner was holding court. I liked the friendly bulk of him, and that amiable smile and those lovely brown eyes. He noticed me hanging around and invited me to sit on his knee. I did, and he went on talking to the others without missing a beat. Eventually I got bored, clambered down, and saw Sophia Loren walk across to the lift, accompanied by her considerably smaller, rather squat husband.

I followed them into the lift, and refused to tell Carlo Ponti what floor I wished to access. They did not want me to know on which floor they resided. The lift went up and down, up and down, Ponti fuming, Loren gazing silently over my head, me standing below her, looking up into her face. I stood my ground. I was at last – oh, glorious hour – in the presence of beauty. She had tawny eyes, flawless complexion, full lips, glossy hair and a magnificent half-bared bosom. I had not come all the way from Derry – me who had spent nights as an usherette, staring at the widescreen close-ups of people from another planet – in order to walk away now from that planet. Eventually Ponti stopped the lift and called a security guard, and I was discreetly ushered out of the hotel. It did not matter. I had achieved my objective and walked with the gods. (The gods don't walk around Cannes so casually any more.)

When I finally put on a pair of jeans, the day school closed, in June, one of the other assistants greeted me with approving astonishment: 'Ça te donne une tout à fait autre allure.' ('That gives you a totally different allure.') I was at ease, at last, with clothes, after nine months' penance. She had been conducting an affair with the school's female nurse, to all our knowledge, but their dignity forbade any malicious remarks.

I spent the summer of 1966 in Greece with Ann, from my university days, who had just finished a year teaching in Africa. I made a circuitous journey via train from Marseilles to the southern tip of Italy. There would not be another ferry for days, so I shacked up with Lance, an American, who had secured room and board in a deserted hotel in exchange for painting a mural on the wall of its restaurant. How we met, I cannot recall. The road was like that, just as Kerouac said. I helped Lance fill in the outlines of his mural. We entered a dance competition – first prize a one-way ticket to Greece – and won. I left immediately.

On the island of Mykonos, to which Ann and I travelled because of its famous white windmills, I checked my bag into the police station, where all hippies were made welcome. When we had secured a sleeping place on the beach, under the protection of a group of American boys, we returned to the police station. My bag had gone missing. 'Such is life,' said the cop with a steely gaze. The next two months were spent in a towelling beach frock and bikini, the sleeping bag stashed away by day under a rock. I saw my first penis on a nudist beach. 'They're not all as long as that,' Ann soothed me. We got occasional work washing dishes in a downmarket restaurant, with tips if I performed the 'Zorba the Greek' dance with a waiter, which I did.

Smashing plates is lovely. We also learned to love small bottles of rotgut retsina, which accompanied the meatballs served as the sun sank, red, under the windmill sails. A New York Jew, all lip and sarcasm, invited me to his bed one night. He was rich enough to rent a room. I hadn't seen a mattress or shower in weeks, and was flattered that he had chosen me above every woman on the island. In the event, his bedroom floor was crowded with hangers-on. He climbed into bed beside me, whipped out his penis and said, 'Suck it.' I was astonished to meet yet another man who had not heard of foreplay, and I was out of the bed in seconds. Another woman instantly replaced me.

Our American friends persuaded us to travel to another island, where there was work for film extras on a Sam Wanamaker movie, *The Day the Fish Came out*, which dealt with the effects of nuclear bombs. Candice Bergen was the star, which was enough for me. She ate every night in the same open-air restaurant, on the same small pier that we all shared. Ann and I customarily ordered one plate of four meatballs between us, and watched Bergen make her stately way every evening towards a lavishly laid table. Eventually, I came to resent her. She could afford food, I could not, and I was breaking my Irish back charming the local peasants who had to stand around all day waiting for 'Action'. We were clad in black from head to toe, and it was hot and she never spoke to us.

In the event, we were all left on the cutting-room floor, and I never did get paid for being an extra to Bergen. I shared a bed occasionally with one of the Americans, John, and appreciated that he did not tell the others that nothing was happening. He didn't even try. He sensitively knew not to. Some men are all right like that.

Chapter Eight

Ann and I returned to Ireland in the autumn of 1966, resolved to save up for another summer trip in 1967. She got a teaching job in Belfast. I got no job in Derry, despite applying for numerous vacancies. The state or Protestant schools would not hire me because I was Catholic, and the Catholics would not hire me because I was not a proper Catholic. 'You haven't even been to see the Bishop,' said Father Mulvey, on a pastoral visit to our house. People did not apply for teaching jobs in Catholic Derry. They sought an interview with the Bishop, kissed his ring, and 'offered' him their services, without mentioning job or wages. I cannot explain why I took it into my head, aged twenty-two, to do no such subservient thing. The lesson drummed into me by my father played a part, certainly. 'The labourer is worthy of hire and must get a just wage for a just day's work.'

I hadn't seen Father Mulvey since confessing to him at seventeen that I was lesbian. I don't know if that played a part. There was no need to mention it anyway, as he had other ammunition primed and ready. Looking round the sitting room where all serious discussions took place – my parents were waiting in the kitchen – his eye fell on a book by Sigmund Freud. He opened it and read aloud the name of one chapter.

'Sex,' he intoned.

Had I asked permission from the Bishop to study this subject at Queen's?

'I didn't know I had to. How could I have known, unless the Church told me before I enrolled at university?'

'You should have known to ask,' he replied.

'Catch-22,' I countered, flashing my learning in his face.

'You blasphemed at Queen's,' he told me, 'in a play.'

What?

'You took the name of the Lord in vain,' he said, and cited my saying 'Jesus' in Eamonn McCann's revue.

Eventually, Mother Gertrude – she who had told me that I might have to live with lesbianism for ever – offered me a temporary job as substitute teacher in the secondary school where she was now principal. Though glad of the four months' work, I was still snobby and ignorant enough to regard teaching in a secondary school as a step down from grammar school and a glittering career. More fool Mother Gertrude, I ignorantly mistook her vocation. Her seeming demotion reinforced my growing belief that the Church had no regard for women. It didn't matter to the Bishop where women taught, or what, provided we kissed his ring.

It didn't matter much, I soon found, whether the girls learned anything; they were destined for the factories. It didn't matter much whether I tried to teach them or not: I had been brought in to replace a series of teachers who had been unable to handle the rowdiest girls in the school. The teachers were followed by a number of women with no teaching qualifications – including, among others, a retired telephonist – who were willing to fill the breach and practise crowd control.

The school was in the Creggan estate, which had been built to take the overflow from the Bogside, where the parents of the girls had grown up. On the very first day, I hit on the idea of letting them know that I knew their seed, breed and generation. This I did by inviting the entire class to come to my mother's house, after school, for a cup of tea. She gave them tea and buns, and soon established who their parents and grandparents were. She was full of praise for the efforts their parents had made to rear them through years of poverty and hardship. She, too, had been that soldier. I was her daughter, as they were the daughters of their parents, her neighbours, friends and acquaintances. They were soon eating out of her hands, and next day they did not bite mine. In one fell swoop, my mother had given them dignity and changed my snobby attitude towards secondary schools.

★

In the autumn of 1966, the hopelessness of Derry was exemplified by the fact that my brother, married with two children, was living in an attic flat, in a slum dwelling. Under the terms of tenancy, his wife was obliged to clean the stairs every day, from the top of the house to the bottom. Most young married couples lived like that. The population was expanding – the establishment of two new factories, attracted by grants, provided a small alternative to emigration – and there was little building going on. Not a house was built in 1967, for instance. Thousands of families were on the waiting list, the majority of them Catholic. My brother's skilled job as a master butcher counted for nothing. My sister Nuala was among the many who made the pilgrimage up to Creggan to secrete a Padre Pio medal in the foundations of whatever new house was being built. Please, Jesus, give our Hugh a house. We understood the refusal to house Catholics to be a matter of pure sectarianism – that we were being punished for being Catholic and Irish. This was puzzling because, the pious aspiration of the Nationalist Party apart, none of us was looking for a United Ireland. That was up there in the pantheon, with heaven, and we, meanwhile, had to get on with it, on earth.

In January 1967, three bad things happened. My teaching job ended; the BSR record-player factory, Derry's biggest employer, closed down when its seven-year tax-free honeymoon ended, putting thousands out of work; and my mother asked me to make the rounds of party politicians in the city, to plead the case for Hugh, Margo and their two infants. Having been at university, and widely travelled with it, I might make an impression. Ours was not a shiftless family that relied on state handouts. Hugh and Margo were only too willing to pay whatever rent was requested for state housing.

The first man I visited was city councillor Eugene O'Hare, who had sold me my first sanitary towels and who held a clinic in the back room of his pharmacy one night a week. There was a queue at the clinic. When my turn finally came, he listened gravely, courteously, took notes and told me not to get my hopes up. He, and we, were nationalists, and the unionists would do us no favours.

I had seen how crowded the clinic was, he said. A queue just as long as the one I had been part of had already formed behind me again, and supplicants were standing in the street, waiting their turn.

Undaunted, I entered the unionist fortress next day, the city's Guildhall, to speak to the unionist mayor Albert Anderson. He was courtesy itself and took notes.

I left Derry in February 1967 and embarked with Ann on a car journey through Europe, heading for a kibbutz in Israel. Anything was better than being an unemployed, educated, allegedly atheist, Derry spinster. And the ideals by which kibbutzim were governed were deeply appealing: they were run as cooperatives; there were no wages; the longer a person stayed, Gentile or Jew, the better her or his accommodation. Every worker was supplied with free food, accommodation, work clothes and cigarettes, and given a monthly allowance. Another attraction was that I would be helping the Jews who had suffered so much in concentration camps (post-war British television had shown some dramas about that). Also, Paul Newman had starred in *Exodus*, which showed Jews settling Israel the way cowboys had settled the West. I would be the Calamity Jane of them thar' Jewish parts.

We bought a car in Germany – an Opel Record – and had a whale of a time sleeping in it, cooking by the roadside on a Bunsen burner, taking in the sights wherever we paused: a concert in Vienna, an empty supermarket in Yugoslavia, a forced halt by oxen crowding the road in Bulgaria, a train station in Belgrade bursting at the seams with migrant workers sleeping on the platform. Ann did all the driving: I didn't know how. In Istanbul we found that it cost little to hire a sleeping space on the roof of a hotel. The place was full of hippies. We were delighted with ourselves. Wherever we were, Ann took time out to practise on her viola. She played the scales nonstop. I begged her for a tune and she refused: the true artist practises her scales. I wrote while she played.

On a mountaintop in rural Turkey snow forced us to a halt outside a speakeasy. Conversation stopped when we walked, freezing, into a large, dimly lit room full of dark, grizzled men. They made us more than welcome, and we had coffee and schnapps. The men gestured that we should not dream of going back outside to sleep in the car. Young and racist and scared, we insisted, and fell into a cold, wakeful sleep. Just before dawn, hammering on the windows gave us both near heart attacks. We were surrounded by Turks, who poured hot water on the glass to defrost it and waved cups of coffee at us. Prudish to the last, we rolled the window down just enough to accept the proffered gifts. The men refused our offer of money, grinned and smiled approvingly, pointed to the snow-free sky, and cheered encouragement as we rolled away.

Damascus in Syria was a flat, disappointing place where nobody understood English, the Arabic signs were indecipherable and we could not find the 'Street called Straight' where St Paul rested after his dramatic conversion. On we went, through the desert, causing astonishment to families in a camel train, who had never seen a car before. We hadn't seen camels, or people so exotically dressed, all long robes and jewellery and scarves hiding the faces of the women. By the side of the road, we all stopped and gazed at each other, they touching the car, we touching the camels.

We arrived in Jericho and could find no walls; our knowledge of the Middle East was derived entirely from our hazy recollection of Bible stories. Treating ourselves to a rather grand meal – chicken roasted on a flat stone and wrapped in bread – we fell in with a businessman who told us how his family had been put out of that part of Jerusalem controlled by the Israelis. We were not nearly sympathetic enough, exercised as we were by the Holocaust. The man pointed out a throne-like chair at a reserved table, which, he said, was where Arab royalty sat. The chair also acted as a commode, and the local prince often used the facility during meals. Then he gave us each a ring set with bright stone and told us about the Arab tradition of hospitality to all strangers for three days – after which the stranger had better look out, or have a clear conscience at least.

In the rose-red city of Petra there was a police station at the entrance to the narrow gorge, which led down to the abandoned palaces. The commanding officer told us the site was closed for the night and offered us sleeping space on the floor of his station. We accepted, remembering how well the mountain Turks had treated us during the snowstorm, but clung to each other as tightly as if we had been handcuffed, the better to show the cop that he would have a fight on his hands if he made a move on either of us. Trepidation increased when he invited another cop to join us for dinner, and went through the roof when he produced a rifle and invited us outside, where he proceeded to shoot dozens of little birds. 'Dinner,' he said, and gathered them up. A delicious dinner it was as we crunched our way through a platter of little roasted fowl, casting caution aside as wine was consumed. The three-day hospitality tradition was a fine thing, we decided.

Next morning we rode down the defile on sway-backed horses. The ruined fabled city, cut into the rock, was a bowl of dull, perfect isolation. Mountains towered all around. We stood on the floor of that silent valley and watched, open-mouthed, as yawning Western hippies emerged from the mouths of palaces and stood between pillars, scratching themselves. I was frightened. The cop asked if we intended to spend the night. Feeling more Catholic than hippy, afraid of the drifting human wraiths who did not greet us and sure that they were all drugged out of their minds, we clung to his company and left.

Then we were in Jerusalem, in the Arab territory, standing precariously on one chair, looking over the wall at the Jews beyond. Once we entered Israel, we would not be allowed back out through Arab countries. The young man, barely in his twenties, who brought us to the wall, was the worst possible advertisement for his race. He wore a ragged jacket and trousers, had few teeth, had lost two fingers and assured us at first greeting that he could give us 'fucky-fucky' anyway with the fingers remaining to him. But he was biddable, and proud to be seen with white women, and, after his sexual proposals were firmly rebuffed, he cheerfully offered us a place in the cave where he dwelt. First, though, we should look over the wall and mourn his exile with him: he pointed into the dark distance to where his family had lived in a proper house before they were displaced after the Israelis won independence in 1948. This took the shine somewhat off my avowed mission to help the Jews settle into a homeland of their own. All the same, I admonished him: as long as he persisted in offering fucky-fucky to white women, he and Arabs like him would give their cause a bad name. Quite what that cause was, I couldn't figure out, as it then seemed to me that the Arabs had loads of countries where they could settle down while the poor Jews had only a small slice of earth called Israel.

I think I could have said anything to him, so pleased was he to have us as guests in his cave. A radio, a light bulb hanging from a flex, and cushions and rugs on the stone bench that ran round the walls were the sole furnishings. As the night wore on, other whites arrived. He produced dope, rolled cigarettes, and I had cannabis for the first time. I sank into a state of sublime well-being. Then I discovered I could hardly move. Making a huge effort, I walked as if underwater to the outside toilet, in another smaller cave, and sat there head in hands, arms on knees, resolving to get up as soon as the music stopped. The radio was playing 'Lara's Song' from *Doctor Zhivago*. It played the song forever. I was borne up and away on a swell of voluptuous strings. 'Somewhere my love,' I sang along. And what the hell if nowhere, no love: this was more than enough, travelling the world, seeing places and people. The song went on and on. And on. Eventually, I believed, I would be able to get to my feet. Ann was outside, she who had lived and worked in darkest Africa, for God's sake, so I was perfectly safe. I was even a hippy, like Kerouac. On the road. Stoned. In Jerusalem.

Next day we entered Jewish-controlled Jerusalem and went to the church that had been built over the place where Jesus had been entombed. Or was it? A bewilderment of such places, in a bewilderment of churches, run by a bewilderment of sects, was on offer. Nothing was sacred, especially not in Jerusalem, where every site claimed a piece of the Son of God. Gethsemane itself may not have been where the original Gethsemane was. Even so, I dispatched to my mother a crucifix-cum-holy-water-font inlaid with mother-of-pearl, and leaves from the alleged Garden of Gethsemane. We drove to Bethlehem, eight miles away, where yet another freelance Arab guide offered 'fucky-fucky' in the bowels of the church that was allegedly the very site where Christ was born in a manger. I'd had enough and went back to Jerusalem. The Wailing Wall was much better. Nobody disputed its authenticity, and I understood the Jewish religious practice of writing a plea on a piece of paper and lodging it in an interstice in the wall – that was what we did in Ireland, where Catholics placed medals, keepsakes, crutches and bandages in holy wells seeking cures and intercessions. How deeply I wish now that I could remember what I wrote on the note I lodged in that wall.

We strayed down a main road that edged the ultra-Orthodox Jewish quarter. We were unmistakably Gentile in our hippy gear. From the warren of side streets, a swarm of young men in ringlets and black hats came buzzing out, shouting and throwing stones at us.

We travelled to an office in Tel Aviv, where a kibbutz was assigned to us in the northern corner of Northern Israel. On the way there we paused briefly on the shore of Lake Galilee. It was smaller than the Bible would have us believe – Christ could have easily walked round it if he was that pushed – and not one bit stormy. Then we turned on to a long dusty deserted road that finally sloped quietly uphill to Kibbutz Maayan Baruch, directly under the Golan Heights of Syria. It was the beginning of March.

A tarmacadamed forecourt, with a parking place for lorries and tractors, was surrounded on three sides by a large communal dining room and offices. We reported to a tall, rangy sandy-haired fellow called Moni, who took our details, pointed out the distant wooden hut, in a grove, where we would sleep, and gave us a chit for work clothes and boots, bed linen and towels from the store. We would work in the apple orchard, miles away, reporting at four the next morning for breakfast, and receive pocket money once a month, free meals and lodging, and a pair of honorary parents to visit once a week. Apart from the hooked nose, Moni could have been a Derry man. We were each given a free carton of cigarettes, and told that there were plenty more when we ran out. They were awful little things, cheap tobacco in cheap paper in cheap blue wrapping. The pocket money would buy us a bottle of wine a week.

Our new home, after weeks of travel, was bliss. A small foyer gave on to a shower on the right and a large room on the left. It had one big window, a bed at each of the four corners, and a table and four wooden chairs in the centre. We hung clothes on nails and showered under the hot water, which, we discovered, was constant. Winding paths took us past other huts and brick houses. In a secluded grove, outside a small house, in a clearing hidden by trees, we saw an old man cobbling shoes. He wore the clothing of a religious Jew, with a prayer shawl round his shoulders. He had a long white beard. He did not glance at us. Instinct told us not to approach him.

That evening in the communal restaurant we were made welcome, and directed to a table that seated half a dozen young Americans and Canadians, all Jewish, all over for a sabbatical year. We had landed into the only secular kibbutz in all of Israel. The old man apart – and, yes, we were right not to speak to him – these settlers were Jewish by culture, not by religion. They had come mostly from England and America, and only a few had been born in pre-partition Palestine. Our 'parents', a youthful English couple, introduced themselves and invited us to tea the following afternoon, after work, when their baby, who lived full-time in the crèche, would be brought home for a few hours. John, our 'father', would be working in the orchard with us, under the foreman Gusman, who had been born in the former Palestine. Gusman was confident, muscular, handsome and dark-skinned. People queued for food in front of long, clanging stainless-steel counters and hotplates, and it was plentiful. Following soup and stew, there was dessert of stewed apples, cooked apples, eating apples or apples in custard, and we could have apple juice, water or weak coffee to drink. People brought their used dishes back to the kitchen, a steamy place, crowded with workers.

Aviva, an assured, statuesque volunteer from Chicago, immediately stood out. She was deeply tanned with almond eyes and a smooth caul of black hair. I developed an instant crush on her. That night, there was a knock on our door, and a huge American came in to say that now there was an actual car on the kibbutz – ours – he could drive us anywhere we liked in Israel during our one day off a week, or the monthly weekend furlough. The car, we realized, would make us universally popular. There were not many private vehicles in Israel; they were expensive to import because nothing could be brought in through the Arab countries that surrounded the state. It was obvious from his talk that this fellow adored Aviva. Apart from her and us, there were no single available women on the kibbutz.

It was dark when we rose next day and made our way to the canteen, where bitter black coffee and old bread – no butter – constituted breakfast. Nobody spoke much. Gusman, John, Ann and I drove off to the orchard in a pick-up truck, the men in the cab, us sprawled in the back, looking at the stars. Dawn broke as we drove through acres of young trees, about five feet tall, with hardly any branches, and came to a halt before a little shed. We were given tools, driven to a distant location and told to weed our way along the hedges that separated the fields. The men would be working nearby, and we would have a proper breakfast around six.

Determined to prove ourselves, we had one side of the field done before John came to fetch us in the pick-up. Gusman was already cooking when John told him how much we had done. The bond that formed was palpable. Our team would outwork everybody in the kibbutz. Breakfast was six scrambled eggs each, pickled herring, coffee and good bread with butter and a slab of halva. Gusman winked. He took care of his team. No other team in the kibbutz ever had a breakfast like this. We thought of the poor slobs working in big gangs in the cotton fields, the battery-hen sheds, the mature orchards – and toasted each other and went back to work with a vengeance. I was deeply happy. If this was communism or communal work – one for all and all for one – it was the future for me, as Lourdes had been the future for the treatment of those who cannot work.

We went home at noon – 'home' already after less than twenty-four hours – because it was too hot to stay out. Lunch was last night's stew and stewed apples. We showered and slept in the afternoon, dropped our work clothes off at the laundry and picked up a fresh batch, returned them to the hut, and set off for John's house. His wife had laid out tea and sweet biscuits on a table, and, nursing her baby, she hardly spoke. The longer a person worked, the more points were built up, so that eventually a couple – invariably they were couples – graduated from a wooden hut to a concrete two-roomed house, then to a larger house in which older children could live with their parents, having been discharged from the nursery when they were old enough to be unsupervised. Goods such as refrigerators were also allocated on a points basis, and pocket money was increased to the stage where a family could eventually afford a rare holiday back in the homeland, failing which they could take exchange holidays in other kibbutzim – the ones in the Negev Desert, near the Red Sea resort of Eliat, were popular.

Nice though they were, we would not often visit John and his wife. With just a few precious hours with their baby, they needed visiting strangers and stilted conversation like a hole in the head. We veered naturally towards the society of young, unattached people like ourselves – volunteers, playing at being settlers. We fell into the routine almost at once. The volunteers congregated in each other's huts by night, there was a movie once a month, and the coffee-shop-cum-library was open a couple of nights a week, but goods had to be paid for there and we were all saving our money for our air fares home.

As winter turned to spring, Ann and I were promoted to daubing tar on wounds left after Gusman and John had pruned branches, though weeding still had to be done. Other volunteers – goyim like ourselves – dribbled in, and we showed them the ropes. Joop from Holland, thin with a weedy beard, killed a chicken illictly and stuffed it with prunes, roasting it over a campfire by moonlight. Carole from New York, large and shambling and odd as two left feet, drove us crazy in the first week, talking nonstop, an intruder in the third bed, but we came to like her crazy ways. Handsome Trapper John, from Canada, brought furs that he had picked up on his rambles through the Middle East, and pressed his intentions gently, but never laid a finger on me, to the relief of Joop, who had no hope of ever getting a girl. Aviva taught me chess, and tactfully ignored what Ann called the 'moony' face I adopted when in Aviva's company. I was beginning to sleep long, despairing unkissed hours again, as I had done at university. Ann was much in demand among the single men. I wrote an ever-watchful note about myself on my twenty-third birthday, 28 March 1967:

Once I recognized the familiar attraction [to Aviva], I . . . behaved according to plan – a plan which I thought to have long since discarded especially since, if I am going to be what I think I am (I fear to use the word and ostracize myself), I should go about it like a woman, not as the child looking for motherly love, the innocent abroad needing care and protection.

I looked and listened, paying court to every word. I followed her around, bumping into her accidentally-on-purpose. I leaned close when she spoke, so that I could catch the warmth of her breath. When she expounded, I asked leading questions – those which would keep her talking, not questions as I usually ask, designed to pave the way for my point of view . . .

I wish I were thirty that I might know finally what I was (when I was seventeen I wished I were twenty-three that I might know) . . . A queer's letter . . . What a waste. Weakling . . .

A fortnight later, after an evening with Ann and Aviva, I wrote again:

. . . My first problem is that I really don't know what to do in the future. Secondly, when someone points this out, I will reject this and proceed to make a concrete defence. Thirdly, tonight's situation suited me just fine. Three people, unaware, start to search, question and admit. But Ann has an unfair advantage. She knows what I want to conceal; every question bearing on this swallows the air between us and I am left in a vacuum with her, my head spinning, embarrassed with my answers which she knows are not true, or embarrassed with my silences, the reason for which she knows only.

Why do I, otherwise, like such nights? Because I love to find out about other people, to plunge straight into the truth, avoiding politesse. So what does it gain me? At the end we are left stripped, exposed, and if there is no love between us, we have laid waste one another . . .

Problem: I must be myself, show myself, be accepted. But how can I?

Second problem: Do I really want to be what I think – know – won't admit – I am?

As summer approached, we were transferred from the orchard to the cotton fields, initially a dreadful disappointment until I realized that I would be working with Aviva every day. With a bag slung over the shoulder, we would race each other down the rows, competing to fill the bag first. Once in a while the Arabs would launch a bomb from the Golan Heights, and it would hopelessly miss the cotton fields, kicking up a spurt of dirt. We were warned to stay watchful when bathing in the rocky stream that ran down from the Heights along the edge of the kibbutz.

At the beginning of June a huge batch of volunteers – young, educated, professional white Jews from South Africa – arrived for the summer. They brought the latest record with them. We forswore sleep and played the Beatles' *Abbey Road* all night. The South Africans also brought dope – we cashed in our monthly allowance on wine and real cigarettes, and we went to work next morning high as kites. That evening we attended the Hebrew lessons which had been hastily arranged for the South African Jews. Learning how to speak the language, never mind write the strange symbols, promised to be a challenge in a kibbutz where the common language was English.

Around eleven on the morning of Monday, 5 June 1967, we were ordered to report to our bunkers. Israel and Egypt had engaged in battle in the Negev. We went down steps into a large, dimly lit concrete room. We were each given a plain white postcard, on which to write messages to our parents. 'Having a wonderful time,' I wrote. They received the card in Derry, amazingly, three days later, just as the war deepened. 'Derry girls safe,' said the front page of the *Belfast Telegraph*, noting that the card mentioned a lunch of egg-and-onion sandwiches. Towards the end of the article, it was mentioned that thousands had died in the fighting.

When I did send a real frontline dispatch a week later, the *Telegraph* declined to publish it, but noted in a paragraph that the Derry girls had come through alive. I titled the article 'A Kibbutz Mobilizes':

. . . For most of us, the war is a question of passing the time underground, of trying to stay clean, of looking for a cigarette. The BBC announces that Syria claims to have occupied the entire Hula valley, where we are now sitting, quite bored, and I wonder what my mother must be thinking. We hear that the Old City of Jerusalem has been taken. For the first time in almost 2,000 years, Jews hold a religious service at the Wailing Wall. There is great national joy, and we gather together in the twilight to drink a celebration glass of wine. Mazala, eyes bright, hugs me and speaks of the day twenty years ago, during the War of Independence, when she stood there with a baby in her arms and wept at the sight of a Flying Fortress, the first and only Israeli plane she had seen defending Upper Galilee. And today, Egypt and Jordan are defeated.

On the fourth morning there is a lull in the fighting. We resume normal duties, though confined to the kibbutz. Abe, twenty years old, who took a year off university to come here with a group of Canadian and American Jewish volunteers, borrows a truck and drives down the valley to the new orchards. For two hours he works alone there, within sight of the Syrian mortars, irrigating the young trees. His companions have spent the night on guard duty, crouched in a ditch by the main road armed with machine guns and rifles. They stop all traffic and ask for the password 'Marat Shimson' (Gates of Samson). If they meet trouble, their orders are to shoot to kill.

After lunch, the siren suddenly wails, loudly rising and falling; I drop the dishes I have been washing in the kitchen and run outside, panic-stricken. My shelter is 200 yards away. Then I overtake my friend Ann and burst out laughing. Asleep when the siren sounded, she is headed frantically for the shelter clad only in a brightly coloured bedspread . . .

On Friday night, at sunset, Shabbat begins. In the shelter a South African boy reads the service and sips the traditional glass of wine. Two lighted candles are placed on an upturned box and we sing 'Shabbat Shalom' (a peaceful sabbath). Outside, on the mountain, our soldiers fight beside brightly burning tanks.

On Saturday morning we awoke to complete silence. The mountain is ours; our troops have gone over the top and into Syria. By nine o'clock we are back in the wheat fields, in the sunshine, gathering hay. A ceasefire has been declared, and the war is over. Shabbat Shalom!

I know now that I should have put into the article the fact that the women were given a few blunderbusses when the war began, to kill ourselves with in the event of rape by Arabs should they overrun the kibbutz. There weren't enough of the big ancient things, which looked rather like the horns on old record players, to allow us one each, and we got a single demonstration – by a man – in how to use them. I kept my British passport at hand, for extra protection, intending to wave it at the Arabs while they had their way with real Jewish women.

What I could not have written about – a first lesson in journalism for me – were the emotional explosions that the war brought on. Aviva and a young South African volunteer had fallen for each other the night before the war broke out, and he abandoned his fiancée, who had come to the kibbutz with him, to join Aviva in her bunker. This news rocked us and broke the young woman. Aviva's widowed Aunt Peggy had also started an affair with Ralphie, who had helped found the kibbutz with her, during the brief war, and when they emerged Ralphie left his wife and moved into Peggy's house. The tension and implications of their affair shook the kibbutz to its foundations. There were only 200 settlers, and the affair was impossible to ignore. Ralphie's wife stopped coming to communal meals. Nobody could figure out what to do. All three were entitled to remain living there, though the woman's poor sad face was a daily rebuke. After two weeks, Aviva's fellow, a doctor, went back to his fiancée, then Aviva was suffering.

My mother wrote to say that during the Six Day War she had a vision of me, as she sat worrying and drinking coffee in the afternoon. She looked to where I normally sat at the table after coming home from school and saw me, clear as day, sipping weakened coffee, sitting on the chair with one foot tucked under my bum and the other swinging back and forth, as I gave her my day's news. I immediately composed and sent her a poem entitled 'Mammy'. What she made of it, I cannot think:

> Foetus-formed I curl me,
> Clutching at the cord
> That binds me still to her.
> I feel her strength come to me,
> Comforting, however distant,
> And slowly I unfurl,
> Trying to stand in her image.
> She casts a sweet shadow,
> Shelters me;
> But if I laid my head upon her breast
> The tears would come –
> And I would not cause her pain.
> So the cord lies loose,
> Though always there.

Jaysus, but I was a lonely little lesbian on a kibbutz.

A welcome escape from the claustrophobic atmosphere came through a tour of the 'liberated' territories. Leaving behind a skeleton staff, we piled into trucks and drove up to the Golan Heights. Pushing further inland, past burned-out tanks and aeroplanes, we came upon an abandoned pharmacy in an oasis of palm trees. Joop suggested that he and I search it for drugs such as morphine. Though we found nothing, I noted the thrill that came from looting, and feeling entitled to do so. We slept in sleeping bags under the stars and ate out of tins. Next morning we searched an abandoned village. I helped myself to a black-and-white keffiyeh, the Arab headdress. We entered the abandoned primary school, and there gazed in silence at a cartoon drawn in chalk on the blackboard. It showed Jews, with great hooked noses, saliva dribbling from their mouths, teeth bared and expressions of hate on their faces, bent over Arab women and girls, preparing to rape them.

The same propaganda about Arabs raping Jews had been taught to us, and the point was not lost on me. It did not stop me from taking part in the convoy that swept into Sharm el Sheik, on the sea. It was a sandy, dust-blown place of wooden huts. We crowded into the shabby restaurant staffed by a solitary sullen Arab and ordered fruit juices, slapping Israeli money on to the counter, the currency of the occupier, which he was obliged to accept; we demanded change in Israeli money. He had it already in the drawer. As we raced into the water, the women in bikinis, I felt a niggling sense of shame at this insult to Arab culture. On the other hand, we were hot and sweaty.

The life as we knew it before war continued to unravel. An elderly South African couple arrived with their daughter, having sold up their home. Within a week, the father had a heart attack which left him in need of round-the-clock care. This promised to drain the kibbutz's financial resources. The alternative was to send the family to make a home in one of the country's main cities. But they knew nobody and didn't speak Hebrew.

I became more curious about how exactly the philosophy of one for all and all for one worked in practice. It emerged that, though many of the kibbutz pioneers had arrived with nothing but the clothes they stood up in, some settlers had left money in bank accounts in Tel Aviv when they first arrived in the country. This explained why a few were able to take weekends in cities, while others took their breaks in other kibbutzim. This new-found knowledge was not entirely upsetting. The kibbutz offered a hard, austere life. It would not have been entirely fair to expect those who had some surplus wealth to hand it over entirely, for use in an experiment which had no guaranteed outcome, and which might indeed collapse. The unanswered question was: How much personal wealth should one retain as insurance against a rainy day? This was a question that was to plague me as I was drawn more and more to socialism.

I learned that I must never ask about the number tattooed on Sarah's wrist. Sarah had a strong Liverpool accent. She was about fifty, so must have been in her late twenties when she emerged from the concentration camp in 1945. She was a short, strongly built woman, of enormous good cheer and energy. You could see the number only when she rolled up her shirtsleeves to set about work with an extra surge of energy. She was in charge of one of the mature apple orchards, a position of considerable responsibility, something which was a source of pride among the other women. I worked even harder for her than for Gusman and John. The faint blue brand on her wrist was a visible reminder of the reason I had come to Israel. When the opportunity presented itself, I would look down from my apple-picking ladder, through the leaves, and stare at it. But no matter how often I sat near her during snack breaks, she never talked about her past.

In early September Ann decided to go back to Belfast to teach. We sold the car easily – and at a profit – which gave us both the fare home and a few dollars to spare. Ann took off.

The apple picking was what broke most of the volunteers. No matter how often we climbed up that ladder, with empty baskets slung about our shoulders; no matter how often we came back down, baskets filled; no matter how many of us attacked the same huge tree – and at times we swarmed through its branches like locusts – we made little visible dent in the amount of its abundant fruit. Sarah drove us like slaves, and Arabs were hired to help out. They sat apart from us during meal breaks. They wore traditional dress and were older than us. They worked on separate trees. There was no communication between us, though I sometimes essayed a smile when I had to pass them. They did not respond. I regarded them with some disdain: they had bad teeth; they had no English; they kept their eyes down; they worked humbly for their oppressors.

That autumn, in quick succession, most of the volunteers packed up and left. Joop and I accepted a lift to Haifa, and a young Swedish volunteer, a Gentile like ourselves, decided to leave with us.

She was nineteen, with straight blonde hair reaching to her waist,

wore a permanently serious expression and hardly ever spoke. The
three of us lay on the covered flatbed of the truck, lounging on our
knapsacks, looking out and bidding a mental goodbye to Israel. I
was afraid for the future: Joop thought we should take a boat to
India. But what would we do there? What would we live on after
our money ran out? He didn't know if it was even possible to sail
there from Haifa. My outstretched leg bumped against Marie's,
who was sitting opposite. A streak of sunlight fell across the blue
jeans we both wore. Hers were beautifully faded and pressed. Her
leg was very long, and she wore soft brown moccasins. Our legs
bumped again, and I did not shift mine this time. She did not shift
hers. We looked at each other and smiled. I fell into a pleasurable
swoon. Joop continued to talk. Marie and I rolled with the bumps
on the road, making sure to keep our legs in contact.

At Haifa, I told Joop I was going back to Ireland, and he accepted
this with a minor grumble. Marie and I continued on to Tel Aviv,
where she had arranged to rent a flat from an old man who had
befriended her, and take Hebrew lessons, and study art. Her late
father, a factory owner, had left her a small inheritance. She did not
get on with her mother, who drank too much. Cheap student fares
back to Belfast were about to end. I booked a flight home.

That night we sat on a sofa in the twin-bedded room, looking
at each other's family photographs, drinking a jug of red wine.
Then I went to bed to read Truman Capote's *In Cold Blood*. It was
sexually violent and graphic. I switched off the light to go to sleep.
Within minutes Marie came into my bed. I was kissed by a woman
for the first time in six years. We went to Jerusalem for a few days
before my flight was due and got a double room with a double bed,
and a balcony overlooking the Via Dolorosa where Jesus had carried
the cross and fallen three times. I was deeply happy and felt normal
for the first time as an adult. We spent all our time in the Arab
quarter, smoking water pipes and looking at the full moon. For
evermore, we promised, when there was a full moon, we would
look at that full moon, and, no matter where the other was, think
of each other. I still do, and always, give thanks that I knew Marie.

One night we went to a disco. We sat in a corner drinking a jug of red wine. The Procol Harum record 'A Whiter Shade of Pale' came on. A young man came over and asked Marie to dance. She accepted, and they moved slowly round the floor. I felt despair and grief as I watched. It was only good manners to accept a dance in a dance hall, Marie said afterwards. A couple of years later, when she visited me in Ireland, and we found ourselves in a drinking den in the hills, where only old men gathered, she accepted the invitation of a ragged old fellow to join him in an Irish jig. I was asked that night also, and I refused because I did not know the steps and didn't want to look foolish. In the event, Marie, jumping determinedly up and down, showered grace upon the gathering just by making the effort to participate in a foreign culture; they applauded the attempt, and were pleased that a young woman would not turn an old man down. I agreed with them, but it did not lessen retrospectively the pain I felt that night in Jerusalem. When I hear 'A Whiter Shade of Pale', even now, that feeling of being excluded comes rushing back.

Chapter Nine

It was raining, as usual, as the plane landed in Belfast. When I got to Derry, our home seemed small, and I registered with shock and sadness that my mother was wearing glasses. Immediately she told me that Hugh's marriage had broken down. It was the worst thing that could happen to a family – or at least to parents. As ever, I wrote to myself about it:

I was upstairs putting my clothes in the wardrobe when I heard him come in, and I moved on to the landing and stood there in the half-light wondering how to greet him. From the kitchen below I heard Mammy say, 'Nell's here. She's upstairs.' Immediately the door opened, and he came running up. I began to tremble – how strange it was, for Hugh and I had always met with shouts of laughter and a smacking kiss – then I was in his arms, and we held each other tightly and he said, 'I need you, Nell,' and began to cry. I could find no reply. So I held him. It was our first adult embrace. He stood back, trying to smile, then he was gone. Was this my brother?

My mother told me that she had been to see the Bishop while I was in Israel to find out why he wouldn't give me a job. I was astonished, and proud of her. Bishop Farren was a remote, snobby man, and parishioners had little or no access to him. Going to beard him in his palace, as she did – and she a woman – was like Daniel going into the lion's den. It was unheard of. She had put on her hat and gloves – she hated hats and gloves – told nobody about her mission and confronted him. I hadn't been to see him, he told her. I had not offered him my services, nor kissed his ring. I had written often enough, applying for places, she responded. What was I doing in Israel, working for no wages, for Jews? he asked softly. Because her daughter was wild upset about what had been done to them in the Holocaust, my mother said, and wasn't it great to see a wee Catholic girl from Derry go out and do her Christian bit for Jews, and go through the war there and everything? And weren't there plenty of jobs in Derry for teachers and 'our Nell' better qualified than most of them, with brains to burn? She got nowhere.

Undaunted she took a bus across the river to the Waterside, to talk to the priest there about the teaching job he had advertised in his school. He referred her back to the Bishop. It would be difficult to exaggerate the courage and self-confidence my mother showed in these battles. I think also that she was just plain angry. The hungry 1930s, when, after the death of her father, she was left, aged twenty-five, to rear her two young brothers and sister, had seared her. The only institution to offer her help, she often said, was a charity funded by a rich Protestant for orphaned boys, and John and Jim, both under sixteen years old, were given a small monthly allowance that made the difference between food on the table and hunger. My mother had also given serious consideration to the offer of a rich, childless Protestant couple who wanted to adopt Nellie. Nellie, a little girl, had childishly agreed – if John and Jim could come with her.

Halfway through the first term of the school year in 1967, I was offered a temporary teaching job in St Cecilia's secondary school, up the hill from our street. The job was to last but two months, until Christmas, and I seized it. Naturally, the first thing I did was invite the girls down to have tea with my mother, who knew all their mothers and grannies. St Cecilia's, like every other secondary school in the town, was regarded as a mere stopgap before the girls went into the shirt factories. Some of the teachers cared about education. Far too many did not and treated the pupils with disdain. The girls were just fodder for the Church – they would marry, have children and produce more souls.

I was glad of the money and sorry to be back in Derry. Hugh and Paddy were in one bedroom, Nuala and Carmel and I were crammed into a double bed and a single bed in the back room. Hugh brought his children once a week to spend the day with our mother. Too old now, at twenty-three, to go dancing – I was practically on the shelf – there was little in the way of society other than going to the cinema. Pubs held no appeal. The height of social activity consisted of going to the Leprechaun coffee shop on the Strand Road after school, to kill a couple of hours with other unmarried teachers.

I considered myself well and truly doomed, and lived for the letters from Marie, who was now back in Sweden. I was spending a fortune on a weekly phone call to her from a public phone box, though she always took the number and rang me right back. To crown my woes, I felt that I stuck out like a sore thumb when I made the trek with towel and shampoo to the public baths every week, passing the girls I taught. At home, we still used the tin bath in the scullery, but the set-up was awkward. The doors between the kitchen and the scullery, and the scullery and the back yard, were at right angles to each other. Whoever was taking a bath tied the door handles together with one of my father's ties. The person taking a bath had privacy, but no one else could get through to fetch a bucket of coal or to use the outside toilet. And my father's ties were wrecked.

One gloomy autumn afternoon, as I headed up Fahan Street, Eamonn McCann came down the street, bursting with energy. I hadn't seen him for three years. He wore a combat jacket and grey flannel trousers, and still had the Elvis sideboards. He had a bundle of pamphlets under his arm. I complained of boredom. Why didn't I come up to the Londonderry Labour Party headquarters that night and help in the forthcoming general-election campaign? he asked. His assurance and optimism and bright belief were infectious.

That night I walked into a large room, packed with women and men, young and old, who sat around long tables, addressing envelopes and stuffing them with election literature. The candidate was, unusually, a woman. Janet Wilcox was English-born. Her sex and nationality told against her in what was already a hopeless cause – standing a Labour candidate in a Catholic majority town against the sitting Catholic, Nationalist Party MP, Eddie McAteer, who had been in situ for ever. The Unionist candidate hadn't a hope either.

What the hell – all the people in the room were delighted with themselves. Derry, finally, was going to rise against unionist discrimination and nationalist pathos. I was made welcome, seated at a table and shown how to mark names off the electoral register as I completed my quota of envelopes. The room ran with energy. I spent a few nights there, went home full of stories, and learned for the first time that my father had once fought an equally hopeless fight on behalf of a Labour candidate in the 1950s, Stephen McGonagle, a local man, who had been dubbed and drubbed as a 'communist'. The door of his election headquarters had been daubed with red paint.

I was enchanted with everyone I met. Big Brendan Hinds, who had a skilled job in Du Pont and was married to a teacher, held himself like John Wayne, and spoke in a stream of aphorisms. 'The unionists cut off our thumbs, kid . . . The squeaking wheel gets oiled . . . Stick with me and you'll wear diamonds.' Cathy Harkin was separated from her violent husband and rearing a son. She lived within the walled city in a cold-water slum flat with her mother, who worked in a shirt factory. The facts belied her cheerful, fierce belief that one day we would run Derry. Anne Keenan, with fiery short red curls, a huge laugh and a total commitment to trade unionism, lived with her mother and sisters in an asbestos-lined hut in Creggan that should have been condemned long since, and was studying to be a care worker with the mentally disabled. Gerry Mallet, middle-aged and between unskilled jobs, had a large family of children and a working man's cut to his jib. Dermie McClenaghan, an accounts clerk in a shirt factory, lived in one of the most famous streets in Derry, Wellington Street, where several families shared small houses, was synonymous with unemployment and had a terrific piece of graffiti on the wall of the corner bookies: 'We want better odds.' Dermie loved Frank Sinatra and worried about his family as much as I did about mine. Willie Breslin was a schoolteacher, serious and affable, and dedicated to issuing statements morning, noon and night. Mr and Mrs Sharkey were implacably respectable, indomitable and inseparable. Ivan Cooper, the only Protestant member of our party, managed the factory where Dermie worked, and thought life was a breeze and victory near at hand for socialism. My parents were pleased to welcome these new friends into the house.

After Christmas, when I finished my teaching stint and contemplated life on the dole, I packed and went to London to seek a new life, or even a job, once again. I brought a typewriter with me:

My father wept sorely as I left the house, and I was moved by the love he showed for me. His face was weak with sobs, the frame of his spectacles starkly strong against it. He smothered me to him, leaning on me, and I realized with sudden despair that he wept only for the sins I would commit once away from home. What life has he suffered that his conscience and heart should be torn so deeply as my own when he looks at me in the kitchen, gaily fighting back his tears? What confidence in me, or ignorance of me, has my mother as she firmly pins the Immaculate Medal on my coat? Between the shame of the one and the trust of the other I am once again resolved to change my ways.

I stayed with Muireanna and Maurice, who had moved from a flat to their first house, with their first baby, a girl, in Croydon, on the outskirts of London. It never occurred to me to ask if I could move in, nor to them to refuse. It was assumed that the family member abroad would help those just arriving to get a foot on the ladder. When I arrived in January 1968, winter was biting and we remembered it ever afterwards as the year of the Big Snow. Maurice had invested in a van and had just branched out as a self-employed builder. He'd leave in the morning, chasing work, as I did, and we'd return in the evening, both empty-handed. The courage of my sister and her husband was unfailing, unlike mine, as school after school turned me down. The civil service and banks declined all job applications, usually on the grounds that, at twenty-three, I was too old to train.

One evening, I walked through the snow to a factory that was taking on night-shift workers and was hired on the spot. The management was male, the workers entirely female, many from India and Pakistan. My job was to solder wires to a wooden plate. None of the women seated beside me on the bench knew what the end product was. During a break for tea, I asked the foreman, who expressed surprise that anyone cared. He immediately took me on a tour of the premises. We were making radios for the blind.

I amused myself by working faster than anyone else, finding ways to shift stuff along the bench more quickly. I'd soon tire of that, the foreman said, warning me, by the by, that if I exceeded the expected quota so much and so often, the other workers would feel under threat. There wasn't any extra money in exceeding the quota, he pointed out. Soon, I was spending more and more time waiting on the others to catch up. I brought in a book to read while waiting, which did not go down well.

One night, Muireanna remarked that I reminded her of the protagonist in a Sinatra song: a rover who never found a home. I thought that a romantic and agreeable image of myself. For reasons I no longer remember – perhaps because the loneliness was unbearable, maybe because I wanted someone to know who and what I was, perhaps because life with a couple and their child held no promise for the likes of me – I told Maurice that I was lesbian. He nodded, sympathetically, but without comment. In March, as the snow faded, and Maurice acquired some proper contracts, I decided to get a bedsitter in the city. At least there would be theatre, movies and museums to while away the days. I left the factory in Croydon and took up residence in a converted bathroom in Kensington. The former soap-holder, in the wall beside the single bed, served as an ashtray. The room also held a table, a two-ring cooker and a cold-water sink. It was just down the road from Kensington Palace, where lesser members of the royal family, those not directly in line to the throne, lived. The first thing I did in my new home was send my mother, who still ached over the breakdown of Hugh's marriage, a bunch of flowers with a saying I had heard somewhere: 'After winter, comes spring.' I was still trying to write:

Today would be a new day. She jumped out of her bed, brushed her teeth, took off her nightdress and smoothed cream on to her large, hanging breasts. Standing in front of the mirror she slapped them vigorously upwards 100 times. Two minutes later they hung red and sore, in their original saggy position . . . a little wine, perhaps. And a little more . . . For six years now she had slipped all her problems under the bed covers, shedding them in sleep. The more problems she had, the more she slept. Half laughing, half crying, she chose a dream. In five minutes she was sound asleep.

I got a waitressing job in a Wimpy Bar in nearby Earl's Court. Eventually, said the manageress, I would be given my own tables, but in the meantime I had to prove myself by working in the windowless basement, ladling tomato ketchup from a barrel into plastic bottles. My sister slave was a large black woman who said absolutely nothing all day long. Being black in London was bad enough in the 1960s but *now* she was stuck with an Irish woman whose pronunciation of English she could not understand. It must have felt to her that she was scraping the bottom of the barrel. I filled bottles far faster than she did and was soon promoted upstairs – where no black waitress would ever set foot.

I resolved to supplement my wages with decent tips, and became the most efficient worker in the place. Soon I had regulars, one of whom tipped enormously. He worked in the building trade and ate there alone every evening, immaculately attired in brown suede jacket, white T-shirt, blue jeans and desert boots. He was over thirty, well built, tall, and his hair was dyed a startling blond. I noticed almost at once that he wore eyeshadow and, touchingly, clear nail polish on his roughened fingers. I batted not an eyelid, spoke not a word, lavished him with instant service, and added extra chips to his burger or steak. I was cheering for the guy, whoever he was – we never exchanged names – and sorry for myself that such an aloof, solitary state awaited me, too. Or would it? I didn't look different to any other woman, did I? A letter from Aviva, about to leave the kibbutz for her hometown of Chicago, dispelled forlorn hopes that I would pass muster in a crowd of women. She had been looking at photographs of our time together. She knew from the start that I was lesbian, she wrote, and she enclosed a poem titled 'The Leprechaun Wears Lipstick'. As rejections go, hers was gentle.

One day I mustered the courage to walk up Chelsea Road, and entered a converted-warehouse-cum-coffee-shop, which advocated free love, dope and whatever you're having yourself. There was a solitary male pimpled youth in its cavernous depths, sitting cross-legged on the floor before a chessboard. I joined him on the floor, played chess in total silence and went home in despair.

On the eve of my twenty-fourth birthday, 28 March 1968, I wrote to Aviva:

> . . . i cannot get a job. i refuse to believe it but after another two weeks walking round london knocking on doors the answer is still no. at first i did not mind because i thought to use the time writing. this morning at 3 a.m. i knew i could not write anything worth a damn . . . i think i have become slightly eccentric. i still don't know anybody and talking to myself is confusing since i never know what i really mean.
>
> today i went to the canadian and american embassies to get immigration forms. the canadians gave me booklets which apologized for the lack of cultural, social and normal intellectual facilities available anywhere else in the world, but promised jobs, cars, ski resorts and casual dress . . . item 'canadian women make their own clothes because haute couture has not yet had sufficient impact on our country.' but at least they pay your fare out. the americans gave me forms in which i was hereinafter referred to as alien, and were most interested in how long, and where, and under what name i resided in israel, since apparently my sojourn there qualifies me to all and practical intents and purposes as a COMMUNIST!!! . . .

I can't remember how I spent my birthday next day. The rest of that stay in London is a blank. I know I returned briefly to Derry for my brother Paddy's wedding and was envious of heterosexuals whose life was fairly clearly marked out for them.

One Saturday morning in October 1968, I rose at dawn, packed my suitcase, left a week's rent for the landlady in the hallway, and walked to Kensington Tube station. I did not have the fare back to Ireland, I tearfully told the black woman who staffed the ticket booth. She gave me a free ticket to Euston station and wrote down the name of a man I should ask for there. He was black, too. He gave me a free train and boat ticket for the overnight journey to Belfast, in exchange for an IOU.

On the platform, waiting for departure, I ran into Christy Sheerin, who grew up in the street next to me in Derry. In our childhood, he had accidentally punctured the skin above my left eye while wielding a plank studded with nails. Standing there on the platform, tears running down my face, trying to smile, I pointed to the scar and asked him for a loan of ten shillings – there would be no black stationmasters in Belfast. Christy hugged me and gave me a pound. He was going home on holiday. I was too upset to talk to him and made sure that I was nowhere near him on the journey back.

Chapter Ten

In Belfast, on Sunday morning, the front pages of the papers were devoted to the riots that had taken place after a civil rights march in Derry the previous day – 5 October 1968. The marchers organized by Eamonn McCann had demanded 'one man, one vote', and 'one family, one house', two simple slogans that went to the heart of the North's politics. The franchise and housing were linked. To vote in local government elections, you had to have a house. The more houses Catholics had, the more votes would be cast for the natural nationalist majority in the city. To prevent them getting on to the electoral register and putting Protestant members out of office, the Protestant-controlled Londonderry Corporation wouldn't build houses for Catholics. It was a vicious circle. The Derry march had been banned, and the Royal Ulster Constabulary (RUC) had batoned people attempting to walk from the Protestant east bank of the Foyle over to the Catholic west bank, and used a water cannon to hose them across Craigavon Bridge. The cops had attacked Labour members of the Westminster parliament, brought over to observe by their Westminster colleague, the Republican Labour MP from Belfast, Gerry Fitt. As night fell, and people regrouped back in the Bogside, there were running battles between the police and rioters. Petrol bombs had been thrown, property burned, and people on both sides of the battle injured.

The taxi driver in Derry was in a state of high excitement as he talked me through the journey to Beechwood Street. Gerry Fitt had been hit with a truncheon and his head split open, right there – he pointed to the exact place on Duke Street. The marchers had been hosed with water, right here. And look at the stones in the road and the broken glass and the scorch marks on buildings in the Bogside.

I asked him to wait while I went into the house to get the fare.

The key was in the front door. I dumped my bag in the hallway, calling out. My mother came rushing in from the scullery; my father got up from the sofa in the kitchen. They hugged and kissed me. My father gave me the money for the taxi. When I came back in, crying and describing myself as a failure, my father said solemnly, 'As long as I'm in this house, you'll always have a roof over your head.' I was not to worry about a thing, he said. While I sat drinking tea, eating a gorgeous thick slice of fresh scone bread lathered with butter, noting the smell of roasting meat, talking ninety to the dozen – Jesus, how I had missed my mother's cooking and the sound of voices in conversation in a warm house around a coal fire – my father glanced at the clock and said, 'It's only five to twelve. If you rush you'll get the last mass.' I hadn't been home half an hour. I hadn't really been home since going to university. I had been halfway round the world and back in the seven years since then. But I was now in my father's house. I rose into the silence and went to mass. Normally I would have walked round the block until mass was over, but on this day the mass-going population was a source of news.

That night, I went out with my Uncle Leo, Mammy's brother, who had just retired from his job as an undertaker in California and come back to settle in Derry. As we headed to the Lecky Road, in the direction of flames, smoke and shouts, he told me that because he had embalmed Spencer Tracy, who was a Catholic, he knew for a fact that Tracy was not an alcoholic and had not committed adultery with Katharine Hepburn. We hung about the dark fringes of the riot, too far back down the Lecky Road to see anything. Uncle Leo said the situation was dangerous for a girl. In the confusion of a sudden rush of people pelting towards us – and away from the cops – we were separated. I could run much faster than my elderly uncle. When the crowd started running forwards again, I hid myself among them and saw Uncle Leo no more that night.

A crowd had gathered and settled round a makeshift barricade at the grey gable wall that marked the end of the tiny terraced houses of the Lecky Road. Up ahead, at the far end of Rossville Street, which was an extension of the Lecky Road, a bulk of cops in dark heavy coats and helmets lined up behind plastic riot shields. They beat the shields with their batons, pushed forward, forced us past the gable wall, taking over our territory, then retreated under a hail of petrol bombs. I had never seen or been at a barricade before – it was a flimsy affair of rubble and bits of wood and metal. I had never seen a petrol bomb before. Jokes about them were already flying about. The petrol was poured into empty glass milk bottles, so people were advised to leave notes for the milkman on his rounds: 'No milk today. Six empty bottles, please,' or 'Throw well, throw Shell.'

I saw a fellow light a fuse – a petrol-soaked rag stuffed into the mouth of the bottle – bring his arm back as he prepared to throw, then burst into flame as the fuse fell out and burning petrol poured down the arm of his jacket. I picked up a stone and threw it, and it fell far short of the cops. The effort made my arm ache. I switched to gathering material for others, piling it at their feet. There was plenty of ammunition around, the pavement having been broken up. I felt terrific. The day before, I had been crying for my pitiful state. The day before – for generations before – the Lecky Road had hosted a respectable, law-abiding community, where people were resigned to a fate of overcrowding in dingy housing. The post office in the Lecky Road was where my mother used to send me to pick up the children's allowance money, a prized addition to the family income. Now we were tearing up the road and throwing it at the Royal Ulster Constabulary, the unionist government in Stormont, and the British government in London. They had beaten us up because we demanded equal opportunity. Generations of pent-up humiliation were unleashed in a show of rage that night. It felt completely, inexplicably right. I felt completely at home.

Uncle Leo, who was still in the house when I finally went home after midnight, could hardly conceal his excitement and satisfaction, though he counselled solemnly against destruction, danger and communism, and reminded us of the impossibility of getting into America if a person had a criminal conviction for throwing stones. Uncle Jim, who had shot his father's apple tree in the long-since demolished Lecky Road police barracks, cautioned sagely that Catholics would never win because we were in the minority in the

North, and my father fondly remembered fighting for Labour – and losing. My mother was itching to know every single thing that had happened in the riot: 'Would yese all give over till we hear what she saw.' There was unanimous agreement that – our lawful instincts apart – this was just great. This would teach them.

I slept like a baby that night, had a late breakfast and went up the hill to sign on the dole. Once, that would have felt like defeat. Now it felt like defiance. I was no welfare sponger. I was a revolutionary and would use the British money to finance my enrolment in the cause. In the coffee shop downtown, the Leprechaun, where teachers gathered after school, the women were buzzing with elation. The destruction was bad, of course, but the cops and unionists were worse, denying us our rights. A meeting of concerned citizenry had been called for Wednesday night, and I turned up on the doorstep of the City Hotel with a female acquaintance who taught in a primary school. As knots of men went through the door, our nerve failed us. We would stand out like sore thumbs. I railed against our sense of exclusion all the way back to this woman's house, where we had tea and waited on the late-night radio and television news. The meeting had not yet finished. I went home, embarrassed at having nothing whatsoever to tell my mother.

We learned next day that a Citizens' Action Committee (CAC) pledging itself to non-violence had been formed and had planned a sit-down occupation of the Guildhall Square on 19 October and a march on 16 November, six weeks hence. Eamonn McCann had been offered chairmanship of this powerful group of the good, the great, the concerned and the radical. He had declined the offer and walked out of the meeting. He dismissed the CAC as 'middle-aged, middle class and middle of the road' – but not as men only. He later wrote that his refusal was based on a 'fit of pique or principle, I don't know which'. He never did explain which or what the principle was. I think he meant the principle of class warfare. Eamonn was never again in his life to be offered leadership of the community.

I was puzzled by Eamonn's refusal to take power; it made no

sense because he continued to speak on CAC platforms and his friends and comrades were in the CAC. Its fifteen members included three members of his own Londonderry Labour Party – Brendan Hinds, Dermie McClenaghan and Ivan Cooper – and two radicals from other groups with which he had worked, Eamon Melaugh and Johnny White. White was a declared Republican – a member of an organization that had links with the defunct IRA, which was dedicated to removing the British presence in Ireland by armed force. All these young men were around the same age as Eamonn, and all were involved in the 5 October march. They felt effortlessly able to represent the interests of the working class from which they came.

Ivan Cooper was elected chairman, and John Hume vice chairman, of the CAC, after Eamonn walked out. Besides leading the fight to have a university built in Derry, Hume was a co-founder of the Credit Union in Derry, and of the self-help Derry Housing Association, a non-profit-making cooperative which sought to give us what the unionists would not – homes. He had studied for the priesthood, but left the seminary after getting a degree, and married the popular Derry schoolteacher Pat Hone. Within a year, this quiet man would wipe out, electorally, the Nationalist Party in Derry and, by 1970, co-found its replacement, the Social Democratic and Labour Party. Eamonn had handed him power on a plate.

The papers noted that the CAC had appointed a woman to design a logo. She was Sheila McGuinness, who had taught me art in school. She had been at the meeting – the only female present – in the company of her husband, Dr Ray McLean. In Derry, in 1968, he was as unusual as was Mr Hinds in our party: a husband who openly shared his political life with the woman to whom he was married. 'I saw a man, he danced with his wife . . .' I used to sing fondly to both men.

Soon, I was back in the ranks of the Londonderry Labour Party, with a ready-made set of friends, a social life and a system of beliefs. We weren't looking for much, really – jobs, universal franchise, and housing. Our demands were for nothing more nor less than full civil rights such as were enjoyed over in Britain. This tactic struck us all as terribly clever, not to mention unarguably reasonable. All the British government had to do was force its provincial Unionist government in Stormont to treat Catholics and Protestants alike. (We turned a blind eye to the fact that only a Protestant could inherit the British throne; none of us was looking to sit in that particular chair.) My sister Nuala joined me in the LLP, busy though she was with voluntary work as a member of the Legion of Mary, which brought her on nightly visits to houses where the elderly lived alone, or illiterate people needed someone to read and write their letters.

In an effort to prove what all-round peaceful, well-behaved, God-fearing people we were, at a sit-down in the Guildhall Square on 19 October, the chief steward, Paddy Doherty, did a pre-speech warm-up in which he asked a series of questions, to which the crowd replied with a dutiful yes or no, as required.

Were we peaceful?

Yes.

Were we law-abiding?

Yes.

Were we communists?

No.

'Thank God,' said Paddy.

Jesus Christ, I muttered in dismay as Doherty treated us like children at a catechism class. 'Fly me to the moon,' Eamonn sang softly. Doherty had an admirable background. Reared in a cramped house, part of a big family, foreman on a building site, and father of thirteen children, he had built his own home on a site he had bought, 10 Westland Street, in the Bogside. The church had thundered against him for working on the sabbath, his only day off. Paddy and his neighbour continued to lay bricks.

He was also one of the co-founders, in the early 1960s, of the Credit Union movement in the city, and he never forgave Eamonn for dismissing the people's bank as a fly on the bum of the elephant, which was capitalism. His anti-communist speech from the plat-form in the Guildhall Square was an ill-disguised dig at McCann and the lefties, all now meekly seated at his feet, a fortnight after they had set Derry afire.

Hundreds of slum-dwelling families had sniffed hope in the flames and besieged the Labour Party with pleas for help. One of my jobs was to visit some of them. The very first woman I called on was surprised that I did not recognize her. She had gone to school with Muireanna and worked alongside her. How could I recognize her? Muireanna was thriving in London, in a lovely home, filled with energy and as attractive as ever. Before me, hunkered in a broken chair by a low fire, sat a crone. There were black spaces where teeth had fallen out. Her skin was grimed, her hair lank. She was about thirty years old and would have passed for fifty. The dampness in her tiny rented cottage in St Columb's Wells had caused the wallpaper to peel off. Her children were sickly. As she spoke, I saw flashes of the young woman she had once been. I remembered her mass of gleaming dark hair, her carefree laugh and her appetite for dancing, dates and romance. 'Did you ever think I would come to this?' she asked.

The solution to her predicament was simple: we piled her belongings into a truck and squatted the family in a vacant house, owned by a landlord. There were not many vacant houses, but that was no bother either. Brigid Bond, chairwoman of the local Housing Action Committee, had come up with a brilliant supplementary strategy. A tenement-dweller herself, and no respecter of the people of property, she read the deaths columns every evening in the local edition of the *Belfast Telegraph*. If the deceased had lived alone, Brigid squatted a family in the house within hours of the funeral and interment. There were nights when a lorry commandeered by her would pass a lorry commandeered by the Londonderry Labour Party; nights when both organizations arrived to view the same vacant house. One night Brigid had an emergency and commandeered us all: she had mistaken the address of a recently deceased person, moved a family into what she thought was an empty house, and discovered that the tenant was only on holiday. 'He's coming back tomorrow morning.' We lent each other ladders for climbing up to second-storey flats and breaking in through the front windows.

We struck gold when the British admiralty vacated an entire housing estate where service families had lived. The estate was across the river Foyle, in the mainly Protestant Waterside, which might have been a problem given the rising sectarian tension across the North. Cathy and I went after midnight to a tenement where a family lived in shuddering misery in one room, huddled over the remains of a fire. They did not hesitate for one second. We helped them pile their belongings and bedding and bits of furniture into a van, and drove off across the river. The bridge was already alive with families pushing prams and carts, trekking towards the New Jerusalem. Around two-thirty in the morning, forty families stood on the green space in front of a row of houses, shivering, under the gaze of two admiralty policemen. They showed no inclination to tell us to shove off. Cathy and I stood beside them for a casual chat.

'If we broke windows to get in, I wonder if these guys would phone the police?'

'We ain't got nothing to do with police, do we? We are the navy, in't we? Navy don't care, do it?'

'If we did break in, I wonder how we'd turn on the electricity?'

'I'd just put in a fuse, if I was trying that, wouldn't I, mate?'

We were giddy with success and defiance, though there was no personal profit for those involved in the Labour Party: the majority of our members had reasonable homes and jobs. And those few who lived in tenements, on small incomes, such as Cathy Harkin and Brigid Bond, had not succumbed to the anomie engendered by that.

The mornings usually began in Cathy Harkin's flat, with tea and baps for those who had no job to go to. Her infant son crawled about, while Cathy's mother was off working in the factory. We drew up press releases on the great issues of the day, which Cathy then typed and delivered. Eamonn's book later dismissed her as 'a housewife whose ability to type at fifty words a minute made her the willing dogsbody of every radical organization'. It could take hours of argument to agree on the statement. Then home for dinner, and back out to the streets to watch the riot of the day. The junction between Rossville Street and William Street which led into the city centre became known as 'Aggro Corner': it was there that young people and the RUC engaged in what had become a ritual daily battle, usually starting at three in the afternoon with a stone thrown at a passing police vehicle, and finishing around six in the evening when it was time to go home and watch ourselves on the local television news. By night, we gathered in the City Hotel, now the home of journalists, or in Labour Party headquarters, and thence to the pub.

On some occasions, Eamonn and I kissed the faces off each other. We took these minor hungers handily enough. He knew all about me and I was under no illusion about him. 'My archetype is a middle-aged, middle-class married woman,' he explained candidly on one of the evenings when I sought political instruction about socialism. Sexual power without responsibility, so — was it a similar impulse which had led him to reject social power, and the responsibility that came with it, through chairmanship of the CAC?

Eamonn wore his contradictions easily, and I identified with them, being burdened with a whole load of contradictions myself. Should I accept a wage for teaching that was twice that of a factory worker who produced food? Or demand that everybody got the same wage, including the unemployed, and in the meantime donate the difference to the Londonderry Labour Party? What would happen, when the revolution came, to the bigger houses around the place? Were we to tear down the homes of the bourgeoisie or demand similar housing for the working class? If everybody had to have a similar house, would we not end up in 'little boxes', as Burl Ives had mocked in his song? My head ached trying to figure out Marx, Trotsky and the whole damn thing.

I eased the intellectual headache of it all with jokes about my own ignorance. The two best books in the world, I would say, were *Das Kapital*, by Marx, and the Bible. Both were very long and extremely complicated, and one day I'd have to read them. In the meantime I settled for reading the *Derry Journal*, which concentrated on the unionist machine we were trying to stop, and watching our progress on local television, and spending evenings in the City Hotel, which was now a hotbed of revolt. Everybody wanted in on the action, and some women even got inside the hotel doors.

Mary Holland, of the *Observer* newspaper, had been the first journalist to smash the media barrier between Northern Ireland and Britain. On 6 October, the day after the march, the *Observer* had published her feature 'John Bull's Other Island' across two pages. It described the North as a political slum. In her article she explained that Gerry Fitt had contacted her asking her to write about the North. She had asked him for factual material, and he had turned up at her London home with a suitcase full of newspaper cuttings and statistics.

Fitt invited Holland to Derry, and because she had witnessed the riot she also got a news piece on to the front page. Now, a few days later, Mary was back in Derry. She brushed aside our congratulations. Her report, phoned in on the hoof from an ice-cream parlour in Duke Street, while the RUC beat rings round them, had declared that 3,000 police were present to counter a couple of hundred marchers. The RUC was quick to respond that the force in its entirety numbered far fewer than that. She had relied on a Belfast lawyer, Vincent Hanna, who had accompanied her to the march, to give her these statistics. He was as overexcited as the rest of us. Get just one fact wrong and the whole article falls, Mary said. Her tone was disdainful and angry.

To her, we were a shambles, not the heroes we perceived ourselves to be. To us, she was a marvel: swanky, beautifully groomed, drifting in a cloud of Estée Lauder. I teased her about getting the police numbers wrong – who did she think she was, queening it over us who had turned the North upside down? – and she froze me with a glance. Later, we had coffee together. She was willing to speak to anybody, to listen, learn, sift, then judge.

A short time later, I received a telegram. Telegrams in our town were used to announce death or disaster. This telegram was from Mary Holland. She was returning to Derry and invited me for dinner in the hotel. I felt flattered, shy and socially inadequate. Mary's cut-glass English accent intimidated me. My sister Carmel, who earned less as an apprentice hairdresser than I was getting on the dole, lent me her best suit. When I was a teenager Muireanna got angry with me when I borrowed an item of her clothing and returned it somewhat stretched by my fuller figure. Happy-go-lucky Carmel didn't mind at all. Was this socialism in action? Was it fair that Carmel's suit, for the price of which she had worked so hard, be ruined? She told me to shut up and enjoy myself.

The hotel dining room was deserted except for Mary. The conversation was heavy going. There wasn't even a riot nearby to divert us, or allow me to talk about what I knew best: local violence, the reasons for it and the motivations of our social betters who condemned it publicly and quietly cheered it on. There were no other journalists about the hotel to amuse us. They were not due back until the eve of the November march. I resorted to the fail-safe solution: I invited her to visit my parents' home next day.

I know now, after decades in journalism, what a boon that was to her. Most of us, covering a story, are left to stand in the streets of a foreign town, wondering what goes on behind closed doors where people lead their real lives, longing for the invitation inside that seldom comes. Soon, Mary was sitting by my parents' fireside, having her hair done by Carmel. She washed her hair in the sink in the scullery, used the outside toilet in the yard, had tea with neighbours and relatives, and debated with whichever party activists arrived for a midnight session. It turned out that Mary's parents came from Clonakilty in the south of Ireland. Her father had served the British Empire, in Malaysia, as an engineer. She was born in England in 1936, and had been sent back to Clonakilty, aged three, for the duration of World War II, to live in a convent which was run by her mother's sister, head of the local order. She shared a room with a young postulant.

One night as we all sat in the City Hotel, Mary silenced the older men who sat round her in a circle, courting her attention, by asking one of them to shift slightly as he was obscuring her view of Eamonn McCann, whom she described as 'the best-looking thing in the room'. She had already described Eamonn in the *Observer* as having 'the looks of a Sean O'Casey street fighter', which pleased him enormously. Mary was married to a diplomat and was thirty-two years old. Irresistible meets archetype. The crush I had developed on her withered. No matter – the conversation was marvellous. I had never been so intimately, for so long, in the company of two such marvellous minds as Eamonn and Mary possessed.

I was still dissatisfied with my lot. I hated the way most women were left out of things. A turning point came on 16 November, when thousands were expected from all over the North, to retrace the steps of the banned march held on 5 October. The police had banned it again. Stewards – all male – were appointed to shepherd the crowds. They met behind the Guildhall and were addressed by the chief steward, Paddy Doherty, who seemed fearless. If any police officer attempted to prevent Paddy doing his civic duty, he said, the other stewards were to 'take that policeman out'. This was getting like cowboys and Indians. I resolved to do a Calamity Jane and stiffly stepped forward to get a steward's armband.

Off we went, all the men – and me – to take up position on the Craigavon Bridge. Behind us was a vast crowd, huge beyond expectation. In front of us were the leaders of the CAC, and in front of them were metal crowd-control barriers, designed to prevent us from walking to the city centre. Behind the barriers were massed ranks of police officers in riot gear. They were pitifully few in number. It was clear that the biggest threat came from the crowds behind us. The CAC had promised them that we would go to the city centre. If the police resisted, how were we supposed to hold back 25,000 people?

The stewards linked arms across the width of the bridge, anyway, in a token show of control. John Hume addressed the massed ranks, without a megaphone, and few could hear him. The members of the CAC walked towards the police cordon. The cops had blocked off the mouth of Carlisle Road, which led up and into the walled city, thence down to Guildhall Square, our designated objective. They did not block off a side road, John Street, which skirted the walls, but also led to Guildhall Square.

The leaders of the march got as far as the barriers. Words were exchanged with the leader of the cops, and some of the more youthful men made a token breach of the waist-high barriers, clambering over them and tumbling into the arms of the cops. Very few people could see this clearly prearranged compromise. There was a long silence, and word of the token breach of the police barrier filtered back through the ranks. People sang the song of peaceful defiance 'We Shall Overcome'. Thousands of them pressed forwards then, slowly, and the stewards moved uselessly ahead. Nothing and no one could hold back the tide of humanity. What happened next was entirely up to the people. With a surge and shouts, they were suddenly all over the police and the collapsed barriers. Many went up Carlisle Road, many went down John Street, and in minutes the city was ours, both within and outside the Walls.

There was some perfunctory rioting. Stones were thrown and shop windows were broken, and the police made some arrests, as thousands of citizens from all over the North took over the streets of Derry. Free at last – but not really. The march had been officially banned. The people had not officially marched. After I ran into the centre of the walled city, to the Diamond and its War Memorial, I looked up at the second-storey flat above a shop where our Hugh's children and his wife were living. The pale faces of his two children were pressed up against the glass, looking at the mayhem. Hugh and his wife were still separated, and he had gone to England. What freedom for them, living in a riot zone, within the citadel? And yet, we were in awe of ourselves. The North had never seen such a huge crowd. The scenes shown on television showed us what we had done. The photographs in the Sunday papers reflected back to us our magnificence.

The unionist government insisted that the law had been upheld. On Monday morning, the shirt-factory women took that law into their own hands and broke it, cheerfully and severally. They downed tools, left their benches, linked arms and walked in and out of the gates of the old walled city, up hill, down hill, along any street of their choosing. They sang, wisecracked and declared ownership of their town. What ban on walking within the Walls? What government? What police force? 'In and out of the dusty bluebells, in and out of the dusty bluebells, in and out of the dusty bluebells, early in the morning,' they sang the skipping song of their childhood as they went in and out of the great open gateways. People laughed and applauded and admired, and the police stood by. Then the dockers heard wildly exaggerated tales of the dangers faced by their womenfolk, and they also downed tools and marched in and out of the Walls, seeking women to protect. The dockers may as well have been trying to rein in new-born lambs. It was springtime in November in Derry.

Now the women of the city had the bit between their teeth. At the slightest alarum – bin lids banging on the pavement to signal a police incursion into the Bogside – my mother and her neighbours would get up out of their beds and march. At three in the morning, four in the morning, in the dark before dawn, the women walked the streets of their town in droves. Most women of my mother's age – she was fifty-eight, then – had never seen Derry so late at night. They had gone home early while young and single. They could not stay out late after motherhood curbed their gallivanting. They adored it, walking about like free people, gazing in amaze, listening to the sound of their feet slapping into the silence, seeing buildings closed that they had only ever seen open during daylight.

The biggest signal of social change was that many women like my mother broke another lifetime habit. My father was used to having his meal on the table at six o'clock sharp, when he came in from work. That meal went out the window. 'I was marching Hughie . . . Couldn't get home through the riot . . . I fed half the revolutionaries in Derry the day. I've been wild busy.'

One Sunday afternoon in October I had opened the door to a knock and was puzzled as to why my father had not just turned the key. He pushed past me, silent, holding one arm, and went straight upstairs. I told my mother. She went up, came down, and sent for the doctor. My father had had a stroke. He had just taken his last driving lesson, prior to doing the test. There had been a flat tyre. For some reason, he had taken hold of the back fender and tried to lift the car up, though it was already on a jack.

He was moved downstairs to the sitting room to sleep. He did manage, shortly afterwards, one last walk, down to the quays, and he introduced me to the dockers, about whose conditions I was to write for *Ramparts*, the Labour Party magazine, but then strokes came in quick succession and he was barely able to manage the walk from his new bedroom to the kitchen, using an iron splint on his leg and a walking stick. Soon he was having difficulty speaking. He roared against his fate one night, rising up in his bed, to swipe at and break the chandelier with his stick. The doctor put him on Valium. The Valium made him a bit of a hippy, quietly stoned by the fire. Before he went to sleep at night, we could hear him sing 'Ave Maria'. He was only sixty.

Simultaneously freed from working to the timetable of my father's job, but trapped by the need to care for him all day long, my mother took it into her head to join the Labour Party, along with my Aunt Nellie. The City Hotel fell before them as the Rialto cinema had fallen when they used to attend X-rated movies which, after midnight, were meant for the eyes only of the all-male corporation censorship squad. The two women seated themselves at the back of the room, a week after the mighty march over the bridge, nodding approvingly as I was elected secretary of the party. They were referred to as Comrade Mrs McCafferty and Comrade Mrs Brown. Every time a vote was called for, they looked to me for guidance – hand up, or hand down – and followed faithfully.

We embarked on a grand tour of the North, marching, usually on Saturdays, wherever a civil rights organization had sprung up. Most of us had never actually seen much of our own country. We had spent most of our lives in whatever town or village we were born in, leaving only to go to Belfast for education or a medical operation, or to catch the emigrant boat from there. Like explorers, we discovered Enniskillen, Armagh, Strabane, Newry and places that we'd only heard about in song – 'where the mountains of Mourne sweep down to the sea'. We were the fastest explorers on record because wherever we went we'd often discover that the fundamentalist Protestant preacher, the Reverend Ian Paisley, and his followers, had got there before us, arriving at dawn to occupy town centres. So we got up earlier and earlier, arriving in the dark, speaking as fast as we could, and getting out before dark. Sometimes it was frightening. You'd arrive in a place and not know if it was cowboy or Injun territory – Protestant or Catholic. Which side streets led to safety? Which to a kicking, or arrest?

You'd hear Paisley and his people before you met them. As dawn broke over Armagh one Saturday, his bellow and his people's growls greeted our arrival. The man certainly had nerve – Armagh was a mainly Catholic town – and we certainly had naivety, expecting the police to move him away. We had served legal notice of the march, hadn't we? We might have been talking to the wall as remonstrating with the tall policemen who gazed stonily over our heads, while Paisley's people, in the background, waved clubs.

We sent signals across the divide. I was dispatched to meet Ferville Wright, who was chairman of the Young Unionists, a group that had taken an interest in the equally dreadful housing conditions of those Protestants who lived in the Fountain Estate, a tiny working-class redoubt which abutted the Walls. The Fountain was ironically symbolic. On one side of it, inside the Walls, stood the courthouse, the Church of Ireland cathedral and the palace of the Protestant Bishop. From within this palace, more than a century before, the wife of the Bishop, Cecil Frances Alexander, had gazed across the valley of the Bogside to the hill of Creggan and been inspired to write some of the world's greatest Protestant hymns, including 'There Is a Green Hill Far Away' and 'All Things Bright and Beautiful', which, on first examination, seems to be about birds, bees and flowers, but is actually about people knowing their place – the rich man in his castle, the poor man at his gate. The people of the Fountain certainly knew their place – outside Bishop's Gate, which gave entry to the inner sanctum. The Fountain was built around the city jail, facing down into the Bogside. The gables of the housing in the Fountain were famous for their murals of the Protestant King William, astride his white horse. Every year, the Fountain was the gaily decorated Mecca of Protestants who came from all over the North to walk under the traditional arch there, and celebrate the fact that the Protestant Apprentice Boys, who had not yet completed training in their trades, had closed the gates in the name of the Protestant King William, against the Catholic King James. The Protestants within the Walls had resisted a six-month siege, being finally reduced to eating dogs and rats. Derry's coat of arms features a skeleton.

The housing in the Fountain was as atrocious as any slums I had seen in the Bogside. Ferville, in a neat jacket, shirt and tie, and flannel trousers, took me round the tenants. They were friendly and as worried as Catholics about their plight. As they told me their tales of woe, Ferville struck a pose of vindication. I brought him to my home – of course – en route to a Derry City football match. He had tea under a painting of Jesus, Mary and Joseph. He was of the opinion that Protestants were not welcome to watch their home team in the home grounds of the Brandywell, which adjoined the Bogside. Nonsense, said my mother, blessing him with holy water as we left for the match. Afterwards he brought me to his house for tea – it was as neat as mine – where I sat under a photograph of the Queen.

This was non-sectarian revolution of the first order, I thought, pitching a plan to him that the Young Unionists and the Londonderry Labour Party unite to agitate for proper housing for the working class. He briefly told me the facts of life from a Unionist perspective. If more public housing were built in Derry, more Catholic householders would have votes, and they would use these votes to elect nationalists, and the unionist-controlled corporation would be defeated. Next thing, there would be communism and a united socialist Ireland. In the meantime, more police were needed to quell us agitators and he, a shop assistant with no prospects but an impeccable political CV, had applied to join the cops. (Which he did. He became a detective, earned loads of money on overtime in a permanent state job, married, had children, buckled under the stress of the job, divorced, drank, and one night killed himself with his service revolver.)

Within weeks of the great November march, the unionist government abolished Londonderry Corporation and set up a Housing Commission to oversee the building of homes for the people. For forty-seven years unionists had solved the threat to their minority rule by corralling most of the Catholics into one electoral ward, the South Ward. Each ward, regardless of population, returned the same number of councillors, and Protestants were in the majority in all the other wards, thus giving the minority unionists control of local government. The municipal election in 1967 had seen eight nationalists returned from an electoral roll of 20,000 Catholics, and twelve unionists returned from an electoral roll of 10,000 Protestants. When there was no more land for building houses in the South Ward, the unionists simply stopped building houses – none at all was built in 1967 – and refused to allocate housing to Catholics in the other wards, where they would have gained votes and majority rule. Furthermore, business people were given extra votes because they paid higher rates than householders, and most businesses were owned by Protestants. There was not one Catholic employed in the city's Guildhall.

Now the Londonderry Corporation was gone. We were ecstatic. After forty-seven years of gerrymandering, we had, in the space of six weeks, brought down the hated heart and symbol of Northern sectarianism: minority unionist control of nationalist Derry. Prime Minister Captain Terence O'Neill went on television to make a broadcast to the people of the North. 'Ulster is at a crossroads,' he said. He wanted a moratorium on marching. John Hume agreed. Eamonn drew up a statement pointing out that we had lost an essential plank of the civil rights movement – one man, one vote – by accepting an unelected imposed Housing Commission. My mother laughed as she gave him his morning tea and baps while he sat on her sofa, furiously scribbling. Anything was better than Unionism, she felt. We would never again have to do the doleful rounds of city councillors begging for a house. The Commission would do, for the moment.

O'Neill also promised to review the North's Special Powers Act, 'as soon as circumstances make this possible without danger to the interests of the community as a whole.' What were these special powers? most of us asked ourselves. If we'd ever heard about them we had forgotten. The answer threw fuel back on to the fire. The 'special powers', which allowed the North since its foundation to derogate from the normal law operating in the rest of the United Kingdom – England, Scotland and Wales – were so draconian that the white prime minister of South Africa, who had his own problems trying to maintain apartheid against the black people, said that he would abolish the legal system there entirely in exchange for even one of the North's 'special powers'. The Special Powers Act allowed the suspension of habeas corpus, internment without trial, and a call-up of an armed 'Special Constabulary' as reinforcements of the regular police. We had been reared on stories of the Special Constabulary, an exclusively Protestant paramilitary force. For Catholic children, they were the equivalent of bogeymen. There had originally been three kinds of Special Constabulary, A, B and C. A-class constables were employed full-time when Ireland was partitioned in 1921, to help the transition from Royal Irish Constabulary to Royal Ulster Constabulary. B-class constables were unpaid volunteers, who drilled once a week in uniform, and were trained to use guns which they were allowed to keep at home. A small sum of money was paid 'for each drill in excess of one a week'. Class C was an unarmed reserve force that was on stand-by for emergencies, received no pay or allowances, and did only occasional drills.

By 1968, the A and C classes had been disbanded, but the B-class constabulary remained, and was viewed by Protestants as a home guard which provided men with a social club and pocket money. O'Neill's mention of the Special Powers Act brought the B Specials back into focus. We weren't as scared of this Dad's Army as we let on, but, hey, it was another target in the alphabet soup of Northern politics – 'SS-RUC, SS-B men,' we could chant.

Christmas was hard. Hugh and his now reunited family were back from England, where he had joined the Royal Navy. They came to stay in our house for the festive season. With my father downstairs, the grandchildren sleeping with my mother, Carmel, Nuala and me in the second bedroom, Hugh and his wife were given the third bedroom. My notebook of the time records:

Hugh arrived with a laugh and a shout, deposited his baggage, wife and children, and went out. He got himself a Christmas job, returned for tea when it was long since over, and went out again to see his pals. His wife was tired, the house was disordered, the children affectionate, irritable, confused. My father smiled for the first twenty minutes, then placed his head in his hands. My mother hugged, hovered, cooked, cleaned, worried. She stood in the scullery whispering, 'Jesus, Jesus.' . . .

[The next morning] the children woke up, looking for food and attention, and my father struck the wall with his stick, and the kitchen was crowded again and my mother knew it would never be tidied up. After Carmel and Nuala and Hugh had gone out to work, she made breakfast in shifts and carried mine up to me on a tray, and wished she was on the beach, far away, by herself, and said it was all right for me, I could go out; I couldn't finish my breakfast or face them, so I turned over and slept again and thought, like my mother, 'Jesus, Jesus.'

If we thought this was bad, what was it like for the thousands of families crammed into Derry tenements for years, two and three generations at a time?

That Christmas, Eamonn gave me a biography of Constance, Countess Markiewicz, the upper-class revolutionary who fought for Irish independence. Why should I study Irish history? We called ourselves the Londonderry Labour Party, accepting the British nomenclature for our town. If we were Irish, why not call ourselves the Derry Labour Party?

Because then, Eamonn said, we would be expelled from the Northern Ireland Labour Party, which was affiliated to the British Labour Party, and thus would be deprived of links with the millions of workers in England, Scotland and Wales (compared with Ireland's relatively small labour force). Also, the Northern Ireland Labour Party accepted, indeed supported, the notion of us being British citizens. Ours was not a fight for independence from Britain, he said; ours was a fight for working-class rule all over the world, and nationalism had no part in it.

The meeting of the Londonderry Labour Party on 30 December was light relief after the sorrowful Christmas with my increasingly ill father. My mother and Nuala and Aunt Nellie were mad to cast a vote for anything, anywhere. The Housing Commission and the promise of more houses was great, yes, but these three women were getting used to, and enjoying enormously, the flexing of female muscles in the political arena. Instead of extending the franchise by housing Catholics outside the South Ward, and allowing them to vote for a Nationalist Corporation, O'Neill had abolished it altogether, so the Labour Party was the only political arena in town. That night we debated a motion that in January we would take part in a march from Belfast to Derry, a journey of ninety miles, which had been organized by the People's Democracy, a radical group rooted in Queen's University. The march would be a show of defiance against O'Neill's minimal reforms and the virtual capitulation to these reforms of the leadership of the civil rights movement. We would walk through the unionist heartland and, as the unionists were bound to object, and the police would probably try to stop us, O'Neill would be exposed as a pretend-liberal emperor with no clothes. The motion was passed by eighteen votes to fifteen.

After the meeting ended, my mother was worried that my participation in the march, starting on 1 January, would cost me my week's dole money. It would last four days, from Wednesday to Saturday; I was due to sign the dole on Thursday, and I would be only halfway to Derry on that day. I pointed out that she, Aunt Nellie and our Nuala had cast the three deciding votes in favour of participation in the great walk. She pointed out that the trio had only voted as they had after I had nodded my head to indicate what they should do. 'It was you that raised your hand, and you looked at us and we followed.' In truth, I was just as worried as my mother about losing a week's dole money. It was my only income, and at £4. 5s. a week wasn't enough even to buy cigarettes and drink.

Nonetheless, the next day, the last of 1968, I set off with Eamonn for Belfast. We had dinner in the flat of our friends Michael and Gráinne, whose marriage I had effectively arranged, if I may congratulate myself upon such brilliant foresight. I had known Michael, also from Derry, since I was seventeen and he was twenty-four. We had signed up as salespeople for *Encyclopaedia Britannica* – me to supplement my income; he to supplement his wage as an architectural draughtsman. We sold not one copy, and the experience was scorching: in a very poor household, a man who wanted education for his children was abjectly grateful for the free brochure I gave him. Michael and I consoled each other after every night's work by playing Monopoly in my parents' sitting room. Gráinne, from Cookstown, had given me a crash course in Thomas Hardy when I found myself, three weeks before the final exams, one author short of the prescribed syllabus. When Michael arrived in Queen's as a mature student, to study architecture, I coaxed him away from poker games and into Gráinne's intellectual embrace.

After dinner, Mary Holland joined us, and she brought her husband along. He was a British diplomat, tall, besuited, quiet and conventionally handsome. Being a diplomat, he gave no hint of what he thought about our politics. He had nice manners. We didn't ask him anything about Britain, our own mannerly gesture. Eamonn and I left early – and sober – a sure sign of our discomfiture, and went off to spend the night on a crowded floor in a student flat. There was no carousing. An endless amount of time was spent drawing up a statement. The Londonderry Labour Party was the minority element in People's Democracy, the leader of whom was a teacher, Michael Farrell. Though I had not seen him for years, I recognized him at once – he was the eccentric atheist I had seen waving a Bible on my very first day in Queen's. He was much more mature now, serious in his deliberations, with an air of authority.

Eamonn and I, both unspokenly deflated by the earlier encounter with the fact of Mary Holland's marriage, shared a perfunctory, despairing embrace in the dark, then turned our backs on each other. I fell asleep feeling lonely and odd. Nobody wished anybody a happy new year.

Chapter Eleven

We were a raggle-taggle bunch, numbering fewer than fifty, and our departure from Belfast was jeered by a motley crew of similar size, followers of the Reverend Ian Paisley, who stood on the pavement as we walked steadily uphill along the shores of Belfast Lough. On this Wednesday morning there seemed little to fear.

That had changed by nightfall, when we stumbled into Antrim. The cops had diverted us hither and yon, all day, off the main road, allegedly to avoid Paisleyites, who nonetheless attacked us from behind ditches on the side roads. They used stones and sticks. I grew to fear the sight of a Union Jack in the distance, as we crisscrossed strange territory which rumbled with the hidden thunder of Lambeg drums.

I had noticed by then that a young female student in the group wore a crash helmet. A small, silly girl, I thought, and badly dressed, too; the helmet did her no favours at all. Her name, it transpired, was Bernadette Devlin. I paid her no attention. Michael Farrell was the man of the moment, fearless, outspoken, eyeballing the police, taking the brunt of blows from loyalists who lunged over police shoulders with sticks. I was not enjoying this march one bit.

Next day, Thursday, we hit the road at 6 a.m., to avoid cops, loyalists and diversions. But they were waiting for us. I ran over the bridge of Lough Neagh. Michael Farrell had given us a lecture on its eel fisheries, which had belonged to locals, been taken over by British colonial interests and were now the subject of dispute. I could not have cared less about eels, did not notice the beauty of the lough, and was aware only that the bridge had been the scene of a relatively recent massacre – in the 1950s – when the IRA was ambushed by the B Specials. 'Young Roddy McCorley's going to die, on the bridge of Toome today' went the lament about a hero of the 1798 rebellion. Though not convinced that the same fate awaited me, I was sure that somewhere en route I would be hurt by the growing number of loyalists, unionists and policemen who harried us, sometimes in obvious collusion. It would be decades before I revisited the lough, after reading Polly Devlin's beautiful evocation of life along its shores, *All of Us There*.

My foot had erupted into a huge blister, and when it burst I was glad to be put into a car at lunchtime and sent off for medical treatment. Conveniently, the driver also had to go to Derry – two hours by car – on an urgent errand, and while there I signed on the dole. Speeding back to the march, the driver proposed to stop in Magherafelt, that night's designated halting spot, and seek out a doctor to dress my foot. The town was deserted. It smelt of fear. We did not dare ask for the address of a surgery, especially as I wanted a Catholic doctor. My companion, a trainee solicitor from the area, managed to sniff one out. I was treated in silence. I wondered how our companions would fare as they trudged into this place. They never did – diverted once again.

When we finally found the group, down a side road, Michael Farrell was magnificent. We all hid behind him as he stood up to the cops. Maghera had meantime erupted in loyalist fury when we failed to show – the driver and I had got out just in time – and that night we lay down to sleep in a community hall on its outskirts, at the foot of Slieve Gallion, than which there is no more republican area in Northern Ireland. We were assured that mountainy members of the Gaelic Athletic Association were on patrol outside, guarding us with hurling sticks. There was much whispering and coming and going. Eamonn told me that it was not beyond the bounds of possibility that the GAA men were armed with rifles and guns. Committed though we were to a peaceful demonstration, I was glad to hear that the local Fenians took a different view. The newspapers, television and radio were full of foreboding about how our march was dredging up Protestant resentment, both of Catholics and of Prime Minister O'Neill's concessions to them.

On the third day, Friday, 3 January, we trudged uphill towards the Glenshane Pass, which would take us over the mountains and down into safe Fenian territory, to Claudy, fifteen miles from Derry. My foot was hurting badly still, and late that afternoon Farrell sent me on ahead to Derry – by car – to check out arrangements for the crowd which would welcome us home. The driver was the lawyer Vincent Hanna, whose late father had been a Labour member of the Stormont parliament.

Ian Paisley had called a meeting in the Guildhall that Friday night. The square outside was packed with Derry Catholics, young and old, come to jeer him and trap him inside. Also inside were Brigid Bond and members of her group who had been squatting in the mayor's chamber. Brigid's epic squat in the Guildhall was later the subject of Brian Friel's play *The Freedom of the City*. The authorities had locked them inside the vast building. The squatters spent most of their days and nights sitting in the cold marble foyer, talking to passers-by through the great wrought-iron gates. At night, Brendan Duddy, who owned a fast-food café, brought Brigid and her troops, or had his staff bring them, trays stacked with hamburgers, chips and hot drinks. (Though he was a capitalist of the sort we were determined to overthrow, we regularly tapped Brendan, and other businessmen, for funds to help pay the bills of poor families we were helping, and he often fed us, for nothing, as we sat in his café discussing the socialist future.)

Some people attending a ball in the City Hotel, attired in full evening dress, formal frocks and black tie, came out to watch the scene at the Guildhall. The mood of the Catholics, young and old, was ugly. No thought was given to the fate of Brigid Bond and the families trapped inside with Paisley. The great doors suddenly opened, and Paisley and his people came roaring out. They had broken up chairs and were using the pieces of wood as weapons. The Catholics scattered. I had to admire the Paisleyites for their courage. In fact, I was glad for them, for they were few, in strange territory, and the Catholics were many, in their own home place.

Afterwards, the City Hotel was littered with people in torn clothes and broken, bloody skin. Cathy Harkin told me that she and my sister Nuala were going to march out with a crowd from Derry next morning and escort the march into town. She expected thousands. Vincent and I caroused the night away in the hotel. We did not get back to Claudy until dawn was breaking. We briefed a wide-awake Farrell, who directed that we should immediately set forth again, to scout the hilly terrain around Claudy, seeking out the enemy.

Up and down and around we drove that Saturday morning. What exactly were we to do if we came across Paisleyites on a narrow side road that did not allow space for a car to turn? A farmer who was as scared as ourselves when we roared into his yard brought us into the house, and his wife gave us tea and scones. Thank God for Catholics, we murmured unashamedly to each other. By the time we arrived back in Claudy, the marchers had departed. When we caught up with them, they were under attack at Burntollet Bridge. Police and men in civilian clothes were laying about them with batons, sticks and bicycle chains. Some marchers ran towards our car; others were scrambling over ditches to get off the road. The road itself was strewn with shoes and clothing and stones and pools of blood.

We got out of the car and stood there paralysed. Mary Holland arrived in her car and proposed we get in and drive through the ranks of the cops. Vincent said no. She said she would go on by herself. We got into her car, abandoning our own, and drove forwards. The police let Mary through, my first experience of the power of a press card. When we finally caught up with the marchers, Mary stopped the car, got out and ran to them. She forgot to put on the handbrake. The car started to roll off the road. Vincent yelled at her. 'It's hired,' she called back. I was struck by her style. I never did find out what happened to either of their cars.

By now there were thousands on the road, the people from Derry joining those who had come from Belfast. As we marched past Altnagelvin Hospital on the right, on the outskirts of town, word filtered back that the Protestants had gathered outside their awkwardly named Irish Street estate, on the left. We came to a confused, milling halt. There were shouts and screams from up ahead. We faced an awful choice – walk back in the direction of Belfast, and the police and the Burntollet ambushers, or walk the gauntlet. There was no question of running. The road was crammed tight. As the green, grassy slope that bounded Irish Street came into view, we could see that the tenants there, women and men and children alike, were armed with stones, sticks, bottles, and buckets of burning coals, which they hurled with hate-filled abandon upon the heads of the marchers. Our crowd moved forwards, halted, moved again, halted; stuck there in the midst of that heaving, frightened mass, missiles raining down, I decided to break away to the right, where the bourgeoisie lived, some of them Catholics.

This was not a great idea. The silence in the leafy streets was menacing. Friend or foe? I could not tell. I didn't know where I was wandering. Neither did the other bloodstained, muddy Catholics, who, it could be inferred from their marching attire and their condition, did not live there. Nobody opened a door to let us in. The silence was worse than the noise in the distance, so I made my way back to the marchers and by a stroke of luck found that they – and I – were now beyond the Irish Street estate. One more half-mile down Spencer Road and we would be on the bridge heading over to the safety of the west bank.

Spencer Road is a narrow canyon of three-storey houses, one side of which was built against a derelict banking of old stone. A nonstop hail of stones soared over the roofs and down on to our heads. The cops up ahead had blocked the bridge. Being small, I sheltered beneath a canopy of upraised arms. We were there for quite a while, yelling and rumbling until I espied a gap and scrambled to stand in a doorway from which I did not budge until it was clear that the cops had abandoned the bridge. We poured over and on into the Guildhall Square.

Bernadette Devlin became a political star that day. She stood on a platform and declared Derry city to be the 'capital city of injustice', which made us all feel like martyrs, heroes and saints. That evening she was driven down to Dublin to appear on Ireland's premiere late-night chat show, hosted by Gay Byrne. When Byrne anointed a contributor, that contributor remained anointed and became instantly recognizable throughout the island, North and South.

The joy of being in the Guildhall Square evaporated instantly when Cathy Harkin told me that my sister Nuala was missing. She had last been seen standing in a stream at Burntollet, loyalists to the left and right above her. They had cudgels studded with nails. At four feet nine, Nuala is even smaller than me. I cried with fear. When she did turn up at home later that day, she told us that two Derry men, friends of hers, had jumped into the stream, hauled her out and up and through a barbed-wire fence and force-marched her over fields until they spotted the main body of marchers on the road.

As the day closed, we learned that the Burntollet ambushers comprised off-duty police, B Specials and Protestant civilians, who had spent the morning behind a hedge, gathered under the benign eyes of the RUC who had, for once, declined to re-route the marchers. Fifty of those who had set out from Belfast or joined en route had been injured. That night, the unfazed Vincent Hanna called to our house and found my youngest sister Carmel standing at the door in her mini-skirt, waiting to take a delivery of potatoes and lemonade from the lorry man. He introduced himself and asked her to come to Belfast with him 'and we'll have a party in my grand piano'.

When Dermie McClenaghan, Eamonn and I left the City Hotel at midnight on Saturday, the town was at peace, riots over, police and Bogsiders gone away. We stopped for a fish supper in Duddy's on the way home. We were saying goodnight to Dermie at his front door in Wellington Street around 2 a.m. when the sound of tramping feet drew our eyes upwards to an unbelievable sight. Wave after wave of the RUC poured through Butcher's Gate and down Fahan Street, which led directly to Wellington Street. They walked in formation; they were clad in black, wielding batons and riot shields; they were silent. I was awe-struck. There was absolutely nobody around but us three. Dermie went inside and closed his door, while Eamonn and I hurried away to our own homes. None of us had telephones. Who would we ring anyway? The police?

On Sunday morning, the Bogside awoke to news that defied belief. The RUC had spent an hour rampaging along St Columb's Wells and the Lecky Road, where the tiny houses were populated mostly by old-age pensioners. They had broken windows, kicked in doors and beaten anyone who had come out to see what was happening. In his report *Disturbances in Northern Ireland*, published in September 1969, Lord Cameron concluded:

... with regret, that our investigations have led us to the unhesitating conclusion that on the night of 4th/5th January a number of policemen were guilty of misconduct which involved assault and battery, malicious damage to property in streets in the predominantly Catholic Bogside area, giving reasonable cause for apprehension of personal injury among other innocent inhabitants, and the use of provocative sectarian and political slogans.

In effect, the non-violent movement for civil rights died the night the RUC came in to beat Catholics in their homes.

That afternoon, the women of the area marched to the police station and told the chief cop that the RUC would not be allowed back into the Bogside until those responsible for the attack were charged. That evening, vigilantes were organized and barricades built across the main roads leading into the Bogside. Eamonn arranged for a local house-painter, John 'Caker' Casey, to write on the gable wall of St Columb's Street the slogan 'You are now entering Free Derry.' The effect was electrifying. The police would not freely come in again, nor would the writ of Stormont run in the Bogside.

On Monday, 6 January, Captain O'Neill attempted to refute the Free Derry declaration, and the organization of vigilantes, with an expression of the government's 'complete determination to bring to justice any person or body of persons who attempt to take into their own hands that lawful authority which is properly vested in the Government of the police'. Most significantly, he said that 'we have considered the possible further reinforcement of the regular police by greater use of the Special Constabulary for normal police duties and have authorized the Minister of Home Affairs to undertake any degree of such reinforcement which may be necessary to enable the police to fulfil the heavy responsibilities placed upon them.' He threatened to fine tune the Special Powers Act with a specially designed Public Order Act which would make resistance to the police a mandatory offence punishable by six months in jail.

The six days since we had set off from Belfast had dramatically shaken our little world. We had marched the breadth of Northern Ireland to dredge up the vile underbelly of unionism, provoked into sight a ghastly law-breaking coalition of cops, B Specials, unionists and Protestants, and now O'Neill was responding by turning the clock back to 1921, when the same illicit coalition gave forced birth to the partition of Ireland and reinforced their rule with the Special Powers Act and the B Specials. While this was, on the surface, frightening, the next five riotous days were shot through with fun. The barricades remained in place. Eamonn and Dermie had acquired a radio transmitter, and it was used to broadcast 'Radio Free Derry, the Voice of Liberation'. The transmitter was installed on the eighth storey of the High Flats in Rossville Street, and some of the broadcasts were pre-recorded in my mother's house. It had good coverage, and we heard it loud and clear.

An awful lot of programme time was devoted to playing record requests from one Bogside citizen to another. These requests provided a source of gossip that my mother and her friends mined to the full. There was the meek young fellow whose equally meek girlfriend went off to be a nun, but changed her mind, came out of the convent in a big, stiff skirt, a beehive and stilettos – 'like the Queen of Sheba', said Annie – and tottered up to his door to announce herself to his parents. The parents, a pious pair, had opposed their son marrying an ex-nun, but now weren't they after turning up on Radio Free Derry requesting a song for the young couple's fifth wedding anniversary. My mother thought a request from a Nora McGuinness to all her brothers and sisters over in the Waterside was 'wild sad'. Mrs McGuinness was a fine tall handsome woman living in the Brandywell who had had to change her religion when she married a Catholic: 'Of course, she stuck out like a sore thumb, bein' that tall, and everybody else that small. The Prods must be reared on the best of meat,' she said. 'She only ever sees her relatives the once a year, around Christmas, when she goes over there to visit. There was nothing to stop them coming over here, but ye know how it is . . . they were kinda rigid, but very decent people for all that. She must miss them; they're her own flesh and blood, and there's nobody like your own.' My mother and Annie told Eamonn off for giving scandal when he said that a retired priest, for whom 'Ave Maria' had been requested, was retired only because he was in danger of getting lynched for touching up little girls.

The barricades came down on Sunday, 12 January. Eamonn wanted the Londonderry Labour Party to protest against an article in a British tabloid which had blamed our march from Belfast for the turmoil that had followed, but at a meeting on 21 January his motion was rejected because of 'the unfavourable aspects of reraking the situation'.

Whatever we had done, it did not prevent me getting a job that came out of the blue – a Protestant teacher in a state grammar school in Strabane, Co. Tyrone, had become pregnant, and the Protestant Dean of Derry came in person to our house to offer me the job. I was not there, and my mother accepted the offer on my behalf. 'He sat on that sofa, same as anybody, and took his tea in his hand and a bun,' she told me.

I was assigned to teach French. I was the only person of a Catholic background on the staff. I got a lift every morning from Willie Breslin, who also taught in Strabane. We would meet outside Dermie's house around 8 a.m., shivering and exhausted from the politics and riots of the night before. Dermie, also on his way to work, would give us a cup of tea, which we took on the pavement, while simultaneously dealing with supplicants who knew that it was a good time to catch us – Dermie, especially – and who wanted to squat in a house, or have an electricity bill paid, or get a little money towards back rent. Those winter mornings were dark and cold and miserable. You can get to hate the poor. Dermie and Willie didn't. Then again, they didn't have to teach *Le Grand Meaulnes*, the French equivalent of *The Catcher in the Rye*, which I could barely translate myself, never mind pass on its rudiments to the daughters and sons of police officers.

The children and the teachers knew my background. Even if

they couldn't smell a Catholic, they could smell the riots of the night before in my hair. Nobody ever said a word to me. Were Protestants just naturally polite, or timid, or – unthinkable – liberal? Were they not even curious to hear tales from the other side? If they were, there wasn't much chance of getting tales from me: I spent every moment of free time, or tea break, snoozing in the staffroom. Maybe that suited the staff as well as me. I liked the teenagers in my class. They were not at all like city children. You could smell the fresh country air off them. I hit on a ruse to entertain them. I divided them into groups of four and told each group to pick an area of France and find out all they could about it. Their travelogues were pinned on the classroom wall, and added to every week. This meant that they had to visit libraries for information, write to travel agents for posters, collect postcards, and labels off wine bottles, and photographs of French film stars (Brigitte Bardot was popular). I invited photographs of the French Foreign Legion and – a daring touch, I thought – of the gendarmes. I played Edith Piaf for them, and Johnny Halliday, the (pale) equivalent of Presley. I was as anxious to escape the atmosphere of the North as they were.

I loved having money. I opened a bank account and went to see the bank manager after lodging the first cheque. He was a Catholic. I told him I wanted a loan to build a bathroom. He asked me how the riots were going, told me to keep up the good work – 'burn the town if you have to' – and loaned me £300, the exact sum it had cost my father to buy the house from the landlord the year before. The builder knocked a hole through the wall that separated the scullery from my father's tool shed and a hole through that to the outside toilet. We had a formal opening ceremony when it was completed, sending my Aunt Nellie in for the first bath, on the grounds that she was glamorous. She dressed solemnly in her best nightie, and dressing gown, cut the red ribbon that we had pinned across the bathroom door, opened it, closed it behind her, ran both taps, got into the bath, called out to us a running commentary, then started screaming. The cold-water tap had ceased to function and she was scalded.

★

Unionists were in open revolt against Prime Minister O'Neill's reforms. He decided to test his support by calling a general election for 24 February 1969. On our side of the divide, the Nationalist Party found itself challenged by figures thrown up by the civil rights movement who now sought parliamentary office and power. Eamonn went up against sitting Nationalist Party MP, Eddie McAteer, and John Hume was standing as an independent on a civil rights platform. One of our party members ran away with the deposit needed to contest the election. Eamonn bought a three-piece grey suit, and Ivan Cooper gave him two shirts, one blue, one pink, free from the factory because the stitching was defective. If photographs won elections, the photo of Eamonn on his election manifesto would have given him a landslide. He was twenty-five and gorgeous. One evening, as we toured the Bogside by car, using a loudspeaker to announce our presence, Eamonn's voice gave out. I took over the microphone and intoned the mantra:

McCann's the man for West of the Bann,
McCann's the man for Foyle.

He took the microphone from me and said that it sounded bad to have a woman's voice declare his virtues. 'People will think that only women are voting for me.'

It was the tradition then to cast votes in the names of the recently dead, who had not been struck off the register, or of those who didn't usually vote, or even ahead of those who had intended to later in the day. 'Vote early, vote often' was the imperative of all parties. It was open to those who staffed the polling booths to challenge all comers, but this was seldom done. I went round many stations posing as Miss X, Y or Z. I voted alongside a cousin who backed John Hume – she, too, was impersonating – and we just glared at each other in high dudgeon.

John Hume won Eddie McAteer's seat, the Nationalist Party began its slide into oblivion all over the North and the People's Democracy, including Bernadette Devlin, polled surprisingly well.

My Belfast Protestant grandmother,
Sarah Duffy (née McAleer).

My grandfather, Sergeant Duffy,
in the Bogside barracks.

With Daddy, Muireanna holding Paddy, Hugh, me and Nuala, 1947. I am, of course,
the one with the gorgeous curls.

Women on Beechwood Street take a break to barter stories.

In pantomine at St Columb's Hall in 1953. I'm second from the right.

All together for Christmas 1961. Clockwise from me (perched beside Daddy),
Hugh, Paddy, Muireanna, Nuala and, in front of Mammy, Carmel.

Me and a friend, Patrick, at the Gaeltacht in Rannafast, August 1959.

Belfast, early 1962

Royal Avenue, Belfast, 1962

Cannes, 1965–66

Madrid, 1966

In January 1969 Eamonn McCann had the slogan 'You are now entering free Derry' painted on the gable wall of St Columb's Street. He once observed that it was probably the most important single sentence he ever constructed.

Protesting against the British army's massacre of fourteen people on Bloody Sunday on 6 February 1972 in Newry, Co. Down, a week after the massacre. My companion on the march, to the right, was the film star Vanessa Redgrave. To my left is the feminist Marie MacMahon. By then we were used to being in the international spotlight.

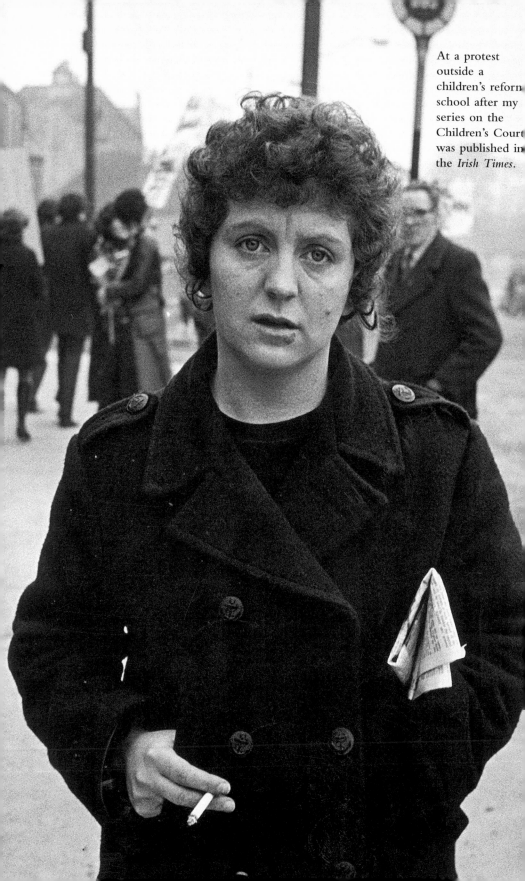

At a protest outside a children's reform school after my series on the Children's Court was published in the *Irish Times*.

Bernadette contested a unionist seat that not been challenged since 1947. Eamonn got 1,993 voters, thirteen short of the number required to recoup his deposit. We were devastated. Walking home that night, he said he had enough spare cash to buy us a few drinks. I declined, sat on the kitchen sofa beside my father and cried.

Gráinne and Michael had returned to settle in Derry, in a spacious house in the suburbs. Importantly, they did not live with their parents, which most of us did. A big house, with no parents present, meant big parties: booze and records and talk and dancing afterwards, especially at weekends. Brendan Duddy also made his house available. Middle-aged, middle class, middle of the road? It was the only way to go, party-wise. We laughed and loved and fought and planned to change the world. When the café closed, Brendan's wife, Margo, and the manager, Bernie, went home, changed into the flamboyant clothes they bought on their annual trips to Spain, and appeared in shawls, flounces, big earrings and stilettos. Brendan used to escort them into the room with a big grin on his face. They were magnificent. One night, my sister Carmel nudged me and said don't look behind you – which I did immediately of course – to see a white horse walk in through the French windows. It was a pet for the Duddy children.

Despite the fall-out from Burntollet, marches were still organized. Coming up to Easter I set off from Belfast with Eamonn and Bernadette on a PD march to Dublin, where it was hoped that we would show those who were commemorating the glorious revolution of 1916 that their business was unfinished – the South had slums as bad as any in the North, and, what's more, it was their own fault. We at least were doing something about our problems. I left the march at the border, fed up with the pseudo-revolutionary carry-on, when a fellow halted dramatically on the Northern side and produced a condom and a novel by Edna O'Brien which had been banned in the Republic. We would not get condoms, or books about sex, in the South, he declared. We wouldn't get condoms in the Church-clenched North either, was my reaction, and they had never been mentioned on any civil rights platform by any of the men present. I was not going to walk a hundred miles listening to them sniggering about sex.

Mary Holland and her husband had driven to the border to see how we were doing. I asked her for a lift back north and accepted, instead, her invitation to go with them to a Fleadh Cheoil in the nearby town of Clones, on the southern side. It was amazing, and joyful, to find the streets of that small place crammed with thousands of people. There was music indoors and outdoors, in the pubs, on pavements; there was singing in Irish and dancing; they played tunes I had never heard on fiddles and accordions. One person would start a melody, another would join in and a band formed on the spot. I could see Mary Holland falling in love with Ireland. I started falling myself. The three of us ended up in an outhouse behind a pub, standing in hay, well after midnight, as music lifted people's hearts to the rafters. Mary ordered a round of drinks for the musicians; her generosity and courtesy left me dead impressed. When she reached for her handbag to pay, it was not there. In the presence of her English husband, I was affronted. I felt Ireland had let itself down. In the North you got hit, in the South you got robbed. He was sanguine. He had served in places where worse happened. 'Yes, but, we're Irish . . .' I stuttered to a racist halt. I felt a flash of hatred for the idiot who had waved condoms and never talked about them in Belfast, where a priest or a minister might eat the face off him; for the becalmed civil rights movement; for Irish robbers; for the English; for everybody.

When another march was proposed for Strabane in the month of April, I took it into my head that this might be one march too far. The government had already waved a red rag to the bull by introducing a Public Order Act which limited even further the right to march. So I made a long speech at the Londonderry Labour Party meeting on Thursday, 20 March 1969, at which it was recorded that Comrade McCafferty:

. . . opposed the march, saying that the civil rights movement had become sectarian and that the mass body of the marchers would march for the sake of marching and to prove to the Protestants that the Catholics controlled the city of Strabane. She was sure that any excuse on Saturday would be used as an excuse to get up the Fountain [the Protestant enclave on our side of the city]. There was no point marching if one were not determined to go all the way. In the event of a police ban, barriers would have to be broken by violent means. Comrade McCafferty did not fear Protestant opposition. She feared Catholic bigotry. Comrade McCafferty felt that British troops would be called in within the next fortnight.

We voted by 30–17 to march in Strabane. There was a riot after the march.

On Thursday, 17 April 1969, Bernadette Devlin won a by-election to Westminster, taking a seat off the unionists and, at twenty-one, becoming the youngest person ever elected to the House of Commons. She was now the British parliamentary representative of Her Majesty the Queen in the heartland of traditional Fenian insurrection, Mid-Ulster. On Saturday, 19 April, the police, chasing Bogside rioters, burst into the home of Sam Devenney, in William Street. Fleeing teenagers had run through his house and out the back; the cops followed them into the house and beat up all members of the Devenney family who were present. Later in the afternoon, a cop drew his revolver and fired two shots. That night, the police entered the Bogside in dozens of trucks and rolled easily over the barricades. On Sunday, 20 April, loyalists set off a bomb at a reservoir, and the Stormont government suggested that the IRA was to blame. On Monday, 21 April, the British government announced that army units had been made available for guard duties at essential installations in Northern Ireland. On Tuesday, 22 April, an emergency debate was held in Westminster at which Bernadette made an electrifying maiden speech. She spoke off the cuff. She described the North as a medieval political slum, told both sides of the House to take full blame for their colony, and generally laid waste around her, closing with the suggestion that Stormont be abolished. The honourable members on all sides cheered her. Home Secretary James Callaghan, who had overall responsibility for the North, lauded her 'brilliance' and hoped one day she would become a member of the British government. She became, instantly, an international star. It was the eve of her twenty-second birthday.

Back home, unionists had to read that they were anything but beloved on what they called 'the mainland' of England, Scotland and Wales. The day Bernadette spoke was the day Prime Minister O'Neill promised to introduce universal suffrage. The enraged Stormont cabinet forced his resignation on 28 April. O'Neill's departing words illuminated the unionist mind-set:

It is frightfully hard to explain to Protestants that if you give Roman Catholics a good job and a good house, they will live like Protestants because they will see neighbours with cars and television sets. They will refuse to have eighteen children; but if a Roman Catholic is jobless, and lives in the most ghastly hovel, he will rear eighteen children on national assistance. If you treat Roman Catholics with due consideration and kindness, they will live like Protestants in spite of the authoritative nature of their Church.

Captain O'Neill was replaced by his cousin Major James Chichester Clark, another member of the landed gentry.

Bernadette Devlin MP arrived outside my mother's house one sunny afternoon. I was sitting at the door, on a chair, enjoying the fresh air. Bernadette's brand-new two-door red sports car – which she could not drive – was driven by her boyfriend Loudon Seth. She was grinning and laconic. He had a frown on his face, and I recognized him at once as being of middle-class Protestant background – the glossy hair, slim build, confident demeanour and swanky accent. He was a radical without street credentials. She was looking for Eamonn, who had given my address as a contact point. My mother gave them tea, and thereafter Bernadette stayed regularly overnight, usually on Fridays. She was lionized wherever she went. She tried to get away by eating over the border. It was then that I had my first real experience of a social pecking order. Where Bernadette went, so, too, went Loudon. Also Mary Holland. Also Eamonn. Also Dermie, without whom Eamonn seldom went anywhere. Also me, if I hung around long enough while the decision about where to go was made. It was much easier if we all just stayed in a city bar, where anyone at all could join in, but such a situation was terrible for Bernadette – everybody wanted a piece of her. This was also my first experience of stardom.

By the summer of 1969 the teaching job had ended, and I was back on the dole. Late one evening in the first week of July, there was a knock on the door. Marie had come over from Sweden, checked into a bed and breakfast, and wondered how I was. After the family had gone to bed, we made awkward conversation. I was consumed with unionism and rioting, she was an artist, and our summer of love in 1967 seemed very far away. I walked her back to her lodgings, and she came for dinner the next day. My mother, aghast at the thought of anyone paying to stay in Derry, insisted that she move in. Another foreigner to talk to was lovely. She had a bedroom to herself, Nuala and I were in another, and Carmel was in with my mother. Marie bought bathroom accessories – towel rail, soap dish, toilet-roll holder – which charmed everybody. My father was wary, though, of the relationship between me and the tall, blonde Swede, then apoplectic when she produced birth-control tablets one morning. She explained calmly that it was for a medical condition, to do, I think she said, with small lumps in her breasts. I could hardly hear her, for the roaring in my head, as my father had to listen to a dissertation on birth control in his own kitchen. Anyway, what would I know about it? We had been as chaste as nuns in my family home. I sat in smugly virtuous reproach of my da.

I was proud as punch when my friends in the Labour Party came to our house and met Marie. She joined in with the crowd, in our front room, helping us staple together the forthcoming edition of the party magazine *Ramparts*. We were high on the whiff of what was to come – the violence that would attend the annual Orange parade of 12 July. Eamonn, the only one, I think, who knew the score about Marie and me – such as it was – was delighted for me. Gráinne and Michael invited us to Belfast, to attend Michael's graduation ceremony. We had a bedroom of our own there, and we spent all day, every day, playing Simon and Garfunkel. I forgot about riots and the North. Michael lent us his Mini. We drove down through the west of Ireland, a vast, open place of blue mountains and green plains and rocky valleys, and villages where people painted their front doors in riotous colours. I could not help but notice how relaxed people were, and how sweet-natured.

We took a boat to the Aran Islands, where we walked between low stone walls, looking at the small bright green fields, and accepted the invitation of an old lady, standing at her door, to come in and have a cup of tea. She wore the famous Galway shawl over her black blouse, and black petticoats under her black skirt. She sat at the open hearth before a turf fire and spoke in Irish to me, she not having much English. It hurt me to see an old woman, living alone, in poverty. Revolutionary socialist that I was, I could not see that she at least had a home of her own, and the confidence to talk to strangers, and her own home-made bread, and eggs from her own chickens, and milk from her own cow. We came back for Michael's graduation on 9 July, and Marie went back to Sweden on the eve of the 12th.

Chapter Twelve

The North pulsated with violence that 12 July in 1969, the annual marching day of Orangemen. They could walk where they liked, Orange parades being, in the eyes of Stormont, just that – parades. They paraded within the law; we marched outside it. We saw things differently – the Orangemen, who included almost the entire government, were parading the supremacy of Protestants, police, B Specials and unionists alike.

Eamonn made a speech in Strabane, attacking the civil rights movement as pan-nationalist, therefore Catholic, therefore sectarian. The incoming chair of the Londonderry Labour Party criticized him in the press, and we had an emergency meeting on 14 July, at which the party barely managed to paper over the cracks between those who wanted to fight for nothing less than socialism and those who wanted to stay within the programme of the civil rights movement.

That night, a pensioner called Francie McCloskey died of injuries sustained during an RUC attack on Catholics, who had themselves been trying to burn an Orange Hall in Dungiven, Co. Derry. His was the first recorded death since the civil rights movement had begun a year earlier. On 16 July, Sam Devenney died of the injuries he had received when the RUC beat him up in his home three months earlier. The Citizens' Action Committee quietly died, and a Citizens' Defence Association (CDA) was set up in its place, ostensibly to defend the Bogside. Its chairman was the venerable republican Sean Keenan, who had served time in jail in the 1940s and 1950s for membership of the IRA. We debated sending representatives to join the CDA. I argued within the party that, while the idea of the CDA was to defend the area and keep demonstrators off the streets, now everybody seemed to be going on the streets. I had heard that 2,000 petrol bombs were being made, and I said there was no guarantee they would be used for defence. I believed that violence was inevitable, and we could not politically sit on the fence. Eamonn said that there was little that could be done in the confrontation between Protestants and Catholics, that people had a right to defend themselves and because most members of the party lived in the Bogside they should defend it against attackers. He also said that we did not need to work whole-heartedly with the CDA, that we had a PA system, a radio system and leaflets, and we need not submerge our identity. We decided to send representatives to join the CDA. It was another all-male committee.

On 2 August, in Belfast, the Catholic enclave of Unity Flats, at the foot of the Protestant Shankill Road, was besieged by Orangemen and the RUC acting in concert. Our turn was next: the Apprentice Boys were due to stage their annual march through Derry on 12 August. We put up barricades the night before. It was just a matter of luring them into the battlefield. They marched through the town and down into Waterloo Square at the foot of William Street, passing the very mouth of the Bogside. There were thousands upon thousands of them, marching to the beat of drum-and-fife bands, carrying huge banners. A line of RUC men stood between them and the hundreds of us who had gone along to watch. The Apprentice Boys were defiant, cocky, arrogant and angry. One of their supporters, a middle-aged woman called Diamond Lil, from the Shankill Road, danced by, clad in red, white and blue, and stopped to flash her Union Jack knickers at us. (Years later, her daughter would kill her in a drunken brawl in their home.)

When they caught sight of us, and we of them, the exchange of roars became thunderous. Steady, now, steady – I stood near the front line waiting for one of our lot to throw a stone. It took only one stone. It was thrown by a teenage boy, Big Eddie Harrigan, a lovable, good-natured rioter. The Battle of the Bogside was on, though it took a few more stones to establish that. The police reacted like lab rats. They charged us, and, as they did, the Apprentice Boys lobbed bottles and stones over their heads. A stone bounced off my shin. It was more frightening than sore. We all ran back to the junction of William Street and Rossville Street, regrouped, advanced again, and found there was none of the promised ammunition. Bernadette Devlin got hold of a loose piece of kerbstone, raised it above her head, and smashed it on the pavement. Now we had ammo. That photograph of her went round the world. Others followed suit, breaking stones.

Bernadette had been in the Bogside all morning with a TV crew. Sensing what was to come, she had gone to our house and changed from a mini-dress into my sister Carmel's jeans. They were far too long for her, so she had turned up the bottoms, giving her that famous John Wayne look. She did not return to our house during the battle. She does not remember where, or if, she slept.

While Bernadette broke stones, I ran on to the High Flats, hoping to meet anyone from the CDA to find out what exactly was going on, now that the police had run – according to plan – into our trap.

I met Eamonn charging towards me. He stopped to say that the Brandywell branch of the CDA had refused to release their stash of petrol bombs and that the Bogside would have to make its own. Did I have any money? I had less than £1 left from my dole, but I obeyed his injunction to buy a bag of flour from the grocery shop under the flats. 'Give us a kiss,' I said, in a fit of emotion. I remember that moment so well: it must have felt like war, wanting to kiss him goodbye before going to the front. Eamonn gave me a dry look, no kiss, and ran on. I was hurt. He could hardly have thought I was making a pass at him. I knew at once that he and Mary Holland were pledged to each other.

I got the bag of flour and ran to Free Derry Corner, where people had already deposited dozens of empty milk bottles. A car had been commandeered and petrol siphoned out of its tank. There was a handful of petrol bombs ready. A horrified roar went up, and I looked back. The police had advanced beyond the Rossville Flats and were charging towards us. A flaming petrol bomb arced through the air. It fell directly upon a cop who had advanced further than his colleagues. His uniform went up in flames. Everybody froze for a second – us and them – and stood in stunned silence at the sight of the burning body. The silence broke. His colleagues came forward and doused him; they were showered with more petrol bombs, and retreated. We chased after them. The riot resumed, but it felt like no other – this time, adults joined the young. As many of the houses off Rossville Street had been demolished, and the place was a veritable building site, there was more than enough material to use against the police, and some flashes of military genius in adopting the rough-and-ready ammunition. Wire fencing was deployed as a shield; iron bars were rammed into the radiators of the police vehicles; a digger was hot-wired and earthen barricades thrown up.

I burst out laughing when I saw my Uncle Jim and two of his pals, average age fifty-something, crouching by a wall with stones in their hands. As they edged forward, I ran over to join them. Uncle Jim said this was no place for girls. 'I can run faster than you,' I said. We ran out into the open, threw our stones, and I was first back behind the wall, the four of us happy as children. By now windows were open in the High Flats, and people were chucking stones and delph down on the police. On the roof of the High Flats, a frieze of young people was outlined. Someone gave me a bin lid full of stones, and I carried them up the eight flights of stairs, behind a stream of similar slaves. I was all of twenty-four, ancient by rioters' standards, and feeling the strain by the time I got up there.

The roof was the length and breadth of a football field, with a tiny parapet running round its edge. From that commanding height we could see people coming down from Creggan, coming over from the Brandywell, moving purposefully like ants. There were people standing in clusters at doors in the Bogside streets. The police – directly below us – were sitting ducks. I took a stone, braced my foot against the parapet, and threw it straight down at the cops. I nearly threw myself with it. I knelt down and looked at the drop – a hundred feet and more. It occurred to me to check escape routes from the roof, and there was only one – the one by which I had entered. If the cops were to quell us, storm the flats, rush upstairs, and corner us on that vast roof – what might happen?

I had seen enough movies where cops had thrown people over such an edge. They had already beaten Sam Devenney to death, hadn't they? Thus ended my career as a warrior on the roof. I ran back down the stairs. I did not know, until I saw a photograph of her in action, in a magazine, that my sister Carmel spent her time bringing bin lids full of stones up to the roof of the High Flats.

I did see, and was frightened when I did, my mother walking with two of her neighbours and my sister Nuala towards Free Derry Corner. They had armfuls of sheets. They set themselves up under the gable and proceeded to organize the milling crowd. Annie's experience on the shirt-factory line came into play. One group poured petrol into the milk bottles and passed them on to another group that poured in flour and sugar, which passed them on to the finishing group of my mother, Annie, Bridget and Nuala. They had already torn their sheets into strips, then smaller strips, then tiny strips. They doused the strips in paraffin, and stuffed them into the neck of the milk bottles. The petrol bombs were taken up, carried away and thrown at the cops, as fast as they could be made. The ones that were thrown from the roof of the High Flats made flaming pyrotechnics against the blue sky. Most did not hit the cops, but made a wall of flame that they could not penetrate.

'What would your father think of you now?' I asked my mother, as we watched some police dance their way out of danger, others put out their burning uniforms.

'My father was a good cop,' she said fiercely and firmly.

When women rise up, giving authority to their children to do likewise, the revolution is unstoppable.

The cops started firing canisters of CS gas, which caused our eyes to stream, our lungs to burn and our stomachs to revolt in retching and vomiting. Eamonn put through a call to London socialists, and Tariq Ali himself gave the remedy – soak a handkerchief in vinegar and hold it to the mouth. Tariq Ali! The revolutionary firebrand leader who had helped launch student revolt around the world in 1968, in protest against Vietnam. Jaysus, but we were somebodies now. Soon there were buckets of vinegar outside most front doors.

I spent quite a bit of time on a little wall on Rossville Street watching the ebb and flow, smoking cigarettes between inhalations of the vinegar-soaked handkerchief. The thousands of CS-gas canisters the cops fired at us created a mist. Bernadette hit on the idea of burning car tyres, in hopes of creating an updraught which would take the gas away. It did not work, and the stench was bad.

The cops were poor strategic fighters. They concentrated almost their entire efforts on a 100-yard stretch of road that led from the junction of William Street and Rossville Street in a straight line past the High Flats to Free Derry Corner. There were forty-two entrances to the Bogside, and they positioned themselves at one. They could have come at us from the back by Brandywell, and from the top via Creggan, and scattered us in a pincer movement. Instead, they conducted themselves like tennis players across one single barricade. They even threw stones themselves. They tore up cardboard and placed it in their socks to make shin guards. They were hampered in their stone throwing by their heavy uniforms, shields and riot helmets, while we swarmed like monkeys in our light clothing. Some scruple stopped them throwing petrol bombs. They were fighting with one hand tied behind their backs. They did have one weapon which we did not – if they caught us, we would go to jail – but, ironically, that would contribute to their undoing: we had an incentive to beat them because otherwise we would go to prison. When we flagged towards midnight, a lie was deliberately spread by left-wing militants that the cops were attacking the Catholic Long Tower Church, up near the Protestant enclave. This got people back out on to the streets. During lulls, the exhausted police lay down to sleep in the street.

Battle having eased somewhat, I made my way home to find my father wide awake in his downstairs bedroom. He called me in and asked me the time. Around 3 a.m., I said. 'Why are you home so early? Get back out and fight,' he said. This from the man who used to go into paroxysms of rage if I was not home from a dance by midnight. So back out I went to fight again, though I chose the safe job of keeping the supply lines going with petrol bombs and stones.

On the second afternoon of battle, I decided to go uptown to see what was happening. This was a ludicrously easy thing to do. You just walked up Fahan Street, which rose steeply from Free Derry Corner. There was fighting on my left in Rossville Street below, Derry's Walls rearing up on my right. The distance between peace and war was twenty-five yards. At the top of Fahan Street I looked through Butcher's Gate and saw that the city centre was entirely deserted and shops were closed. I walked down Waterloo Street, saw the police lying on the ground at the foot of the street, sleeping or eating, and went into the Gweedore pub halfway down. There were only four customers – two married couples, all teachers – sitting before a coal fire. They had come over from the Waterside to see the battle, but couldn't take the CS gas. They were drinking hot whiskeys and invited me to join them. I had graduated with their daughters. I told them all the news; they fully supported the rioters; I went home for my tea, to hear what they had to say about us on television. My mother told me that Father Mulvey had been round, knocking on doors, offering to evacuate the elderly to the cathedral. Ettie Deeney had told him it would be freezing there, and she was warm at home.

That second night, the police opened up a second front, further up William Street, trying to sneak into the Bogside in the dark, via Abbey Street, headquarters of the Credit Union. It was pitch dark, and the usual exchange of stones, petrol bombs and CS gas canisters was taking place. I met Bernadette there and agreed to walk with her into the space between the police and rioters. She had a loud-hailer, through which she called for both sides to halt while she spoke. The police agreed. The rioters agreed. Everything went still and silent. Bernadette turned her back to the police and addressed the rioters directly.

'I notice that you are all aiming your stones at the heads of the police. That is stupid. They raise their shields to their heads and the stones bounce off the shields. I suggest that half of you throw stones at their heads and the other half throw stones at their legs. That means forming two ranks . . .' The rest was drowned by a deafening roar from the police, who rushed forward. There was a six-foot-high backyard wall along that street. I scaled the wall, dropped into somebody's yard, lifted the lid off a garbage bin, climbed inside, and pulled the lid down over my head. When I got fed up smoking inside the bin, I climbed out, opened the door of the back yard on to the now deserted Abbey Street, continued to William Street, and found a stand-off between the police and hundreds of people at its upper end, some of whom were trying to break into petrol pumps at the garage. The city's Roman Catholic cathedral, St Eugene's, dominated the top of William Street. The Bishop's palace adjoined it. Bishop Farren, a remote man at the best of times, was inside, helpless and confused. (Ettie Deeney, snug at home in our street, had made the right choice.)

A Protestant mob, remnants of the Apprentice Boys who had by then departed the city, was behind the police ranks, and the cathedral was their objective. Or so we convinced ourselves. Father Mulvey arrived down. The man who had said I would not get a job unless I kissed the Bishop's ring, who had criticized me for reading Psychology in university without Church permission, who had torn strips off me for saying 'Jesus' in the McCann revue, now pondered another moral dilemma. How to ensure protection of the cathedral without destroying commercial property? Do not burn the garage, he said, and take only as much petrol as you need from the pumps. I made sure that he saw me as he issued this edict. The police were soon driven back by this fresh flow of ammo. The cathedral was, for the moment, saved.

Down in Rossville Street, I ran into Dermie. We stood chatting while watching people strengthen the barricade and lob missiles at the police. The police made a sudden dash forward, and it was too late for us to run with the crowd, so we dashed down a long back lane. It was a cul-de-sac. We could see the police at its entrance, backlit by flames. Some of them decided to check out the lane and slowly entered it, banging batons on their shields. As they progressed, I felt true fear. What would they do with us when they found us? 'Let's pretend we're a courting couple,' said Dermie. Never have I clung so hard to a man. With my back against a gate, Dermie's face pressed into my neck, his arms wrapped round me, I watched the police come closer and closer. 'Jesus, Jesus,' I whispered. 'Shut up,' said Dermie, fervently. Then came a roar and a rush forward of civilians, an answering roar and retreat by the main body of police. Dermie and I and a few cops were now trapped in the cul-de-sac. The silence was deathly. Police appeared again at the mouth of the alley, the cops who had been searching the lane ran to join them, the surging crowd drove them all back, and Dermie and I ran to join them. Free at last; dear Jesus, keep me free, I was not cut out for war.

A middle-aged countrywoman asked me where she could get help. She had been trapped in the city by the rioting, had been caught up in a headlong race away from a police charge, stumbled and cut her leg on an iron bar that protruded from a barricade. I looked at the wound in her shin and saw the white of the bone, gleaming between two thick fresh red slices of human flesh. I directed her to Dermie's house, in nearby Wellington Street, which had become an unofficial frontline headquarters for everything. The headquarters of the Citizens' Defence Association, in Paddy Doherty's house, 10 Westland Street, a hundred yards further away, was impractically deep behind the line of battle.

I went up to Number 10 to hear what was going on, and stood outside with Bernadette and Cathy Harkin, three women at the gate waiting for the men inside to conclude their deliberations. The men included Eamonn. Three men who had arrived from revolutionary groups in Britain sent in a representative. It was maddening. We knocked at the door and were refused permission to enter: there was a meeting in progress. I was angry that Bernadette should be treated in this way; myself and Cathy also, for that matter. The Citizens' Defence Association expanded by the hour, with any available man being co-opted to replenish ranks depleted by men who needed sleep. The association was supposed to keep in contact with the street fighting by using four walkie-talkies. When the batteries ran out, the machines were discarded. Bernadette knew more about what was going on in the street fighting than the men inside Number 10.

On the second night the prime minister of the Irish Republic,

Jack Lynch, announced that he had moved the Irish army to the border to set up field hospitals. This was a double-edged sword. If we needed the Irish army, then we must be about to be killed by the unionists. If the Irish army came into the North, the country would be united, and we would all lose the free health and education and the incomparably higher welfare benefits that the British had given us. The border and the Irish army were four miles from our house. Among other things, our family was dependent on the free house calls which doctors were now making regularly to attend to my father's rapidly deteriorating health.

On the whole, I felt lonely, mainly because I didn't know what was really going on. The Londonderry Labour Party had, to all intents and purposes, disappeared, and many of its members were now part of, and bound by, the secret deliberations of the CDA – such as they were. Many of the CDA men were republicans with whom, increasingly, Eamonn and Labour were forming a faction. Derry women didn't count. Mary Holland, whom Eamonn talked to at the end of every night, knew more than we did. Years later, when I asked her why he had talked to her, and not to Bernadette or me or Cathy, she said with pithy crustiness: 'We became lovers during the Battle of the Bogside.'

During the second night of battle, both sides exhausted, a scorched-earth policy was introduced. The best way to keep the cops at bay in their lair of Lower William Street was to burn buildings. The biggest building in William Street was the Star shirt factory. Before he helped start the conflagration that burned it to the ground, I had a conversation with the man who was first to break into it. He was a mature, middle-aged, dedicated trade unionist, fully and permanently employed, an amiable fellow who went home to his wife and children every night after the pub closed, while the rest of us went in search of a party. He supported civil rights and did not – then – want a united Ireland. 'We gotta do it, kid,' he said, petrol can in hand. I hadn't the nerve to join him. The flames lit the skyline. The cops, as well as us, were dumbfounded. Hundreds of women's jobs went up in smoke, before our eyes. (My godmother, Sadie, who worked there and often gave me pocket money even when I was an adult, was in Dublin on holiday at the time, and her family did not have the heart to phone her and tell her that her job was gone. As it happened, she saw the fire on television in Dublin.)

I was on the way home around four in the morning of the third day when I came across a plump, begrimed man sitting all by himself on an empty plastic milk crate, leaning back against the wall of the slaughterhouse. His nickname was Chocolate. He was staring at the smouldering embers of a post office sorting branch, the grounds of which abutted William Street. He shifted, over on the crate to make room for me when I asked him why he was sitting there, all alone. 'There's a safe inside that building,' he said. 'When the fire goes out and the steel door of the safe has buckled and cooled, I can break it open and take all the money inside. If you give me some of your cigarettes, we'll share fifty-fifty.'

This was a great bargain. Anyway, I was too lonely to go home to bed. So we sat there, and watched the flames go out and the dawn break, and we smoked amid the drifting CS gas and clouds of ash. It was peaceful. He had stories galore about betting on greyhounds and horses, and dreams about making a rise one day – maybe this new day dawning – just one lousy rise that would see us both well off for once in our lives. A door opened and a woman in nightdress and dressing gown came out to collect her milk – which was, incredibly, still being delivered. She saw us and asked if we wanted a bottle to drink? It was lovely stuff, cool and thirst-quenching. She pointed out with a smile that we could have stolen it. We looked suitably offended at the very idea. 'When you're finished, give me back the empty bottle; I'll wash it and leave it back out for the petrol bombers.' She bade us cheerio.

We returned to the crate and waited and waited. Around 8 a.m., Chocolate adjudged the moment right for making our move. All that remained of the post office was its buckled metal frame. We crossed the road and picked our way round piles of smouldering rubble. Sure enough, there, on the ground, was a little flame-scorched steel safe. I was vastly excited, and a little ashamed that I had ever doubted the man who couldn't pick a winning greyhound in a one-dog race. Chocolate took off his jumper, wrapped it round his hands to protect against scalding and bashed that safe with every brick he could find. Then he hammered it with a metal rod. The safe remained intact. We decided to lift it. I took off my jacket, wrapped it round my hands, and together we heaved, pushed and shoved. The thing did not budge. The fire brigade arrived. We went back on to the road and bade each other goodbye.

When I got home, my father hammered on the wall with his walking stick. Would I ever waken my mother and tell her he was hungry and would like some breakfast? I went upstairs and found my mother asleep, fully clothed, under the sheets, in the parental marital bed. On either side of her, also under the sheets, also fully clothed, were a male professor from Magee College and a young priest from God knows where. I woke them, and we had a chat about the progress of battle. The professor had an English accent; the priest a strong Southern brogue. Then I remembered that my father wanted breakfast. I went downstairs and told him that my mother had been sleeping with two men and would be along shortly. He gurgled with laughter as I described the sight. The priest and the professor bade him good morning. I went up to the shop and got baps, and we all had breakfast, moving between scullery, kitchen and my father's bedside. The priest gave my father the blessing of the sick before he left the house.

I went up to sleep in my parents' bed. Nuala had already left for work, which she assiduously attended by day, despite her duties at the petrol-bomb station. 'We need the wages,' she said when I teased her about this. Carmel did not reveal that she wasn't going to work at all.

I couldn't sleep. I had no political understanding, much less knowledge; I had neither money nor cigarettes; and I was living off my parents. Luckily, the CS gas had given my mother such a sore chest that she could hardly smoke at all, and I helped myself to her packet. Around one o'clock in the afternoon I got up, ate the dinner my mother had made, and decided to go up to the welfare office, via the riots. It was women's dole day. I don't know how people can go through war without money. The riots were going at full daylight strength. There were rumours that the B Specials were on their way across the bridge into Derry, heading for the Bogside. There was panic. B Specials or no, I walked up to the dole office, beside Bishop Street. It was open and completely deserted, apart from staff.

With the precious £4.5s. in hand, I decided to celebrate before going back to war, and walked up Bishop Street to buy cigarettes and lemonade in a little shop. I was the only person in the street, and the man's only customer all day, he told me. I decided to walk on up Bishop Street to get a sense of how the Protestants were doing on the other side of the street, behind the great walls of the jail, within their little enclave of the Fountain Estate. I had the bottle of lemonade to my lips when I saw a group of mostly young masked men come out of the sole entrance to the Fountain, up beside Bishop's Gate. There were about fifteen of them. They had petrol bombs in their hands. They halted, glanced about, saw only me and lit the bombs. Holding them, they ran silently across to the other side of the street, where Catholics lived in the small houses, tossed them in through windows, and bounced them off doors and roofs. They were so quiet – not a word out of them – that it was like a pantomime. I walked backwards, quickly. The deliberate burning of houses, and people in them, was by far the most horrible thing I had ever seen. I turned and ran downhill into the Bogside to get help.

Free Derry Corner was deserted. Rossville Street was deserted. There was nobody on the roof of the High Flats. There were no people or police about. I ran towards the noise coming from William Street. It was filled with cheering Bogsiders. The British army had arrived, and erected coils of barbed wire across the street's width. The police had retreated. We had won. And I had missed the whole thing. Paddy Doherty was up front negotiating with the troops. (I saw him later, on television, shout across the barbed wire to them, in majestic tones: 'I, Patrick Laurence Doherty, in the name of God and of the people of this city . . .')

There was nobody in authority that I could tell what I had seen in Bishop Street. A section of the crowd broke away and surged up through side streets, to Butcher's Gate, at the top of Fahan Street.

The British army stood across the mouth of the gate, their backs to us, facing the RUC. We jeered, 'SS-RUC.' A disgruntled, furious cop lunged forward. A soldier used the butt of his rifle to dig the cop in the stomach. It was true, then! The British government had sent the army in to defeat unionism and its armed wing. We cheered the soldiers and jeered the cops. I made my way back to Bishop Street to find the Protestants gone, Catholics outside their homes, and the army helping to put out the fires.

Down in Wellington Street, Bernadette was in conference with Eamonn. Afterwards, she clambered atop a little barricade outside Dermie's house, and gave an impromptu speech to a small crowd, using her loud-hailer. She asked her listeners not to make the British army welcome, and talked of British imperialism and its ruinous intervention in Cyprus and Aden. The people went home for their tea and to watch themselves on television. Eamonn went off with a fellow recently arrived from Scotland, to produce Barricade Bulletin No. 2, which declared: '. . . This is a great defeat for the Unionist government. But it is not yet a victory for us.'

The news on television was frightening. Eight males were dead, six of them Catholic. The dead comprised a Catholic man shot in Armagh by the B Specials; three adults, one child and a teenager (all five were Catholic), shot in Belfast by the RUC; and two Protestants shot by Republicans in Belfast. The child, Patrick Rooney, had been killed in his bed when a bullet fired by the RUC had gone through the window of his family's high-rise flat off the Falls Road and ricocheted off the wall. Catholics in Belfast had risen up in response to our call that they revolt, keeping police busy there, thereby preventing reinforcement of the cops in Derry, who we thought were going to kill us. Catholic Bombay Street had been burned out in its entirety by a mob of B Specials and Protestants, while the RUC gazed elsewhere. Bombay Street ran parallel to the Protestant Shankill Road, and abutted the Catholic Clonard Monastery, and it was there that fifteen-year-old Gerard McAuley died. Many houses in nearby streets, occupied by Catholics, were also burned. The families fled to parish halls. One hundred and fifty-four people were wounded by gunshot; 1,800 families in Belfast had moved home – of which 300 were Protestant. Thousands of Catholic families had been evacuated from Belfast to Irish army bases across the border. It was the largest migration in Europe since World War II.

In that context, it was difficult for left-wingers to argue that the British army was an imperial threat. Eamonn later wrote dismissively that 'women squabbled at street corners over whose turn it was to bring tea to the squaddies.' He was not similarly scathing of the fact that the day after the army arrived in Derry, he was part of a Defence Association delegation which met the two soldiers in charge – Brigadier Lang and Colonel Millman – and that the men from the Bogside took private refreshments with the two officers and gentlemen. Until we read his 1974 book *War and an Irish Town*, most of us did not know that.

If I had known, I might not have been so frightened about leaving the Bogside after the soldiers arrived. For the first couple of nights I cowered in the ghetto, afraid to leave lest the police were waiting outside it, to arrest us. But I was dying to know what was going on downtown in the City Hotel. And I was supposed to be free. So I walked with Eamonn and Dermie down to the main exit from Bogside, William Street. The army had erected a canvas tunnel, through which we had to pass. There was a table inside the tunnel, and on it was a ledger, and behind the table stood a soldier. He asked us all to sign the thing, for purposes of security – our own security, he assured us, so he would know who was missing if we didn't come home, and could send a search party to find and rescue us. He read my signature and address, and thanked me politely for my cooperation. I had signed myself out as Constance, Countess Markiewicz, and given my address as Dáil Éireann, Éire.

There were no police about the place. We had a great night in the City Hotel. I signed myself back into the Bogside as the radical black American Angela Davis, address Oakley Drive. This farce ended within twenty-four hours.

★

Within days of the Battle of the Bogside, Bernadette disappeared to America. In an unpublished memoir of the time, she bleakly recalled that after a second attempt to rouse Bogsiders against the troops, the leaders of the CDA pushed her off the platform outside the High Flats. 'No one came to my defence.' The CDA was by then in daily negotiation with the British army; Bernadette said that it was negotiating the dismantling of the barricades. Paddy Doherty held up a document. He said it declared that the barricades would remain until the British government had disarmed the RUC, abolished the B Specials and thrown out the Special Powers Act. It had just been submitted to the army and, to acknowledge having read it, the officer commanding had signed it. He showed the signature. Doherty counselled that everybody rest on their laurels for a bit and not rush into anything they might regret.

That night, at a CDA meeting, Doherty criticized Bernadette's opposition to the organization's strategy. No one spoke in her defence. She felt betrayed. A fierce row raged in Paddy Doherty's house, but had to be covered up as a number of parliamentarians from Dublin were arriving to meet the leaders of the Bogside community. 'In this situation my departure to America to do a tour for the Civil Rights Association was engineered,' she wrote in her memoir. 'I am sure that it was set up to get me out of the way, although I do not know to this day who did it or how it was done.'

In his memoir, *Paddy Bogside*, published in 2001, Paddy Doherty wrote that Bernadette retired to bed after he had 'brutally asserted' his authority during a meeting between himself, Bernadette, Eamonn, Loudon Seth, John Hume and Ivan Cooper. 'McCann remained silent. He knew I meant business. Bernadette began sobbing uncontrollably. During the confrontation Hume and Cooper left. Eileen [Doherty's wife] consoled Bernadette and took her upstairs to a bedroom to rest.' Bernadette was exhausted and fell asleep in Paddy Doherty's house. Even when she left the house she didn't know that plans were afoot to organize her trip to America. She went to collect bits and pieces that she had left in Dermie McClenaghan's. Before she could leave Derry, she ran into

Dermie outside the Bogside Inn. A meeting between left-wingers and republicans was in progress inside. He told her that it was planned to send her to America and that the trip had been organized.

'The way I felt then, if Dermie had said I had to go to the moon, I would simply have said, "OK, that will do me. Point me in the general direction." I was put in an ambulance and taken across the border into the Free State. Irish army personnel took me from Donegal to Shannon airport.'

Mary Holland was in the ambulance that took Bernadette to Donegal. She left in the clothing she had worn during the battle. She had no luggage, passport, visa or tickets. Nobody, to this day, will say who organized the trip.

While in New York, Bernadette was given the freedom of the city by Mayor John Lindsay. On Eamonn's advice, she gave the keys symbolizing this freedom to the Black Panthers. Irish America was not impressed with what seemed to them to be a rejection of mainstream America's offer to help Ireland.

Of Bernadette's effective expulsion from Derry, Eamonn makes no mention in *War and an Irish Town*. Almost immediately after she left, he was part of the four-man CDA delegation which welcomed British Home Secretary James Callaghan to the Bogside, where they reiterated Doherty's demands and asked for jobs for the city. Eamonn's CDA faction was supposed to organize a counter-demonstration against Callaghan's arrival, to show the British that the Derry left was not soft, but, as Eamonn wrote in his book, 'Fairly typically, by the time Mr Callaghan arrived we had not decided what form this demonstration should take and it never happened.' Of course, this was partly because Eamonn and his faction were all sitting in Paddy Doherty's house with the rest of the CDA, waiting to hear the place and time of the meeting with the man who represented all he wished to protest against.

We did manage to do one thing, though, those of us who were not party to the deliberations of the great and good men of our town. Cathy Harkin and I persuaded a fellow who was waving an Irish tricolour to stay away from the thousands who had congregated outside the tiny Lecky Road house, from which Callaghan addressed them through a second-storey window. By God, we did not want the Protestants, or the British, or the left, to be upset by such an unseemly display of backward Irish nationalism.

August closed with Bernadette still in exile. Paddy Doherty lost his excellent job as foreman in a Protestant-owned building firm where he had worked most of his life. Mary Holland drove him to a plush house on the outskirts of Derry where his boss made it clear that the services of the man who, he suspected, was fighting for a united Ireland would no longer be required. And the Dubliners came to the Bogside and performed on a platform near Free Derry Corner. Luke Kelly sang a song that was strangely prophetic, and totally contradictory. 'The West's Awake' was a rousing, defiant lament about how one section of Ireland would rise up and strike against British occupation.

Sing, Oh! Hurrah! let England quake,
We'll watch till death, for Erin's sake.

The moon was up over Derry's Walls that night, and we cheerfully joined in the chorus, shaking friendly fists at the British soldiers looking down on us. They probably enjoyed the music, too – we had no intention of harming them. The Dubliners had landed into my mother's house before their concert, looking for Eamonn, and she offered them tea, coffee, milk, water . . . anything at all? She was as puzzled by their polite refusals as they were by the offers. My mother had never heard of Ireland's hard-drinking five-man answer to Bob Dylan.

After the concert, around two in the morning, I went to Dermie's house. Eamonn and Mary and Dermie were in the kitchen giving the band members beer and whiskey. Eamonn was proud of having pulled off the great coup of getting them to Derry. Mary and he were clearly in love. I sat on the stairs, weeping and paranoid about what I interpreted as my exclusion from what was going on. Though you never needed an invitation to go through Dermie's door, this night was clearly different: Eamonn and Mary were having a private party to which I had not been invited. Bernadette was not mentioned.

The barricades came down in September, after several public meetings, and the British army was allowed entry into Free Derry with a token two-man unarmed military police patrol. At one of the meetings held to discuss this proposal Mary Holland urged me to speak in favour of keeping the barricades up. 'We need a Pasionaria,' she whispered. I had never heard of Dolores Ibarruri, the Spanish revolutionary who had famously said of Franco's troops 'No pasarán' – 'They shall not pass.' Anyway, I hadn't the nerve to speak. That was the kind of thing that Bernadette did, and she wasn't there, and Eamonn and his faction had lost the vote at the CDA for taking them down. Later that night, I stood on the main barricade in Rossville Street with a small crowd, led mostly by foreign lefties – the Bogside was now a revolutionary tourists' paradise – before being swept aside by dockers, among others, whom Paddy Doherty had called in to do the deed. He had asked for help at a meeting facilitated by the union to which the dockers belonged. (Sometimes, workers just did not listen to the Londonderry Labour Party, or invite us to important meetings such as this one, and sometimes we did not think to consult them: we specialized more than somewhat in making demands from a distance via manifestos, pamphlets and press releases.)

The man who pulled me off the barricade was neither a docker nor a trade unionist, but a sixty-something man from our street who had been drawing sickness benefit for years. When I told my mother about this, she snorted, 'That wee skitter has been pestering Mrs Barber for years, and I had to go up to her house one night, lie in wait for him, and tell him to lay off her.' Mrs Barber had been widowed for decades, and lived alone, and the man's unwanted attentions – knocking on her door every night, affecting to check if she was all right – were an affront, and a source of fear. Truly, the goings-on in my street were as mysterious to me as the goings-on of the male political activists in Derry. It was not until 1974, when I read Eamonn's book, and 2003, when I read Paddy Doherty's book, that I found out that, while negotiating with the British army, both men had simultaneously trained in armed warfare in September 1969. Neither man knew what the other was up to. An IRA man from Cork gave Eamonn, some Labour Party members and a few republicans small-arms training in a house in the Brandywell. Eamonn wrote in *War and an Irish Town* that they 'learned how to dismantle and reassemble the Thompson and the Sten, and how to make a Mills bomb. We went across the border into the Donegal hills for practice shoot-outs. It was exciting at the time and enabled one to feel that, despite the depressing trend of events in the area, one was involved in a REAL revolution.'

Paddy and his handful of volunteers, mostly his brother and sons, trained across the border, also in Donegal, with the Irish army's FCA – An Fórsa Cosanta Áitiúil, a part-time force similar to the British Territorial Army and the B Specials. Paddy was proud when he was invited to kneel on a prie-dieu, alongside the OC, during a mass on the base. If and when necessary, and with the sanction of Irish authorities, Paddy planned to use guns for the defence of Northern Catholics; if such action should inevitably lead to armed struggle for a united Ireland, he would be working within the Irish constitutional aspiration to unite the national territory. The Irish government soon denied that official training had been formally given to the little group.

When they weren't training, the two men supervised the dismantling of the barricades in Derry and painted white lines across the road in place of them. The agreement the CDA had struck with the army was that the British soldiers would not cross the white lines without the association's permission. Sometimes I laugh now when I think of Eamonn and Paddy, white paint in one hand, metaphorical gun in the other, negotiating with the soldiers, while simultaneously showering abuse on the tiny local IRA contingent. Its aged membership had only a handful of old guns, but the sight of British soldiers had them muttering in favour of launching an armed struggle for a united Ireland.

Whatever the men were all up to in September 1969, nobody told us Derry women. Bernadette came back from America with a bag full of dollars and cheques, which she deposited in the wardrobe in my mother's bedroom, and promptly forgot about. The month ended shamefully when, during a sectarian confrontation within the Walls, a Catholic mob kicked William King, a middle-aged Protestant, so badly that he died later of a heart attack. I was there, with Cathy Harkin, the two of us part of a group who had taken it on ourselves nightly to try to talk the mainly teenage Catholics away from Bishop Street and the Fountain Estate. William King was forty-nine, married with four children and had a good job in the Du Pont factory. There was nothing we could do as the man went down. He lay face-up on the ground, his arms around his head as feet thudded into him. It was over in seconds. The mobs evaporated. Cathy and I ran away, too, that night of 25 September.

In October, the Hunt Report, an inquiry commissioned by the British government into things Northern, recommended the disarming of the RUC and the abolition of the B Specials. That same day, Home Secretary Callaghan brought the new chief of police for the north into the Bogside. 'He's going to look after you,' Callaghan told us. 'Oh, no, I'm not,' replied Sir Arthur Young, from London. 'They're going to look after me.' Our cheering response to this patronizing talk was unedifying. The next day unarmed military policemen took a symbolic stroll past Free Derry Corner. The RUC would be next, we speculated, prompting my agitated mother to remind us all about Bernadette's dollars in her wardrobe, which were supposed to be distributed among those who had suffered in the summer.

We decided that some of the money should be given to Protestants, to show our non-sectarian credentials, and that I was the woman to do it. So I was given a brown paper bag that contained $4,000 in cash. First, though, I had to sign on. That Thursday afternoon I virtuously paid my own train fare to Belfast out of the precious £4.5s.

I stayed with Gráinne and Michael, and telephoned various Protestant ministers, whose names and numbers were listed in the phone book. None of them wanted our filthy lucre. Twenty-four hours after I got there, a Church of Ireland minister finally agreed to my frantic pleas that he take the money – and shove it up his jumper, for all I cared, or better still, distribute it among needy Protestants without telling them where it came from, if that was the only way to get rid of the dough. The nice minister with the modulated voice hadn't a clue who I was or what I might represent. It took quite a while to convince him that a few dollars in the pockets of the poor could brighten their day. I didn't point out that I was in a position to know, having just paid my own bloody train fare. I said I wouldn't even look for a receipt. We met by appointment at the corner of the street where I was staying, in a mixed area near the university. The man in the white clerical collar and grey suit was a polite, handsome fellow. I don't suppose he was used to accepting money from Catholic strangers at street corners. I gave him the brown paper bag of cash and walked away. The transaction took but seconds to complete – just like the kicking to death of William King. I no longer remember the minister's name.

Chapter Thirteen

The day after I got rid of Bernadette Devlin's American money, Mary Holland arrived in Belfast to check Protestant reaction to the Hunt Report. She used her press pass to get us through a police cordon to the Catholic Unity Flats at the foot of the Shankill Road. A policeman had just been shot dead – by the Shankill Protestants, we were told. Constable Victor Arbuckle was the first RUC officer to be killed in the Troubles. The army shot two Protestant civilians dead on the Shankill later that night. As we stood there in the dark, listening to the roar of thousands of Protestant militants a hundred yards away, their bulk on the crest of the road backlit by flames, we heard the sound of gunfire. We flung ourselves to the ground, as did the police and other journalists. I heard the bullets whistle and whizz over our heads. I was dead impressed by Mary, who lay there in her lovely clothes, cool as a cucumber, chatting away to calm me. It seemed as if a press card gave people immunity from bullets, petrol bombs, cops, Prods and Papists.

Though the shooting made me nervous, I found the night exciting. With a press card, a person got to see and learn many things, and didn't have to worry about being arrested. People on all sides talked to journalists.

By then, many of the journalists who came to Derry were looking to talk to me, not least on the grounds that I gave the facts first, then my own interpretation of them. I never forgot what Mary Holland had told us: one wrong fact can bring down an entire story. One journalist, clearly an American, did not approach me. I saw him sitting in the City Hotel, in a leather armchair, all by himself, watching the crowds come and go. I felt sorry for him, being alone, and went over and asked if he needed anything. He introduced himself as Jimmy Breslin. The name of the Pulitzer prize-winner meant nothing to me. He asked me to sit down and have a cup of coffee with him. I gave him our party magazine, *Ramparts*. I adored his New York accent. He was tough and funny and had wavy dark hair, smiling eyes, great big fat hands and clean fingernails. He would use both hands to push back his hair, then rub his eyes, as though he were distracted and trying hard to understand something (not least, my accent). He asked me finally to cut the socialist crap and take him into the Bogside to meet 'young people'. So I took him to an ice-cream café in William Street where a gang of unemployed teenage boys and girls were wont to spend a whole afternoon, killing time with pennies spent on coffee. Just before we entered the café, Jimmy noticed a line of graffiti, guffawed in delight, took out his notebook and wrote it down. It read: 'My vulva is for you.' 'These kids will be all right; these kids have more than just riots on their mind,' Jimmy pronounced.

I took his point, but, even though I knew where it was located, I wasn't at all clear what a vulva was. I asked him to explain. 'Go home and look it up. You wanna be a journalist, you gotta do the work,' he said. I think he was just shy about sex.

I hadn't thought about being a journalist, I told him. 'So why are you writing in that friggin' Labour Party magazine? Is that friggin' socialism – you don't get paid for your work? Me, I'm a 10 per cent socialist: 10 per cent for the poor, 90 per cent for me because I do the friggin' work. In America we admire work. Any work, long as it brings in the bucks. The work you do is journalism. Just drop the friggin' socialist lectures when you write – lemme read the story and, if it's that good, I'll get the point without you friggin' spellin' it out. If it's that good, maybe you'll get paid some day.'

He went into the café and made himself right at home.

Some time later he brought his wife to Derry. He introduced her as 'the former Rosemary d'Attolico'. Amazing – a man who ran around with his wife and used her full name. The two of them filled my mother's sofa, and she was as bemused by the sight of them together as I had been. She gave Jimmy a million stories. Happily we never saw the intimate details about our neighbourhood life which he unveiled to his readers in the United States.

Some afternoons when he called, I would still be in bed. He would come right up to the bedroom, bringing me a cup of tea, sit himself down, and make pointed remarks about the joys of a socialist life – 'You get to sleep all day, live off your parents, riot all night, collect welfare, write for friggin' nothin', and tell the workers of the world to unite and overthrow the boss class. Listen, Nell, the workers are a little busy workin'. Particularly the Protestants. They can't afford to unite with the Catholic unemployed. When you've nationalized the banks and guaranteed wages to the friggin' Protestants, give them a call. Just as soon as you get up out of the friggin' bed, right?'

Mary Holland introduced me to Fergus Pyle, Belfast-based editor of the Northern edition of the *Irish Times*. I took Pyle round the streets a bit. He was sweet, civil, dead swanky and Protestant. A Southern Prod was not a real Prod, I told him. Southern Prods did not support the Northern unionists. He commissioned a piece about our half-built bathroom. My left-wing comrades considered the article, 'Bathroom in Bogside', to be sentimental and not at all Marxist in analysis.

Between the night that the Protestants killed Constable Arbuckle, 12 October, and the end of December 1969, one Protestant paramilitary died after the bomb with which he was trying to blow up a power station in the Republic exploded; one IRA man died in a car accident; and a Catholic man died as a result of his injuries, four months after being severely beaten with a police baton. On 3 January 1970 an Irish policeman, Richard Fallon, was shot dead in the course of a bank robbery carried out by a rabidly left-wing republican group Saor Éire – Free Ireland. The very name invited ridicule. We heard that the Sinn Féin party had split in two. The 'Official' wing favoured Marxism, civil rights agitation and restraint; the 'Provisionals' wanted an armed uprising in the North. Sinn Féin's armed wing had also split into 'Official' and 'Provisional' IRA factions.

The rest of us yawned at the antics of these armchair revolutionaries. While they feinted in the shadows, we were basking in the worldwide fame and glory which a young Derry girl had just brought to our city. When eighteen-year-old Dana from the High

Flats won the Eurovision Song Contest in March 1970, Bogsiders gathered in their thousands outside the Flats. Millions of people in Europe had seen the fetching, endearingly innocent, gap-toothed schoolgirl – Rosemary Brown – sing 'All Kinds of Everything', a song about snowdrops and daffodils and dances and romances. We sang the song again and again to her family, high up in the Flats. I rang Mary Holland in London from the public phone box, held the kiosk door open and put the receiver out on to the street so that she could hear us all singing.

Fergus Pyle asked me to follow Ian Paisley, who was running in a by-election for Westminster, to be held on 16 April, and write about it. Paisley's agent agreed to let me follow the Big Man, and gave me a ride in his jeep until Paisley noticed and told me to use a taxi. The *Irish Times* had told me in advance that I could charge expenses for a taxi – but I had only my dole money. My father, sitting semi-paralysed in the corner, had taken enough money out of his pocket to see me through the weekend. The bill for the taxi was equal to two months' income on the dole.

Paisley was running for the seat that former Prime Minister O'Neill had just vacated, so he was effectively running against the unionist government itself. I did not bother with any of that. I stuck to Jimmy's injunction to 'tell the friggin' story' and let readers figure out what was going on. I wrote what I saw – that Paisley was adored, that he cut a fearless swathe through the Protestant highways and byways, that people literally looked up to him and tried to take courage from him, that they believed that he would rescue them from the Fenian civil rights onslaught, that he made them laugh when he mocked the captains. I was impressed by his conduct towards petitioners after his Sunday-night church service. He was as good as any Catholic priest, especially towards an unemployed youth who was about to emigrate to London. Paisley rang a London minister on the spot – it was after 10 p.m. – and arranged lodgings for the boy. It was strange to meet a Protestant who was unemployed and forced to emigrate.

When the article was published, I was high as a kite. My cup did runneth over when, shortly afterwards, a woman took me in her arms. She had come from England to work in Derry, had a flat with no proper plumbing, and used to come over to our house for a bath. (That bathroom was a great investment.) One night she invited me back to her flat. We smoked dope. Bob Dylan sang in the background. She was great. She laughed out loud at the unexpected – to her – pleasure of being with a woman. She said she liked small, gritty men and small, feisty women. She was about to marry. We were together about a fortnight when Marie arrived unexpectedly from Sweden. The woman bade me a good-natured farewell, and Marie came with me on the train to Dublin, where I had a job interview with the *Irish Times*.

I was socially inept, shy and had no experience of being interviewed for a high-class job. To make matters worse, the news editor, Donal Foley, told me almost straight off that he had been reared in an Irish-speaking district and was fluent in both Irish and English. I didn't speak, never mind write, fluent Irish. I asked how could Ireland be united if Northern Protestants, not to mention Northern Catholics, had to be fluent in Irish? Foley put me at ease by saying he had worked most of his life in London, a forced emigrant like so many. I relaxed even more when he said he had married an Englishwoman, Pat – I had some glancing understanding of English people. This, however, was my first time speaking to an adult in Dublin. On my previous visit, at eighteen, I had met only students.

Donal, a teddy bear of a man, was much amused by his own reflections on life. He went into a long story about a cocktail party on board a yacht on the river Thames with a member of the aristocracy called Lady Docker, who wasn't really a lady at all, in Donal's opinion, given her behaviour. Did he have an affair with her? I asked. *Irish Times* folklore has it that he decided to give me the job there and then for cutting straight to the chase. The fact of the matter is that, like many an Irish person, I had had fantasies about bedding royalty – of either gender. I thought Foley might have some insight. And I didn't know what else to talk about.

I got the job, at a vast 20 guineas a week. Other papers paid £20, but the *Irish Times* had a Protestant Establishment background and was older than the Irish Republic: hence the usage of old British money terms, Foley explained. What the hell, we agreed, 20 guineas was £1 more than £20, and the *Irish Times* management could be as affected as it liked with the likes of us workers, as long as we got more money out of its pretensions.

He introduced me then to the paper's most left-wing journalist, Dick Walsh, a grave fellow with an owlish look. Dick explained that I would need a union card to work as a journalist, and that you could only get a union card if the majority of your income came from journalism. So that was my career finished five minutes after I was hired: I had earned several hundred pounds in the previous twelve months, as a teacher, and about £10 for the article on Paisley. Not to worry, Dick grinned, the union had ways of getting round its own rules, and my card would be waiting on me when I turned up for work, a fortnight hence. Would Marlon Brando have accepted such union corruption on the waterfront? Goodbye, friggin' Brando; hello, Jimmy Breslin. I wanted to work.

I was dazed. Now I had a guaranteed job for life. I had never conceived of such a thing in the North. Women got married, or became teachers, or both, and had to publicly practise their religion to become either. That night, Marie and I booked into a bed and breakfast above a fish and chip shop opposite the Abbey Theatre. We hadn't the price of tickets to the Abbey, but our first-floor bedroom gave balcony views of its foyer, and we sat in the dark and watched the people come out after the show. We were eating fish and chips out of paper bags. Later, a sensation ran through my body that made me sit up in joyful shock. I described it to Marie as electrifying. We figured out that this must be what was known as 'orgasm'. As we couldn't remember what we had been doing, it proved impossible for me to return the pleasure. The blue neon lights blinking outside our window spelt out the name of our abode: Del Rio. Years later, I bought a print of Edward Hopper's painting of three diners in a late-night café. It was remarked to me that I had a fondness for paintings that exuded loneliness. Far from it, I am inordinately fond of intimate places such as Del Rio.

Before I moved to Dublin, I went on a mission with Eamonn

and Bernadette to Omagh, thirty miles from Derry. Omagh was the main town in Bernadette's constituency. The waiting list for houses built by local government was awful. Unionists still held the majority on the County Council. Catholics, as usual, were at the back of the queue when houses were allocated. While the councillors sat in session in their County Council chamber, we disrupted their meeting. They filed out furiously while we parked ourselves on the floor, waiting for the RUC, who obligingly came and arrested us, thus publicizing our cause. We were summonsed to appear in court the following Monday, 19 May, the day I was supposed to start work. I had not the nerve to ring Donal Foley. Anyway, I didn't have the *Irish Times* phone number. And I thought that I could just turn up a day late and say that I was sick, which is how people in Derry explained absence due to pressing engagements.

I arrived in court with a suitcase. We were charged with failure to comply with a direction to leave the chambers, not having any lawful business there. After the cop finished giving evidence, each of us was invited in turn to cross-question him. I was last to rise to my quaking feet. I was halfway through asking the cop if he was aware of the number of Catholic families who were on the housing list when Eamonn tugged at my skirt. I stopped and bent down to listen to him. Don't mention Catholics, he whispered sternly; we want houses for everybody. I was embarrassed by my failure as a socialist to pursue the non-sectarian line of asking the cop if he agreed that baking a bigger cake was better than the sectarian slicing of a small pie – something like that. I was embarrassed at letting Eamonn down. And I was annoyed with him because common sense dictated that, all the same, it was right to point up discrimination against Catholics. I felt myself blush. I indicated that I had no question to finish, never mind no further questions. We were each given a three-month suspended sentence, and fined £20 and given a month to pay.

After we left the court, I caught the bus to Dublin. My parents, not realizing that professional people such as journalists were paid by the month, had given me £10 to see me through what they thought would be one week until I got my wages. 'Sure, you'll be back up on Friday night, for the weekend,' my mother said. The woman who had taken me in her arms in Derry, who still took her weekly bath in our house, had given me a massively generous £30. Mary Holland had bought me a bright red handbag to go with my new bright red high heels, and told me to entrust myself to Mary Maher, a Chicago-born *Irish Times* journalist. The neighbours had bought me packets of cigarettes and given me holy medals. I wore a new coat and mini-frock. I felt lovely enough, but worried about money – would £40 see me through the month, or could professionals get a sub on their wages like everybody else? – and scared and lonely. I was effectively going into exile. I knew virtually nothing of the Republic of Ireland, and they didn't throw petrol bombs. But it was a job. A job, a job, a job.

Lelia Doolan and Jack Dowling met me in Dublin. Like so many others, they had checked into my parents' home when they came up to write about the North, and now they were returning the hospitality. They were famous for having resigned from their prestige positions at the national broadcasting station, Radio Telefís Éireann, and for having written and published a book *Sit down and Be Counted*, about the stifling of radical journalism on the airwaves. I had not read their book because it concerned affairs in the Republic, and had nothing to do with the centre of the universe, the North. That deterred the cheerful duo not one whit.

I was to have a room in the house where Jack lived with his wife and daughter. Though I had been absolutely confident with them in Derry, I now sat tongue-tied in the bar to which they took me for a drink. Not that Lelia or Jack was given to drinking much – their abstinence from alcohol in Derry had impressed my mother no end. She was fond of saying that Jack was 'a gentleman'. He was a former Irish army officer, had a military bearing, and looked like the colonel in the Kentucky Fried Chicken ads. Lelia, a former actress and theatre producer, was always shouting with laughter and optimism. My mother liked her because she swam against the tide – no husband, no children, and a job. I liked her because she had had the good sense to mention – and quote – me in an article she had written months before in the *Irish Press*. Nobody had ever quoted me before she did that. She wrote that I had a 'golliwog' hairstyle. This fame had gone straight to my head – two sentences in a newspaper that few people in the North read, and I was a hero to myself.

Jack drove me to his house in the suburbs. His wife was at a meeting of the Irish Labour Party. He didn't know where his daughter Gráinne was. I hadn't a clue where we were, in the vastness of Dublin, population one million. I did not sleep well. Next morning, I got no breakfast. Jack didn't cook, and his wife was still asleep after her late-night politics. The centre of Dublin was half an hour away by car. Jack brought me to the *Irish Times* office. Before I went in he insisted that we have a cup of coffee and a sticky bun in Bewley's Café. I was not to plead illness to Foley, he said. It would be foolish to go into a newspaper office and hope the newspaper was unaware that I had been convicted in court the day before, along with Bernadette Devlin. I was sick with anxiety. I wasn't just a day late for work: we were now into the second day and the office had opened half an hour ago. 'You're a journalist now,' Jack said. 'Journalists don't punch clocks.'

The man who met me in the newsroom was not Donal Foley, but his deputy. The balding, mild-mannered wee man clearly did not know what to do with me. So he brought me across to what he called the 'Women's Page' desk. There were no women there. He told me to read this 'Woman's Page' and get an idea of what I would be doing. It was devoted to cookery, fashion and babies. I knew nothing of these things and had no interest in them. I sat there, miserably, pretending to read. Eventually Donal Foley arrived in, late. He came over with a wide smile and said he had read about the court case. 'You're a journalist now. You'll have to give up that kind of thing,' he said. I was panicking inside. He had hired me precisely because I came from the Bogside, and now I was being told not to act like a Bogsider any more. I sat there, doing nothing, and the clattering of typewriters, by dozens of people, the majority of them men, made things worse – how could anybody concentrate with that level of noise?

Gradually, Maeve Binchy, Mary Maher and Mary Cummins

took their places at the women's desk. The four of us went to lunch with Donal, in the nearby Harp Bar and Restaurant. It was a liquid lunch, my first ever. I took to it like a duck to water, and went back to the office half-cut. This was great, but it could hardly be called work. We were joined at lunch by Mary Kenny, Women's Editor of the *Irish Press*. She was like no woman I had ever met. Her dress sense was eclectic and colourful – a mixture of granny's attic, high street, and tat. I put out my hand to shake hers, and she kissed me on the cheek. She was from a middle-class Dublin background, but she spoke like a sailor, when the mood took her, in an English-tinted bourgeois accent. She was the same age as me – twenty-six – and had cycled to Paris when the students rose up there in 1968 to write the story for a London paper. The *Irish Press* was fiercely nationalist, but otherwise staid; the editor, Tim Pat Coogan, had brought her from Fleet Street to shake it up. On her first day in the job she had taken one look at the desk in a newsroom corner which had been assigned to her and said, 'Put me on the payroll and call me when you've got my office ready.' Then she walked out. Apart from not turning up for the first day on the job, we could not have been more unalike: she was champagne and perfume, and I was whiskey and petrol fumes. She quoted Emma Goldman: 'If I can't dance, I don't want to be part of your revolution.' She took Karl Marx out of context to justify refusing alms to beggars: 'Charity perpetuates the system.' Men lit up when she walked in that day, and the women sat back to enjoy themselves. 'Oh, Mary!' was said often, in praise, shock or despair.

Around 6 p.m. we all adjourned to the Pearl Bar, just down the street from the office. Towards ten in the evening, I found myself stumbling across the bridge a few yards away to Dublin's main thoroughfare, O'Connell Street. I was arm in arm with Mary Cummins and a distressed male journalist. He had just legally separated from his wife. I had never met anyone whose marriage had been ended by a court order, not even a Protestant. I knew two Catholic men from Belfast whose marriages were annulled by the Catholic Church. Anyway, divorce, though legally available in the North, was only ever granted on very narrow grounds. I knew loads of adulterers, of course, in Derry, in the highest political and business ranks, but it was mildly interesting to be with a legally separated, married Catholic man. This was an honourable course of action, I thought – inasmuch as I gave it much thought because, if he was no longer in love with his wife, why was he crying? It would be decades before I learned that you cry because love has failed.

On this night, however, I totally failed to understand the poor fellow. I was revelling in the exuberance of Mary Cummins. She was the red-haired Kerry-born daughter of a garda sergeant, a fact which she told everybody at the first opportunity, usually within seconds of meeting them; I was the granddaughter of a sergeant, albeit a Northern one. 'He was a good cop,' I intoned my mother's mantra. So was her father, Mary said. It was my second night in Dublin, and I had finally found something in common with someone. Mary was a great drinker, and a great singer. She had only one song really, the words of which consisted mainly of chanting the names of villages in Kerry, 'Abbeyfeale, Abbeyfeale, Abbeyfeale, Abeyfeale, Knocknagoshel and Douagh.' Mary liked to sing in the street, as did I.

She and the sobbing man took me to the General Post Office in O'Connell Street from which Pádraic Pearse had declared independence from Britain. I gazed at the bullet holes in the granite pillars which had been pointed out to me on my first visit to Dublin, as a student. The ancient history was grand, but it had nothing to do with our struggle for civil rights under British rule in the North. Anyway, as Donal had said, I wasn't supposed to be actively engaged with that kind of thing any more. I busted the budget by taking a taxi back to Jack's.

Next day, Wednesday, I was sent off on my first assignment. I had to bring back the results of the Texaco Children's Art competition. At 10.30 a.m., I stood in a hotel, gazing in dismay at crayon drawings done by six-year-olds. A journalist from the *Irish Independent* introduced herself and spat fire at our lowly lot in life. Mary Anderson then brought me over to the drinks table, introduced me to other journalists, and I was quaffing gin and tonics by eleven. 'We can get the results from the afternoon edition of the *Evening Herald*,' Mary reassured me.

On Friday night, I took the bus to Derry. A general election had been called in the United Kingdom. Eamonn was running as an Independent Labour candidate, the unruly Derry branch having been expelled from the Northern Ireland Labour Party. I campaigned every weekend for a month, putting my less-than-stellar career in Dublin to one side until Monday morning rolled around. The paper did not ask me to cover the election, which was puzzling and worrying. Why had they hired me?

One Sunday morning as we hung about, avoiding mass, the sight of Eamonn's father coming down William Street sent us both dodging into an alleyway. I got my own back for the court case: how did Eamonn propose to confront the world as a member of parliament when he couldn't even tell his da that he didn't go to mass any more?

Eamonn lost, and the sitting MP, Robin Chichester Clark, brother of the Stormont prime minister, won handily. Bernadette retained her seat with an increased majority.

On Monday, 22 June 1970, Bernadette lost her appeal against a six-month sentence in Armagh Jail for leading the Battle of the Bogside. It was agreed with the cops that she should hand herself over to them the following Friday evening at the police station in Derry, after a public farewell at Free Derry Corner. I got the bus from Dublin at once, and was due to arrive at 6 p.m., in time to hear her speak. The cops, or the government, changed their minds, and plotted secretly to intercept her at Dungiven, twenty miles from Derry. Ivan Cooper, by now an independent member of the Stormont parliament, heard of this and rushed to my mother's house. He bundled my mother and my sister Nuala into his car, and arrived at Dungiven twenty minutes later. He drove very fast, my mother reported dryly. They waited outside a hotel. The cops stopped the car in which Bernadette was travelling. She was allowed to say goodbye on the open road before being put into the Black Maria. It was an awful sight, my mother thought. 'I looked at her, and her only an orphan.' She was the only person ever jailed for that battle.

When word reached Derry about what the cops had done, thousands of people raged, rioted, and attacked the British army, en masse, for the first time. The army responded with rubber bullets and CS gas. That night, in the Creggan estate, there was an explosion in the house of Thomas McCool. He and his two companions, Thomas Carlin and Joe Coyle, had been making a bomb mixture in the bath. The three men and McCool's two young daughters, aged four and nine, died in the fire that swept the house.

I knew Carlin. Invariably dressed in a cloth cap, frowning behind horn-rimmed glasses, he had been a member of the Unemployed Action Group for decades, and had confronted James Callaghan on the issue of jobs for Derry when the Home Secretary had visited the city after the Battle of the Bogside. I knew – everybody in the Bogside knew – Coyle's older brother Vinnie, a glorious six-foot block of a man and the self-styled chief steward of all the marches in Derry. A ship's chandler, he was unmistakable in any crowd, with his drooping Zapata moustache, broad-brimmed black hat and three-piece suit. He was invariably of good cheer, and tongue-lashed teenagers who did not do his bidding – 'Your father never had underwear.' Just the week before, I had done a sketch of Vinnie in the *Irish Times* diary column, quoting his famous malapropisms: 'There's no jobs in Derry, and the young are corrugated round lampposts every night of the week.'

As dawn broke next morning, I sat round a bonfire at Free Derry Corner with the youngest Coyle brother, Micky, and a group of men, all of them drinking beer from cans, and mournful and crying. 'He died for Ireland,' Micky said. Then he fiercely cursed his sentimentality. 'He died for fuck-all.' Nearby, a boy who might have been all of fourteen, careened about the wreckage of the Bogside in a dumper truck, hotwired and stolen from the building site where slums had been demolished and the foundations of the new housing we had craved were smoking ruins.

Being the only *Irish Times* reporter there, albeit unofficially, I got to write about it. A priest cited my description of the riots in a stern sermon at Sunday mass. 'If it's dry, burn it; if it's wet, drink it; if it moves, hit it.' There was surprise throughout the town when the Provisional IRA later claimed the three dead men as members. They were, in fact, the core of the tiny nascent organization. The riot in Derry lasted from Friday night to Sunday night. In Belfast, ominously, shooting broke out as Orange parades triggered sectarian confrontation, mainly around the tiny Short Strand Catholic enclave which was under attack in East Belfast. Seven Protestants and one Catholic were killed over the weekend. And still, it was difficult, if not impossible, to see the IRA as other than an ad hoc, badly organized, poorly equipped group who sometimes fired rusty guns when ghetto Catholics were in fear of their lives.

The following Friday evening, 3 July, the British army found guns in a house off the Falls Road. The search party was stoned; soldiers responded with CS gas and imposed a curfew on the Catholic area. They shot their way through the curfew, killing three men. They searched house to house, street by street. They smashed through doors, pulled up floorboards, and ripped fittings off walls. No one was allowed out, even to shop. The curfew lasted until Sunday. Hardest to bear were the televised scenes of the Stormont Parliamentary Secretary, Captain John Brooke MP, son of former Stormont Prime Minister Lord Brookeborough (who 'wouldn't have a Catholic about the place'), triumphantly touring the deserted Catholic streets in an army Land Rover. The British government introduced a new law that month, whereby disorderly behaviour – rioting – was punishable by a mandatory six months in jail.

Orangemen had a great 12 July.

In August, a new political party was formed, which drew together six Stormont MPs and was instantly recognized as the new force in Catholic and nationalist circles. The Social Democratic and Labour Party (SDLP) effectively sidelined the Northern Ireland Civil Rights Association and moved the focus from street to parliamentary struggle. It absorbed three civil rights MPs, one Nationalist Party MP, the tiny Republican Labour Party, and the one dissident MP of the virtually moribund Northern Ireland Labour Party. Its nominal leader was Gerry Fitt of Belfast, who had been elected under the Republican Labour banner, which gave a respectful nod to militarism, but had no tradition of physical force republicanism. Its philosophical leader was John Hume. It was all-male. Even if she had been asked to join it, which she was not, the imprisoned Bernadette Devlin would have refused the invitation. We who saw ourselves as socialist revolutionaries scorned parliamentary dancing with unionists. It seemed to us, in 1970, that the SDLP had stopped the revolution in its tracks and reduced the North to a province once again.

I left a dispirited Eamonn to Dublin Airport, and he flew to London to live with Mary Holland (though in time he moved back and forth between London and Derry). I moved out of the Dowling house, rented a bedsitter in the student flatland area of Rathmines, and resigned myself to a whole new life in the Republic. It began badly enough, when I walked into a shop to buy a record player on hire purchase. The man in charge told me that no woman could sign an agreement without the co-signature of a male guarantor. I told him that I didn't know any men in Dublin. It was just a formality, he said, and I could choose any man walking along the street. I stepped outside, asked a male stranger to come in and do the necessary, and he agreeably obliged. He was unemployed, he declared truthfully. 'No problem,' grinned the store manager. 'Just sign on the dotted line.' When the stranger, who had produced no proof of identity, departed, I pointed out that my wages were five times greater than his welfare entitlements. 'Ah, but you're only a woman and he's a man. That's the law,' came the genial reply.

Soon I discovered a refuge for misfits that became a haven – Mrs Gaj's restaurant on the corner of Lower Baggot Street and Pembroke Street. I had been told about her by a Dublin woman who had joined the Derry Labour Party, Liz O'Driscoll (now McManus, and deputy leader of the Irish Labour Party). Liz said, 'She sits at a table in the corner, every night, like a big black spider inviting you into her parlour.' Margaret Gaj was Scottish by birth and Polish by marriage. She was huge in girth and presence, dressed indeed in black, wore a coloured patterned scarf over her shoulders, and had lively dark eyes and a wicked grin. Her food was famously cheap, nourishing and tasty. Her female staff had carte blanche to shoot verbally on sight, if she hadn't beaten them to it. The huge room, one flight up, had picture windows, a wooden floor and bare wooden tables, each of which had a daily centrepiece of fresh flowers in a small jar. There were shelves of wine behind the serving counter. The bottles were covered in dust. Mrs Gaj charged about ten times the normal rate for wine because she didn't like drunks.

The restaurant accommodated cabinet ministers from the nearby Dáil, business people, professionals, students, beatniks, crooks, ex-jailbirds, republicans who may or may not have been in the IRA, office workers and solitary souls. I fell in with members of the Dublin Housing Action Committee who were squatting people in vacant properties, and felt a bit better in their law-breaking company, but I failed completely to understand the students who had occupied Georgian houses that were due for demolition by property developers. Beauty, aesthetics and conservation meant nothing to me. The students got miles more coverage in the *Irish Times* than did the squatters.

I ate in Gaj's every weeknight that I wasn't on the tear with Mary Cummins and whichever other journalists had congregated in the Pearl Bar. Mary and I would drink from left to right off the shelves, working our way through the rows of bottles. 'We'll have a glass of that one, then that one next to it, then that one, third bottle along.' We didn't know what we were drinking, but it was fun, and some of it tasted nice.

Mary was not with me the night I went up to the Phoenix Park with some of the younger *Irish Times* journalists, an intriguing bunch of Protestants and one Quaker, to have a party outside the presidential residence of Eamon de Valera. We had taken it into our heads to mock the old man's proclaimed vision of Ireland, wherein people lived frugally round cosy hearths, and happy maidens danced at the crossroads. As we jived and drank on the grass, a young guard came over to caution us. I asked him to join me under a tree. He dropped his trousers and pressed me against the trunk, but before anything could happen his superior's voice rang through the darkness. He bolted back to duty, trousers round his ankles, white underpants gleaming, calling his badge number out to me – 'K-...' – over his shoulder. He would be on duty for the rest of the week if I cared to come back. I didn't.

One night in the Pearl Bar a male journalist followed me into the ladies' toilet and produced his penis. Was it not, he asked amiably and proudly, the biggest penis I had ever seen? He left me home and came inside. As he reared above me on the bed, I panicked and told him I was lesbian. He was most agreeable and left at once. Next day I was assured by those who knew about such matters that, yes, indeed, his was the biggest penis in the *Times*, if not the country. After another escapade, Donal Foley assured me that I did not have to sleep with photographers who accompanied me on assignment: the man had knocked on my bedroom door the minute we landed in the west of Ireland, come into the room and made himself welcome, and said we had to sleep together. 'Why?' I asked. 'Because that's what we do on tour,' he said. 'But you don't even fancy me,' I protested. 'That's beside the point,' he said.

I met a young government minister in the late-night drinking haunt, Groome's Hotel, and he drove me home. When we walked into my flat, I saw with relief that a man I had met in Derry had already made himself at home. I introduced the minister to my friend, who was a member of Saor Éire. The minister made his excuses and left.

Another fellow, a really nice – and talented – journalist, offered to have sex with me so I would know what intercourse was like with a man. It was six o'clock in the afternoon and we were both sober. I lit a fire in the bedroom, drew the curtains, undressed, lay back and waited. And waited. When I opened my eyes, he was tenderly wiping a glistening little spot of fluid off my tummy. He said we'd had a good time. I said nothing had happened. To this day I am mystified by that encounter. I say we didn't do it. He says we did. When I see him, I joke that I am still waiting. He does not see the joke. I appreciate that he at least made the effort. Whatever it was.

Chapter Fourteen

At the end of August 1970, five women met in Bewley's Café to discuss Betty Friedan's book *The Feminine Mystique*. They were all radicals and left-wingers: Margaret Gaj; Mary Maher; Máirín Johnston of the Communist Party; Máire Woods, a medical doctor; and Máirín de Burca, then general secretary of Official Sinn Féin. Eamonn had told me about Máirín de Burca: 'She lives alone, doesn't socialize, and has a poster of Che Guevara on her wall. She's absolutely dedicated and very set in her views, but she's not that well read in socialism.' Máirín had me round for tea to her flat. The invitation was a rare honour, and was never repeated – she did not indeed socialize. She lived frugally on the small wage paid by her party.

The women decided to meet every Monday night, to discuss the liberation of Irish women. The group expanded to twelve, by invitation, and I was one of them. The first meeting was held in Mary Maher's house. I don't remember a single detail about the agenda of those early meetings, but I recall vividly the sense of peace in my head when I walked into Mary Maher's little living room. I would never again have to stand helplessly outside a door while the all-male gathering within decided what was best for the human race. I felt immediately at home among the women. I knew exactly what they meant, and I had a lot to say myself. We quickly discovered that we didn't know the half of it. Oh, but we were a repressed sex altogether – though we didn't use that kind of language.

What stands out in my memory was a remark made by a woman who was often the *bête noire* of our gatherings: Nuala Fennell was the epitome of the middle-aged, middle-class, middle-of-the-road bourgeoisie. She remarked wistfully that I had lovely hands. I was astonished. This groomed suburban mother, who had just recently started freelance journalism, held out her own hands. They were red and roughened from years of housework. Mine were, by comparison, as soft and pink as a baby's bum. So much for class warfare. In 1970, in Ireland, 96 per cent of married women worked, unpaid, within the home, and their situation did not feature in any plans for the workers' revolution.

Mary Maher, pregnant for the second time in two years – to the amused surprise of herself and her husband – set the ground rules for our gatherings. There would be no cakes or canapés. She would make coffee or tea, and one of us would wash up. We agreed from the outset that we would not include the North in our deliberations, bearing in mind Brendan Behan's dictum that the first item on any Irish political agenda is the split. This was a great relief to me. There were as many views on the North as there were women present, and I was fed up being the slightly sulphurous outlaw who had actually used violence for political ends.

I thought the North didn't need help from the Republic anyway, and that the best contribution women could make was to change the South to make it more acceptable to Northern Protestants. That would pave the way towards cooperation on a divided island. The Republic of Ireland, for instance, recognized in its written constitution the 'special place of the Catholic Church', an almost exact mirror image of the unionist definition of the North as a Protestant state – not to mention the British requirement that only a member of the Protestant faith could become monarch of the United Kingdom of Great Britain and Northern Ireland.

We decided to call ourselves the Irishwomen's Liberation Movement and drew up a short pithy list of six demands, based on what we saw as the greatest obstacles to freedom. Those demands were: equal pay; equality before the law; equal education; legal contraception; justice for deserted wives, unmarried mothers and widows; and one family, one house.

It is a measure of our utter innocence that we did not include divorce. It just did not occur to us that marriage could or should be legally terminated, even though one of the twelve founding members was June Levine, who had been divorced in Canada;

though Irish-born and bred, June was, after all, Jewish. Neither did we think to make demands about abortion, battered wives, rape or incest. In truth, we hadn't a clue about these matters. And nobody, but nobody, had heard of 'gay rights'. Even if I had, I wouldn't have mentioned it. It was enough to be inside the door, among women, and I wasn't about to risk being shoved outside it. Sexual liberation was not then an issue. We were more interested in avoiding pregnancy than achieving orgasm.

It was the law that women in clerical jobs in service industries – banks, local authorities and state and semi-state bodies – were required to resign from their jobs when they married. The principle was followed even where it was not legally imposed. The nurses, teachers, bank employees and such who resigned were often immediately rehired in a permanent-temporary capacity, with consequent reduction in wages, opportunities for promotion, and pension rights.

Not that anybody much cared, including women. Wives who had paid work constituted a mere 9 per cent of the female labour force. In that regard, most of our little group were freaks – married, with children, and with jobs to boot. The Constitution reinforced the concept that woman's rightful place was at the kitchen sink. Article 41.2 declared (and still does) that:

In particular, the state recognizes that by her life within the home, woman gives to the state a support without which the common good cannot be achieved.

The state shall, therefore, endeavour to ensure that mothers shall not be obliged by economic necessity to engage in labour to the neglect of their duties in the home.

The situation for unmarried women with children, or widows with children, or deserted wives with children, was bleak. There was no welfare payment for the unmarried mother. She could obtain money from the state through the Poor Law, though this was at the discretion of its agents. In practice, most unmarried mothers just disappeared into nursing homes run by nuns and gave their children up for adoption. If a woman walked out of an un-happy or violent marriage, she was deemed to be the guilty party and was not entitled to state aid. If a woman committed adultery, her husband was entitled to sue the other man for financial com-pensation for 'loss of services'. If a husband deserted his wife, she, like the unmarried mother, was reduced to dependence on the Poor Law.

The stay-at-home married mother was totally dependent on her husband. The children's allowance was officially paid to the father – though he could sign a release form that allowed his wife to walk with the book to the post office and collect it for him.

The list of grievances was long and woeful, but what resonated most with women, instinctively and immediately, was the demand for legalized contraception, to end what Nuala Fennell described as 'the unremitting nightmare of unwanted pregnancy'. The only legal way to obtain the contraceptive pill in 1970 was to have it prescribed as a 'menstrual cycle regulator'. Ireland, then, had the highest rate of irregular menstrual flow in the whole world, and this was, unsurprisingly, a phenomenon almost exclusively confined to middle-class women who had the money, nerve, knowledge and contacts. Even at that, most women, including myself, did not understand the menstrual cycle at all – the fact that it usually came every twenty-eight days was generally unknown.

Within a month of that first meeting, we had turned over all the women's pages in the national newspapers to the cause of liberation. This was easy because six of the twelve founding members were in journalism, and three of them were editors of the women's pages in the three national papers – Mary Maher in the *Irish Times*, Mary Kenny in the *Irish Press* and Mary McCutcheon in the *Irish Independent*. All of them had full- and part-time female contributors, both staff and freelance, who were either in the movement or enthusiastic supporters of it – such as myself, June Levine, Mary Anderson, Nuala Fennell, Anne Harris and Rosita Sweetman. As of September 1970, I was finally a journalist with a cause. (The previous month I had been mortified when I ran into Mary Holland on the street and she asked how I was getting on. I shrank against the wall with shame: I was returning from the Royal Dublin Horse Show, my latest, greatest assignment.)

I sat silent and blushing one day, heart thumping, as Mary Maher set off with fanfare to interview a 'lesbian'. She brought Maeve Binchy along for protection, lest the 'lesbian' get the wrong idea about Mary being on her own. There were jokes with Douglas Gageby, the editor, about him producing money, guns and lawyers if the two did not come back to the office by a specified time. They might have been going on safari. Still, I was curious to know what they – and I – would make of a woman who described herself as 'lesbian'. The article was as flat, boring, plain and uninteresting as was, it seemed, the 'lesbian' they had interviewed. Still, that meant that I had not been spotted. Boring? Me?

While I had been telling my mother and every other woman in Derry about their need for liberation, my mother had been counselling one of the wives of one of the men who had been fighting for civil rights. I did not know about the counselling until she, in exasperation, told me that there was much about which I, and my new women friends in Dublin, had not got a clue.

This woman had come to my mother after hearing that her husband was spending talkative nights in our house. Until she did, my mother hadn't suspected that the man, whom she liked, was having an affair with one of the women who was part of the political salon in our house, whom my mother also liked.

I hadn't suspected anything either. Nor had I known that my mother had been counselling the wife in our house. When? Where?

'Ach, ye're stupid, ye never notice anything about these things. How would ye, and you always out on the barricades while the wives suffer?' my mother snorted. The wife always came to her in the afternoon. 'I leave your father washed, dressed and fed in the kitchen, and we go into the sitting room.'

And the neighbours never interrupted?

My mother stared at me in silent derision. Had I not yet learned that neighbours always sensed when not to come into a person's house?

And did my father ask what was going on in the sitting room while he sat neglected in the kitchen?

My mother was beyond patience with me: men knew when not to ask.

And what made the woman think that her husband was having an affair?

I sat dumbfounded as my Irish Catholic fifty-nine-year-old mother told me how the woman had produced irrefutable proof: two ticket stubs from the cinema, found in the pockets of her husband's suit, which she had been checking prior to taking the suit to the dry cleaners; receipts for two tickets on the train to Belfast where he had been supposedly going alone on business – stuff like that.

And what had my mother said?

'I told her to stick it out; he'd be back. He had wains and a marriage to think about.'

And how did my mother feel about this man and the woman, who often came into her kitchen?

'I say, "Jesus, protect them all this good day and night."'

Her letters traced the running affair.

Dear Nell,
Mr X and Miss Y were here on Saturday and Sunday with the crowd, and never left until 2.30. I was waiting to see X's wife up here the next day . . .

Dear Nell,
X's wife was up with me on Thursday, and Nuala and your da was here, I had to take her into the sitting room, you talk about a bit of bluffing I had to do, but Nuala was very hard to convince it was a private matter. I have not seen Miss Y so she must know Mrs X was up. Anyhow, Mrs X told me, she asked Mr X to go to a solicitor with her as she was going to get a separation, he asked for another chance, she gave in, I says you will be having another wee wane now but she got a lot of damning evidence for a separation, she still does not trust him – who is after walking in just now, Miss Y and

Mr X. I nearly shit myself with embarrassment. They were taking Nuala up to Coleraine for a meeting. Miss Y is a very bad colour. I says to myself why did I ever have to get mixed up with it anyhow, as I worry about the whole bloody lot of you . . .

Though my mother had made it irrefutably clear that I was useless as a chronicler of the human condition, unless it manifested itself right before my eyes, news editor Donal Foley spotted a slot that was perfect for the kind of journalism that suited me best: he sent me to have a look at what was going on in the Children's Court. Before joining the staff, I had already been exercised, and written for the paper, about the mandatory imposition of six months' jail on conviction of rioting in the North. An orphan boy in Derry, aged sixteen, whom I had brought home to my mother, who fed him regularly and had given him a bed, had been picked up for throwing stones at soldiers. We visited him in the local barracks that night. Urine and shit ran through the open sewer of the dimly lit cell. The smell embarrassed the boy. My mother sat on the concrete shelf that served for a bed. He pleaded – truthfully – guilty to a further charge of stealing cigarettes from a burned-out premises. He was sent to a children's reformatory in Belfast, walked out and came back to Derry. Fear of being picked up and returned to prison had confined him to the Bogside. His pals roamed freely outside it, and he felt like an animal in a cage. The Christian Brothers agreed not to notify the authorities about his escape from custody and promised normal remission for good behaviour if he voluntarily returned. I made him face the awful decision: finish the jail sentence and he would be free for ever. He agreed. I described this lost boy, who had slipped through the net of the civil rights struggle, as a child in no man's land. This was hardly a Marxist analysis. Just as it had when I wrote about my family's new bathroom, the left-wing in Derry dismissed me as sentimental and politically soft.

In the Republic, the age of criminal responsibility was seven. Children were being sent to reformatory from that age until eighteen, if convicted of skipping school; of stealing sweets from a shop; or of playing football in the street. A 1969 report had recommended that the age of criminal responsibility be raised to age fourteen. The woman who wrote it, Justice Eileen Kennedy, was still presiding over the Children's Court. Foley sent me to cover her deliberations and contrast them with her recommendations.

The Children's Court was located at the corner of a quadrangle of dilapidated buildings that formed the courtyard of Dublin Castle, the erstwhile seat of British rule. As the names of the child defendants were called, they left their parents – if any parent had turned up – and stepped into the dock. The dock was the mouth of a huge, empty fireplace. The children cowered under its mantelpiece. Many were sent away to reform schools, some for years, for not going to school, or for playing football in the street. It was staggering – though nothing at all compared to the revelations, decades later, that many of these children were physically and sexually abused by clerics in these schools, and that the state was aware of it. In 1970, the series I wrote, about the mere fact of the imprisonment of these children in remote rural areas, caused a sensation.

This was just as well for my ego because towards the end of the series I suffered a terrible humiliation when the paper sent me to Armagh to cover Bernadette Devlin's release from jail. She was freed in October having served four months of her six-month sentence. Eamonn McCann, who had flown regularly from London to visit her in prison, was due to be there when she stepped into freedom. The article that was published did not hint at what happened with my friends that day. This is the real story, which I wrote and kept for myself:

On the morning of Bernadette's release, I travelled up to wait outside the jail. Both local and international media were gathered at the gates to record the walk to freedom of the most recognized and acclaimed young revolutionary in the world. I was slightly embarrassed because I was going as both new reporter and old friend, and I had never met her as a reporter. I hated the thought of asking her personal questions for public purposes. I thought to hide behind the battery of questions from others and record her answers.

I was looking forward to seeing her. She had been brave and dignified, and there was, in all of us who had fought with her, a sense of guilt that she had been the one to go to jail. On the other hand, she had been the best of us, and it was logical that she would be the victim. Jail never harmed a revolutionary – politically.

It was cold in the square outside the prison gates, at 6 a.m. The awakening birds could be heard clearly cheeping and trilling above the stamping feet of the reporters. I was surprised and a little hurt that her supporters were not there, in thousands, to greet her. She had become very much the property of the media as her fame spread, but she still walked the streets a lot. The public does not make history, however. Eventually they form only the backdrop to photographs and stories.

The other reporters were looking forward to seeing her, too: she was outspoken and humorous and photogenic, and it would be an excellent story. Countess Markiewicz had made similar, stirring history fifty years earlier.

The scheduled time of her release came and went, and rumours began to flow. They would push her out the back door, ignominiously, and deny her to history – as they had arrested her, ignominiously, on a back road, miles from her waiting supporters. We noticed, too, that none of her family was around, or relations, or political colleagues from her hometown. Everywhere she had gone previously, she had been escorted by self-appointed bodyguards, hangers-on, advisers and friends.

I had been used to tactical disasters in my experience of her, and it would not have surprised me a bit that the amateur revolutionaries had slept in, or broken down in a car, or messed up plans in the most casually horrific way. We never took ourselves seriously enough to act with ceremony, and the ceremony others had accorded her had disappeared as her actions threatened the status quo.

So I went to a telephone kiosk and called her political mentor, Eamonn McCann. He was there, to my relief, and I told him, panic-stricken, that I was the only person present who knew her personally. If he could not arrive in time, I would drive her to the hotel in my car and arrange a press conference for her there. He said not to worry, that he would be along soon. But he should have left already, I pointed out. If he was not in time, he said, I should take her to my hotel.

The minutes dragged by, and there was talk already that they would keep her in all morning. We were determined to wait anyway, and I was relieved. The thought of her coming out, after a prison sentence, to find no one at all was mortifying.

There was a sudden shout and a wave of relief when Eamonn arrived in a car, driven by Mary Holland, the reporter who had written most about her and who had become a personal friend. The others looked at me with a smile, pleased that I had not in fact been standing in front of the prison as a decoy while she had been spirited privately away.

They got out of the car in a hurry, and Mary had to get back in and apply the handbrake as it continued to move. I knew there was something wrong when Eamonn did not speak to me. I went over to him, willing to believe he was mistaken, and he gave me a perfunctory nod and went on talking to those who surrounded him, eagerly posing questions. Eamonn had been a close friend of mine until that moment. I had never known acute embarrassment until that moment. I was blushing, I knew, and I knew I was, right then, cruelly outside the fold. He went on talking, the way you have to when you have mortally wounded a friend and there is no way of retrieving it.

Mary Holland did not speak to me at all. I had been betrayed by two friends, and no one else knew it in that dawn crowd. Eamonn called aside a photographer from the British *Daily Mirror*, and everyone sensed that something was wrong, but Eamonn was in control and no one wanted to cross him lest a story be lost. Mary got into her car and Eamonn joined her, and they roared off, swiftly, and the photographer walked quickly away and into his own car, and he, too, was off, while we stood rooted there. We knew Bernadette had been released from prison, but of course we did not believe it, as she belonged to the world.

So we stood on, and we were not all that angry even when the prison gates opened, and a warder came out to say that she had left the prison by a back exit some thirty minutes before. There was sufficient affection for her to know there had been a mistake.

Some reporters went back to the hotel, to await the next communication, and some others remained outside the jail, promising to let us know if she did come out after all. We would do the same for them, if word came to the hotel. There was solidarity in frantic loss. They looked at me a little strangely when I went back to the hotel with them, wondering what the ploy was. As breakfast time came and went, a few of them made sympathetic noises to me, as they realized that I knew as little as them. They were sure there had been some mistake, but covered their certainty with curses at the luck of the *Mirror* photographer.

A disgruntled television journalist broke the bounds of good taste by observing to me that I certainly had nice friends. My pain was most acute when my own photographer put his arm round me and said you could only ever trust yourself in this world. We both accepted Bernadette was gone when he mentioned sadly that he was disappointed in her.

News came that she was indeed gone home. The tabloid photographer Cyril Kane had returned to the hotel, smiling widely, patting his camera. A world exclusive, he said. We could eat our hearts out. I had to join the rush to her hideout, a professional now, a real reporter after nine months on the job. It hadn't been so long ago that I had refused to name a dead person in Derry to my paper until the relatives had been informed. My paper had been astounded. Names were everything in journalism, they said. But they had let it go because background was important, too, and I was trusted in Derry where other journalists were not.

In Bernadette's hometown of Cookstown the streets were crowded, as her own supporters waited to see her. Disenchantment spread when they learned that she was giving an exclusive story to her friend Mary Holland for the *Observer*. Bernadette would not appear publicly until both her own story and Mary Holland's interview had been printed in the British Sunday papers, two days hence. 'Newspapers are more important to her than we are,' they said. There would be no picture for the history books of her standing outside the prison. I knew she did not know what was happening to her; that her judgement was fudged by her prison stay; that she would speak to me, her friend.

I took courage and telephoned the house where she was staying, asking to speak to her. She was not there, a country voice said. I gave my name, confidently, sure the horror would not be added to by dismissal. She was not there, I was told. I rang back and asked to speak to Eamonn. A different voice answered, recognized me, told me in a friendly manner to hold on, and I heard Eamonn being called and my name given. It was all right, then. Friends do not behave like that to each other. The embarrassed voice told me that Eamonn was not there.

I rang my paper and told them about my friends, speaking stiffly. News editor Gerry Mulvey, a hitherto diffident man who would not have said boo to a sheep, was abrupt. Write the story – a straight report on Miss Devlin being released and in hiding.

I wrote the story in Armagh. That night, I went on to Derry and sat in the kitchen, and told my mother, and I cried. Bernadette did not know; she was not like that, my mother said, trying to believe the best.

As for Eamonn and Mary . . . words failed her. You do not curse friends out of hand. There would be an explanation. There had to be. The alternative to friends was God on this earth. God does not exist in person on this earth. Therefore, you had friends. Therefore, there had to be an explanation. My mother's friend and neighbour, Annie, sat stolidly there, listening, supportive, smoking and – significantly – silent. I could clearly hear what she was not saying: that such unbelievable shit happens.

On Saturday morning the colour photograph of Bernadette appeared in the tabloid. She was seated, smiling, on a child's swing chair, legs in the air, in a mini-dress she had crocheted herself in prison. The photograph demeaned her. The brightest hope in our Western world, the politician and revolutionary, was, after all, in her home-made, prison-made dress, a young girl. She remained for a long time afterwards, in the popular mind, a young girl for whom they had once had affection.

On Sunday, the *Observer* devoted a full page to an interview of Bernadette by Mary Holland. The exclusive interview was a stilted dialogue of Marxist rhetoric and compassion for ordinary prisoners. I travelled up that morning for Bernadette's press conference to those few who remained of the rest of the world's media. Eamonn did not speak to me at all now. Mary was as happy as a scoop reporter can be.

We gathered in an empty ballroom, excitement gone, but curious still to see Bernadette in the flesh. Legends do not die out entirely, overnight, even if it had been two days already since this one began to die. She came into the ballroom, slight and smoking, but there was no great applause, or good-natured excitement, the way there usually was when she made an entrance. The reporters resented her now.

She came straight over to me, and I knew in that instant that it was all true. She made a point of coming to me. 'I'm sorry,' she said, and she smiled, childlike, as she was always was. 'Will you forgive me?'

She looked at me, still smiling. She had very winning ways, and I had seen her betrayed myself on many occasions previous to that. 'It's all right,' I said, embarrassed, meaning: 'It's all over.'

My photographer, seeing some kind of news picture, asked us to pose together. She was more than pleased and put her arm round me. I said no, and moved away, urging her to begin the already delayed news conference. She moved off at once, smiling again at me, but the rupture was there.

A few days later I received a letter from my mother, who had been talking to Eamonn:

> . . . Kathy [Cathy Harkin] was up in Cookstown with Bernie, she says she is in a bad state over it, and is coming to see me. I never heard from Mary but now, I realize Clothes never did make a lady. Now not in her private life I mean. It was the rotten mean thing she done, and I suppose sometime I will meet her. I finished my argument with Eamonn 'I thought Friendship was one soul in two people' he was left dumb.
> Love and God bless
> Ma. X
> I am going to, if I ever see Mary just say 'Mary it does not take lovely clothes to make a True Lady . . .'

She never did say anything to Mary. (Nor did I, until thirty-three years later, when she was very ill and we were reconciling our differences.) A few weeks after Armagh, Mary Holland came to my parents' house. She had persuaded Cathy Harkin to accompany her as she came to face the music. Though the key was in the door as usual, Cathy rang the doorbell and pounded the knocker. Having caught our attention, Cathy then came down the hallway, calling out that Mary was with her and looking for mercy. Then she stood in the doorway to the kitchen waving a white handkerchief, saying that Mary was suing for peace. Mary stood behind her, smiling, anxious, affecting laughter. Lovely Cathy, who hated personal rows, talked her way through a tense night. My mother was trapped by the demands of courtesy; I was trapped by misery and compromise.

After Christmas, I had a kind of resurrection. A radical magazine, *Hibernia*, named me as Journalist of the Year for the Children's Court series.

A letter arrived from my mother:

Dear Nell,
Your articles were great and I have to say you were great at telling all about the poor wanes, your pop was all charmed when he heard about the award you got. it is getting very like Xmas here if everybody was better.
Love and God Bless
Ma xxxx

Chapter Fifteen

The news that I was lesbian was announced – there is no other word for it – at noon, on New Year's Day 1971, at a media jamboree. I was not there. The day before, Marie had flown in from Sweden – unannounced – on a one-day return trip. She burst into tears in my bedsitter. She had fallen in love with another woman, in her hometown, and was shocked to discover that such a thing could happen. She apologized over and over. She had thought she loved me, would love me for ever, hadn't looked sideways at anyone else, but had fallen, in seconds, in love with this other woman, an artist like herself. She could not stop crying as she told me this, talking in halting English about the jolt to her code of honour, and truth, and true love. If true love itself could be overturned in seconds, could we believe in anything? Where did this leave socialism, the Jews, Palestine . . . the human race? I have never been so stylishly rejected in my life. (Marie and Thina are still together.)

That night, after she flew home, I went to a New Year's Eve party given by a Dublin radical. It was the usual dull affair, all booze and dance and lights off, and couples in mild sexual grapple, the rest of us dozing off after midnight wherever we could find a space to sit or lie. A woman stretched herself alongside me on the sofa. She kissed me. I was astonished, attracted, and did not care one whit that she might denounce me in the sober hours of daylight because I was sad that I would hold Marie no more. I had been sure that I would never be held again.

The woman invited me to her flat when I should return from Galway, where I was due next morning to write about a legal conference. We parted at dawn, and off I went on the train.

At the Dublin hotel where the media were being entertained that New Year's Day, she kicked open the double doors of the reception room, stood on the threshold, arms in the air, and yelled, 'Happy New Year, everybody. I'm in love with Nell McCafferty.'

Though it became the talk of Dublin, the media never reported such things back then.

From Galway, I went by car on a late-night spree out to the wilds of Connemara. The four student lawyers with me, all male, are now judges in the Irish courts. We smoked dope. We all got food poisoning from eating oysters. We threw up over walls, we had diarrhoea in the vastness of the bog, we danced to rock and roll on the radio. I got back to Dublin much weakened, dressed in a black woollen frock, and went to the woman's apartment.

The apartment was candlelit. She had already prepared and laid supper out on the table – two dozen oysters on a bed of ice on a solid silver salver. She fed them to me with her own hand. I did my best. She wore a necklace of real pearls in bed. She had prepared by reading a manual on lesbian sex, obtained from the library. She was daring.

I was in a state of joy. Nobody would say anything against this woman. She was iconic and people admired her. She was one of the first single women in our age group to have an apartment – bedroom, bathroom, kitchen, living room and hallway – as opposed to the standard dingy bedsitter. She had two telephones, one in the bedroom, one in the living room, at a time when there was a three-year waiting list for a private telephone. I would be under her protection. Nobody ever did say anything against her. Free at last, dear God, I was free at last.

She brought me breakfast in bed, on the silver tray, now covered in Irish linen and adorned with a fresh flower in a tiny Waterford glass vase. We had coffee and croissants and honey, and scrambled eggs with smoked salmon, and strawberries. She was already on the phone, fully dressed and making appointments, while we ate. She left me to sleep late. 'You were born for bed, darling.' She kissed me goodbye. I knew I was dumped when she did not turn up for my twenty-seventh birthday, three months later. I went round and threw stones at her window, angry and dejected and drunk. She let me in, finally, and explained why she had not come to see me. 'I just wanted to see what it was like, being with a man again, darling.' She didn't even fancy him, I protested. 'True,' she conceded, with that giggle she always deployed after kicking over the traces.

I got over it quickly enough, helped by the fact that I was busy speaking all over the country as the women's movement gained momentum, that I had left the lonely bedsitter and was renting a room in the house of the fabulous Patsy Murphy, and that, crucially, the woman who had entranced me left the country.

Patsy claims that I arrived on her doorstep clad in a white mackintosh that needed cleaning (I reluctantly agree); that while she was making tea, I asked her if she had heard of John Hume; and that I had nothing else to say. I claim that nobody gets a word in edgeways once Patsy starts talking. (In one singular way, she is like my mother: I like to introduce people to her, then sit back and watch her monologues surge seamlessly around their astonished heads.) Patsy was then a production assistant in the drama department of RTÉ. She was one of the very few women in Ireland then who had had a baby outside marriage, kept and reared the child, and simultaneously worked outside the home. Her baby daughter Clare was in a Montessori nursery. The three-bedroomed house, with a small back yard, was one of four in a terrace in Hatch Place, near Stephen's Green, the green heart of the city.

She intimated that she might introduce me to her mother and aunts, but, then again, perhaps not, because I might say the wrong thing. Her grandfather had been governor of Mountjoy Jail during the Civil War, her father a doctor, and her mother, before marriage, was secretary to the first President of Ireland. Patsy had been reared in England and come home to University College Dublin with an accent that could have passed her off as an Anglo-Irish Protestant and student of Trinity. Her daughter is the great-granddaughter of the revolutionary Maud Gonne MacBride, the muse of William Butler Yeats.

Patsy, too, had that most prized possession – a private phone. Plus, she had a washing machine. Plus, her house was home. She even had her own furniture. I took to her because I had never met until then – or since – anyone so utterly indifferent to social class. She took to me because she needed a lodger who could afford to pay full rent. Even now, she is apt to take in a lodger, preferably younger, whom she can boss about, when she is actually in residence, which she often is not because she likes to range about the country.

Sometimes Patsy cooked, and once I did. It was an attempt at pigeon breasts. By the time Patsy arrived back from the pub – after a series of phone calls declaring that she was on the way right now – it was near midnight, and the pigeons were burnt little corpses in the oven. Sometimes I babysat. Sometimes I never came home. Sometimes I knew her bedroom was strictly off-limits. Sometimes she pointed out that if any of us in the women's movement were unmarried mothers, we'd have half a clue. She had a point: when we were compiling our information pamphlet *Chains or Change*, the poet Eavan Boland, also a founding member of the movement, had rung Mary Robinson to ask if she could give us seven examples of legal discrimination against women, and Robinson had asked, 'Why only seven?'

By 1971, Gay Byrne had only to nod his head in the direction of a topic on the *Late Late Show* and it became the staple of national conversation. On 6 March that year, six months after we had formed the Irishwomen's Liberation Movement, he gave the whole show over to us. The panel of five women comprised Senator Mary Robinson, talking about law; Mary Cullen, historian, to make the case for working mothers; Lelia Doolan, on education and social conditioning; Máirín Johnston, trade unionist, on discrimination at work and jobs barred to women; and myself, on deserted wives, widows and unmarried mothers. The audience was packed with the sisterhood.

Byrne introduced Mary Cullen as 'the wife of a psychiatrist'. Halfway through the show, he brought on a man who had left his fireside television to rush out to RTÉ to make the case for elected male party politicians. Garret FitzGerald, the liberal Fine Gael TD, sat himself down and declared his 'fury' that Mary Kenny had dismissed the national parliament as a male bastion which did not give a damn about the condition of Irishwomen. Byrne sat back, the women sat up, and the show ignited.

I got a letter from my mother, poking fun at the TV show and worrying about the police who had come looking for the fine imposed the year before:

Dear Nell,

Just a ween of lines for I am sure you must be very tired, after all them dishes; well anyhow them boyos were up here looking for you again, a plain clothes man yesterday morning at 9 o'clock. hello he says is Nell here. O no she is in Dublin. I took him for some reporter not like a cop. after a few questions I says who are you. he says I am the Police. I put him aside and looked up the street and there the Van was parked up at Ettie's door full of them. he says tell her to pay something of that Fine or they will now be on the outlook for you when you come to Derry. OK Buddy I will tell her so that is that.

Your articles were great but you now have started me on womans' lib and I am going to have it and I will be taking the shits if you appear in Derry. you can get a wig. no word of Michael and Grainne
McCann, Willie, and Cathy were over to see the programme.
This is all
God bless and I hope to get my Liberty
Love Ma X

I could not bring myself to tell my mother, in person or in writing, that Bernadette was pregnant. Shortly after speaking on behalf of 'unmarried mothers' in Dublin, I went to London to address a meeting and, while there, had discovered that Mary was pregnant. She and Eamonn were joyful. Bernadette, who had split from her boyfriend before going to prison, was spending a lot of parliamentary time in that city, and I met her, too. She and I were in a taxi; it was raining, late at night, in Soho. She was sad. As I was about to get out of the taxi, in the dark, I noticed a plumpness about her. 'Are you pregnant?' I asked. She was, she said. I named a man, and asked if he was the father. He was, she confirmed. 'Are you going to have an abortion?' I asked. She was not, she said. And that was the end of our conversation. I stood in the street, looking after the departing taxi.

I was staying, on that occasion, with Mary Cummins, who had moved to London to open an *Irish Times* office there. Next evening I told Mary that I wanted to visit a gay nightclub in Chelsea, which Radclyffe Hall had reputedly frequented. After fortifying ourselves in a Fleet Street pub, we taxied to the destination. The women guarding the door would not let us in. Mary told them indignantly that she was the daughter of an Irish police sergeant and we were Irish journalists on a mission of investigation. The police arrived, seemingly within seconds. I have still not figured out why they carted me off to Chelsea police station in the Black Maria, while letting Mary go. At the station desk, I could not remember her address, so I gave them the address of Mary Holland. I had the wit to give the name on my birth certificate, Ellen Pamela. I spent a couple of hours in a big, brightly lit cell, all by myself. I was terrified and affronted. I sang to comfort myself.

Around 4 a.m., they told me that Mary Holland had confirmed by phone that she knew me. Still not knowing Mary Cummins's address, I went to Mary Holland's house, and, mortified, stood at the foot of the bed wherein she and Eamonn reposed, and gave an account of my movements as one Ellen Pamela. They were easy enough about it, and clearly did not believe that it was all Mary Cummins's fault. Next morning, early, I went to court, alone, and the police put me into a holding cell with all the other defendants. It was a huge, white-tiled place, full of women facing charges of prostitution, vagrancy and such.

When my case was called, the policeman who walked me to the designated courtroom asked how I was going to plead to the charge of drunk and disorderly behaviour. Definitely not guilty, I told him, and the police who had arrested me would have no evidence. They weren't even in court. The officer said smoothly that I could fight the charge and have my name all over the papers, or plead guilty, in which case it would be over in seconds, and, he assured me, a guilty plea meant that I'd be let off with a caution. An unusual case, he added, me being a journalist with a major Irish newspaper; just the kind of offbeat story the tabloids might like. I told him I would plead guilty. I could not hear the charge, but the officer leaned heavily on the name of the gay club. The magistrate threw a look of disdain in my direction and – I think – let me off with a caution. I didn't hear him. I was thanking Jesus that nobody in the English court was much interested in my insignificant, Irish, lesbian self. I would have pleaded guilty to anything to avoid such exposure.

I knew that the whole thing was unjust, and I did not give a damn. I just wanted out of there. I could not bear the shame. My precious job and my family's reputation had come within column inches of disaster. I left for Dublin without saying goodbye to anybody. Not that anybody was interested, everybody being pregnant or guarding their careers.

One month after the television debut of the Irishwomen's Liberation Movement, we called a public meeting in the Mansion House in Dublin. (This was where the first Parliament of Ireland – the Dáil – had been set up, illegally, in 1917, to declare independence from Britain.) Women came in their thousands; tables were quickly set up at the entrance, where they registered according to their district postal address. I chaired the panel: Máire Woods, Máirín Johnston, Mary Maher and Hilary Orpen, a researcher on RTÉ. Mary Robinson sat in as our legal adviser. We went through the formalities of stating and explaining our six demands. We were teaching our grandmothers to suck eggs – even as we spoke, a queue of women had formed in front of the platform, eager to speak.

They were the word made flesh. They embodied the inequities, and more, of our demands. Few women claimed that they were doing this on behalf of other women. Practically every woman was speaking on her own outraged behalf. There was a standing, cheering ovation that drowned out most of what one Helen Heaphy said after her opening sentence, 'I am an unmarried mother . . .'

That single sentence was our epiphany. You could feel, hear and see the dam break. It could not but help that she was relatively mature (all of about thirty years old), lovely-looking with it, dressed in gypsy style, and had an authentic Dublin accent. Helen never spoke publicly again.

As the night ended, we helplessly, hopelessly, appointed one woman from each postal district to contact the others, set up a group, and appoint a delegate to come to Gaj's. When we assembled there the following week, the room above the restaurant was not big enough to accommodate us all.

The tensions between those of us who leaned towards socialism and those who did not became apparent after a decision was made to take part in the May Day march. We had come out in sizeable enough force – several hundred – and were allocated a slot, with our home-made banner, well at the back of the many thousands of trade unionists, mainly male, who marched behind venerable banners that defined their magnificent history. Our welcome was functional and polite. There was a distinct feeling of being – how disappointing, this – a minority. We were strangers to each other, the 'women's libbers' and the 'paid workers'. We were not invited on to the platform to speak.

Shortly afterwards we staged the demonstration for which the Irishwomen's Liberation Movement is most famous: we took the 'Contraceptive Train' from Dublin to Belfast and back, illegally importing contraceptives into the Republic. It was almost a year to the day since I had objected to a member of the Northern Ireland civil rights group waving a condom at the border and sneering that French letters were illegal in Dublin, and I saw a chance to draw the eyes of the world to Ireland and its punitive laws against the use of birth control: we would go to Belfast, purchase contraceptives, show them to the customs officers in Dublin and challenge them to arrest and charge us, or let us pass, thereby proving the law both hypocritical and obsolete.

Forty-seven of us turned up to catch the 8 a.m. train on 22 May, a date chosen because it was International News Day and the global media were in Ireland. Of the original founders, there was only

Maírín Johnston, Mary Kenny, June Levine and myself. Nuala Fennell thought the action would destroy our reputation. Maírín de Burca thought participation should be confined to married women only, but agreed to organize a reception committee for our homecoming. Mary Maher was in hospital, in the throes of labour. Margaret Gaj's husband was ill, and she was needed at home.

We had informed the international media of our intentions, and TV crews were there to film our departure from Connolly station, including crews from America and Japan. I was very glad of the cheerful laughing company of Maírín Johnston. She was as rosy-cheeked as an apple-seller, had a long history of trade-union defiance on the factory line, and was both a mother and separated wife.

We had arranged that free legal aid, from willing solicitors, would be available to us. Mary Anderson and I had drawn up a leaflet outlining choices which every woman could make upon return to the arms of the customs men:

1. Declare nothing and risk being searched.
2. Declare contraceptives and refuse to be searched.
3. Declare contraceptives and refuse to hand over.
4. Declare contraceptives and hand over with protest of infringement of your constitutional rights.
5. Declare contraceptives and throw over barrier to sisters waiting beyond. Many people who couldn't come today will be demonstrating at Amiens Street in solidarity with our action.
6. Declare contraceptives and sit down in anticipation of customs action.
7. Declare internal contraceptive. Allow search from female officer only and shout 'April Fool' before entry.

There were no Irish media to see us off; their attention was focused on Belfast, where a soldier had been killed during the night. Corporal Robert Bankier, of the Royal Green Jackets, was twenty-four, married, with two children, and he had been but three weeks in Belfast, having been transferred from Germany where his wife still lived in army quarters. His was the first army death for which the Official IRA admitted responsibility.

I was more than somewhat disappointed at our small number, as we congregated in two carriages, interspersed with shoppers. From twelve women in September, to a national television audience in March, to thousands in April at the Mansion House, to hind-tit on May Day, to forty-seven going to Belfast as that month closed.

There was a chemist shop opposite Central Station in Belfast city centre. Before we marched over, I gave the women, most of whom had never been in the North, a succinct geography and history lesson. If they stuck to the city centre, they'd be grand. Anywhere beyond that and they'd be shot, I said, sending up their fear about the fabled North. Then we crowded, complete with TV crews, into the shop, behind the counter of which presided a tall man with an admirable ability to keep a straight, grave face. I told him that I would like a packet of contraceptive pills. He asked me for my doctor's prescription.

I didn't know these things required a prescription. I asked in succession for a coil, a loop, any item the name of which I could vaguely remember. He kept asking for a doctor's prescription. I called 'June, June,' and our redoubtable Jewish saviour sailed like a galleon to the front of the scrum. She subsequently wrote of this debacle in her book *Sisters* (1982) that:

. . . there now followed an amazing display of ignorance of the facts of life. For reasons I have never cared to examine, then or later, they cast me as the authority on such matters and I was pressed with questions such as 'What does gossamer mean?', 'What do you do with this jelly stuff?', and, from one woman, 'Would I take the same size Dutch cap as you, do you think?'

Uninformed I was, but stupid I was not. I did not fancy us returning to Dublin armed only with condoms, which would have concentrated the mind of the nation on male nether regions; on sex; on anything but birth control. Unthinkable. So I bought hundreds of packets of aspirin.

The scrum left the chemist's shop, the TV crews left for lunch, and some women who had gone straight to the Family Planning Clinic returned to report that it was closed. We went our separate ways until it was time to catch the afternoon train back. I found myself alone with June, the others having disappeared into shops. Astonishingly – to me – nobody was interested in going into a pub. I longed to take a taxi over to the Falls Road and hang out with militants, but June is not the easiest person to be with when soldiers with guns are walking around. June is only truly at ease in her own home.

She wanted to shop for things for her children. I hate shopping, but I was grateful to her for having saved the day so I went with her. I said that I wouldn't mind getting a coat, clothes that fitted tiny people like me being hard to find. This was a mistake. Now June was a woman with a mission. As editor of a fashion magazine and 'beauty columnist', she knew exactly what I needed – which was not at all what I wanted – and I trailed glumly in her majestic wake. I do believe I broke her will to live that afternoon. (She recalls that I bought her a bunch of tulips to make up for the nightmare I put her through.)

We got back on the train, wondering if we would be hauled off and taken into custody at the first opportunity across the Irish border, out of sight of what we hoped would be a welcoming party in Dublin. That would be a public relations disaster, and frightening with it. Ordinary shoppers who had been in Belfast for the cheaper British prices, and wanted to avoid paying duty on their purchases when they got back to the Republic, were putting on layers of newly purchased clothing and concealing contraband about their persons. Word came that Mary Kenny was blowing up condoms in another carriage, and letting them zoom around the aisle.

We did not know, as we travelled to Dublin, that one Bishop Dr Ryan was preaching against us at an afternoon service in the Knock shrine to the Blessed Virgin. Not since penal times, he said, had the Catholic heritage of Ireland been subjected to so many insidious onslaughts, on the pretext of conscience, civil rights and women's liberation.

And then we were in Dublin. On the platform, arrayed behind tables, was a group of customs officers. 'Anything to declare?' they were asking, as per standard procedure. The normal day-trippers swept past. We held back, raised our banner, marched forward and came to a halt at the tables. From beyond the gates at the top of the platform, about fifty yards away, came the sound of voices singing the anthem 'We Shall Overcome'. We could see a heaving mass of people, placards waving, hands in the air, calling to us, cheering for us, and the song bounced up to the vaulted roof and the notes fell down upon us. Máirín Johnston was saying to a customs officer, 'Jelly. I've got jelly, and you're not getting it.' For once she was not laughing. She was stern and not for moving, an example to us all, especially to me, for I could not make my mind up whether to stand, declare, refuse and be arrested; or march past the customs men, 'contraceptives' held high. The customs men themselves clearly didn't know what to do. 'Anything to declare?' they asked, stony-faced, eyes fixed on an invisible spot above our heads.

We declared everything, waved everything at them, and refused to budge. The singing was louder now. The song was like a siren call. 'We shall overcome . . .' Had we not overcome, already? How many hours would we have to stand there, making our point? Would the crowd eventually go, and would we be rounded up after dark on the platform, all alone by then?

We had already taken the wrapping off many of the packets of aspirin. 'These are birth-control pills, and we are taking them and you're not getting them,' we told the officers. And the plan worked, it seemed to us, like a dream: for all they knew, we were taking birth-control pills, right in their faces. Excitement and noise grew, and, simultaneously, nothing was happening. Somebody among us shouted, 'Loose your contraceptives,' and packets of condoms flew through the air. As did packets of aspirin. And containers of spermicidal jelly. They landed beyond the barrier. The noise from there grew, and it sounded like victory.

Night was falling outside. I did not want to go to jail. I wanted to go outside where the fun was. Mostly I did not want to go to jail. We had a huddled conference, and I produced the statement I had drawn up on the train, to the effect that by our actions we had rendered the law obsolete. We decided to walk past the customs officers, read it out, and run to the bosom of Maírín de Burca and the huge crowd she had delivered.

And then I did something I have regretted ever since. In a fit of egalitarianism – or a Machiavellian ploy to show the world that we were indeed just ordinary women, not a bunch of uppity commies who had infiltrated and taken fiendish control of women's pages in the media – I decided not to read the statement, but to give that honour to a woman nobody knew. She was Colette O'Neill, a member of the newly formed Sutton Group, in the eponymous suburb of Dublin. The Sutton Group, under the leadership of Hilary Orpen, had been the most organized, coherent and constant unit among the newcomers who had signed up in the Mansion House in April.

Colette stood in front of our 'Irishwomen's Liberation Movement' banner, read out the statement and entered the history books. Photographs show her up front, reading the statement I had written; a person with a magnifying glass would be able to make me out behind the banner, smaller than anybody else, the tip of my head showing. Thus did I lose my place in history as the apotheosis of Irish womankind. I should have known better, given my lament that Bernadette Devlin had not been photographed for posterity outside Armagh Jail.

The statement read, we surged towards the platform barrier, through the gate, and out into the crowd. It was a much bigger crowd than we had realized. Should we not have stayed with the customs men and forced an arrest? Nobody criticized us. Nobody wanted to end the party. So we walked and ran and tumbled down the road to the nearest police station, in Store Street. As cops looked out the windows, I stood on the steps, read out the statement again, and everybody took up the chant: 'The law is obsolete.'

We waved our contraband and challenged the guards to come out and arrest us – with Maírín de Burca there, I, for one, was willing to face tanks. However, the police would not come out to play. We dispersed and drifted home, to watch Mary Kenny and

Colette, both of whom had been whisked from the train station to RTÉ by staff of the *Late Late Show*.

The Sunday papers gave us massive coverage, though none of the reporters had bothered to travel with us to Belfast. That evening, as I prepared to check in for the night shift, I lingered outside the back door of the *Irish Times* in Fleet Street, talking to Mary Kenny, who was on her way to the nearby *Irish Press*. It was only then that we considered the three most important facts of life, all of them above and beyond contraception. What would our mothers say? What would our editors say? Would we still have jobs? And I worried that my father, although by then increasingly infirm, would vent his disapproval on my mother.

We kept our jobs. My editor, Douglas Gageby, a liberal Northern-born Church of Ireland Protestant, winked as he walked past my desk. I got a letter from my sixty-one-year-old mother. She always wrote to me care of the *Irish Times*, that being my only constant address:

Dear Nell, got your letter today and I was glad to get it, but anyhow Grainne was over on Monday, she saw the state I was in over it all, she understood how I felt but pointed out to me it took some guts to do what was done, I did not mind the whole thing if the single girls had kept out of it, and I kept asking myself the question why did them girls husbands not come with them, it looked so bad on TV. everything came into my head all you had done in Derry and what in hell thanks did you get from any of them, all you went through to get a Job, and all you went through in this house. anyhow Michael and Grainne came back here last night after Pop went to bed. Michael took me in hand. explained the whole thing to me. he thought you were great, he says next year, over it all, you will come into your own and will come out tops. all I could see from Saturday was you getting stoned out of Dublin, anyhow now I am settled down more over it all. Pops has not spoke about it at all which to me is worse. I think it was shock that happened to me but why in hell did all that bloody carry-on have to go on in the station could they not have done it a bit more reserved and Lady

like. I wish to God I did not think on the whole lot of you so much, now I am sick worrying over Paddy he gets no dole for six weeks . . .
Love and <u>God Bless</u>
For God help me yous are all I think on. I keep saying Dear God the Babies you sent me are awful nice and sweet.
Ma. X

Meanwhile, in the Dáil, the deputies were assured by the Minister for Health, Erskine Childers, that the Customs Office had upheld the law and impounded all available contraceptives. I could not understand why the newspapers did not howl with derision at this. What I did not realize was that, outside the women's pages, the media did not take us seriously.

Mary Robinson introduced a bill to legalize contraception. We stood outside the Dáil with placards. Mary Kenny sang 'We shall not conceive' to the tune of 'We Shall Overcome'. You couldn't just walk into parliament and sit in the public gallery as they do in Britain. You had to be signed in by a TD or senator, who had to leave the building, walk down to the security office and do the necessary. Few of us knew the names of our local representatives. Five of the picketers – Maírín de Burca, Mary Kenny, Hilary Orpen, Marie MacMahon and Fionnuala O'Connor – decided to walk in anyway. When an usher chased after them, Marie MacMahon broke away in a feinting manoeuvre. The others spotted an open window in a basement room, climbed in and found themselves in the gents' toilet, where a solitary startled man was going about his business. The ushers arrived, and a member of parliament was found who agreed to sign the women in. Outside, Senator Joe Lenihan was telling the rest of us that we 'should be fucked on our hands and knees, like animals'. Inside, Mary Robinson was being treated like a parliamentary leper, as she spoke the unspeakable.

With no hierarchy and no structure, the movement started to collapse under its own weight. There was unease at the increasing concentration, by some of us, on opposition to the government's proposed Forcible Entry and Occupation Act, which would sentence squatters to jail. To women who lived with their families in their own hard-earned private housing, this sounded more and more like socialist opposition to ownership of private property. And right enough, some of us were given to quoting Karl Marx: 'All property is theft.'

We were more likely to preach Marx at movement meetings in the city centre than to teach Marx to broken-down, work-worn housewives who lived in tenements or in public-housing projects in the outer suburbs. We were already being dismissed as dissatisfied middle-class hussies. If middle-class women had the free time and energy and money to devote to a cause that would also benefit working-class women, I didn't see anything wrong with that. Contraception alone would lighten their burden. I undertook to travel by bus every Monday night to Ballymun, near the airport, to talk to women who lived in a cluster of high-rise flats. The journey across town took nearly an hour. I went with Marie MacMahon and Fionnuala O'Connor, two young women who worked as waitresses in Margaret Gaj's restaurant while waiting on their careers to develop. Marie was that rare species, a female printer, and Fionnuala had just quit a teaching job in the North and was trying to break into journalism.

The seven towers of Ballymun stood in a cold, windy, badly lit wasteland. The lifts often broke down. When they did, some women had to climb up to fourteen storeys with several children and a load of shopping. And still, a little group of them wanted to discuss liberation. They were broke, some had marriage problems, and none of them had the fare into town, never mind a train fare to Belfast. They might have been living on Mars.

Before we knew it, Marie and Fionnuala and I were like social workers. We were spending more time trying to help the women get welfare benefits and money for bills than we were spending just meeting them on Monday nights. It was hard and sad going, and I fell by the wayside. Ballymun went on to produce one of the most vibrant feminist groups in Ireland, led by the late Kathleen Maher. They oversaw the demolition of the flats and the erection of model housing.

After the Contraceptive Train, the movement did not quite know what to do for an encore. The beginning of the end came in August when several hundred people, the majority of them women, picketed the Dáil, where the Forcible Entry and Occupation Act was being forced through after a guillotined debate. Women, as Maírín de Burca never tired of insisting, were the primary victims of the housing shortage. The proposed left-wing solution – of nationalizing banks and cancelling the debt on money borrowed by the government to build more homes – was not entirely acceptable to our members, to put it mildly, and the left wing was very much in evidence that night.

There were kerfuffles in the dark, at the entrance to the Dáil, as ministers were leaving. We shouted at the line of limousines, not realizing they were empty – the ministers had decided to leave by a back entrance and meet the chauffeurs there. Maírín de Burca and Mary Anderson were soon in the arms of the law, charged with breaching the peace, and quickly after that in the legal embrace of Mary Robinson, who was to represent them in court. The two women opted for trial by jury. Jury service was confined to property owners: they would have to face twelve property-owning men. Maírín, who had already done time in jail for an anti-Vietnam War protest and been deeply marked by the loss of the privacy she cherished, wanted to be tried by a jury of her peers and wondered how she could insist on that, in court, without being sent down for contempt. Robinson thought they could take a constitutional action to challenge the Juries Act. They did. They won. Women now serve on juries.

It took years to push the challenge through the courts, but Mary Robinson was like that – tenacious. She took the long view and believed that justice and social change could be won by legal means. She played the Constitution like a violin in her decades at the Bar, steadily having it reinterpreted on the great social issues of the day, such as contraception, divorce and abortion. She practised until 1990, when she was elected President. In 1971, most of us could not, would not, take that long view. There was an entirely valid, different one, which I loved pushing at the meetings that we sometimes addressed together: that law reflects the sanctions of society, and laws would change to reflect the social change we were intent on bringing about. Where we led, the judges would follow. 'When the law is unjust, the place of every just person is outside that law,' I quoted an unknown source at one such meeting, where Robinson and veteran legal eagle Seán MacBride were urging caution.

MacBride treated my exhortations that we storm the social barricades with arch good humour, as well he might: nearly four decades earlier he had been chief of staff of the IRA, but now he was engaged in activities which would see him receive both the Nobel Peace Prize (in recognition of his role in founding Amnesty International) and the Lenin Peace Prize. He and Robinson seemed amused when the crowd showed a preference for the street tactics I advocated. This reinforced my suspicion that the more action we alleged outlaws took, the more they could seize the day in the courts to widen and update interpretation of the Constitution – or drive a coach and horses through obvious holes in it, and force the insertion of new provisions. I was young enough back then to think MacBride very old indeed: he was nearly sixty. And yet I admired him for bothering to turn up. MacBride patted me on the head that day, presumably because my little stone-throwing self reminded him of his times past.

On the August night when we stormed the Dáil, our action was a step too far for such law-abiding citizenry as Nuala Fennell. She resigned with a coarse rhetorical flourish that echoed the Establishment's unease at the sexual revolution which was bubbling under our prosaic demands for housing, birth control and welfare payments for the unmarried mother which would allow her to keep and rear her own child. Fennell's statement to the papers declared that: 'Women's Lib has not only lost her virginity, but has turned into a particularly nasty harlot.' She said the Irishwomen's Liberation Movement required adherents to be 'anti-American, anti-clergy, anti-Irish Countrywomen's Association, anti-police, anti-men.' Her high-profile exit did not do much damage – the Irishwomen's Liberation Movement was already petering out.

Germaine Greer's scorched-earth book *The Female Eunuch* had just been published. I consoled myself that I had already gone further than her battle cry: 'You haven't lived until you've tasted menstrual blood.' And in one of those consciousness-raising exercises which women all over the world were engaged in, I had also tasted breast milk. An obliging female had squeezed some into a teaspoon. It was thin and weak. I felt like a cannibal. You truly haven't lived until you've tasted mother's milk one more time. You won't do it again. It is not at all as nice as wine or brandy.

I went further still. The Boston Health Collective Book *Our Bodies, Ourselves* suggested we indeed have a look at ourselves. I found myself looking up my own vagina. The objective was to find and study the cervix. We were all strangers to each other. Each woman had to remove her knickers, lie on the floor, spread her legs, use the left hand to hold a mirror against the vagina, the right hand to shine a torch up it, and spot the cervix. It was dark up there. Even had I known what the cervix looked like, I just could not spot mine. Those who had spotted theirs were instructed to let me look up their vaginas. I lay on my tummy, looked up the birth canals of strangers and still saw nothing. Then everybody got to look up my vagina, and all were agreed that I had a cervix just like them. I still haven't found what they were looking for.

My mother had written me a letter, expressing innocent concern about Bernadette:

> Eamonn was over here last night . . . Bernadette stayed here last night, and God knows she is failed, she says it is the flu has her like it but I don't know there is something changed in her. anyhow she went back today again to London. You were great on TV only you lose your rattle too easily. Michael was telling me he was speaking to Hume in the Catholic Club. Hume says did you see Nell on the TV. She is as rude as ever. It was then Michael says that is how she got the award of the year. Hume was shocked and said no more. That is all I have to tell you, let me know how you are.
> Love, Ma

I went to Derry and waited until the house was cleared of visitors, my father was sound asleep, and my sisters had gone to bed, before telling my mother about Bernadette's pregnancy. I did not tell her the name of the father. I told her about Mary also being pregnant, that Mary would probably get divorced and that Mary and Eamonn would not, as far as I knew, be getting married. I caught the early-morning bus back to Dublin.

My mother sent me another letter later that week:

Dear Nell, words could not tell you how shocked I am at the news. I keep thinking all day long, it cannot be true. God almighty, how do these things happen. Mary I am heartily sorry for. She was married, had no children in that marriage, why? It could not have been on the rocks from the beginning. Now she has landed herself with a divorce and a baby on the way. She has a chance to cover up things a bit, why under God did she let things go so far, it is all right saying she is happy, how could she be? Anyone in their right mind about the whole thing could not be happy. I am sorry to the heart bone for her, I wish to God I could see her for myself. I am just as bad about it as if I was her Mother, what would I say to her if I wrote, all I could say was my heart was sore. About Bernie I keep saying to myself is she taking a hand at Nell, or is it true, what Nell is she going to do. I know a hell of a lot more about these things than you all. all Mothers like to know, Nell, that Babies need to have a da and so does a girl like to have a man beside her at a time like it. I would not be sore on anyone that got themselves into a Muddle like it, but Mary and Bernie such two people, I cannot think how they let it happen. Such a Mess and a Mess it is, no matter what you say about them being happy over it all, they just cannot be. If they only knew how I felt about both of them. Bernie needs somebody, who will she have. look how it is going to affect her whole career but what about the wane, all this comes through my head, and I end up by saying God almighty don't let it happen, it is when the bubble bursts, and all this gets around, I say to myself, I will say she was not a bad girl or she could have done what every one else has done in the same plight. there is no good in me talking

about it any longer, but who is the Fathers to both of them. Mary is at a bad age to have a first child, but she could go to Canada to her mother, where is Bernie going to go, London, and who will be with her? God and the Blessed Virgin protect you all. Nuala will be in an awful state if it ever gets out, for to her Bernadette was out of this world. I could roar my head off about them both. When I think of Mary and her coming back here after all I gave them both about you, but there was always something about them both with me, that I cared for. Nell, I am worried. Maybe God will see a way to things for them both. I wish I could talk to you. Your pop is far from well, there is a specialist coming to the house to see him, he has taken a bad knee and cannot walk. I have an awful handling, but he is pitiful to look at, he cannot put on his clothes now, all this I have to do, but I would do twice as much more if only God would see some way for them both, I would make all the sacrifices I could. Nell, they could not be happy, who could, and they are so much involved. Don't answer this letter, or speak about it, until I see you. Kathy was up and telling me she was going to put this in Ramparts for the next issue, I told her not to do it, give her all the advice I could about it, but she put it in and was worried about what I would say. She came up last night. I started her but she came over and kissed me when I was done barging, and all I could think on was mary and bernie, maybe I am taking it too serious, but all along you know how I stood up for them, but it is not us and people that matters, it is just them two girls. Will bernie get stopping at home or what will she do. It is getting late and I have to go to bed. Grainne has gone to Burnfoot. I cannot be bothered writing any more.
Love and God bless you.
Ma xx

I started spending more weekends in Derry. It was fun to stand around and watch the stone-throwing, especially when the soldiers unfurled a banner which advised that rioters had three minutes to disperse, or action would be taken against them: the soldiers would fire CS gas or rubber bullets. You'd have to get up really close to read the words.

In early July the *Irish Times* revealed that Bernadette's child was due in the autumn. I was asleep when my sister Nuala rang me from Derry to say she had read the paper. She had started work at nine, and was in tears by ten. Why hadn't I told her, prepared her for the shock and the fear and the worry about Bernadette? I was shocked myself that the news had finally been broken. The interview she gave to the *Irish Times* presaged the public reaction.

Mary Cummins asked if she expected to lose some support.

'Yes,' said Bernadette.

Mary Cummins asked if she had thought of having an abortion.

Bernadette said, 'I personally did not consider it. My moral position on abortion is that I would not be able to justify it to myself. This is something that people have to decide for themselves. My decision was: No.'

Mary Cummins asked if it would not be fairer to have the child adopted.

Bernadette said, 'I recognize the practical difficulties. I feel that it is my right and duty, not somebody else's, to bring up my child. Society is wrong in penalizing illegitimate children and that very term is a misnomer. There are no illegitimate children, only illegitimate parents, if the term is to be used at all. The self-righteous argue that every child has a right to be born and therefore there is no right to abortion. Yet they call children illegitimate and imply that they have no right to exist, and give scandal by the very fact of living. My child has a right to live and I do not think that, in supporting this right, I give scandal or set an example that is likely to be followed.'

Who is the father? Mary asked.

'I am not saying,' she replied.

Why are you not saying?

'I am not prepared to answer that question either.'

Eamonn shepherded her next day through the international media scrum that followed her around London. I caught the bus to Derry that weekend. That Sunday night, 8 July 1971, events in Derry took Bernadette off the front pages. I was watching a riot in the company of Willie Breslin, who often took conscientious mental note of these proceedings. Still wedded to the Londonderry Labour Party, he was both taking the political pulse of the Bogside and keeping an eye on the soldiers, to see that they continued to act within the law. I was just taking my mind off Bernadette and the further news, which shattered my mother, that our Paddy's marriage had ended while he trained to be a teacher in England.

The riot was lasting longer than usual; these things were usually over by five in the afternoon, and it was now approaching eleven at night. Since the 12 July parades were imminent, it could be argued that nationalists were just letting off steam and venting their anger on the only people around – the soldiers, who had replaced the police. Plus, the rioters were collecting souvenirs – a used CS gas canister could fetch a few pounds. Journalists and revolutionary tourists bought them as souvenirs.

I saw a fellow I knew who was much older than the average rioter and did not fit the profile. Seamus Cusack was twenty-eight years old, in full-time well-paid employment, and engaged to be married. I knew him to be a steady, mature man. Willie and I laughed at his souvenir-hunting antics: a soldier's helmet lay just in the mouth of an alley that divided two blocks of new houses. The soldiers were sheltering behind the end house, and peeking out from it. Seamus was sheltering at the front of the same house, and peeking back at them. He was crouched down, gauging whether it was safe to dash across the mouth of the alley, picking up the fallen helmet en route. A couple of young fellows had already tried and failed. Willie and I stood at the far side of the road, directly opposite the alley. Seamus finally ran out, bent down to grab the helmet, and as he did a shot rang out. Seamus fell to the ground. We all knew he had been shot, and none of us believed it. Everything halted. The soldiers seemed as surprised as us. Rioters and soldiers stared at each other. A howl went up from our side. 'Unfair' would be a good word to describe the nature of the sound. Soldiers were not supposed to shoot bullets. Not during a riot, anyway. Not during a good-natured, souvenir-hunting end to an evening where both sides understood that the engagement was not personal, just political.

We all ran towards Seamus; the soldiers ran away. He lay on the ground, blood pouring from his left leg. This was not so bad – a flesh wound to the upper part of his leg – but still there was an awful lot of blood draining away. A passing driver offered to take him to hospital. There was a vexed dispute. If Seamus was taken to Derry's Altnagelvin, a twenty-minute drive away, the cops would pick him up and he would be given the mandatory sentence of six months. Another man volunteered to drive Seamus across the border to the hospital in Letterkenny. This hospital was twenty miles away. Seamus would be a well man in no time, and a free man for all time.

The riot ended, of course. Nobody was so foolish as to risk being shot by soldiers who clearly did not understand the unwritten rules of engagement. We all went home. I was making coffee for Willie – both of us in a state of mild shock – when the phone rang and we learned that Seamus had died from loss of blood within minutes of reaching hospital.

An hour later, around two in the morning, there was a quiet knock at the front door. John Hume was standing there, tousled and rumpled as usual. Though we met often in the City Hotel, he had never come to my house before. I made coffee for him. He sat frowning, totally silent, listening to the account we gave of the shooting. He crosschecked with a few questions, but, being John, he made no comment or assessment of what had happened. He just stood up and said, 'If you say it was so, Nell, it was so,' and he left the house. In the midst of tragedy, I was egotistical enough to be flattered. Now I was a real reporter. And if John Hume took a thing seriously, it stayed serious.

Seamus Cusack was a good person, and now he was a dead person, and he wouldn't have died if it hadn't been for the mandatory sentencing policy introduced by the British government to appease the unionists from whom they had taken control of law and order – because the unionists could not be trusted with law and order. And yet the unionist police force still had the right to send Seamus to jail. And he would have lost his job. That precious job – he died because of that? Loss of blood, loss of job . . . the mantra came easily, and the argument came full circle in my head as I managed to arrive at the conclusion that Seamus died because of unionism and British rule in Ireland and the forthcoming 12 July commemoration of that bitter historical fact.

When dawn broke that Monday morning, Willie went home to get ready to go to teach in school, and I went on the early bus to Dublin. I had a job to keep. That afternoon, in the Bogside, during a riot of rage against the army for killing Seamus Cusack, the soldiers shot dead Desmond Beattie, aged nineteen. Next day, the SDLP withdrew from Stormont, a huge and serious step. And still I did not grasp the gravity of the situation: the North would be fine.

I wanted to be in Dublin because Mary Kenny was leaving for a big job in Fleet Street, London, on 12 July, and I cared not about the Orange parades on the same day. You could feel the excitement drain from the Irishwomen's Liberation Movement with her departure. It would not be nearly so much fun. She made a ship-to-shore phone call to me as her boat sailed away, describing the night and the stars and the sea and the fast-disappearing lights of Irish homes. Nobody before or since has made a ship-to-shore call to me. It was typical of her style.

While I was in Dublin, Bernadette visited our house in Derry and had a private conversation with my parents. My mother was less anguished. She would tell me nothing of the visit.

The *Irish Times* continued to broaden my scope and education by sending me to cover the Yeats Summer School in Sligo in August. Both wings of the IRA had started shooting in July, but it was pea-shooters against an army, and the summer school offered a pleasant break from my obsession with Northern politics. I didn't know what to make of the professors or how to report on their multifarious theses, but there were no petrol bombs, loads of foreign people, a small undercurrent of feminism, and I was getting paid to stay in a lovely hotel, with great food and wine. One morning at breakfast, the organizer of the school came by my table and expressed sorrow for my troubles.

What troubles?

Internment had been introduced during the night, and hundreds of Catholic males had been taken from their homes by the British army.

I caught the first possible bus from Sligo to Derry that day, 9 August 1971. I gave no thought to the precious job. We were supposed to change at Letterkenny, for a connection to my home-town, but bus services into Northern Ireland had been suspended. I took a taxi to the border, beyond which the driver would not travel, and walked the four miles to our house. The main road was deserted. There was nobody on the side streets. There was rubble and broken glass and the smouldering remains of hastily erected barricades. People had been fighting and resisting the army since 4 a.m. I got home in time to watch the television news at 6 p.m.

Now this was beyond belief: the British government had given the unionist government, under yet another new provincial union-ist Prime Minister, Brian Faulkner, permission to use the army to round up Catholics and intern them without trial. The army relied on RUC intelligence. The RUC rose to the opportunity of paying us back for beating them off the streets.

We had no right to know where the internees were, how they were, for how long they'd be there – years, maybe; the internees had no right to trial or to a lawyer.

The army had broken down doors in the pitch dark, taken men from their beds, clad only in pyjamas, and run them barefoot into waiting Jeeps. Many were pensioners; some were teenagers; all were of a Catholic background. A sizeable number were radicals and activists in the civil rights and student movements; few were in the IRA.

Among the internees were Michael Farrell, who had led us from Belfast to Derry in January 1969, and John McGuffin, his teaching colleague in Belfast. Derry had yielded up about twenty people, including Sean Keenan, the veteran IRA man who had been interned in the 1940s and 1950s, and had led the CDA during the Battle of the Bogside; Micky Montgomery, who had been there the night my sixteen-year-old cousin John Duffy died while cleaning an IRA gun; Johnny White, the young leader of the barely operative Official IRA. A Derry father, in his sixties, had been taken when the soldiers could not find his son, and they fired a rubber bullet at point-blank range into his stomach. Derry had got off light compared with Belfast and rural areas, but we were frightened. The action was beyond our understanding. Unionist explanations of an IRA and communist plot were risible. What struck real fear into us was that the British government had agreed to it.

That night in the City Hotel, the atmosphere was hysterical. I spent a while in the company of Hugh Herron, a dark, handsome, flirtatious, irreverent, curly-haired rogue, who was married with two young children. About an hour after I was with him, around midnight, news came back to the hotel that the British army had just shot him. But how? Why? According to the army, he had left the hotel, and gone to the disused jail in Bishop Street where the army was billeted. He had stood there, drunkenly waving a gun, then – the army said – he fired it, and they shot him dead. We still don't know where he got the gun. He probably didn't even know how to fire it properly. There were fifteen deaths in the North during the twenty-four hours of 9 August 1971.

A short time later, Bernadette gave premature birth to a daughter, Róisín, and my mother and Nuala went to see her in hospital in Cookstown. I cannot explain to myself why I didn't go, or why I went to London to visit Mary Holland when she gave birth to her daughter, Kitty, in October. I stayed in the house with her and Eamonn, and loads of Derry fellows who had came over to celebrate. Mary recalled crisply that we were useless, which indeed we were. I was embarrassed enough that after I left, days later, I had a crate of wine delivered to her from the famous Fleet Street pub El Vino, a favourite haunt of hers.

The details that seeped out of the internment camps would make a person squeal, as the internees did squeal at the hands of the British army. A handful of internees was subjected to what the European Court of Human Rights later condemned as torture, and cruel and inhumane treatment. These men were forced into boiler suits and helmets, made to stand against walls and subjected to 'white noise'. Many suffered nervous breakdowns; many died prematurely, years after release. Though hundreds of others remained imprisoned without trial for years, the majority of internees were released within days or months.

Michael Farrell was quickly set free. He had been made to run barefoot over broken glass, down a gauntlet of snarling army-trained Alsatians and their handlers, who beat him with batons. He was thrown, blindfolded and handcuffed, from a helicopter. He was not to know, as he went into free fall, that the helicopter was two feet above the ground.

In the Bogside that August, Johnny White, just released, told the avidly curious masses that the internees had been fed 'pigswill'. A young unknown said that it was now a 'fucking united Ireland or nothing at all': Martin McGuinness was an unlettered teenager. The two young men lacked oratorical skills. If this was the best both wings of the IRA had to offer – and this was our first public sight and sound of the emerging leadership of the modern paramilitary movements – they were neither inspiring nor engaging. The vice president of Provisional Sinn Féin Maire Drumm came from Belfast to declare in a repellent speech that British soldiers were 'Barnardo's bastards' and should be sent back to the eponymous orphanage in coffins. The barricades went up again anyway, and two IRA volunteers died within days, during gunfights with the British army.

Northern Catholics embarked on a rent and rates strike, those in public housing withholding rent, while the business class and private house owners withheld rates. Many strikers held out for five years, and paid dearly for it, when the British government struck back by deducting the money from their welfare payments.

On 6 September, as my brother Paddy, home on holiday, walked through a gunfight between the IRA and the British army – normal rioting was also in full swing – a fourteen-year-old schoolgirl, Annette McGavigan, died at his feet, shot by the army. She was a pupil at St Cecilia's, where my friend Gráinne was a teacher.

We developed a new addiction: listening to the British army's radio traffic on the television after 'God Save the Queen' was played and transmission ended. We'd stay tuned in to the blank screen, watching the blizzard of snowy dots, listening to the soldiers talking to each other, and to their central command, from their various bases in occupied buildings and fields throughout the city. The reception was terrific. On 13 September, a Saturday, we heard a soldier say that he was watching a man approach the barricade at the junction of Lone Moor Road and the top of Westland Street. This barricade was about 200 yards from our street. The soldier's base was in a disused factory in a field above the barricade. The field separated the Bogside from the Creggan. The soldiers had been billeted in the factory since shortly after they first entered the city, but they respected local rules: they could stay inside, but not come outside, except for such exceptional purposes as internment. They looked at us and we looked at them, and that was it.

We heard the soldier describe the man's approach to the barricade below him. There were plenty of people at the barricade. It had become the locus of late-night social gatherings, though ostensibly its function was to keep the soldiers penned into the factory. The soldier described the man's clothing, demeanour and gait. He was middle-aged, he said. We were amused, my mother, Nuala, Carmel, and I: as a social commentator, the soldier did not pass muster. Anybody in the Bogside could have named the man at 100 paces.

The soldier's voice tightened. He had the man in his gunsights. The change in tone puzzled, then alarmed us. I don't remember which of us said that, Jesus, the soldier was going to shoot this man. It was a stupid conclusion, of course – soldiers did not line up people in their rifle sights and shoot them of a calm night – but Carmel and I shot up out of our chairs, bolted out of the kitchen and ran to the barricade. We had to go down to the foot of our street – 10 yards; left along the flat Elmwood Terrace – 150 yards; left and up Westland Street – 50 yards; and we'd be at the barricade – 210 yards in all, one minute maximum, if we pounded at full speed. We pounded. Just twenty yards from the barricade, we heard the rifle shot. We ran on. Seconds later, we were standing in an astonished crowd, looking down at the dying figure of William McGreanery, a shop assistant who lived with his mother.

There was a friend of mine there, the jazz singer Helen Quigley. We stood looking down at Mr McGreanery. My sister Carmel had melted into the shadows, on the nod of a young priest who was hanging about in civilian clothes. He feared for Carmel's safety. I did not know then that the British army had a marked interest in rioters such as my sister. Helen and I both knelt over William McGreanery, leaned our faces to each of his ears, and attempted to whisper the Act of Contrition. Neither of us having been to church for years, Helen and I had to help each other out with the words: 'Oh my God, I am heartily sorry for having offended Thee, because Thou art the Chief Good; and because everything that is sinful is displeasing to Thee, I am resolved, with the help of Thy holy grace, never more to offend Thee, and to amend my life. Amen.'

William McGreanery died on the way to hospital. He had offended nobody in the British army, and his family was later awarded compensation. Hours before the army killed him, a soldier in the factory from which the shot had been fired had been wounded by an IRA sniper. This soldier, Sergeant Martin Leonard Carroll, died in hospital after McGreanery died. Because the British army was close-mouthed about such matters, we had not known that a soldier had been hit before McGreanery until after the sergeant's death was announced. The IRA said that it had carried out the attack in retaliation for 'brutality to young children on their way to school by the British army' – that was the girl Paddy had seen shot eight days earlier, Annette McGavigan.

Helen Quigley switched from jazz to Irish rebel songs in Derry pubs. Barricades were thrown up everywhere in the Bogside, Brandywell and Creggan, and were reinforced now with steel girders sunk in concrete. The British soldiers stationed in the disused factory, and in the new Nissen-hut camp above Creggan, remained confined to their posts, occasionally making a screaming sortie in reinforced Saracen armoured cars.

Photographs started appearing in the *Derry Journal* of young fellows, in masks, wearing camouflage jackets, posing with rifles.

Small in number, they constituted the two Irish Republican Armies. And still, though they walked openly around the streets bearing arms, and were becoming efficient in killing soldiers and cops, we regarded them as our young fellows, the neighbours' children. Knowing them as we did, looking at their street shoes and ordinary trousers, it was hard to think of them as other than that.

I knew a number of members of the Official IRA, mainly because many of them had defected from the Londonderry Labour Party. The Officials set up a shoulder-high sand-bagged sangar against the front wall of a house near Free Derry Corner and installed a machine gun. It was loaded with a belt of bullets. Locals were invited to step into the sangar – how quickly we had learned to use military terms – feed the belt through and look down the sight at the end of the barrel. The machine gun pointed straight into the Bogside. We could take aim at our own people, walking towards us, unsuspecting, and growl, 'Bang.'

Unionist rage was mounting against the no-go Fenian areas in the North. For ourselves, the no-go areas were sociable and enjoyable. By general consensus, every street set up its own commit-tee, which in turn was given the task of setting up a street barricade. I went with my mother and our neighbours up the street and into the bookie's shop in the back lane, to do precisely that. The bookie's was a wooden hut with a tin roof, a gloriously ramshackle establishment, with sawdust on its ancient wooden floors. Women went in there to place bets on the annual Aintree Grand National, or – in the case of such as my mother – to place bets for their bedridden husbands. All the same, women never stood around the place, for hours, chewing the fat, like the men.

Now we were in there, after hours, sitting on the benches that lined the walls, in discussions alongside the men about the placing and erection of a barricade. We drew up rosters of vigilantes to staff it and of people who would deliver refreshments round the clock to the vigilantes. The average age of the group was sixty. There was a pub at the top of our street opposite a shop, and the pub and shop were divided from the houses below by a laneway. The suggestion of a barricade across the lane that separated residents from merchants was scornfully rejected. 'The vigilantes need the laneway for an escape route' . . . 'I'm not climbing over a barricade to place a bet for my man' . . . 'How will the milkman get up and down the street if the top is blocked off and he can't reverse into the lane?'

The women stressed that they wanted a clean barricade – no rubbish on it that would attract rats – and a nice barricade: 'We'll have to look at it all day.' The pavements on either side of the barricade were to be left clear: 'Jesus, how will any woman get a pram by, or get to the shop for the paper?' Otherwise, they were delighted that no more cars or lorries, especially beer lorries, would come thundering down Beechwood Street, using it as a shortcut to main roads. 'Remember that day the barrel broke loose and Mrs McBride had to dance like a dervish to get out its way?' Children would be free again to play outside the door. Also, somebody would have to put out the street lights, so that the soldiers stationed up on Derry Walls, looking down on us, would not have a clear view of our nocturnal activities. Our barricade was indeed lovely. You could look at it all day long, so you could, it was that neat and strong, its foundations sunk firmly into the tarmacadam. Our street felt peaceful and protected. The soldiers couldn't come roaring down in their Saracens.

Chapter Sixteen

After the Irishwomen's Liberation Movement had disbanded in the autumn of 1971, a few of us regrouped and launched the Women's Liberation Movement, Ireland. The politics behind the renaming boded ill for our future. It was thought that the term 'Irishwomen' would offend Northern women of a unionist background. However, the term 'Ireland' was also offensive to them, as, in unionist minds, Northern Ireland was part of the United Kingdom, not of Ireland. My attempt to explain that, and the WLMI's attempt to understand that, led to many a boring meeting. This merely confirmed my initial instinct that any movement for the liberation of women in the South should avoid Northern politics, until feminism was firmly rooted south of the border. The WLMI lasted about two years and mostly consisted of a very good Saturday-night poker school.

Nevertheless, invitations kept flowing in. I spoke all over Ireland, in small towns, in major cities, in villages – wherever a group of women was willing to gather. Sometimes I spoke to crowds of three, sometimes to packed halls. I travelled by bus and train, after the day's work was done at the newspaper, and returned by milk train at dawn. Lovely things happened. As I walked to a meeting one evening, in beautiful, quiet Ballydehob in West Cork – I was enjoying the foreign travel – a woman standing at her door invited me in for a meal. She made a salad in no time. I admired the dressing. She made me up a bottle of it, to bring home. 'You don't strike me, Nell, as a woman who knows how to cook.'

The English-born playwright Margaretta D'Arcy, living in the wilds of Connemara, asked for a deputation to travel there and show the people actual contraceptives. I went by car with Frank Crummey, a social worker and voluntary bagman in the Family Planning Association, which had worked out a way to circumvent the law: contraceptives could be given in exchange for a donation. The only thing was that anybody going into its Dublin office would be known to be going in for only the one thing, so the office did not lure many visitors.

During the five-hour drive to Connemara he told me things to which I did not – would not – pay much attention. I even assumed he was exaggerating, the way a person might do whose whole world is reduced to crisis work. There was a lot of incest in Ireland, he said. He talked of overcrowded slums and of isolated families in the countryside. He even mentioned sexual abuse by priests of children in reform schools. I wanted only to hear of the bright new world that awaited women – and men – once contraception was legalized.

We arrived in Connemara in the pitch dark, around nine at night. We were utterly lost in the little side roads that wandered through its vast expanse of bog and lake. We looked at the moon, but Frank no more knew east from west, north from south, than I did. D'Arcy appeared in the headlights, standing at a crossroads. Where she was going, the car could not go, so we walked a short distance and stepped into a thatched cottage at 10 p.m. The cottage was crowded. Every pensioner in the district was there, all fifteen of them. They had walking sticks and false teeth, or no teeth. They were, in a phrase, past it. Also, these lifelong Gaelic speakers did not speak English.

Frank, professional to the fingertips, dispassionately opened his bag of tricks, and produced pills, intrauterine devices of coil and loop, jellies, and condoms. His audience murmured as he demonstrated in sign language how to use these things and where exactly to put them. The pictures and charts helped. These old people were among the first people in Ireland, most Irish-trained doctors included, to see the whole kit and caboodle. I was seeing things myself. I couldn't say much in broken Irish beyond 'Is an-mhaith na rudaí seo ma's níl paistaí a dhít oraibh ar bomaite' – these things are terrific if you don't want children immediately.

The old people pronounced themselves satisfied. They did not hang about or debate. They went straight home, mission

247

accomplished. I could not decide if I should kill D'Arcy. An egalitarian, she genuinely could not understand my reaction. People were entitled to knowledge, regardless of creed, class or age, were they not? She clearly thought me something of a shirker. Frank flew in the face of reality and declared that we had done a tremendous thing and learned a tremendous amount. He could not wait to tell Dublin that Connemara was relaxed about the sexual revolution. We got back in time for breakfast, singing 'The West's Awake'. We were laughing, still.

I unveiled my own version of the naked truth during a debate in University College Dublin a month later, in October 1971. The hall was packed to overflowing. Three of us sat at the table beside the lectern, looking up at the serried rows. Mary Anderson was the child of an unmarried mother; Sister Benvenuta, or Sister Ben, was a religious radical; and I was the public face of women's liberation.

We had not worked out the order of speaking, or which aspect of feminism each would address. Mary suggested that each of us make a short opening statement about the specific personal difficulties under which we laboured as women, and that she go first. Sister Ben and I had no idea what was coming next.

Mary Anderson said: 'I am a bastard.'

I said: 'I am a lesbian.'

Sister Benvenuta said: 'I am a nun.'

The audience erupted in yells of pure, unadulterated pleasure. The exchanges that evening were a runaway train of untrammelled speech. The students were rapt and rapturous, and so were we. The debate ended with a contribution from the actor Siobhán McKenna. She had remained anonymously up at the back, but now she declaimed from the doorway a poem which she deemed entirely suitable to the occasion: 'The Mother', written by the patriot, the only begetter of Irish independence, Pádraic Pearse.

Pearse had put the words into the imagined mouth of his mother on the imagined eve of his execution by the British:

> Lord, though art hard on mothers:
> We suffer in their coming and their going

Yes, well, some mothers do suffer – though fewer children would henceforth add to their suffering lot if we three on the platform had our planned way on legalizing contraception.

There were no working journalists present, so I didn't have to worry about my spontaneous declaration. That was to happen time and again. The media just did not cover mere women, who talked off the top of their heads. And when, perchance, they did, I relied on the paper barrier between North and South to protect my parents. Northerners read British newspapers because Britain controlled their lives, jobs, and pensions. When the *Irish Times* was brought into our house in Derry, my parents went straight to my article and disregarded the rest of the huge broadsheet, with its coverage of things foreign: the doings of the Irish government, which affected Northern livelihoods not one whit.

Their experience of the many people I was now bringing from Dublin to Derry for the weekend did not, in any case, inspire them to look South. The journalist Anne Harris suffered from asthma: when my mother heard just how much she had to pay for medication, she swept my asthmatic father's (free, British) medication into Anne's handbag. 'Sure, there's plenty more where that came from, daughter.'

Eamonn decided to take umbrage at a satirical revue by Tomás Mac Anna, about our Northern troubles, held in Dublin's Abbey Theatre. He rang the *Irish Times* to ensure coverage and my personal assistance. I told the news editor, abandoned work and went down to the theatre. He had leaflets for us both to hand out at the interval. As the second half drew to a close, he went to the bar and ordered fifty brandies, which the unsuspecting barman dutifully poured, on credit, and for which, in the event, Eamonn never paid. Before the final curtain fell, Eamonn interrupted the revue by walking onstage and giving out about the South making light of our Northern troubles. It was, looking back, a trifle precious, but the audience was thrilled by his intervention, hailed it as a *coup de foudre*, loved being lashed, and Mac Anna wisely regarded it as brilliant first-night fireworks.

Eamonn and I handed out more leaflets as patrons left, the

cognoscenti and cast joined us for the brandies, somebody else settled the bill, the *Irish Times* got a minor scoop, and I kept my job yet again. Mac Anna invited us all back to his home on the Hill of Howth, which formed one of the embracing arms of Dublin Bay. The party must have been wild because it ended with me sheltering behind a hedge with a fellow called John Kelly from Belfast, as another man fired shots in our direction. The previous October, Kelly, a senior member of the Provisional IRA's Northern Command, had been found not guilty of smuggling guns into Ireland; his three co-defendants, including former cabinet minister Charles Haughey, were also acquitted. The man who fired shots at us was Paddy Kennedy, a Republican Labour MP at Stormont and former colleague of Gerry Fitt, and I know the gun was not Paddy's, if only because he hadn't a clue how to use it, and most of his bullets went skywards. Kelly told me not to worry as we crouched behind the hedge. He and Kennedy were convulsed with laughter.

Sometime in the autumn of 1971, I opened the front door of Patsy Murphy's house in Hatch Place to find Cathal Goulding, the Chief of Staff of the Official IRA, standing there. He asked could he come in and talk.

When Sinn Féin and the IRA had split the previous year, Goulding, a Dublin builder, had led the majority Marxist faction, which favoured political development over armed struggle. They called themselves Official Sinn Féin and the Official IRA to emphasize their seniority. The members of the breakaway faction, which emphasized armed struggle over politics, called themselves Provisional Sinn Féin and the Provisional IRA – they were on stand-by to claim the legacy of the 1916 Easter Rising, which marked the start of the modern campaign for Irish independence. Inevitably the name was shortened to 'Provos'; the Officials were then dubbed 'Stickies', after the style of paper lily they sold to commemorate the Rising. It was affixed to the lapel by adhesive (the Provos' lily was attached by a pin). Notwithstanding the seismic effect of internment, which pitched Northern nationalists against the British army, the nicknames of these two organizations summed up, as far as I was concerned, their politics: they were split over a pin.

I had a nodding acquaintance with Goulding around Dublin, where he kept company with leftie and liberal journalists, and I liked him well enough. He was short and stocky with wavy hair, laughter wrinkles round his eyes, a handsome pixie face and buckets of laid-back charm. When he arrived at Patsy's door, it was bright and early, and I was still in my nightie. I ushered him in. He wanted to know about the men in the Derry branch of his army. Their numbers had grown considerably, and he had no idea who the new men were or what they were like.

I gave him tea and toast, and a fond account of the ham-fisted exploits of the Derry fellows, whose enrolment in the Official IRA I did not take seriously because they lived on a different planet from that of the stereotypical murderous gunman portrayed by the media. They were mostly former members of the Londonderry Labour Party. There was Red Mickey Doherty, a street trader who had a car, with whose father, Boojums Doherty, a bookmaker, my father had often worked at greyhound race tracks at night. There was Barricade Joe, a garrulous, happy-go-lucky tradesman, who delighted my parents with his nightly renditions of 'Joe Hill' and 'The Banks Are Made of Marble'. There was John, the poacher, who shared his catch of whole wild salmon, the taste of which – sauced by its provenance – my father loved. And there was Seamus, a teacher, who, like myself, was unofficially blacklisted. His mother was a chambermaid in the City Hotel and was very fond of her regular guest Mary Holland.

I did not think that the Official IRA, as a whole, took its job in Derry seriously. By their own reckoning, they were at war with the British army. By mine, they were socialist boys with toys. For instance, I was one of a group that was invited to stand, in broad daylight, on a patch of waste ground directly opposite Con Bradley's pub at Aggro Corner, at the junction of William Street and Rossville Street. We were told to watch what happened when the bomb, which they had planted behind the window of the pub, went off. We stood there nonchalantly as a squad of six soldiers came down

William Street. One was on point duty, leading the way. One brought up the rear, walking backwards. The four in the middle swivelled their rifles this way and that. They came abreast of the pub, and nothing happened. The soldiers walked on. Minutes later, an abashed and cursing Stickie told us the bomb hadn't worked.

How we laughed at him. How immature about war, and how foolish and stupid, we all were that day. If the bomb had gone off, the flying glass alone might have maimed or killed us. Many deaths were later to occur from no-warning bombs. We, however, had been warned. And what would I have done if bits of the squaddies had gone up in the air and landed at my feet?

Cathal Goulding was not best pleased. He had served time in jail in England and Ireland for his IRA activities. I reminded him that he had been young and foolish once. Never that foolish, he said. I allowed that there were some Derry IRA men whom I considered headstrong.

Goulding asked me to keep in touch. What did that mean? I asked. If I heard anything I thought he ought to know, he would like me to get in touch, he said. He gave me his phone number, with a warning never to give details over the phone. A casual suggestion that we meet in Bowe's pub, opposite the *Irish Times*, would be sufficient to alert him.

'Does that mean I'm in the IRA?' I asked him, in jest.

'If you think you're in the IRA, you're in it,' he replied, with a smile.

'I'm not in the IRA,' I declared.

Grand, he said, but proper intelligence from Derry would be helpful: socialists such as me had a part to play in the North's revolution.

We met about once a month thereafter, usually in the company of three other journalists: my colleague Dick Walsh; Eoghan Harris, Anne's husband, who worked as a current-affairs producer in RTÉ, dominated the trade unions there, and advised Official Sinn Féin; and Ciaran McKeown, who worked as a journalist in Belfast, and was later to become guru to the Nobel prize-winning co-founders of the short-lived Peace People's movement, Betty Williams and Máiréad Corrigan. None of us was a declared pacifist.

I wore my different hats and contradictions easily, but my heart was in the women's movement. It was far less confusing and rigid and ideologically driven – and riven – than the male-dominated left. The theory of class warfare, especially, was driving me nuts, not least because its exponents were well educated and in professional jobs. When the bourgeois Hazel Boland, chair of the Council for the Status of Women, broke down while talking in public about the strain of caring for her ailing husband, I cheered her courage and sacrifice. Still, I got a great kick out of walking around with Mao Tse-tung's *Little Red Book*, which was then the rage. I listened dutifully – believingly, even – when Eoghan Harris, an enchanting, amusing, intellectually energizing exponent of socialism, told me fiercely one night that only members of the IRA wore the 'red badge of courage'. Eoghan has a habit of repeating (and, in the moment, believing) himself, though this deficiency was tolerated, given that the repetitions came from the melodiously high-pitched, Cork-accented, moustachioed mouth of a man who looked the epitome of the handsome, civilized desperado.

He was not in the IRA. When he praised yet again those IRA men who wore the 'red badge of courage', I told him I already knew about such things, having seen Alan Ladd star in a movie called *The Red Beret*, based on World War II. I was bored with tales of the IRA, which, as far as I could see, was wrecking the North. He took the hint, relaxed his rant and directed our homebound taxi to another pub.

One night in Dublin, my social life changed drastically as I was coming out of yet another pub. Eimer Philbin Bowman stopped me, offered me supper, and drove me to her house. She had driven into town specifically to see me. I didn't ask her why. Life was like that then. I was pleased and flattered that anyone should care enough, or deem me interesting enough, to bring me home and give me a home-cooked meal.

Eimer, one of the twelve women who had founded the Irish-women's Liberation Movement, was nobody's idea of a radical (our notion of radicalism, then, was limited and rigid). She was a quiet-spoken bluestocking who actually wore woollen tights. She had applied, and been turned down, for a hospital internship, without which she could not get her doctor's licence to practise. She was turned down because she was married. The job, as ever, was open only to men, single women or widows. The interview panel didn't even get as far as being pointedly sniffy about the fact that she had two babies.

She lived in a mews house in a back lane in the centre of Dublin. A large wide black gate opened on to a plant-studded patio, beyond which a door divided two picture-window rooms. One room was a study where her husband, John Bowman, a broadcaster, was writing a thesis on Eamon de Valera. The study walls were lined with books, the floor knee-deep in piles of newspapers. The other room, a dining room which gave on to a kitchen, was where Eimer sat up late, during the free night hours after the children and her husband had gone to bed.

She roasted pigeon breasts. She poured half a bottle of wine into a decanter. (She always did that, always half a bottle at a time into that little glass decanter, even if I had just persuaded her to open the third bottle of the night.) She showed me a landscape painting by Camille Souter. I asked how much it cost. They had paid the equivalent of a year's wages, a fortune to my mind. Outside of museums, I was looking for the first time ever at a properly painted original.

Some nights we talked until dawn. She wanted me to write an article on the health benefits of brown sugar. Or was that the health threat posed by processed brown sugar? I wondered what brown sugar had to do with the women's movement. She invited me to supper parties given by her and John. Her regular guests included the poet Eavan Boland and Senator Mary Robinson.

On 6 November 1971, as soldiers entered Creggan in the dark to search houses, Kathleen Thompson stood in her garden, banging her bin lid to warn the neighbours. The soldiers shot her dead. She was married, aged forty-seven, and had six children. In Belfast, a soldier, standing in the garden of Emma Groves, fired a rubber bullet at her at point-blank range because she was playing republican songs out her window at him. He blew out both her eyes. Television footage of her daughters, holding their blinded, bloodied mother by both arms as they zigzagged down the street, seeking help, was deemed so upsetting and potentially inflammatory that it was not broadcast until after the final IRA ceasefire of 1996.

The day after Mrs Thompson was gunned down, both wings of the IRA put up posters in Derry warning against 'fraternization'. There was no doubt what they meant: during the ensuing riots, I heard a friend of mine, a businessman, say to the group around him, 'And what are our girls doing while the lads are fighting? They're up on the Walls, down on their knees, sucking the soldiers off.' Within a week, as our Carmel was returning from work, she untied the ropes that bound a young woman to a lamppost, the third girl to be punished since the death of Mrs Thompson. She was shaven-headed, doused in red leaded paint, tarred and feathered, and had a placard round her neck that proclaimed her 'soldier-doll'. The teenager, it turned out, was our cousin Deirdre Duffy, whose IRA brother had died while cleaning a revolver in 1960. The factory girls with whom she worked had already punched and beaten her. She knew one of the young masked women who had judged her at the all-female kangaroo court.

I knew this 'judge' myself. I had taught her, seen her march for civil rights, fight the RUC in the Battle of the Bogside, and fight the soldiers on the barricades. The community had, at all times, applauded young people like her, just as it had nodded benignly when the soldiers of 1969, in the honeymoon period, had dated young Bogside women and gone to their homes to meet the parents.

There was no formal community condemnation of the tarring and feathering, though both wings of the IRA publicly disavowed the method, rather than the principle, of punishing fraternization. The professional classes, at an anti-internment meeting called shortly afterwards, did not mention the tarring and feathering. Those present — architects, doctors, dentists and businessmen — went so far as to reject, overwhelmingly, a resolution deploring violence from whatever quarter. The *Derry Journal*, which had prominently condemned violence, the IRA, Communism and all things anti-Establishment, reported the incidents without a word of rebuke from it or any named source. There was no repudiation from the organizations that represented the civic life of the Bogside, Brandywell and Creggan – three tenants' associations, two women's action committees, five political groups and autonomous street-defence committees.

I interviewed a friend who had watched the public tarring and feathering of Deirdre. He didn't know at the time that she was my cousin. It made no difference when I told him. In the piece that was published in the *Irish Times* I quoted him:

This is no time to talk of civil liberties. You get civil liberties in the political situation. This is no political situation. This is a war. If these girls who go out with soldiers never consciously give any information, every word they say is a piece in the military intelligence jigsaw.

And if they never said anything, they're giving comfort to an army which nightly comes into this area to fight with the people. Man, woman and child, no one is safe. People are dying, people are being interned; children go to school to learn that their classmate was killed the day before.

We spent the last few years on the barricades, night after night, protecting who against what? So these girls can sail safely through with their soldier boyfriends? Have you any idea what we've gone through, you who make moral judgements from the comfort of London and Dublin?

That firm which sent wigs to the girls who were shaved – what have they sent the children of Kathleen Thompson? Sweet damn all . . . There are 35,000 people in this area and not one of them feels safe. They could shoot anybody and they have done so. And you want to worry about the judicial refinements of three girls who were having a good time?

I interviewed a young woman who was about to flee to England with her soldier boyfriend:

Look at all those Derry girls who married soldiers and there's some of them now who've been living with their husbands in Derry for a long time. Nobody tells them they're wrong because they met their boyfriend when Derry was peaceful. Well, I met my boyfriend when Derry was peaceful . . . it wasn't the British army started the trouble in Derry. It was the police and I hate the police.

Her mother said:

I'm all mixed up. I'm on the side of the Bogside against anybody that attacks us, but I know Tom is a good fellow . . . Didn't the IRA themselves say the wee girls have a right to love?

A man who used to live in our street, a railway worker, stepped on to the tracks and stopped the train as it left Derry. He asked his daughter to come home. She refused. She was going away to England, she said, leaving this bitter place to marry her soldier. She was eighteen. My cousin Deirdre Duffy also went to England.

I ended my article: 'And what Solomon will judge the moral, military and political morass into which Derry has been plunged?'

Chapter Seventeen

Patsy Murphy was getting to like Saturday nights in Derry very much. There were noisy parties in either Gráinne's or Brendan Duddy's house. There were raucous sessions beforehand in pubs, especially if Helen Quigley was belting out 'James Connolly, the Irish rebel'. Somewhere out there, the IRA (both wings) and the British army and the RUC might exchange fire, but not so much that you'd notice.

Patsy and myself arrived in Derry on 29 January 1972 in a car driven by Patsy's great friend, the RTÉ Irish-language news reporter Nuala Ní Dhomhnaill. It is a harsh fact that I did not find many people to be troubled by the IRA killings of two policemen two nights previously, though they were the first policemen to be killed in our town, and such killings were not a normal fact of life. The RUC chief superintendent even acknowledged that there had not previously been any such hostility to his men. Sergeant Peter Kilgunn was a twenty-six-year-old Catholic from Fermanagh who was married, with one child. He had joined the RUC in 1966. Constable David Montgomery was a twenty-year-old Belfast Protestant. He had been due to transfer out of Derry the week before he was killed, but had asked to be allowed to remain until June, when he planned to marry a Derry girl.

The next morning I scouted the town with Nuala Ní Dhomhnaill to test the atmosphere before the anti-internment march planned for that afternoon. It was not a march against the police, but against the British army and British government which were enforcing internment without trial. Marching had been banned since August, and the army had put its toughest regiment into Derry to supervise it – the First Battalion of the Parachute Regiment, known for their red berets, rough ways and sharpshooting skills.

The Paras were everywhere on the Bogside perimeter, lying on footpaths, ensconced behind school walls, faces blackened, fingers on triggers. We tried to get words out of them. 'It's a nice day for a killing,' one of them said. Silly macho bugger. There had been several anti-internment marches, and our side was not looking for a gun battle. We were used to soldiers blocking our route, and essaying the odd baton charge, after which the marchers would retreat to home ground, and there would be a riot. It was just like the days of marching against the RUC and the unionist government – but the death toll was mounting.

This march had been called by the Derry branch of the Civil Rights Association, under chairwoman Brigid Bond, and the main speaker was to be Bernadette Devlin. Bernadette had dinner in our house with the family, Patsy and Nuala Ní Dhomhnaill. As we left our house, my mother gave Carmel and the neighbour's daughter Teresa Cooley leftover potatoes, still hot in their jackets, to keep their hands warm. Afterwards, we walked uphill to Creggan, from which we proposed to walk back down again, in a glorious scenic route via the Brandywell and Bogside, to the forbidden city centre. The weather was stunning: dry and sparkling, a few clouds in a high blue sky.

The prelude to marches in those times was still lovely. People streamed through the streets en route to the starting point. You'd know this and that one – the usual suspects; nudge each other at the surprise participation of another; swell with optimism when it became obvious that successive generations were joining in together: grannies, sons and granddaughters. The numbers that day exceeded the wildest expectations of the organizers. There were about 20,000, as big as Derry had seen since 1969 when John Hume led a similar number, demanding housing and universal suffrage. They were, by and large, the exact same people, still peacefully resisting the North's iron anti-Catholic fist.

In 2003 I testified before the Saville inquiry, the second inquiry called by the British government into the massacre that took place in Derry on Sunday, 30 January 1972. I managed to give three contradictory accounts of exactly what I had seen that day – in which house I had taken shelter, where exactly I saw the dead bodies, and whether I saw gunmen before the march, or on a different march altogether.

The march was stopped, as anticipated, by the soldiers at William Street, who blocked entry to the city centre. There was a riot at the front of the march, a bottleneck at the back, and the soldiers used tear gas and water cannons which stained rioters with dyed water. Eventually, people retreated to Rossville Street and regrouped at Free Derry Corner. There was a lull while they assembled and microphones were being tested on the back of the coal lorry where Bernadette already stood with an elderly Englishman, the liberal Lord Fenner Brockway.

Thousands of people stood with their backs to a small group of teenagers, a hundred yards behind them, who were trying to get a riot going at Aggro Corner, where Rossville Street and William Street met. It was my habit, as usual, to keep one eye on the crowd, and another on the minor riot, so I stationed myself beside the barricade at Glenfada Park, directly opposite the High Flats. The front gardens of the park were surrounded by a low wall, about a foot high. I stood on this wall, and the extra height afforded a good view of proceedings to either side of the barricade. Patsy and Nuala Ní Dhomhnaill stood below me.

There was a flurry of shouts, and the riotous teenagers ran towards us, pursued by armoured cars, which did not stop at Aggro Corner, as they normally did. The armoured cars came on and on, then stopped, about twenty yards away from the barricade. I could not understand why the soldiers had driven so far into our territory. Soldiers jumped out. The high-pitched cracks did not make the dull thud associated with rubber bullets. I made Patsy and Nuala run with me up a ramp which accessed the second storey of Glenfada. From there we looked down at the barricade, and whatever we saw, which none of us remembers at all, made me say that we had to get out of there; the press cards which Nuala and I held would be no use to us. We ran back down the ramp and into the courtyard of Glenfada Park. There were three houses on the left, and I banged on a door. An old lady opened it, and we rushed past her, into her living room.

Inexplicably, we put on her kettle and made ourselves tea. There was more banging on the door: 'For Jesus' sake, missus, let us in. They're shooting.' The old woman opened it and three youths ran in, straight through, and out her back door. It was, Patsy testified to Saville, 'like a French farce'. I looked out the window and saw soldiers pick the bodies of four young males off the barricade, one by one, and toss them by the arms and legs into the back of an armoured car. I assumed the teenagers had been knocked out by rubber bullets. I saw a group of men and women herded against the gable wall of the courtyard, among them the young priest Denis Bradley, who was subsequently to leave the priesthood and help negotiate the IRA ceasefire in 1994.

Patsy and Nuala and I sat on the woman's floor, me under her window. She stayed in her armchair.

There was the sound of pounding, running feet. I got up, looked out the window, and saw Jim Wray fall headlong on the garden path that led to the front door. A second fellow, running behind him, fell on the pavement beyond the fence. I knew Jim Wray's father from many civil rights meetings, but Jim I knew only by sight and name. He was tall and well built. He lay on the ground, head raised, calling out to me to open the door. I shook my head. 'No.'

I cannot say why I believed I would be killed if I did open the door, because I cannot now remember hearing rifle fire. Patsy still does, as does Nuala. I do remember that the sound of silence prompted me to stand up, finally. I looked out the window and saw a young woman in Red Cross uniform run diagonally across the courtyard. The shots which soldiers fired at her were the only ones I clearly recall. They fired at her feet and made her dance. One of the soldiers, at the far end of Glenfada Park, was crouched on one knee, his eye trained along the rifle barrel. He was not a slim fellow. He had a low, dark brow. I could not have picked him out at an identity parade. Another Red Cross official dragged a body away.

There was more silence. When it seemed sufficiently extended, I looked out the window again. I saw Dr Ray McLean walk through the mist that had fallen. Whatever it was, it was over. We left the house and walked through cordite smoke: there had been no mist.

Patsy and Nuala assure me that we looked at Jim Wray's body; that we crossed the road to the High Flats and looked at the body of an older man; and Ray McLean records in his book that I collapsed, crying, into his arms. This much I do know, and it is agreed by those who were there that day: Derry people went straight home, straight past those dead people who were lying on the ground. That is not in our culture. People gather round the dead and pray for them. On that day, it was only the priests and identifiable medics who stayed at the scene. And the soldiers, at a distance.

I do not remember why I hurried away. I suppose that I must have been scared stiff. I do not remember the route I took home. When we got there, the house was crowded. Bernadette, who took shelter under the lorry, does not remember how she made her way to my mother's house. Neither does Eamonn, who was pinned to the ground at Free Derry Corner, alongside everybody else. Michael and Gráinne remember that, after people first flung themselves to the ground, Michael stood up, calling out to them not to be afraid, that these were rubber bullets, then, realizing that they were live rounds, threw himself down beside Gráinne. My sister Carmel lay hidden in an alleyway with her future husband, Kevin. The alleyway was at right angles to the distant Paras, and they did not know that the shots bouncing in among them all had come from Derry's Walls, above and behind them: another regiment had decided to join in the duck shoot. My sister Nuala remembers running all the way home after the first shots were heard, and having to tell Teresa Cooley to leave behind the shoe that fell off Teresa's foot. Loads of shoes were lying around next day, and Teresa found hers. My mother remembers that she left my father briefly to dash down to the meeting, and that the tail-end of the huge march had still not reached Free Derry Corner when she arrived there, so she started off back home before the meeting began. She was with Teresa's mother, Bridget, and Annie, at the Credit Union building in Abbey Street, just beyond Glenfada Park, when they heard shooting. Bridget hesitated, out of curiosity, and my mother pushed her forcefully in the direction of home. 'For God's sake, Bridget, we're not fit to run if anything happens.'

More and more people crowded into our house after the shooting, and none of us had a clue. How many were dead? Two, anyway: Jim Wray and Barney McGuigan. Bridie McDaid arrived from the street next to ours, frantic and in tears, to say her young brother Michael had not yet come home. Carmel said she had seen Michael near Free Derry Corner, all dressed up, making his way against the stream of the marchers, heading towards Aggro Corner, beyond which lay the bus station from where he intended to get a bus to go to see his girlfriend across the border in Buncrana. Carmel had given him her handkerchief to cover his mouth against the CS gas which soldiers had earlier fired at us. The shooting hadn't started by then. Still, Bridie wanted to be sure and thought she would go to the hospital.

The six o'clock news came on: an unknown number of people had been killed in Derry; they were all in the IRA. Standing there looking at the television, I said the worst, most vile word I could think of about the soldiers. 'Cunts,' I said. I had never cursed in front of my father or mother, and never used that word before. I was aghast at myself and looked at my father, sitting paralysed in his armchair by the fire. He shook his poor speechless head, to indicate that he understood the reason for this unprecedented outburst, and he was crying.

There was not enough food in the house. None of us wanted to leave. Where would we go? What would we do? Gráinne and Michael drove off to the Chinese restaurant, and came back with takeaways for thirty people. My parents had never eaten Chinese food. Another news bulletin said that Bernadette Devlin was over at the hospital, protesting. Bernadette went out to the phone in our hall and rang the hospital. Our staircase was packed, people were in my father's downstairs bedroom, and there were people standing all the way to the front door and people in the kitchen. There was dead silence when we realized that the hospital authorities had agreed to give Bernadette names. She had a pen and a sheet of our Nuala's swanky writing paper. The list seemed interminable. We presumed she was also writing down the names of the injured. She was not. Thirteen people were dead. Michael McDaid was one of them. Ten of the dead were under the age of twenty.

That night I phoned a few shocked, limp paragraphs to the *Irish Times* about the two deaths I had actually witnessed. As I spoke, bin lids were banged on the pavement outside our house, a warning of troops in the vicinity. I could hear the news editor in faraway Dublin shout to staff, 'Jesus, they're shooting again.' They weren't. The Paras were back at base, and officers, as television later showed, had set up kegs of free beer for them. Both wings of the IRA were in shocked conclave and agreeing not to retaliate until after the dead had been buried. Bernadette and Eamonn were drawing up a statement, in our house, about the massacre being 'our Sharpeville'. What was Sharpeville, I asked, and the Dublin journalist Vincent Browne, who was sitting on the edge of my mother's kitchen table, explained. I tried unsuccessfully to convince Bernadette and Eamonn that nobody had heard of Sharpeville. God forbid that the imprisoned Nelson Mandela should have been depending on the likes of me.

Eamonn met with the republicans that night, and the next day he asked me to write the front page of the *Starry Plough*, newspaper of the Official Republican Movement and mouthpiece of the Official IRA, which was bringing out an emergency edition in time for the funerals. Like him, I was happy to write for a paper which would allow us free political expression. A black-and-white photograph of the bloodstained banner of the Derry Civil Rights Association was struck along the top of the front page. The blood was that of Barney McGuigan, whom I had looked at earlier. He was forty-eight – the last to be targeted in that ten-minute shooting spree and by far the oldest to die. He had stepped out from the shelter of the High Flats, arms upraised, appealing to the Paratroopers to let him tend wounded, dying teenagers. The banner had been used to cover his entrails, where they lay on the street after his body was removed.

Under the mast, the headline read 'There'll be another day.' I wrote:

Bloody Sunday was carried out with one objective. The British army decided coldly and deliberately to shoot the risen people off the streets. We were shot with our backs turned, in some cases with our hands in the air as we went to rescue the wounded. We were killed on the barricades, in the courtyards . . . and a few died God knows where. The vultures picked them up first. But the siege goes on. The 808 acres of Bogside, Brandywell and Creggan remain free. Forty of the forty-two entrances to Free Derry remain barricaded.

Sunday, bloody Sunday, was a fine day and a foul day. It was a fine thing to swing down Southway, thousands of us singing, to pick up thousands more of our comrades at the Brandywell. And then to swell through the Bogside where it all began four years ago. Do you remember?

We asked them to ban the Corporation, and they said no, and then they banned it. We demanded houses and they said no, and then they built them. We demanded that Craig should go, and they said no, and then he went. We told the police to leave the Bogside and they said no – running all the way to barracks. And when Sam Devenney died, paying the price of it all, we thought it more than we could bear, but we did. Death was strange then. Death is no stranger now, but the price is higher, and no easier to bear. No one who died was a stranger to us.

What impossible things did we demand this time? That our internees be freed? That we walk on our own street, that the Stormont cesspool be cleaned up – even the SDLP couldn't bear the stink? For the least of these and the best of these, thirteen men were murdered last week. Let it be said of them with pride, they died on their feet and not on their knees. Let it not be said of us they died in vain.

Stay free, brothers and sisters. There'll be another day.

Eamonn knew rightly that I wouldn't be drawing global parallels. I was asked to write the front page because I, and most natives, were wholly bound up in our own grief. We had eyes for none but ourselves. Apart from a snide remark about the SDLP, I got the tone just about right. We were howling silently with pain and looking for comfort from each other, and hope. What hope? We did not expect anyone else to understand. How could anybody else understand that which we did not understand ourselves? That the British government would have its own citizens shot.

I spent a week in Derry after Bloody Sunday, returning daily to the scene of the massacre, retracing the places where men and boys died. It was like doing the Catholic ritual of the Stations of the Cross. John Johnston apart, the others were shot in a fairly straight line that could be traced from Glenfada Park along the barricade, then into the courtyard of the High Flats. My defiant article in the *Starry Plough* had been wrong in one respect: some were indeed shot in the back, one with hands raised, but one man was shot through the buttocks as he tried to get away on hands and knees.

It took years for photographs to emerge. There were two of Michael McDaid. One showed him in his sports jacket, shirt and tie, and flannel trousers, hair cut in a neat back and sides, heading towards Free Derry Corner. He had not managed to get past the soldiers to the bus station. The photo shows him returning, in mid stride, on the pavement right alongside the barricade at Glenfada Park, hands in pockets, looking down as he was passing at a body around which a few men were crouched. Michael does not look worried. Seconds later, Michael was dead. Was he in mid stride because he thought the teenager was stunned, just another casualty of a rubber bullet? Did he halt, realizing that the body was that of a dead boy, not a wounded boy? These are the kinds of questions we ask as we pore over photographs of Bloody Sunday. Michael was shot in the forehead and chest. His back was to the Paras. He was killed by a soldier firing from the Walls above. His was one of the four bodies I had seen being tossed into the armoured car. His mother, who used to make and sell doughnuts from her house, kept his lovely jacket, with the neat bullet hole through it.

There is a photograph which shows Jim Wray sitting cross-legged on the ground in William Street, hands on his head, in a pacifist stance, even as the soldiers sprayed people with gas and water. He would have been one of the last, then, to leave William Street, and one of the last, then, to get into Glenfada Park. There are several photographs that show the body of Jim Wray, and – head almost to Jim's feet – the body of another fellow, on the pavement outside the wicker fence that surrounded the garden of the house where I had found sanctuary. Jim's body was not on the garden path. How could I have seen him lying on the garden path? Several eyewitnesses told the Saville inquiry that they had seen a soldier walk up to Jim, while he lay wounded and alive on the pavement, and fire several bullets into his back. Had Jim and the other fellow inched themselves backwards out of the garden? Patsy remembers Jim lying on the pavement, after the massacre, and that he wore a T-shirt emblazoned with the words 'The Incredible Hulk'.

As with the photographs, it took years for details to emerge about what happened on our side. Though it was our understanding – and belief – for decades afterwards that neither wing of the IRA had engaged with soldiers during the march, and that all weaponry had been taken out of the Bogside the night before the march, we know now that the Official IRA did fire briefly on the soldiers. After John Johnston and Gerry Donaghey were shot, two enraged members of the Official IRA had taken rifles from the boot of a car parked in Glenfada Park – they had been supposed to ship them out the night before, but were late as usual. Given their cowboy record, about which Cathal Goulding had been so worried after I told him about their antics a few months previously, this is entirely believable. The two men ran through alleys towards William Street, and one of them fired a single bullet at soldiers stationed in the ruins of a factory opposite. The thousands of us who had already swept by knew nothing of it. No soldier was hit, but the shot, clearly, would have made them jittery and given substance to the notion which the British army claimed to entertain, that both wings of the IRA were intent on a gun battle that day.

About halfway through the massacre proper, another member of the Official IRA had taken out his revolver and fired a single bullet. He did not know that one of his colleagues had already fired a rifle. He had a revolver on his person, he told the Saville inquiry, because he was a commanding officer, and officers were allowed to carry a weapon at all times. An amateur video shows him inching along a gable wall, gun held before him, then he pokes his wrist and his gun round the corner and blindly fires off a round in the direction of the soldiers and their armoured cars. 'What else could I do?' he told me. 'People were already dying, and I was the only fellow there with a gun. I thought they were going to kill rings round them, and I hoped to stop it a little.' Those of us who know Barricade Joe personally believe him absolutely and sympathize with him: the Derry man who might be blamed for contributing to the mayhem on Bloody Sunday. Relatives of the Bloody Sunday families know who he is. They have not posted his name or that of the other two on their website (nor have they named those soldiers who fired that day, some of whom they have met privately).

Joe was granted anonymity at the Saville inquiry, like the others, and I poked fun at him: 'We'll all be sitting there in the public gallery saying, "Speak up, Joe, we can't hear you."' He collapsed under strain during testimony, and was taken to hospital. He can smile ruefully himself at how the lawyer for the soldiers helped him out of the witness box, laid him on the floor, and comforted him, 'Stay with us, Joe, stay with us.' Before he testified, Joe told me that, on the night of Bloody Sunday, he still had the revolver in his coat pocket when he crowded into my parents' home.

Nothing alters the fact that all of those killed were unarmed.

Peggy Deery was the only woman to be shot on Bloody Sunday: typical of the rotten bad luck that had dogged her as a widowed mother of fourteen. I first met Peggy's family in 1969, when Cathy Harkin and I – patrolling the town as so many Labour Party members did after a small riot, trying to round up teenagers – met her eldest child, thirteen-year-old Paddy, in the city centre. He had, unusually for one so young, wandered far beyond the Bogside turf, and it was nearly midnight. We took him to his home in Creggan. The overcrowded damp cold bungalow reeked of poverty and of the open cancerous sores on his father's back. With Bernadette's help, we gathered enough money to pay most of

Peggy's bills. Our Carmel and her friend Marie were enrolled to scrub the house. Peggy's husband died in 1971, shortly after she gave birth to their fourteenth child. Two others had died – one in utero; one in stillbirth.

On Bloody Sunday, Peggy put on her finest clothes – a black mock-leather wet-look coat and black wet-look boots. She went out to march, as much for her right to a bigger, better house as for the sake of the internees. She was shot in the leg, and the injury left her with a permanent limp. Soldiers called her 'chicken leg' for the rest of her life. Months later, on 19 May, her nephew Manus Deery, aged fifteen, who lived in the street next to the late Michael McDaid, was shot dead – also by soldiers stationed on the Walls. He had been bringing home a fish-and-chip supper. On 9 August, Peggy's birthday, and the first anniversary of internment, Peggy's son Paddy was blinded in one eye by a rubber bullet. In 1987, Paddy, by then in the Provisional IRA and married with three children, died alongside IRA man Eddie McSheffrey when a bomb they were transporting in a car went off prematurely. Peggy, the great survivor and hustler, was broken at last; she took to her bed and died a year later, aged fifty-four.

The first inquiry into the events of 30 January 1972, conducted weeks afterwards by Britain's highest judicial authority, Lord Chief Justice Widgery, and boycotted by most, exonerated the soldiers, with a slight slap on the wrist for some careless shooting. Eddie McAteer remarked of Widgery: 'At least he didn't return a verdict of death by suicide.'

In a rebuke to the British, who claimed that many of the dead carried arms or bore traces of explosives on their hands, Dr Ray McLean said that the autopsies showed that they possessed nothing more than 'the remains of their dinners; meat, potato, and two veg'.

Bloody Sunday altered our entire world. It is not a myth that all of us there were changed for evermore by the experience: it is a fact. It went deep into us. It is in the Derry air. It is limned in our blood. Hundreds of young people joined the IRA in its aftermath. Four hundred and ninety-six people died as a result of political violence in Northern Ireland in 1972, more than in any other year during the Troubles. Bloody Sunday brought us over the brink into full-scale war against the British.

Less than four weeks after Bloody Sunday, I received a call from Washington, inviting me to testify there before the Subcommittee on Europe of the Committee on Foreign Affairs, House of Representatives. America! I said yes. The visa and ticket were waiting at the airport, the hotel pre-paid and booked at the far end.

At Dublin airport I discovered who my travelling companions were to be. Brendan Duddy was there, and we fell on each other's necks, amid a crowd of the great and the good, which is to say, people with more obvious credentials. If Brendan and I were the fish-and-chips brigade, the others were fillet steak. Father Edward Daly, the priest who waved the white hankie on Bloody Sunday as he faced into soldiers who were still shooting, was there. The wealthy businessman Michael Canavan, who had supported John Hume's politics – and, later, those of the Citizens' Defence Association during the Battle of the Bogside – was there. So was Father Denis Faul, the country priest who fought for civil rights through clenched teeth, and Kevin McGorry, executive member of the still extant Northern Ireland Civil Rights Association.

Our eagle had barely landed in Washington on Sunday afternoon before our egos took over. An invitation to address an Irish-American organization had been delivered to hotel reception. They wanted one speaker. We fought for the honour of speaking. We all went along, then found ourselves in a primary-school room, sitting on children's chairs, before an attendance of twenty. We who were used to the company of thousands in the North fought again about who would take on a task beneath our eminence. McGorry was chosen to be the sucker – he was an executive, was he not?

The evening was interminable. The audience wanted to ship guns to the IRA, or drive the Protestants out of the North, or unite Ireland at once. We returned, chastened and aghast, to our hotel. I was having a drink in my room with Brendan, in the early hours, when the receptionist mistakenly put through a call to me that was meant for Brendan's room. It was Father Daly. I explained that Brendan was in the room with me: 'Why don't you come down and join us?' Which is what the Holy Man did. Brendan and I lay on the bed, and Brendan poured a duty-free whiskey for the future Bishop of Derry, who stayed seated, and startled, on a chair.

On Monday we were asked to line a corridor on Capitol Hill. There came a hubbub and kerfuffle, and Senator Edward Kennedy, surrounded by a media scrum, came striding along. He glowed with power. He did not pause to greet us, his chorus line. We trooped into a room after him, and he launched into a peroration on Northern Ireland which was informed, fluent and commanding. (His description of British internment without trial reads, after all these years, like a description of the American detention process in Guantanamo Bay after September 11, 2001: 'The nation that gave the Magna Carta and habeas corpus and due process to the world imprisons hundreds of citizens of Northern Ireland without warrant, charge or trial, often on evidence of the rankest hearsay and deception.')

When Kennedy left the media went with him. The American legislators, stuck with us, maintained considerable composure, though there was the occasional slip, as when Senator Wayne Hays of Ohio declared, 'The more I think about it, the more I can tell you that my ancestors left Derry exactly 200 years ago next month, and I am thankful to the Almighty God that they didn't miss the boat.'

He was addressing Austin Currie, of the SDLP, who had appeared out of nowhere that morning, straight off the plane, at the invitation of the Irish embassy: his appearance pushed the rest of us even further down the chorus line. Mr Frelinghuysen, a New Jersey representative, remarked that Austin was 'not listed as a witness. I am curious how he happened to cross the ocean and happened to be here. Has there been a mass migration across of people who are going to testify voluntarily?' Americans are no dozers: Frelinghuysen had detected the fine hand of Jimmy Breslin, who had testified before Currie took the stand.

In the immediate aftermath of Bloody Sunday, Breslin had published a fierce criticism of the Irish Embassy in Washington, which, in his opinion, was mistakenly cosying up to the Nixon administration, which itself was anxious to maintain good relations with its ally Britain. In the aftermath of Bloody Sunday, Nixon referred to the 'bad Irish'. Breslin wrote that the Irish Ambassador had tried to prevent a meeting between Senator Kennedy and the Irish Minister for Foreign Affairs, Patrick Hillery, lest Kennedy upset the British. 'Mr Warnock's reasoning was that Kennedy is a political opportunist. Beautiful. So were the brothers before him . . . What has the Irish government done to help its own case over here? It has done exactly what Ambassador Warnock has done. It has done eff all.'

In the event, Austin Currie's approach was no different from Kennedy's. Maybe the Irish Embassy thought that we were going to persuade America to help throw the British out of Ireland, leaving the Irish government to foot the bill of unifying the country.

After Austin left, the gallant Committee listened patiently as, one by one, we natives, who had been talking to each other for years, proceeded to bore each other stiff with woeful tales of oppression. When it came to my turn I was determined to show those fellows who were left – American and Irish alike – a thing or two. Just as I got into my stride, a bell rang loudly. The Committee got up and left for a vote. They were gone for more than an hour. The original chairman didn't come back. When I finished saying my piece the Committee didn't ask me a single question. They didn't put questions to Brendan either, nor Father Daly. The three of us had a few more drinks in my bedroom that night.

Next day, as a consolation prize, our delegation was brought to the office of Senator Kennedy. Capitol Hill is so vast we had to use a little underground train to get there. His office was so vast we had to go through three rooms to get to the inner sanctum. His staff lined us up like sheep to have our photographs taken individually with him. Fed up by now with trying to get my photograph into the history books, I declined the opportunity. (Years later, when Eddie Daly was made Bishop, I sent him up rotten for having a huge picture of himself and Ted hanging over the fireplace in his palace.)

Brendan and I hotfooted it out of Washington and up to New York to stay with Jimmy Breslin, Rosemary and their six children in Queen's. The first thing I noticed was that Rosemary took for ever to unload bag after bag after bag of groceries from the boot of her estate car. The massive fridge still looked empty.

Jimmy did not like the high life, preferring the company of cops and dodgy characters on his home turf in Queen's, but it did not take long for us two Derry desperados to find our level – the Lion's Head in the Village, where the journalist Pete Hamill held court most evenings. Among those he courted was a flirtatious Irish woman in civilian dress who turned out to be a nun. Hamill hadn't a hope after I shamelessly sang 'Lake Isle of Inisfree' for Sister Rosemary. She sang 'Guantanamero' to me in the taxi that took us over Brooklyn Bridge. I knew I hadn't a hope when she invited me to lunch in her apartment and served fish because it was Friday, with lashings of iced water.

It was time to get politically serious, so Brendan and I made a foray by subway to Harlem, to meet the Black Panthers. Bernadette had met them years before so we knew we would be welcome, too. Emerging from the station, we saw that everybody in Harlem was black. This was no problem to us, their Irish soul mates, who were also suffering under the jackboot of the oppressor. I led the way into a bar, Brendan being a basically shy kind of fellow with whom foreign travel does not easily sit. The man sitting on a stool of whom I enquired the address of the Black Panthers did not reply. We were Irish, I explained, from the Bogside. Still no reply. I led the way out of the bar, feeling suddenly white, stopped a taxi and asked the driver to take us anywhere he liked as long as he took us out of Harlem. Brendan refused to come with me. His story, to which he still sticks, is that after I left he found the Panthers and got a great reception.

It was in the Lion's Head that I saw a fellow at the end of the bar who stared back: my cousin Jimmy McGuinness, whom I hadn't seen since childhood. Within minutes we were talking about Uncle

Brian, the banished brother of his mother and mine, and it was Jimmy who told me that the mysterious crime which our Uncle Brian had committed in America, for which he served twenty years in jail, was the murder of a woman. Brian had died in London in 1970, Jimmy said, and Jimmy's father had buried him. Uncle Brian had been working in London while I was there in 1963, 1964 and 1968. I could have found him through Jimmy's father, but I didn't know the man was in London at all until Jimmy told me in the Lion's Head. Uncle Bill had never said so, nor Aunt Sadie, nor Jimmy's sister Sheila.

The Stormont government was abolished in March 1972, and the British instituted direct rule, which was to last until 2000. In the absence of unionist control over the British army – which they no longer totally regarded as their army – loyalists had formed a paramilitary arm, the Ulster Defence Association, whose violence was directed totally against Catholics. Many Catholics reluctantly accepted the Provisional IRA as their protectors against both the British and the loyalists.

The Official IRA was disbanded soon after Bloody Sunday, and it was not before time. It was bad enough that they set off a car bomb in Aldershot, England, headquarters of the Paras, which killed five women cleaners at the base, one male gardener and the regiment's Catholic chaplain, a soldier. The deed which finally prompted Cathal Goulding to disband the organization was the capture and killing of the Derry youth known as Ranger Best, on 21 May, two days after the killing of Manus Deery.

Ranger Best was a nineteen-year-old from the Creggan estate who had joined the British army's Royal Irish Rangers as a boy soldier, had never served in the North, and was home on leave from his posting in Germany. He hung out for six days with his pals at the barricades and disregarded warnings by the Officials to leave the town. His pals saw him as an ordinary Derry fellow; the Officials did not. They picked him up, eventually, put a hood over his head, and shot him dead on waste ground near William Street.

I was sleepless that night, and shocked, and had a fair idea who might have been ruthless and callous and stupid enough to have killed a local boy. Just after dawn, I walked uphill to a 'safe' house in Creggan where Official IRA volunteers on the run often spent the night. The man who opened the front door was in his underpants. There were several men sleeping on the floor in states of undress. The place stank of stale socks. The windows were closed and the curtains drawn. I knew two of the men very well indeed, and one of them was a fellow I had long thought trigger-happy, to put it mildly. He was apt to boast about his exploits with a gun.

The men were taken aback at my rage. They could not see that the killing of Ranger Best would cause revulsion in the community. They could not see that they could have picked him up, put the fear of God in him and given him a couple of hours to leave town or else. As far as they were concerned, he was a British soldier. I was shocked at how cold they were because I had had good times with some of them. I walked back downhill, caught the bus to work in Dublin, and that night met Cathal Goulding in Bowe's pub. I told him the names of everybody in the room whom I had recognized, and emphasized one man in particular. If Goulding did nothing else, he should drum this guy out of the IRA.

The reaction to Ranger Best's murder had already started: in the afternoon, several hundred women had marched on the Derry headquarters of Official IRA/Sinn Féin. Twenty-five priests and Bishop William Farren concelebrated at his funeral mass. Goulding called a ceasefire three weeks later. The killing of Ranger Best had added to the increasing unease of the Dublin Marxist leadership that its left-wing politics were being subsumed into paramilitary activity which provoked sectarian confrontation in the North. Hopes for revolution through civil rights had long since died.

With the Officials gone, and the Derry Labour Party soon to disband, those of us who adhered to left-wing politics were left standing on the sidelines. That vacuum was filled by the Provisional IRA and by John Hume's party, the SDLP, led by Gerry Fitt, which aspired to a United Ireland by means of unarmed nationalism.

The Provisional IRA had the republican paramilitary field

effectively to itself. Its leader in Derry was twenty-one-year-old Martin McGuinness, who lived in Elmwood Street, the street next to ours. I had interviewed Martin after Bloody Sunday, in a bedroom in our house. The article, which named him and was accompanied by his photograph, was published in the *Irish Times* in April 1972. In it I portrayed Martin tenderly enough. He was more than the neighbour's child: when his mother, Peggy, first came to Derry from Donegal, to work in the shirt factory, she had lodged with my father's sister and her large family. She and my mother were – and remain – friends.

I quoted the ever-prescient Jimmy Breslin, who did not see the tall, slim, blond, curly-haired youth as a dictator. 'Jeez, that boy would be hot on the coast. Can you see him, six feet tall, in a dinner jacket, raising funds?'

The neighbourhood had been astonished when it first became known that Martin was in the IRA. He had grown up so quietly that it was said approvingly of him that he had the makings of a priest. In the interview Martin told me his mother was 'panic-stricken' when she found out he was in the IRA. 'A few months after I joined she found a belt and beret in my bedroom, and there was a big row. She and my father told me to get out of it, and for the sake of peace I said I would and they calmed down. But now they have to accept it. They've seen the British army in action and they know I'd no choice.'

His mother, though, had started smoking again, 'which she hasn't done in years . . . I know her health has failed and she's always worrying about me. If I'm not around to tell her myself, I send word that I'm all right. I don't discuss my business with her and she doesn't ask.'

Peggy McGuinness told me that she was worried about Martin giving up his job as a trainee butcher. 'His trade's been interrupted. His father is a welder, his brothers are at the carpentering and bricklaying, but what will become of Martin? That's why they'll have to get an amnesty, so's he can get back to work and not always be on the run.'

Sitting on the edge of the bed in his hobnailed boots – the

footwear of a fellow on the run – Martin exuded sadness as he reviewed how his life had changed in the previous two and a half years. He had been an eighteen-year-old stone-thrower in August 1969. He was now Officer Commanding of the Derry Provisional IRA. He still sometimes joined in the riots. 'It relieves the pressure and it's a way of being with my mates, the ones who have not joined the movement, and I feel ordinary again.'

When Martin joined the IRA in 1969 – by invitation – Sinn Féin had been one party, with one armed wing. (Its arms consisted of three guns.) He defected to the Provos after the split because the Stickies:

. . . wouldn't give us any action. For three months we attended policy and training lectures in a house in the Bogside. You could see the soldiers just settling into Derry, not being too worried about the stone-throwing. Occasionally the Stickies gave out Molotov cocktails which wouldn't even go off . . . It seemed to me that behind all the politics and marching it was plain as daylight that there was an army in our town, in our country, and that they weren't there to give out flowers.

The IRA took care, he said, not to harm innocent civilians:

. . . but sometimes mistakes are made. There was an explosion in Derry some time ago and I read afterwards that a man had been trapped in the basement. He lost a part of his leg. Then you read that he's a cyclist and you feel really sad.

The worst I ever felt was Bloody Sunday. I wandered about stunned, with people crying and looking for their relatives and I thought of all that guff about honour between soldiers. The British army knew right well we wouldn't fight them with all those thousands of people there, so they came in and murdered the innocent. I used to worry about being killed before that day, but now I don't think about death at all . . . you know how much life has changed when you're having a Republican's tea – a bottle of orange and a bap – in the back of a car, just a few minutes from your own home.

He was not, the day I interviewed him, the articulate man he is now. His naivety and idealism in 1972 were affecting, his vision uncomplicated – simplistic, even. He knew where he wanted to go, but not how to get there.

I want a United Ireland where everyone has a good job and enough to live on . . . The Officials [were] all views and no support. I wish we [the Provisionals] were getting more press coverage for our political beliefs, but we don't have the talkers in our ranks . . . I have a lot of respect for Bernadette Devlin, but I think maybe people are too greedy. I'd be willing to sweep the roads in my world, and it wouldn't seem like a bad job if they got the same wages as everybody else, but do you not think now that people are just too greedy? Somebody always wants to make a million. Anyway, before you can try, you have to get this country united. We'd make sure that Protestants are fairly treated.

After 1972, I never again spoke to Martin McGuinness about his role in the IRA.

Chapter Eighteen

A steady stream of Northerners began to venture South to have a closer look at the capital of the United Ireland to which, one distant day, we separated brethren aspired. Unlike me, who had a secure place in the women's movement, Northerners were not always welcome in Southern society. Our accent alone marked us out, and our rapid-fire way of talking was associated with war. Many of these tourists and transplanted Northerners stayed overnight in Patsy's spare bedroom, and she, exceptionally, made them at ease. It helped that she had stayed in the North, in our house, and had come to see us, I believed, through our own self-regarding eyes.

One night Patsy turned over her room, which contained the only double bed in the house, to a honeymooning couple from Belfast. Being in the IRA, the new husband was not in steady work, and it was my pleasure to treat the newlyweds to dinner in Nico's, a great Italian restaurant, where an added attraction was a man who played piano. I invited a lively journalist friend to join us, so that the happy couple would have the further joy of meeting a real, uncontaminated Irishwoman who had never been to the North. She was great company, and it was a grand night, and when it was over we were all astonished to find ourselves, once we stepped back out into the street, surrounded by Special Branch officers. They were arresting me, they said, for not paying the dinner bill. I waved the receipt, to no avail, because by then a waiter was dancing around me in a rage, speaking Italian, and another of the restaurant's staff had taken off his shoe and was trying to thump us.

The cops put me in their wagon and minutes later I was standing before a garda sergeant in Pearse Street station. I again produced the receipt. The sergeant took it and put me in a cell. Two hours later he gave me back the receipt and released me without charge.

When I got back to Hatch Place, Patsy was in the living room with the husband. I told them my story, but they were not as interested as I thought they might have been. They greeted it with silence, in fact. I asked the man where his wife was. She's upstairs, he said shortly. Where was my friend, the journalist? Upstairs, he said abruptly. Silence resumed. Into that silence fell the unmistakable sound of Patsy's bed shaking vigorously above our heads. The husband's leg was drumming like a jackhammer. He kept one hand jammed into his pocket. 'Does your lady friend upstairs, the journalist, know that I'm in the IRA?' he asked me. I had not, in point of fact, told either Patsy or my journalist lady friend that he was. This was a honeymoon, after all, not a political foray into the deep South. And it was news to me that my lady friend was other than a raving heterosexual, with a track record to prove it. I had sensed, once, at a meeting about feminism in Belfast, that the brand-new wife upstairs had a mild crush on a woman of my acquaintance, but that had become practically par for the course for women who were discovering liberation.

I excused myself to go to the toilet. I knocked on Patsy's bedroom door, opened it slightly, and whispered urgently to the journalist within, 'For Christ's sake, her husband's in the IRA.' By the time I came out of the toilet, she was out of the house. Downstairs once more, I remarked that I was tired and was going to bed. Patsy remarked icily that she was a little tired herself. The husband said he was tired, too, bade us good night and made his way up to his wife. They were gone before Patsy or I got up next morning. The hostess with the mostest was still a little icy over breakfast. The lady-friend journalist, when I got in touch with her, was laughingly dismissive. 'You Northerners are too uptight. And he should be grateful that his wife won't die wondering. I did him a favour.' The couple are still married. They dote on their grandchildren.

The Northern stream through Patsy's house became a flow. My sister Carmel and her two friends stayed in Patsy's house while they did an extra course in hairdressing. My cousin and some of his pals, desperately seeking work because of a prolonged strike in Derry, stayed with us. Eamonn and Mary stayed with us. Men from the disbanded wing of the Official IRA stayed with us. Marie and her partner from Sweden stayed with us. A bohemian woman who lived down the little street with a violent husband occasionally stayed a few hours with us, once coming in through the ground-floor window, while he, hatchet in hand, came through the front door. Patsy's friend, the historian John A. Murphy, stayed with us. Nearly twenty years later, as the Northern war dragged on, he shunned me in the Merriman Summer School and called me a 'Provo-lover'. The house was often full of directors and presenters from RTÉ, and actors who followed Patsy all the way home.

One night after the pub closed, and me happy as a lark, I knocked on Patsy's bedroom door, and put my head round it to wish her an exuberant good night. I didn't even get a glimpse of the man – and sure what did it matter? Next morning she gave me notice to quit. I was devastated. Two years in paradise had come to an end.

The first night I spent in the flat to which I moved, to live alone, was awful. I was twenty-eight years old, and I did not know how to cook the pork chop that I'd bought for my solitary meal. I didn't have my own telephone. When the communal phone rang in the hallway, and someone knocked on my door to say it was June Levine, I poured my miserable heart out to her. Get into a taxi and bring the pork chop to my house, she said. I went round there like a shot. Her children were in bed asleep. She cooked the chop expertly, then put me into the bath. It was a bubble bath, scented with oils. She lit candles round it, and sat on the edge of the bath, talking to me. She wrapped me in fluffy heated towels and put me to bed.

A few nights later, on the bus home after talking to a group of university students, a graduate student tapped me on the shoulder and invited herself back to my flat. It was lovely. The flat was lovely. I felt lovely. Our affair ended the afternoon she joined me in a hotel lounge after I had completed an interview with an Italian television news crew. The presenter, deeply tanned and bearded and gorgeous, put a flirtatious finger into the tear above the knee of her jeans. She smiled. On the way home, I struck her full in the face. I had never hit anyone before, and never have since. I was rather less sweepingly condemnatory after that when talking about male violence towards women.

I met her again, from time to time, but I was watchful and terrified and felt sexually inferior when any man joined us. In every other respect I enjoyed male company (so long as I met them outside their homes and didn't have to suffer the sight of them sitting idly while the woman of the house tended to the company). It was the nature of my job that I moved in a wide circle of men. Meeting men outside their homes was like taking a holiday from feminism – and from women. Men did not talk about the plight of the single mother, or the washing piling up, or the parent needing to be nursed.

Senator Paddy Wilson was the kind of man to whom I enjoyed talking. I met him a few days before a local election in June 1973, which I was covering, and we stood smoking cigarettes outside City Hall, Belfast. He was the election agent for Gerry Fitt, and he had the jaunty air of a working-class man whose fortunes have taken a turn for the better. His white raincoat matched his pale face, and he wore his hat at an angle. He gave me tips for horses, and I gave him stick about his leader – and his hat. That night he was stabbed to death by loyalist paramilitaries, as was the woman he had been drinking with in a bar – Irene Andrews, a twenty-five-year-old civil servant, a Protestant and a member of the Northern Ireland ballroom dancing team who had taken part in the BBC's televised ballroom dancing competition *Come Dancing*. Thirty years later I met his killer. I got on grand with him.

I was terrified of being killed. Loyalist paramilitaries had started picking up Protestants whom they judged disloyal, and Catholics at random, taking them to back rooms in their drinking clubs and torturing them to death. They called these venues 'romper rooms' after a popular children's TV programme. The Shankill Butchers gang had also sprung up. Its members' speciality was the capture, slow torture and death by a thousand cuts of whichever Catholic they could snatch as they cruised the streets of Belfast. Teeth were pulled, flesh sliced off by the inch – a butcher's knife was used – and victims were hung upside down, still alive, moaning and

Myself, my mother and
Nuala at Rossville Street,
after the usual Saturday riot
against the British Army, 1970.
(*Photo by Marie Falksten*)

In Derry, 1978, during rioting which followed the shooting of Denis Heaney, IRA, by the British Army. (*Photo on this page and opposite, top, by Marie Falksten.*)

My mother, Lily, in 1969 and myself in 1983. My mother has always had
the best hair in our family – something she never lets us forget.

Mammy and me, at home in Beechwood Street, 1974.

Clockwise from me: Carmel, Paddy, Hugh, Muireanna and Nuala, 1990.

The cream of Irish women gathered together in 2001 at the joint sixtieth birthday party of Maeve Binchy and Mary Maher. I am seated on the ground in front, at Maeve Binchy's feet. Also included are Mary Kenny (*front row, far left*), Mary Holland (*second row, fourth from left*), Mary Maher (*front row, third from right*), Sylvia Meehan (behind Maeve) and Nuala O'Faolain (right-hand side of the picture, to the rear, beneath the green bush).

Being embraced by Belfast woman Mary McAleese, at her inauguration as President of Ireland, 1997.

At Staffordshire University to receive my honorary Doctor of Letters degree, 1998.

Life at sixty. I run an open house and I never know who will turn up.

Patsy Murphy (*below*) is a regular visitor.

I share a front yard with my neighbour Gregg (*see next page*), and we are easy in each other's company.

begging for mercy. Mercy meant death by bullet. Bullets were seldom used.

When news of the romper rooms and the Shankill Butchers broke I never crossed the border, by bus or car, without swallowing a Valium prior to the journey from the British army's first check-point at Aughnacloy village to the safety of nationalist Derry, all the while fingering the stash I had in my pocket, to be taken if I was captured. They were my father's tablets, prescribed to keep him calm and happy in his dreadful physical imprisonment, as he deteriorated to a paraplegic state. An awful lot of people living in the North were by then on Valium, prescribed free of charge by the National Health Service, to help them as their nerves crumbled. My father was not in that category, and the stash I stole did not deprive him.

I did not tell anyone. My cowardice and hysteria were my own private business.

In late 1973 I met a much-travelled woman who was born gay. Angelina preferred the exclusive company of women. My social life narrowed to the bone, as I fell into a lesbian ghetto at the age of twenty-nine, in 1973, until 1977. Angelina had charm. She was daring and edgy. She took one look at my record collection and swiftly replaced it with black Americana. She persuaded me to buy a car, a bright-yellow Datsun. The night I took possession of it, I was so excited that I rose from my bed, drove to the west of Ireland, saw the dawn rise and returned in time for work. She insisted on maintaining her independence by renting a room elsewhere, in a shared house. She was a naturally skilled cook. She despised frocks and skirts, so I always wore jeans in her company, though I drew the line at a trouser suit – I was afraid of looking butch. She had a silk trouser suit that she wore with panache. She wore jeans otherwise – and Doc Marten boots when no woman did. After succumbing to her spell, I never again had a proper wardrobe. The one mark which she left on me, which I have always regretted, is that I virtually gave up frocks.

The relationship had hardly started when I knew I was in trouble.

She took drugs and stole from shops. I was in a dilemma: she liked wine or beer, lots of it, with every meal, and I couldn't afford to buy alcohol in the quantities she liked. However, I did like, very much, the great wines she stole and placed on the table – a fact to which she tartly referred when I, initially, objected to her method of producing such abundance.

Shoplifting was a mania among the women she hung out with, many of them gifted, all of them finding difficulty in getting a job in those times of high unemployment. It was excused by Angelina and her friends as a strike against a system that doubly discriminated against them: as women and as lesbians. I could well understand their terror of the straightjacketed workplace, though I think the prospect of being bored in such surroundings was also a big factor. These women had tasted freedom in the movement, and a frugal lifestyle was a small price to pay for it. They were wildly generous with their shoplifted spoils: one doting couple often gave me jars of the best coffee.

At a trade exhibition in Dublin, the women spread out and helped themselves liberally. I lifted a toothbrush. As I walked away from the stand, a garda tapped me on the shoulder. I blustered that I had not yet left the premises and that I intended to pay. I was weak with shame and fear. The garda looked down at me and said, 'Now, Nell . . .' I brought the toothbrush back and paid for it. The near-ruinous experience of being caught shoplifting – outright theft – left me homophobic. I blamed the lesbians for my behaviour. I blamed everybody but myself – just as the lesbian women did. I hated the term 'lesbian'. And I came to appreciate the meaning of the term Garda Síochána – guardians of the peace – and the subtle distinctions they made between law and order.

One night Angelina asked me to bring a candle into the bedroom. I did, and I lit it. She asked me to bring in a carrot. I scraped it before offering it to her to eat. 'You don't get it, do you?' she asked. I recoiled when I did. She told me then that she often picked up male strangers, the bigger and more brutish the better. She had been sexually abused as a child. I had no idea how to cope – child sexual abuse was not talked about in the 1970s. I reached a low point the night I tried to emulate her and asked a taxi driver if he wanted sexual intercourse. He took the fare first, then clambered into the back seat and lay on top of me. I was out of there in seconds, filled with self-loathing, the deed not done.

This woman took a great deal of pleasure in seducing other women and made no effort to conceal it. I knew that they meant nothing to her emotionally. For a while I competed with her, though I did not go to bed with any of my 'conquests'. At that period, a lot of women flirted with lesbianism. There would be a party every Saturday night when women danced and kissed and swapped partners with, at times, deliberate and casual cruelty. I knew I was debasing myself even as I simultaneously queened it, cashing in on the fact that I was the only one in the ghetto with a satisfying job, and that I had a growing measure of fame, due to a successful print journalism career and a burst of television and radio appearances: women of all ages and dispositions used to fondle my Afro hair for the fun and thrill of it. Publicly, I was wildly popular and feisty. Privately, I was pathetic.

Derry was a sanctuary at that time. No sex, no romance, no lesbian ghetto – just a straightforward war. On Christmas Eve 1973, I gave Angelina a present of snails and a snail-cooking set, and went to my parents' house for the season. At dawn, after Christmas, bulky soldiers with big guns invaded our little house, and we had to sit there in our dressing gowns. I wrote about it later in the *Irish Times*:

On Boxing Day, the family in number 14 (Ettie Deeney's) noticed that the key to their front door had been removed from the lock, shortly after a British army patrol had passed. On New Year's Eve, shortly after another foot patrol passed, the key to number 16 (Annie Harrigan's) was missing, and also to our house, number 8.

My mother rang the army and asked them to return the keys. As a matter of fact, said an officer, one of his foot patrol had indeed found two keys lying in the gutter at midnight. He would send them down. A six-man foot patrol, in jungle fatigues, and with blackened faces, carrying loaded rifles, came to return the keys they had found in the darkened street. One of the keys fitted number 14. We rang the army and asked how the key to number 14, which had been missing for a week, had been found alongside the key to number 8, which had been missing for a day, and how they had found them all at the exact same spot – and where, by the way, was the key to number 16?

No comment from the army.

Next morning at 7 a.m., the foot patrol appeared in the back lane armed with a ladder, and they climbed over the wall and into all the yards. They were looking for something, they said.

That night, a friend who was coming to our house was stopped, arrested and questioned for two hours about the occupants. On the following day the army appeared in our street at 8.30 a.m., rang our bell and said they wished to search my parents' house. 'Why didn't you use your copy of my key and not be getting me out of my bed?' my mother asked. They came in and went out to the back yard with their tracker dog, and he sniffed around the bushes. Then he peed in our dog's kennel, which our dog could do nothing about, the affront having been committed courtesy of the Special Powers Act.

One soldier stood at the front door with his gun and refused access to all visitors. One officer stood at the kitchen door and surveyed the family. Two soldiers with guns searched the bedrooms, and their leashed dog sniffed about. They read my books and my letters and went through the wardrobe and under the mattresses and prodded stuffed teddy bears. They read my sister's love letters, briefly. Then they climbed up into the roof space where no one had been for years and obediently reported, after my mother enquired, that one slate was loose.

I asked the officer which regiment he represented and he refused to answer. Special Powers. Who were we and we had to answer. Special Powers. The officer called us 'love'. Special Powers.

The two soldiers came down and went into the bathroom, and looked under the bath plug. They searched the cornflakes. They looked into the washing machine. They examined the refrigerator. They looked up the chimney in the kitchen. 'Have a titter of wit,' said my mother. 'Would I have gelignite up there and me with the fire lit?'

Would I get up from the sofa while they searched the cushions? They looked in the teapot. 'Have a titter of wit,' said my mother. They had once found an Armalite in a man's wooden leg, said the officer. 'Have a titter of wit,' said my mother, and she went out to the bathroom where I saw her giggle.

The two soldiers looked through her books. 'Those are my debt books and they are private,' said my mother. 'Nothing is private,' said the officer. Special Powers. 'Kindly return them in the order in which the debt men come,' said my mother.

The officer picked up a shiny cartridge from the mantelpiece. 'You wouldn't take an empty shell,' said my mother. 'Sure, have a titter of wit.' The soldier noted the number of the old shell. 'The brass in that cartridge is as good as the brass in your neck,' said my mother.

The two soldiers were looking through the sugar bowl. We were in dressing gowns, and they were in jungle fatigues and big boots. We had tea and toast, and they had Special Powers and guns. The soldiers were examining my mother's letters. 'Would you do that in your own mother's house?' asked my mother. 'This isn't my mother's house,' said one soldier, continuing to read.

They examined the telephone in the hall. 'Is it working?' the officer asked. 'Do you think it's an ornament? Have a titter of wit,' said my mother.

A soldier removed the ferns from the vase and shone his torch inside. He replaced the ferns one by one. 'You would make a good housekeeper,' said my mother.

They asked her to sign a form stating that no damage had been caused. The soldier wrote, incorrectly, that the search had commenced at 9.55 a.m., and he neglected to say when it had ended. 'Sure they haven't a titter of wit,' said my mother.

Then they removed themselves and their boots and their guns and their Special Powers and their dog from our house. On the way out they wished us a Happy New Year. That night the Irish police raided the house of Derry boys who had been living across the border in Donegal. That night, also, the British army stopped my friend again and asked him who lived in our house.

And the next night the soldiers with their guns and blackened faces came round the houses in our street and asked us to list the occupants in each house. Otherwise it was a peaceful Christmas season.

Our house in Derry was raided often. I was frightened, every time, and feared their huge rifles. Shots had been fired in people's homes. If the soldiers came at an hour when we were fully dressed, we feigned indifference while they clunked through the house. One of us was usually allowed to accompany a soldier when he rampaged through the bedrooms, to ensure that he didn't plant evidence. 'Eat your dinner,' my mother would insist to those seated at the table. This was no mean achievement in a room full of hungry armed soldiers. 'Shut up and eat,' my mother whispered once, when we pointed out that she had made gravy for the roast chicken out of the chocolate powder reserved for my father's evening cup of cocoa.

Many households suffered far, far more than we ever did. In the next street, Peggy McGuinness, mother of Martin, stood up to a woman soldier who wished to give her a body search. Peggy would not let the woman touch her. She said, 'You're bigger than I am, and younger than I am, and in a fight you'll bate me, but fight me you'll have to, because I am not letting you lay a finger on me.' The officer in charge told the woman soldier to drop the matter. If you resist them, they'll back down, was Peggy's counsel. But what if they didn't?

One officer was known in the area to be more polite than any other when it came to house searches. Paddy Ashdown, who later went on to become leader of the Liberal Democrats in Britain, knocked on doors to bid a personal farewell to each householder when he finished his tour of duty in Derry. 'Right enough, he was a gentleman,' my mother reflected with a grin. Peggy was formal with him. 'I just said, "God bless you," the way I'd say to anyone.'

In March 1974 Eimer Philbin Bowman held a thirtieth birthday party lunch for me and presented me with a round white delph plate on which was engraved the blindfolded statue of justice, a huge compliment to the column 'In the Eyes of the Law', which I had then been doing for nearly two years. The column's strength was that I reported verbatim the remarks of the judiciary. The judges often showed themselves to be a vain, abusive lot, lording it over the poor who came before them.

Emboldened by pre-lunch gin, and wine with the food, I asked Mary Robinson a question about her sex life. 'If you discuss the absurd, you end up sounding absurd,' she said. 'Think about it, Nell, the positions people have to adopt – all those arms and legs flying about.' She was laughing and dignified and firm. I began to understand that loads of people did not discuss in graphic terms their own – or other people's – sex lives, and I felt much less burdened about the unspoken details of my own.

That thirtieth-birthday lunch was the last time I was invited to such gatherings, by Eimer or by anybody in Dublin. It was not that anyone deliberately cut me off. It was the deepening, hardening, murderous war in the North that came between me and most people in the South. People died by the dozen from bombs placed in pubs and restaurants and hotels; or individually in lonely places; or as they went innocently about their work because that work marked them as unionist/British/nationalist collaborator; or Catholic or Protestant or unionist or nationalist.

Many people that I had counted as comrades and colleagues, and in some cases, friends, stopped talking to me. They were, for the most part, members and associates of Official Sinn Féin, and they conducted themselves towards me with the fury of zealots. I was *persona non grata*, even to those who had partaken of my mother's hospitality. She never saw them again, but I had to – many of them were journalists. I refused to condemn the neighbour's child, therefore I was a murderous Provo, in thought if not in deed. If I could not talk about the North, I could not talk at all, and it was easier to be with people who had a faint glimmer of understanding – or with ideologically unbound feminists who tried to avoid such discussions. I gradually lost social contact with most of those who lived outside the ring of sulphur.

The North was brought to a standstill that May of 1974 by the Ulster Workers Council. The UWC was an ad hoc group of Protestant workers that closed down industry and vital supply services in protest against Britain's latest desperate political wheeze.

It had been agreed, at the Sunningdale conference in England, that an unelected Executive would be appointed to rule the North, comprising unionists and nationalists who had agreed to share power and, crucially, to include an all-Ireland dimension in their governance. This, ultimately, was the basis of the Good Friday Agreement, 1998, which brought an end to the war between Britain and the IRA, but it was foisted on us in 1974 without an election to determine its merits, and loyalists understandably, and rightly, resisted it. Their vigilante methods of resistance caused terror to Catholics: loyalists set up roadblocks in every town and village, and armed masked men decided who could pass freely. Buildings and cars were burned, and people were killed. In the South, car bombs planted by loyalists killed thirty-three people in Dublin and Monaghan.

The strike showed where Ulster's true strength lay: essential services such as gas, water and electricity were controlled by the majority Protestant community. The British government stood idly by, paralysed and stunned: its army did not have the will or strength to resist the workforce and was pitifully lacking in skills to keep essential services functioning.

The power stations were being run down to the point of no return, we were told, in what became hourly bulletins on the BBC. The supply of electricity became erratic and intermittent; areas ran out of gas for cooking and heating; there were queues for petrol. The weather, luckily, was fine, and some people took to having makeshift barbecues in their back yards; in our house, we were reduced to candlelight, and cooking on a small camping stove, fuelled by paraffin. My sister Nuala, incredibly, made her determined way to work every morning, to the headquarters of local government, passing through loyalist blockades. My mother insisted that I take hot baths several times a day, using to the full the two hours of daily electricity which was allocated to the town: 'Wash yourself while there is time.'

The British Prime Minister Harold Wilson decided to address us on a Saturday night, and the lights went out and the television set died just as he came on the airwaves. We turned on the battery-operated radio and listened in the gloomy dark while he referred to the people of Northern Ireland as 'spongers'. It was the only occasion in the history of Northern Ireland when the entire people rose up as one, united in pure rage. Who? Us? Spongers?

The strike ended after fourteen days when the newly appointed Executive resigned. The war deepened.

The stories from the romper rooms got worse. During the course of an afternoon on 24 July 1974, while her six-year-old daughter cried in an adjoining room, Ann Ogilby was placed in a chair, blindfolded and battered in the face with a brick – by women. It was thought that she had been having an affair while her loyalist paramilitary partner was in jail. Afterwards the women who beat her to death went for a drink and on to a disco. Another Protestant woman, mistaken for a Catholic, was brought to a drinking den and beaten to death with billiard cues. A Catholic woman who drank too much one carefree night went to a loyalist party, and was killed in the bedroom while women and men alike drank downstairs, knowing what was going on.

I used the car to take my father out on trips at the weekend, which gave respite to my mother. He loved the car. I was sadly conscious that he had been cut down just after the last training lesson before taking his driving test. I keep his provisional driver's licence among my family heirlooms. On the trips around Donegal, he used a medicinal bottle to pee into. There was no embarrassment at all between us when he performed the intimate act; it just made me sadder still to think of how, in my youth, he would glower and darken when there was kissing on television. All those years of angst and worry and anger and suspicion about the sexual development of his teenage children might never have happened, so easy were we as we drove through Donegal, father and daughter, side by side.

He liked me to drive fast, so I did, when there was a wide, open road. But even as I did, I was aware that if a child or a dog stepped out I would have to brake, and maybe my father's head would bounce off the dashboard and he would die, then my mother would not have to carry the burden of his illness, and neither would he.

He was not embarrassed when I had to push and pull and shove him out of the car into his wheelchair, when we stopped for refreshments. It gave him pleasure to put his hand into his trouser pocket and bring out his wallet and lay it on the table to pay for what we might order. He insisted, often, that I have a drink – a glass of wine, or beer with the meal. This was the man who had offered me a Babycham at Muireanna's wedding, when I was sixteen, then cried by the fireplace that night because his daughter drank alcohol. He would smile now as I drank, a father with his grown daughter, on a day out together. For a treat, I sometimes gave him half of the Valium tablet I carried everywhere with me, in case of emergencies. We travelled in companionable silence, listening to the radio, looking at the places to which he had dreamed of driving. He saw the funny side of a visit we made to a holy well, when a priest happened upon the scene to find me on my hands and knees. I had spilled my father's afternoon quota of pills after drawing water from the well with which he was to wash them down. We often stayed out until the moon had risen. Sometimes, if I was working on a story in Donegal, I would bring him with me; he would sit patiently in the car, peeing into his bottle when necessary.

Sometimes, I would have a woman friend with me, up from Dublin for the weekend, and I worried at what might be going through his head, but there was nothing I could do. I could hardly say, 'I'm not sleeping with this woman, Daddy.' That would mean I might be sleeping with the other one. I couldn't mention it at all – it would have been cruel: me, with the power of speech and movement, versus him, helpless and speechless. I reasoned to myself that if such a situation was upsetting for him he would have declined to go out on a trip. I argued with myself that he would settle for anything, just to get out of the bed and the house, and that reasoning made me feel cruel because I was now mistress of the master's fate. I called him Kojak when he removed the cap that kept his head warm and ran his hand – as best he could – over his completely bald skull. I exulted that my mother had had a day off.

★

I managed to hold on to feminist sanity in Dublin through involvement in a radical feminist group called Irishwomen United, which was formed in 1975. Dozens of us met every Sunday afternoon, for years, in a free-thinking ferment of ideas. It was a relief to be in a group that did not fear discussion of the North. Before Irishwomen United, in the dog days of the remains of the Women's Liberation Movement, Ireland, we had taken the struggle to the heartland of the Dublin working class, Ballyfermot, then the biggest public housing estate in Ireland. The local cinema was hired and a broad platform of speakers invited. I was delighted that Bernadette Devlin accepted. The other speakers pulled out when they heard of this, fearful of her sympathy to republicanism and armed struggle (which at that time amounted to no more than a refusal to condemn the IRA in the wake of Bloody Sunday). We spoke to a small audience in the echoing, cold and dusty cinema. The hard-pressed working women of Ballyfermot were simply not interested in the revolutionary tourists who had come to spout theory. The afternoon was notable for two other things: such interest as the media showed was concentrated on trying (and failing) to obtain a photograph of Bernadette's daughter, and the WLMI stuck me with the bill when the cinema owner demanded cash up front. I wrote a cheque that cost me a month's wages. The others did not donate a single penny.

It was courageous of Irishwomen United to dip their toes in the inexplicable, dirty political water of the warring North. There were times when I gave up explaining the North to people in the South, and times when I gave up explaining it to myself. You had to live there to fully understand, and I did not. For instance, how did my sister Carmel put up with what was happening to her? While businesses were being blown up on a daily basis, she had decided at the age of twenty-one to set up her own hairdressing business with two equally young colleagues. They had persuaded their parents to give them the seed corn: £300 each for the renting and refurbishing of premises. They were blown out of their premises several times – 'but we always got a warning'. The warning was occasionally less than five minutes' notice. When I went to watch an evacuation once, I found the three young women out on the street, putting the finishing touches to the hair of their clients: putting in and taking out rollers, combing out, wrapping towels ever tighter round the dripping tresses of those who had been whisked from under the tap. They managed, despite all, to buy their own place. Fellows who were on the run continued to come in for a haircut.

Irishwomen United never actually worked out a coherent position on the North, and indeed the founding charter of the group did not even pay lip service to what was known as 'the national question', but it was courageous of these feminists even to talk about it. Talking could cost jobs and damage careers, at that time, in the Republic. It even threatened the cohesion of our movement, as witness the somewhat stiff tone of reproach in a letter by Betty Purcell, a radio and television producer, and herself a member of Irishwomen United, to the editors of our magazine, *Banshee*:

It is simplistic in the extreme to accuse Republican women of being 'distracted and divided' or 'side-tracked' by the struggle for National Independence. Ireland's economic backwardness has been caused by Britain's political and economic stranglehold over her. This has led to the inordinately strong position of the Catholic Church in education and social legislation (such as contraception and divorce). To see the struggle for the liberation of women and the struggle of national liberation as mutually exclusive shows a complete lack of understanding of the effects of the latter on the former. No one could deny that Irishwomen are in a far worse position than their English or American counterparts, and this is obviously caused by Ireland's domination by Britain.

None of this undermines the need for women to rely on their strength rather than that of their Socialist or Republican brothers, in fighting their oppression. In the words of James Connolly – 'There is none so fit to break the chains as those who wear them.'

That letter appeared in the same issue which reported that members of a Dublin branch of Provisional Sinn Féin were distributing leaflets alleging that abortion was a 'British plot' to decrease the production of children for Ireland.

Irishwomen United occupied the offices of the Federated Union of Employers, demanding the immediate adoption of equal pay for work of equal value. When we entered the FUE building, we were quickly locked into one room and warned that the police would be called if we did not agree to leave quietly and immediately. We disagreed and remained in the building until the employers finally agreed to meet us in their boardroom. The discussion took a bizarre twist about shoes – they could be made more cheaply abroad, or something, and therefore women had to take lower wages in Ireland in order to remain competitive and keep their jobs. We put our feet up on the table, examined our shoes, danced on the table, and occasionally addressed the gathering crowd outside through an opened window. We got the front page of the papers.

Equal pay was subsequently introduced on 1 January 1976, by order of the European Economic Community. The government, astoundingly, sought to derogate from the introductory deadline, but we were out on the streets like rockets and the EEC brought the government immediately to heel.

I cannot think now how I got the nerve in those days to break or flout the law and expect to keep my job in the *Irish Times*, writing about the courts. I was not afraid of the gardaí, though. We were often on the same side. The guards were regularly humiliated in the petty criminal courts by an unrestrained judiciary, and many told me that they appreciated my criticisms of the bench – though the criticism usually consisted of a straightforward recording of the uncouth remarks of the judges. I just let them open their mouths and put their feet in. I always named the judges, never the guards or the criminals. The guards who worked in the drug squad used to ring me if a recalcitrant teenage female had left home for a dangerous walk on the wild side, and I was occasionally successful in having her returned home, without charges being brought.

Though I had sworn off stealing after my brush with the law when I attempted to take the toothbrush, I decided that stealing electricity from my landlord was in the tradition of robbing the rich to help the poor and didn't count. I learned how to do this from a couple of striking Drogheda electricians who slept on my floor for a night before going on a protest in Dublin the next day. In exchange for bed and board, the electricians showed me how to disconnect the meter in the hall outside my flat. Landlords, they persuaded me, set the meter to charge more than the domestic rate and kept the little bit of profit for themselves.

I was mindful of Derry, where my mother often got a few pennies back from the man who checked her consumption of gas – she was legally entitled to the rebate and was glad of it. I was also entitled to any rebate going, I thought, given my great service in subsidizing the hungry workers of the world in their gallant struggle against capitalism. Aine O'Connor and her husband, Larry Masterson, who both worked in RTÉ, had brought round the striking workers knowing that I would let them stay. The more people I gave floor space to – electricians, feminists, hippies – the more rebate I awarded myself, until the landlord wondered if I lived in the dark. When he discovered the ruse, calling at an unexpected time, I pretended ignorance, and never again stole electricity; meantime, the workers of the world ate me out of house and home.

A former prison officer came to see me at the *Irish Times*. She had become infatuated with a republican woman, a friend of mine, who was serving a jail sentence. During night shifts, she had slept with the prisoner. When trysts had been impossible, the warder had pushed packets of potato crisps under the cell door, which action turned them into crumbs, but which the prisoner gladly ate. The warder wondered if she were now a lesbian, and asked if she could sleep with me. I slept for Ireland that night because I was fond of the prisoner and grateful that not all prison warders were brutal. It was the first time that I had ever slept with a person for whom I had no feelings at all. Sex without affection was a disconcerting experience that I never repeated, though it was not sordid. When the prisoner was released she asked me to fund an abortion for a young woman, also a republican. Neither of us knew the cost of the termination, so I made out a blank cheque in the name of the woman going to London. The amount later cashed seemed inordinate. The young woman had decided to treat herself to a new outfit after the abortion. That was the end of me and blank cheques.

Abortion was still relatively unknown territory, though 'self-determination' and 'control of our bodies' were, as ever, Irishwomen United's main themes. The language showed both a deepening understanding and a desire to avoid the crude terms of argument used by the opposition, most of which went unreported in the mainstream media. Trinity College's Professor of Obstetrics and Gynaecology, John Bonnar, who was to become a leading anti-abortion spokesman, attributed the occasional failure of natural methods of contraception to the fact that women were reluctant to watch for the vaginal secretions that indicate ovulation. 'There seems to be a natural revulsion to mucus. I know for instance how my children detest being presented with a half-boiled egg.'

The 'singing priest' Father Michael Cleary, one of a group of priests who sang for charity, was abusive when we met him while leafleting his parish in Ballyfermot. He said that the campaign should be renamed the 'Durex Action Programme', though wearing Durex, he said, was like 'going to bed with your socks on'. Cleary, a Catholic marriage counsellor, said that 'perversion' rather than contraception was the main problem in marriage because some husbands wanted to have intercourse with their wives 'up her back passage'. We now know that by 1977 Cleary had had two children by his housekeeper, who lived with him.

At that time, Senator Mary Robinson was receiving packets of excrement through the post on foot of her attempts to introduce a bill legalizing contraception, albeit in limited circumstances.

The Irish Censorship Board banned the sale in Ireland of the British feminist magazine *Spare Rib* on the grounds that it was 'obscene and indecent' – the magazine carried advertisements for contraception. Simone de Beauvoir's book *The Second Sex* was also banned, as was the lesbian novel *Rubyfruit Jungle*. Irishwomen United organized another train to Belfast, and brought back copies of *Spare Rib*. The police stepped aside when they arrived in Dublin, declaring later that: 'An attempt was made to seize *Spare Rib*; the attempt failed.'

We notified the gardaí that we were going to sell the magazine at a meeting in the Mansion House. I chaired the proceedings, hundreds of copies of *Spare Rib* were sold, the police noted our names and addresses, and nothing happened – other than I got to sing a duet with Mary Black. As she sang lines from 'Hit the Road, Jack', I would interpolate words of my own. 'Yeah, fuck off,' I'd say. And as she sang that Jack should come back no more, I'd repeat emphatically, 'Just fuck off,' nodding my head and throwing shapes. There were, alas, no TV cameras present.

Contraception apart, some of our aims were in retrospect (and even at the time) laughable, particularly Article Three of our charter which declared that we wanted the 'Recognition of Motherhood and Parenthood as a Social Function'. Specifically, it demanded 'State support for programmes implementing the socialization of housework, i.e. community laundries, kitchens, eating places, etc.' The 'et cetera' was revealing: we simply did not have a clue about running a home and family, and even less interest. The demand for 'twenty-four-hour nurseries, provided free of charge' by the state showed an alarming ignorance of motherhood, not to mention the needs of babies. Had we had our way back then, sleeping children would have been plucked out of their beds in the middle of the night and carted off to a neon-lit crèche; people would have queued like prisoners to eat en masse in the basement of tower blocks, or the local parish hall. The gulags in Siberia would have had nothing on us. Evelyn Conlon was the only woman among us who was married with young children; two other, older women had grown families and were separated.

But many of the things we called for actually happened. There are state-financed birth-control clinics; there are women's studies programmes at third level; there are state-funded women's centres in major population areas; we do have divorce; though we coyly did not use the term 'lesbian', the right of all women to 'a self-determined sexuality' is proceeding apace, following the decriminalization of homosexuality; and Ireland is slowly, painfully, legalizing abortion.

Significantly – such was our ignorance of Irish domestic and

intimate life – our group's charter made no mention of wife battering, incest, the sexual abuse of children by clerics and lay staff in
orphanages and reform schools run jointly by Church and State,
and the entombing of single mothers in Magdalen homes where
they worked as unseen, unpaid washerwomen all the days of their
wretched lives, the survivors to emerge blinking and infantilized
octogenarians when the Magdalen homes finally closed.

It was Nuala Fennell who rolled back the stone on domestic
violence against women through an organization which she set
up, Women's Aid. Contrary, cantankerous and bourgeois, accompanied by women dismissed as middle-class do-gooders, Fennell
borrowed a derelict city-centre house from a male business acquaintance, and I watched her scrub out the shit-encrusted toilets before
the first women and children arrived seeking refuge. I knew, of
course, that it would not work – that Nuala would not last the
pace. I was, of course, wrong. Fennell, who had split from the
original women's movement because of its resistance to the anti-
squatting bill, subsequently squatted in a derelict mansion beside
the residence of Micheál Macliammoir. Women's Aid refuges, with
state funding, are now established throughout the country.

Compared with such things as domestic violence, some of the
concerns of Irishwomen United were madcap froth, and our activities entertained and irritated. We were defined by cheek. We had
no respect for the powers-that-be, and our lack of respect was often
welcomed by other women's groups which were constrained to
act within socially acceptable and legal parameters. The Council
for the Status of Women, for instance, was mortified when Charlie
Haughey, the Minister for Health, arrived into their headquarters
to present them with a chain of office which he had personally
commissioned. They wanted equal pay; he offered them chains.
Our group attended the ceremony, and, when Charlie went to
wrap his offering round the neck of the chairwoman, I stepped
forward and denounced him, asking those who agreed with me to
clap their hands. Most of the women did.

It was easy enough to run rings round the government in such
public display. Or, maybe, Ireland was just easy-going then: after

the Contraceptive Train, I happened to be passing through the foyer of the Shelbourne Hotel when the Minister for Foreign Affairs, Patrick Hillery, arrived to attend some function or other. I grabbed him by the tie, backed him up against a wall, and told him Irishwomen wanted contraception legalized – yesterday. The doorman approached me afterwards and said the staff had laid on brandy for me at the bar.

We decided to take umbrage at those bars where women were deprived of the right to drink pints. We could order half-pints to our heart's content, and drink them one after another, but the sight of a pint glass in a woman's hand was considered unladylike. The fact that two half-pints cost more than one pint was neither here nor there. Inspired by Eamonn McCann's protest at the Abbey Theatre, when he ordered brandies and refused to pay for them, I went into the actor's pub, Neary's, accompanied by thirty women, and ordered thirty-one brandies. When the barman had set up the drinks, I then ordered a pint of Guinness. He refused to serve. We refused to pay. We drank up and left the pub without paying. The publican did not seek redress – or the unwelcome publicity. Women are served pints now in every pub in the land.

That night had an odd postscript. Luke Kelly from the Dubliners was among the crowd that applauded us when I stood on a table in Neary's and made a speech, asking for support. I met him some time later, both of us wandering along the quays at twilight, and we took a taxi to see Joe Dolan in cabaret at the foot of the Dublin Mountains. Afterwards, Luke invited me to his home. He was separated from his wife. We were both sober. I went with him like a lamb to the slaughter, and while he spent a discreet length of time in the bathroom I undressed and got into bed. He came out in his underpants, climbed in between the sheets, propped himself up on one arm and looked down at me. 'You don't want to, do you?' he asked. Indeed I did not, I said. He grinned, rolled away, put out the light and fell fast asleep. When day broke, I looked at the back of his wonderful head of red Afro hair and thought of what a great life I could have, if only . . . When he woke up I told him that my rendition of 'Peggy Gordon' was better than his. It is a song of love lost, for a woman. There was no food in the house, and he took me for breakfast to his local pub. Breakfast was a coffee, cigarettes, several newspapers and total silence. On rare occasions after that, he would ring me at the office and suggest a late-afternoon movie. We met inside the Screen cinema in D'Olier Street, adjacent to the *Irish Times*. He took a seat on one side of the aisle; I sat on the other side of the aisle, across from him. He passed me sweets and popcorn. We maintained what was by now a customary silence and parted in silence after the show.

Irishwomen United continued to grab headlines. We climbed a high wall to invade the exclusive men-only Fitzwilliam Tennis Club and played sets badly. We invaded the men-only deep-water bathing pool in Dublin Bay known as the Forty Foot (after the British battalion that had started using it for swimming). The Forty Foot was a beautiful clean-water haven. Voluntary contributions from the men had been used to build rocky ledges, ladders and diving platforms. Round the corner was a filthy beach where women and children were meant to pass their days. To reinforce their hold on the territory, custom and tradition had it that men could bathe and bask naked in and around the Forty Foot – no sight for ladies, and the guards turned a benign blind eye.

We invaded it on a Saturday by land, sea and air: we marched in on foot, some jumped off the rocks using umbrellas, and two women rowed in by boat. The men did not take kindly to us. Some waved their genitals as weapons of shock and awe; some told us in graphic sexual terms that we needed 'a good seeing to'; others attempted the hoary old insults of 'lesbian', 'whore' and such. We undressed among them, forswearing the usual Irish tradition of using a towel as a tent. The weather was lovely, the water bracing. Our cause was helped by the presence of the respectable suburban Fennell family – Nuala, Brian and their children – who posed in swimsuits. (I gladly returned the favour years later by publishing a rave article in support of her in the *Irish Times*, on the day she put herself before the electorate as an independent in the general election. She nearly won, and the seismic shock of that paved the way for the embrace of feminist candidates by established political parties.)

The prohibition on women in the Forty Foot ended that Saturday. I went back there in the summer of 1995, when the sun shone for weeks and the population had taken to wearing shorts. Nuala O'Faolain and I had parted that June, after a fifteen-year relationship. The great rock pool was filled with the bobbing, peaceful heads of women, men and children. A smiling man swam up alongside and said that he had been there twenty years previously when I had parachuted off the rock face with an umbrella. It was the best day's work I ever did, he congratulated me: the Forty Foot was a great place now for conversation, with all the women about, and the picnics were better, and nobody minded the presence of gay men, who used to meet there after dark, but now consorted openly. I put on a cheeky grin, and swam underwater when the tears came.

Chapter Nineteen

Angelina left the country in April 1976. I was so anxious to be free of her that I paid most of her passage. Her departure saved us both the trauma of formally separating, though we were already separated in most respects. Nonetheless, I made it my business to go to the flat where I knew she was spending her last night with another woman, and I broke the window there at dawn and stood shouting in the street. Then I followed her to the airport and apologized to her. I excused my behaviour as a gesture of desperate romantic love. It was not. It was the demeaning, jealous act of one who had lost power.

A few days after Angelina left, I attended a farewell party for the woman with whom Angelina had spent her last night. This was a ridiculous pretence by me, that I was above the mundane, sordid fray. This woman happened to be leaving the country, too. Early next morning, one of the women who had been at the party called to my flat. I went back to bed while she made breakfast. She brought me a bowl of cornflakes, produced a naggin of whiskey, poured it in on top of the milk and told me that the woman to whom I had bade a gallant farewell the night before was not going to America, as I had thought, but was going to join Angelina.

Everybody at the party had known. That left me reeling: I had been an object of ridicule, pity and *schadenfreude*. Shame at seeing me hung out to dry had brought the woman round. If I had paid the party more than a fleeting visit, the truth would eventually have come out. I reeled again. What a sight that would have been. I sent the woman out for more whiskey.

That afternoon I went into Bowe's Bar and found Donal Foley sitting with a colleague from another paper. 'My heart has been broken. I need time off, immediately,' I said, and burst into tears. Foley put his arm round me, and said I could take as much time off as I wanted. I went straight back to my flat and spent a month there, drinking and taking Valium. Nuala Fennell saw me walking the roads during this time, picked me up in her car, and brought me to her home for dinner. I went to Derry (where my father's tablets were) and straight to bed. My mother brought me breakfast, dinner, tea and supper. On the second day she said to me, 'Would you not be better off going to stay with Gráinne and Michael?' She was frightened for me, and frightened of what might be hurting me. It was wise of her to send me to people who could cope with what she could not face.

Carmel, who had married and was living in her own home, was sent for, and she drove me to my friends' house. I told her nothing en route, but I told Gráinne and Michael everything, and I told them exactly what I needed: I was due to make a television appearance in Belfast in eight days' time. In the meantime, I wished to sleep for a week, using Valium. I would like them to waken me for meals and wine – to be taken in bed, alone. I would like to be reminded that I had to go to Belfast, to appear on television, when the time came.

Gráinne and Michael were both working, and their two children went to a nanny by day, but both came every lunch hour to check on me and feed me. They came separately, and Michael was usually last, and this was a matter of some curiosity to the workmen who were painting the house that week. Standing on scaffolding, they had a perfect view into the bedroom where I insisted that the curtains and windows be kept open – I hate dark, stuffy rooms. The workmen's interpretation of what was going on, as Michael came and went every lunch time, to feed the naked woman in the bed, can only be surmised. Such matters would not take a wrinkle out of Michael, a person of great equanimity, but I do remember him finding me naked on the staircase, making a phone call. Somehow, I had got through to the office of the Spanish Prime Minister and was asking his secretary for an appointment with General Franco, when Michael took over the call. Franco was, of course, dead.

On the eighth morning, Carmel came to fetch me before she went to work. On the way home, I told her I was lesbian. 'I know

304

you are,' she said. She had been told years before by Malachy McGurran, Northern Chief of Staff of the Official IRA, with whom she had a brief romance in Derry. Malachy was a sensitive man, and I knew he would not have revealed my secret maliciously.

'Why didn't you say?' I asked.

'I was waiting for you to mention it,' she replied.

I briefly considered pointing out that that meant that my condition was unmentionable, but I found the intelligence to be glad that she was being so sweet. Apart from my brother-in-law, decades earlier, and my parents, Carmel was the only person in my immediate family to whom I spoke openly about my sexuality.

I went into the house, told my mother that I was all right, collected the car keys, and said that I was driving to Belfast to do the television interview. Her face was creased with worry. She blessed me with holy water and hugged me at the front door and said, as ever, 'God bless you, daughter.' Wanting to reassure her that I truly was all right, I stood on the doorstep and said that I had done a rotten thing, but that it was over now and I would not do it again.

'Were you an informer?' my mother asked, coming up with the worst thing that any person could be or would do.

'Ah, no, Mammy,' I said. She knew from the vehemence of my response that I was telling the truth. Her face cleared. The years dropped off her. I drove round the corner, stopped, and cried at her childlike innocence.

I arrived in Belfast with but minutes to spare, parked illegally outside an office block, got out, locked the car, and ran down the street towards the studio. I heard people yelling and shouting behind me. They had poured out of the ground floor of the office block, thinking that I was a car bomber. One of them recognized me. I gave him my car keys, press and credit card, and ran into the studio and took part in a debate about the RUC.

When I got back to Dublin that afternoon, I told Donal Foley that I needed more time. He reasonably refused. 'We've all had our hearts broken. You've had more time off than anybody for a broken heart.' I had been off work for six weeks.

In July 1976, I took six months' leave of absence. I was involved with a new woman, Christina, a member of Irishwomen United. We had met on the rebound: me from the *femme fatale*; she from a short-lived marriage. Quite simply, she rang me up. She was a safe haven from my recent past – kind, ambitious and fiercely principled. She earned her own way, even doing a job she didn't like; she enjoyed homemaking and cooking; she did not do drugs or get blind drunk; she cleaned my car, which she used for her work. She was a blessed relief from the company I had been keeping; I wanted to get out of the lesbian ghetto. A lovely thing happened that gave me hope: when she came on a work assignment with me, and we were stuck with a single bedroom, the *Irish Times* sports correspondent Paddy Downey insisted that we have his double room, while he moved into the one allocated to us. Christina's job was taking her to America, and it seemed like the perfect chance for me to make a break. Though I did not fully realize it, I was in crisis. My 'In the Eyes of the Law' column had become predictable. I had begun to weary of the same social misfits and recidivists turning up in the dock. The paper did not know where to slot me, and I did not fancy being a reporter without a cause. I wanted to attempt fiction because a thousand words on anything could not begin to catch complexity.

There were warning signals that life with Christina might not turn out to be perfect. She had a difficult relationship with her mother, a gallant working widow who had reared Christina for better things and did not approve of her leaving her marriage; she thought me too concerned about my own mother. She never got used to the violent atmosphere in the North and was jealous of my frequent trips to a place where she could not function. Through no fault of her own, when we socialized outside the women's movement, people ignored her and talked to me as if she were not there: I was famous, she was not. I had no idea then (and still don't have any) of how to cope with such bad manners. I was also open to approaches from the needy, as ever, and from the merely chatty: I liked to know what people were thinking.

We went to Cambridge, Massachusetts. On our very first night in an all-female communal household, a female plumber called to fix a broken pipe. Then a female electrician called. This was more like it. Next morning, I bought a broken-down car for a few hundred dollars, and the commune helped me push it to a garage where I signed up for a course as a car mechanic. Our teacher, a little Scotsman, sat inside the bonnet of a huge American car, perched on the engine block, and he announced that, 'Whatever goes wrong with a car, it's a simple matter to fix it. It's always simple.' Within weeks, I had changed the clutch, put in brakes, and tuned the engine, using strobe lights. It was indeed simpler than I had thought, and it was exhilarating. I was in love with my old banger. On the slightest excuse, I would leap out of the car and retune it.

The one thing I could not do was get a job: I was a journalist, not a bartender. Christina had told me that when she worked in Boston as a student, she discovered a corpse in the bedroom of the hotel where she was a chambermaid. Imagination ablaze – raw material! I thought – I succeeded in getting a similar position. The boss woman and I abraded each other on sight. I was an illegal immigrant, and she established her superiority immediately by showing me how, after vacuuming the shag carpet that was standard furnishing in the bedrooms, I was to rake my way out of the room, backwards, using an actual rake, leaving not a footprint behind. The boss woman left footprints everywhere, and I had to shag along behind her, back bent, eradicating all traces. She made me go round in circles after her. She would never guarantee me another day's employment: 'I'll ring you tomorrow if there's any work available.' And she would ring at 5.30 a.m., to say yes or no, giving me fifteen minutes to get to the hotel.

There was no source material for the great book. There was never a sign to indicate the character of the person or people who had spent the night there. It was the pubic hairs in the bathroom that broke me; there was always one I had missed. I got the sack after collapsing into a crumpled bed one morning and drinking the remains of a bottle of champagne. The client hadn't even left the fabled tip which, I had been told, Americans always left for humble backroom staff. (Ever since, I've left a tip on the bedside table for chambermaids, and worn myself to a shred trying to remove pubic hairs from the bathroom I've just used.)

I was a kept woman, living off Christina, and it was no consolation that I had paid her bills in Dublin. I had lost the only thing that had kept me going: a job. It was all right to be a hippy when I was young, with no real intention of working, or notion of what I might work at, but here I was in America, in green shorts, a pink sleeveless T-shirt, pale skin and hairy bandy legs. And nobody was interested in Northern Ireland.

We decided to finish the six-month stint with a drive to California. We did not consult a map. I wanted to see Georgia, and Jimmy Carter's mother rocking on her porch, shelling peanuts. This was an enormous detour (I now realize), and we never saw Miz Lillian. But the red earth was inspiring, and I got to sing 'Country Road' driving along the ridge of the Virginias. There was a diner, in the dark, off a highway somewhere in the South, where the waitress told a black family that service had stopped for the night, then turned to us, who had arrived after the blacks, to take our order.

After a smashing night of gumbo and jazz in New Orleans we finally took out the map and saw that Texas was as long again as the enormous mileage we had just travelled. We turned back. We were within 100 miles of Memphis, decided we'd see Elvis some other year, and arrived back in Dublin in December 1976. Elvis died in August 1977. I tore his picture out of a newspaper, went on a pub crawl, and Christina was not best pleased when I arrived home the worse for wear. The generation gap showed up that night – Christina, six years younger than me, was four, and I was ten, when Elvis had his first hit in 1954.

June Levine visited my family while I was away, and my mother showed her a letter I had written from New Orleans. It was one long apology for enjoying myself, June told me later.

When I returned to Derry after my wanderings, I noticed that my father's thumb was red and raw where it lay in his lap, as he sat, in a world of his own, by the fire. I remarked on this to my mother, and there was a slight silence. I looked again and realized that my father was fondling his penis. Carmel, who had come to visit, said with a grin, 'He's checking to see that he's all there.' The shock and tension evaporated. The situation became perfectly normal.

On her wedding day in 1975, Carmel had insisted that our father escort her up the aisle, and he leaned on her arm as she more or less weaved him to the altar. Being the youngest, Carmel had an easier time with our father than the rest of us did, but she also had a greater sense of family ritual. She gave my father his due manhood on her wedding day. Carmel has great gifts.

I couldn't settle back into the *Irish Times*. Donal Foley sent me out to do a series on foreigners in Ireland: the Italians, the Chinese and the Indians. I visited the restaurants that were their main source of employment and was blanked. It didn't occur to me to go to their embassies for help, and it didn't occur to Foley to check on my progress. I had never received basic training as a reporter and that didn't help. When I finally confessed that I was getting nowhere, Foley gave me a punitive assignment: the status of the Irish potato, the cultivation of which was declining in face of foreign imports. I did not care about potatoes. I did a good enough job – at least the people I interviewed spoke English – but it was far from potatoes I was reared, and I was affronted by my fall from hotshot court reporter, reeking of Northern sulphur and Southern feminism, to the vegetable patch.

Douglas Gageby, the editor of the paper, came to the rescue by sending me round Ireland in the summer to cover local festivals. At first I thought that, too, was beneath me, but I was scarcely out of Dublin, and on the road, before I fell madly in love with the Republic and its people. Away from all the political and social ghettos, on my own, released from emotional turmoil, I tapped into pure joy and communal goodwill: country markets, shark-fishing competitions, harvest thanksgiving. I wrote about fresh brown eggs, a midnight tug-of-war in a field between lawyers and farmers, after-hours drinking in shebeens, the worship of a wild goat at Puck Fair, the ploughing of a straight furrow. I relished a society well at ease in simple pleasures.

On my return from America I found that Irishwomen United was crumbling. There was no formal dissolution. The more committed women spent less time at marathon meandering Sunday meetings and more time elsewhere in pursuit of single-issue agendas, the foremost of which was the setting up of Ireland's first Rape Crisis Centre. Evelyn Conlon, Betty Purcell and Anne O'Donnell, with others, met in the regulation dank basement room, and their legal adviser was Mary McAleese, the young woman who had succeeded Mary Robinson as Reid Professor of Law at Trinity College. Unpaid, unheralded and unsung – they studiously avoided publicity – the women spent months acquainting themselves with the facts. At that time, the ghastly joke about rape was, 'If you can't avoid it, lie back and enjoy it.' This attitude was not confined to men. The group was focused and determined. They took the groundbreaking step of meeting with the police. When they emerged from the dark, their revelations shook the country.

I started roving the feminist landscape again, speaking and agitating. My motto was: 'You do not ask the prophet for a blueprint.' Details were for others to work out. Arrogant and lazy though that position was, I wasn't idle: I was bogged down in extracurricular social work, expending a horrendous amount of time on individuals. My rule of thumb was that, if a woman bothered to contact me, she was worth working with. I quickly came to understand that a client was a client for life.

Mary heard of me through a fellow part-time cleaner in Trinity College, who had seen my work in papers and magazines she was throwing out. Mary wrote to me care of one of the magazines. She had a long, sad story, and I believed every word out of her mouth. She said she was a deserted wife with one child. It was not until the evening before I was due to represent her at the social welfare appeals tribunal that she told me the full truth: she had had three children by her husband, two of whom were in care. She had met her future husband through a lonely hearts column in the wholesome Catholic family magazine *Ireland's Own*. He was a minor civil servant. On the first afternoon they met they had sexual intercourse and she became pregnant. The child died in her womb, and she became pregnant again. They married immediately. The ceremony was attended by neither kith nor kin on either side. He soon broke her jaw. Then he broke her arm. After a few years, she fled their council house. Though the Catholic Church annulled her marriage, Mary could not claim the welfare benefits to which a single mother was entitled because she was still a wife in the eyes of the state, and she could not get the benefits to which a deserted wife was entitled because she was deemed to have deserted her husband.

It was my intention to argue constructive desertion – a new legal concept, whereby a wife pleaded that she had been driven by violence to leave the family home. I had learned of this concept from Colum Kenny, a young lawyer with whom I had once taught literacy in the slums of the inner city. At that time, two senior lawyers, Mary Robinson and Paddy MacEntee, and a handful of newcomers, Kenny, Máire Bates, Barbara Hussey, Garret Sheehan, Michael White and Pat McCartan, were the sole sources of support in the legal world. I relied on hints, advice and succour from the newcomers.

I need not have worried about the strength of my argument. Mary's husband entered the civil court swishing an outsize pair of rosary beads in one hand and waving an outsize crucifix at Mary with the other. He was literally foaming at the mouth. The sorry fellow was also a hunchback. The panel of lay judges found immediately in Mary's favour.

She spent the award – retrospective welfare payments equivalent to one year of my own wages after tax – on a glass-fronted walnut sideboard which stretched the length of the living room in the public-authority house I had successfully negotiated for her. I had been there several nights previously, when Mary had moved in. On the mantelpiece she had placed a copy of one of my books – the better to frighten and impress the social workers, who had contempt for her, she said. While I drank wine, she took the old carpets out of the house, laid them on the lawn, and shampooed them – at midnight. I said nothing about the monstrosity on which she had spent a fortune.

Over the years Mary fed me information on a need-to-know basis, in times of crisis, when she had run out of other avenues of relief. I learned that she had had a child after parting with her husband and placed the boy with foster parents outside of Dublin, bringing the total number of her children to four. She got pregnant yet again. She told me that the man in question had fed her a Mickey Finn. I told her to stop kidding me. I told her that I was no virgin, though unmarried, and I explained my relationship with Nuala O'Faolain. She was uninterested. She was worried only about what she would do, pregnant yet again. She had no intention of having an abortion.

Mary said she had not yet recovered from the premature birth and immediate death of her first child. (Six pregnancies by three men, I silently counted. How did this woman, with false teeth, mottled legs, bad health and a nervous disposition, maintain a love life, however tawdry, I silently wondered.) She had not been allowed to hold her first-born baby because she was unmarried.

In 1992, I attended the birth of Mary's last baby, which, she had been told, was already dead in her womb. The nurses in the Coombe were lovely. The dead child's head had been squashed into a peak as it passed through the birth canal, and blood had congealed on its nostrils, and skin had torn off its flesh. The little alien was her baby, and she was given peace to hold the tiny corpse in her arms, in a private room. They were photographed, and the child was given a baptism and a funeral in the Coombe chapel, and a grave in the Angels' Plot in Glasnevin, which had been consecrated in the aftermath of a referendum that outlawed abortion. Mary put a photograph of the child, complete with little peaked head, in her walnut sideboard.

I attended and gave out prizes at her graduation at the local school where she had taken a basic course in adult education. I brought her cash every Christmas courtesy of those who responded to the occasional articles I penned about her anonymous struggle against the odds – she understood that, if I wrote about her, she might get donations. She never asked me to bring the articles, and she couldn't afford the price of a daily Irish paper: the cheaper British tabloids gave her gossip and the daily TV schedules.

I was on Mary's case for fifteen years. It was never going to end, and she was never going to get a job, though I had often driven her to interviews for poorly paid cleaning work, where the employer questioned how she would possibly get from the distant suburb to the city centre by 6 a.m., and pay childcare for her son, the sole child she managed to keep by her side.

Mary had a brain haemorrhage in 1996, and I last saw her in hospital, curled up like a foetus, paralysed, whimpering, speechless and dribbling. Three of her teenage children were by her side. She knew us all. I gave the children money. I did not go to the funeral. I could not take any more. I should have gone.

I helped a man I came across in Dublin's worst slum, Benburb Street. He was a gentle fellow, a father, and bewildered about the unemployment hole into which he had fallen. I wrote about him, accepted a job on his behalf, bought him a jacket and trousers, and drove him to his new workplace. It took a long time afterwards to understand that the culture shock was too much for him: not everybody is allowed to drink the first few months' probation away, after years of unemployment, as journalists are allowed to do.

I learned another hard lesson in 2003. An agreeable young man had been panhandling outside the wine shop in Ranelagh. Every week I had given him money, and books to read. Every week, I had offered him a room in my house nearby – a permanent address from which he might qualify for unemployment benefit and a place on the housing list.

He left Ranelagh, relocated to a begging pitch in the city centre, and I approached and reproached him once more: why had he not taken up my offer of a temporary home? He didn't know me, he pointed out; he had different tastes than I did; he was shy about moving into a stranger's house and being bound by her rules and aggravating her; he had nothing and I had everything, and he would be humiliated; what's more, he dreaded the sight of me and the sense of failure I had inflicted upon him by making him an offer he could not accept; and that was how I had driven him out of Ranelagh into a new environment where he had to start, painfully, all over again.

I have concluded now, at the slow-learning age of sixty, that it is more effective to support organized campaigns than take individual action. It is my harsh analysis that individual charity perpetuates the system. I dread phone calls from people in need.

At the end of 1977 I gave my notice at the *Irish Times* and we went to Crosshaven, West Cork. I was going to write the great novel. Leaving a job did not seem that enormous a step. I knew that I would be welcomed back with open arms. I believed I was good enough to write a novel, having already turned down tentative offers from English publishers. My mother did not share my confidence. 'What are you going to work at after this novel?' she wrote. 'I do keep wondering and, no need to say, worry.'

In Crosshaven, a village at the mouth of a sleepy warm estuary at the edge of the Atlantic, I immediately joined Weight Watchers. Anything was better than sitting down in front of a typewriter. I lost half a stone in six months. I met the poet Paul Durcan, who praised and encouraged me – how I have held on, down all the years since, to his generous words. I joined the Irish Countrywomen's Association and left almost immediately, following a visit to an old people's home where we sang, badly, at them. The memory tortured me in 2003, when it was my dolorous turn to find a nursing home for my mother. I was invited on to a committee set up in Crosshaven to prevent the village's historic fort being turned into a dump for waste, and advised them how to build barricades, and pointed out the folly of appointing a male-only roster to keep a twenty-four-hour vigil. The men were affronted when I asked them who was going to give up paid work to keep the vigil going. I signed on the dole. I grew lettuce.

When Malachy McGurran died in the North and I did not go to the funeral – a ten-hour journey by car – my mother was aghast. I raced up there when word came that my father was dying. He rallied as we all gathered round his hospital bed. We scattered back to where we lived. My father died two weeks later, on 6 July 1978. My mother had left his hospital bedside to go home for lunch, and he died while she was away. He died as she walked in her front door. She had been nursing him for ten years.

I got to Derry at seven in the morning. There was a black ribbon on the door. Mrs McBride arrived as I turned the key. She liked to pay her respects when no other neighbours were present. I was awfully tired, and embarrassed that my mother felt obliged to apologize for waking me a few hours later: 'The Bishop's here. Can you go down and talk to him?'

I was acutely self-conscious about deliberately not going to communion during the funeral mass. As we left the cemetery, after the funeral, my mother cried out in fear: 'What shall I do about money?' My father's old-age pension had died with him, and her income had been halved. I was stunned that she would be afraid – Nuala was living with her, the house was fully owned and furnished, and the rest of us would contribute, I pointed out. But how would I? I was on the dole and couldn't support myself. 'I'll be going back to work soon,' I babbled. Her fear was a salutary lesson to me, though I had vacuously preached for years that every woman needed an income of her own. There had been £15 in my father's bank account when he had the stroke that laid him off work, in October 1968, the month he was due to take his driving test. There was £100 in my father's bank account when he died. It had been my intention, should he pass the driving test, to help him buy a car, just as I had helped to pay for the bathroom. My father was a good provider, a steady earner. When I was in the *Irish Times*, I was earning more than enough to lavishly return the compliment, but there was nothing I could buy for the paralysed man in the corner.

There was a family row the night he was buried. Paddy quarrelled with Hugh, I intervened, and Muireanna joined in – the four exiles. My sad, shocked mother left us to it and went to bed. Nuala looked on glumly. Carmel put such manners as she could on us. We have never dared quarrel so openly since.

I stayed longer than intended in Derry to comfort my mother.

Christina was furious because, without our car, she had to make a twenty-six-mile return journey by bus every day to work, which necessitated a very early rising. I could not see her point: I was looking after my mother. Christina was further irritated when the whole Derry branch of the family arrived down to Crosshaven shortly afterwards, a sad little caravanserai seeking desperately to distract my mother in her grief and shock. I had asked them not to bring the dog because our cat had just given birth. They brought the dog. My mother remembers how my face froze when the dog leaped out. She remembers which of the many friends I had brought through her house did not attend my father's funeral. Practically brain dead he may have been for years, but he was her husband: I had not realized how much store my mother placed on marriage, nor understood the love that twines around marriage and family. Feminists knew more about sex than love.

My mother discovered the pleasures of reading a book – or at least finally had time for it – after my father died. Neighbours would remark with pleasure as they glanced up at her front bedroom and saw the light on, 'There's Lily reading.' Her favourite book of all the ones I gave her was *Elena*, the story of a Greek woman living in a village during the resistance. Novels about families, and about people struggling against the odds, absorbed her. She liked Zora Neale Hurston's *Their Eyes Were Watching God*. She ventured a criticism once of Maeve Binchy, a former colleague of mine in the *Irish Times*. Round about Maeve's fifth book, my mother snorted, 'Everybody in her books always ends up happy. She should read your man that wrote *Home before Dark*.' (Hugh Leonard, who used to express distaste for my feminism and nationalism in his newspaper columns.) After I sent Maeve a money order and asked her to send my mother an inscribed copy of her first novel, and she had gone to considerable effort to do so, always thereafter her books arrived, unprompted and inscribed, the week before publication, in my mother's house. They were passed round the neighbours, then returned to take their proud place on the top shelf. My sister Carmel pointed out to me that my mother was quite vain in such matters. She liked it that the Bishop called to her house; and the chiefs of staff of the IRA; and the leading politicians of the day; and all the journalists and TV crews. And if my mother was vain – which I came immediately to see after the bleeding obvious was pointed out to me – what did my mother think of me? I asked her once. 'You're gullible,' she responded immediately.

Christina bought a cheap old house in Cork city in the autumn of 1978. During the week, she worked in Dublin and I stayed in the house. She commuted from Dublin every weekend, and we renovated the building together. I loved learning to plaster walls, lay down tiles, install wiring and plumbing. I loved having the place to myself from Monday to Friday, and did not mind that Christina was having relationships in Dublin. The great novel was not going well. My mother was still worried:

. . . last night I kept thinking on the whole lot of you. I never closed my eyes the whole night and every one of you came into my head, wondering how in the Lord you pan out, all the time on the dole . . . Mary Holland and the man from the BBC was here. She wanted me to go to Dublin to her and then go to Cork as she is dying to see your house but I said I would let her know, she gave me her phone number but I don't think I would ever make it . . . The weather here is awful, rain all the time and dark very early. This is a time when I cannot take in about your daddy, times I think he is here, anyhow I suppose time heals everything . . . how is your house coming on and how is Christina coping. Bobby Stitt says youse were plastering all wrong . . .

The hang-up I had developed about clothes – frocks or jeans – came to a head when I got a call from the *Late Late Show* asking if I would agree to be made over by the fashion designer Pat Crowley, who was instructed to create a Victorian-style confection of crinoline, satin and lace. I looked a fright. I used the occasion anyway to make a political point about the North, where a song called 'The Men behind the Wire' had publicized internment. In my padded bra, I told Gay Byrne, I was the woman behind the wire. As to my apparel, which he rightly ridiculed, Gay could do with a codpiece himself, I suggested, gazing pointedly at his crotch. Then, significantly, I took it upon myself to make a surprise reappearance in jeans and a T-shirt just before the credits rolled. I realized bleakly, after I did that, that I was cornering myself into being the woman behind the jeans.

Soon after I was invited to return to Dublin to speak at a Reclaim the Night march in October. There had been a series of rapes in the capital, in particular a gang rape by adolescents of an adolescent girl, which left her severely wounded. The Minister for Justice, Gerry Collins, had advised females stay indoors at night, for their own protection, or go about in numbers, or ensure a male escort after dark. Former members of Irishwomen United were about to open a twenty-four-hour Rape Crisis Centre. It is a measure of the fear then prevalent that all of them insisted on remaining anonymous. One of them explained to me, 'For all that we trained for a year, we were still foolish enough to announce that if any woman rang us we would go to the scene of the rape. That was, we realized almost immediately, an open invitation to hoax callers to lure us there.'

Gay Byrne had backed the march in his daily radio broadcasts, and his support alone guaranteed a huge turnout. Thousands of women, the biggest number ever seen on the streets, gathered that night and marched through the capital.

There had been some argument beforehand with male trade union leaders whose offer to escort the women, in a show of solidarity, was refused. One of them was Des Geraghty, whose wife, Mary Maher, was reporting on the march for the *Irish Times*. I even had an argument myself with the organizers, who rejected my suggestion that the march be led by the forty prominent women who had publicly sponsored it, among them Dáil deputies. There was to be no elite, I was reprimanded.

As we addressed the massive crowd, a rumour swept through it that the girl who had been gang-raped had died. The mood became angry. There was a hint of hysteria. Many were heard calling for castration. One of the organizers wished to announce the girl's death. Ever the reporter, and aware of how false rumours had many a time inflamed the North in times of tension, I asked her for proof. She had none, and I dissuaded her from saying anything.

The march was the lead story in the next day's *Irish Times*. On his radio show that morning, Gay Byrne took great umbrage at the refusal to let men play their own part against rape by allowing them to escort the march. Quoting from the *Irish Times* article, he read out my remarks in heavy tones. Thinking of the attitude of the Church and State to women and sexuality, particularly in the matter of contraception, I said, '. . . there isn't a woman on this march who hasn't been abused physically or mentally. Every woman has been raped in thought, word or deed.' Then I finished on what I thought was a sensible note: 'The streets are ours. We are not looking for jail for men; we are not looking for castration for men; we are not looking for men at all. We are looking for fresh air.'

The fresh air bit was dropped in Mary Maher's front-page report, which made my words sound harsh. She rightly observed that there were, amid the general cheering and applause, some chants of 'Not all men are rapists,' but I thought this gave the impression that I was arguing otherwise.

Byrne certainly wondered on the airwaves about how many women were 'not looking for men at all' or if it was wise to refuse male support. The discussion on rape that had dominated his programme for weeks disappeared in a welter of debate about whether it was right to refuse gestures of solidarity from men. The *Irish Times* columnist Kevin Myers weighed in, criticizing me for playing to the gallery that angry night. I'd had many a friendly conversation with him, particularly after he felt obliged to resign from RTÉ, which he considered censorious of his reports from the North, years earlier: RTÉ had thought him biased in favour of nationalists. At the time of the march, he was anti-republican and was arguing in favour of unionists. I thought his critique of my feminism was informed by fury at what he thought were my republican sympathies. Maher, Geraghty and Myers were part of the group of left-wing media, trade unionists and party politicians who fiercely opposed the Provisional IRA and Provisional Sinn Féin: I had never questioned their sincerity on that, but, whatever the disagreements between us on the North, I was truly upset that they would question my feminist credentials. I was wounded at being portrayed as anti-man and wrote a letter to the *Irish Times* suggesting that Byrne, Maher, Geraghty and Myers hold a meeting with their supporters in the back of a small car.

Christina and I returned to Dublin in late 1979, after selling the Cork house at a profit that owed more to rising house prices than our efforts at restoration. The profit was enough for Christina to put a deposit on a grand house in Dublin. On the day we moved in, friends called, I poured wine for them, and Christina was agitated: a precise, tidy person, she had wanted to unpack and settle the place. We persevered. I began to play poker every Saturday night, all night, because I did not want to stay at home. I was feeling tied down. I had great hopes of the novel and dismissed as not literary enough the reminiscences of another card player Katherine Kavanagh, who had married the poet Patrick Kavanagh late in life: truly, I was as arrogant as I was ignorant.

I was soon brought low.

I applied for my old job with the *Irish Times* and was turned down. Assistant editor Conor O'Clery took me out to lunch and said there were no vacancies. There was a hum in my ears during the rest of the meal. When O'Clery had joined the *Irish Times* as a sub-editor he had come to me for advice on how to break into journalism. As far as I knew, no journalist had ever been refused back into the fold, and I had been among the best of the *Irish Times* journalists. The paper had nursed drunks and hacks until retirement. One woman had been reduced to sleeping her way back in, though the two executives between whose hotel rooms she had passed back and forth in the space of a single night insisted to me, when I privately reproached them, that the three of them had just been having a good time. These two men actually believed that. (They had many years previously left the paper, nobody else knew what I knew, and the refusal of my cocky offer to do the *Times* a favour by rejoining it had nothing to do with that infamy.) I was too embarrassed and ashamed to ask O'Clery exactly why I was *persona non grata*.

It was not until sixteen years later, in 1995, that I picked up the phone and rang Douglas Gageby at his home for an explanation. Nuala O'Faolain and I had just broken up. I was trying to understand what had happened to my life, which was in bits. Gageby was astonished. He had never seen my application. 'I often wondered why you never came back to us. I thought you found us too tame.' He promised to ring O'Clery, who was by then running the office in China, and get back to me. He didn't. I picked up the phone again and rang Conor O'Clery. Conor told me that it embarrassed him to say, in 1995, that he and another assistant editor, both of them in charge of hiring in 1979, had then considered me 'too radical' to handle. He mentioned my campaign for contraception, divorce and abortion, the speech I had made at the Reclaim the Night march, and radio interviews I had given excoriating the Pope, who had flown into Ireland. 'It all seems tame now, and how right you were, but back then it was ground-shaking.' He was solicitous and apologetic; he had had no idea, he said, that I would mind being turned down by the *Irish Times*.

Mind? I was thirty-five years old in 1979, I came from a culture that prized the good permanent job, I had had one for most of eight years, and now I thought I would never work again. I was a feminist, I was on the wrong side of the moderate Northern tracks, and I was lesbian. I did not ask O'Clery in 1995 if my sexuality had anything to do with it, no more than I had asked in 1979. I was paranoid, still, after all those years.

My expulsion from the fold coincided with Pope John Paul's arrival in Dublin. I was one of the millions who extended a rapturous welcome to the head of the Catholic Church. I saw absolutely no contradiction in opposing his daft policies on birth control and cheering the great day for the Irish. It was a cheerful fingers up to Cromwell. The whole country had come to a standstill: traffic stopped in Dublin city centre; airports closed; workplaces shut down. I had never seen anything like it before. I love being part of an ode to joy, wherever I find it. I love the theatre and drama and spectacle of religion. Plus, my mother wanted to see him.

She and my sister Nuala came down from Derry by bus, and I took them to the house that atheist friends had loaned me while they fled the country. We had the time of our lives. We rose at dawn and, as we queued for the special buses into town, John Paul's plane, painted in papal colours, appeared over Dublin Bay, moving so slowly that it seemed at times to be suspended in the sky. Everybody, including the cops, looked up, and cheered and laughed and applauded.

In the Phoenix Park, which had been divided into metal corrals to contain us all, we were happy and carefree as a bunch of babies. We were too far away to see the Pope conduct mass under the newly erected (and very ugly) cross which reared above him, couldn't hear a word he said, and consequently conducted ourselves like pagans, eating and drinking from the snacks we had brought: we had been up and on the move for six hours. We also knew that, when mass should end, the Pope would be driven through our serried ranks in his Popemobile.

In truth, it was seeing him, not attending mass, which was the point of it all. Mass was available any old time. And anyway, if the central part of mass was the consecration of the host, the turn-ing of bread and wine into the body and blood of Christ — what matter that we missed it, as we were now in the bodily presence of Christ's nearest relation, John Paul, who had a direct line to God the Father.

The Popemobile came within feet of our corral. I loved the Pope's frock and his jewellery and his handsome masculine looks.

Afterwards, there was benign chaos and no bus to take us home. Hundreds of women queued for portaloos in the Park, and my mother broke ranks to go into the nearby gents' toilet, before which stood but a handful of men. The other women, shocked at first, poured in after her, laughing at another small step for womankind. We walked six miles to another friend's house for dinner. My mother vomited from nerves, exhaustion and shyness.

We were driven home and sat up late into the night to watch the replays. Next day, Nuala and my mother went back to Derry.

As he progressed through Limerick, Galway, Knock and Drogheda, the Pope shot himself in both feet. Years later I described how he had single-handedly, in the course of a weekend, destroyed the Roman Catholic Church's hold over the Irish people:

. . . Women, he said in Limerick, should return to the kitchen sink. Paid work outside the home was bad for them, for their offspring and for their husbands. Contraception was no good either. This was the equivalent of telling children they shouldn't have pocket money or buy Smarties.

Murder is murder, John Paul declared confidently in Drogheda, looking North where he had not the nerve to go. 'On bended knee I ask you to stop,' he asked the Provos, and everybody in possession of a telly could see that he was sitting on a chair as he said this, and there was no way, however much the nation still clung to the faint hope that somehow, somewhere, he would show himself infallible, that the viewer could be persuaded that a Pope sitting on a chair could also be on bended knee.

Shortly afterwards the people of Fermanagh elected Bobby Sands, Officer Commanding of the IRA in Maze prison, as their Sinn Féin member of the British Parliament at Westminster; Kieran Doherty, also of the IRA, was elected TD for Cavan; and Paddy Agnew, also of the IRA, was elected for Louth. Cardinal Ó Fiaich's explanation that people saw their elected Sinn Féin representatives as helpful in matters such as gardening was seen as so much ecclesiastical shamrock.

The Pope's visit, said Eoghan Harris at the time, would set Ireland back sociologically for about three weeks. He was wrong. John Paul brought us right smack into the twentieth century. And there is every indication that the people came of secular age right on the button of the 21st. The Pope untied the Gordian knot of Church and State, and personally exposed the fallacy of infallibility, leaving her Holy Men in frocks in tatters, for which let us give thanks. God Bless the Pope.

The critic and columnist Fintan O'Toole subsequently wrote that my critical writing on religion broke radically new ground in Ireland. (I have treasured and hoarded such accolades since I was cast out of the *Irish Times* paradise in 1979.) The curious thing about my article is that it was not written until 1986. I had not been that acerbic, or outspoken, about the Catholic Church in 1979. However, in the year after the Pope's visit, there were political earthquakes North and South, and a personal upheaval in my own life.

The year 1980 opened with the news that IRA prisoners in Northern jails were going on a dirt strike. That meant that they were refusing to wash or slop out. Women and men alike smeared the walls of their cells with their own excrement, and poured urine on to the floor. The vomit and diarrhoea caused by disease were left in their chamber pots, and emptied on to the prison-wing floor when they were released to fetch breakfast. They had to walk through this swamp to get their food. They had a change of clothing, including underwear, once every three months. There were no sheets on the beds.

The dirt strike was a dramatic escalation of the position obtaining since 1976 when they had refused to wear prison clothing and were forced to wear blankets. I remember explaining to Jimmy Breslin, who called me from New York, just why they refused to wear a convict's uniform. The British government, I told him, had withdrawn special category political status from all paramilitary prisoners and decreed that henceforth they should be regarded as criminals. 'They've cancelled the war and announced that the whole thing is a criminal uprising.' Breslin got it in one, in 1976. Most people still hadn't got it when the dirt strike erupted in 1980.

I had been in contact with some of the prisoners since 1 March 1976. Those convicted before that arbitrary deadline were still regarded as political and were now living alongside those categorized as criminal. The 'politicals' were still allowed to communicate with the outside world; the others were forbidden books, newspapers, radio, television and letters. The 'politicals' kept the 'criminals' in touch by shouting messages every night. Some of the

Derry politicals asked me to send them in books about feminism. They were the neighbours' children, particularly Donnacha Mac Neilis, with whose mother, Mary Nelis, I was on friendly terms.

She lived three streets from our house in Derry. She had had eight children. She had won the local heat of the Housewife of the Year competition in 1967, had missed the first civil rights march in 1968 because she was in labour, had joined the SDLP and opposed the IRA, and, on a wintry day in 1976, had found herself standing outside the Catholic cathedral in Derry, barefoot, clad only in knickers and a bra underneath a blanket. She had abandoned modesty in a plea for help for her son, who was freezing in jail. She had two IRA sons in jail at the time. She toured the capitals of Europe in that blanket.

Apart from sending books and letters to some of them, I had done and said little about these prisoners. The IRA itself had said repeatedly that death or prison was the inevitable price of soldiering in its ranks. Sinn Féin would not support Bernadette when she campaigned for a seat in the European elections in 1979, on the platform of return of political status, because the party was opposed to elections. The republican mothers who had campaigned for political status, and who wished to campaign for Bernadette, were told that, if they did, their imprisoned sons would be ordered to denounce them. Sinn Féin also felt that undue focus on prisoners diverted energy away from the IRA campaign. And the party did not, anyway, have the confidence to stand before the electorate.

I regarded a prison sentence as a tax on the fruits of paramilitary activity service, just as I regarded it as a tax on the profits of criminal activity. Many prisoners' relatives heaved a sigh of relief when sentence was passed because imprisonment meant life, not death. Our street consoled a mother thus when word came that her son had been captured in possession of arms. She had been screaming and roaring in grief and pain. She had not known – nor had we – that he was in the IRA. We did not know how else to calm her. 'Mary, Mary, we'll get him a lawyer. At least he'll be safe now. Nobody will shoot him in prison.'

As we consoled her, two women, all unknown to us, were going through Mary's house, looking for guns. They knew the soldiers would soon arrive to conduct a search, and even more guns meant an even heavier sentence. While Mary cried on the pavement, inconsolable and frightened, the two women came out with revolvers and bullets concealed about their frocks and jeans. Front doors on the other side of the street from Mary were open. Some back doors had been deliberately opened, for these two women knew what they were about. They walked in a front door, out a back door into the laneway, in the back door opposite, out the front door, and so on, until the armaments were three and more streets away. Neither of these two women, and none of those who opened doors for them, was in the IRA: they were helping the neighbour's child, who was no criminal. (The IRA had its own methods of which we were unaware. Much later, after the ceasefire, a joyful, relieved IRA commander revealed one of its operational secrets: when arms or explosives were being transported around the Bogside, volunteers signalled that the coast was clear by standing at a front door with a copy of the *Financial Times*. The pink paper on which that august paper is printed is unmistakable, but it seems that no British intelligence operative noticed that people in an area with 50 per cent unemployment were reading the *Financial Times*. Outdated copies, at that – rather than arouse suspicion by placing a daily order at the newsagent's, volunteers used the same copies for months, until the paper faded.)

In 1980 a ghastly scenario reared its head: nobody was safe in prison. The republican females, all of whom were lodged in Armagh Prison, were particularly vulnerable in the dirt strike, due to menstruation, which increased the risk of infection. The ration of sanitary towels issued monthly to each of them was inadequate because they used the towels outside the menstrual cycle as masks round their mouths, and as extra sanitary protection against their dirty knickers and jeans.

In July I went to the United Nations Conference on Women in Copenhagen, in the hopes of publicizing the cause of the Armagh Women. My fare had been paid by a left-wing, Scottish-born woman, then teaching in Dublin, who supported the IRA. Vincent

Browne, editor of the political magazine *Magill*, provided me with a letter of comfort which declared that he had commissioned me to write about the conference. This ensured that I would be given a media pass, access all areas. No fee was agreed. Or offered. Vincent had accepted at face value my desire to write about Copenhagen. And, sure, it was at the back of my mind. Still, Vincent's sudden interest in the international dimensions of feminism was commendable.

I travelled by boat, to save money. A left-wing Swedish organization put a flat at my disposal.

The objective was to garner as much support as possible from the women of the world. Or at least to tell them about the plight of the Armagh Women. I introduced the Swedish left to the concept of the traditional Irish split: they wanted me to lobby Yasser Arafat's Palestine Liberation Organization; I wanted to lobby the Americans. The Swedes opposed those representatives of capitalism. I needed the PLO like a hole in the head, given the careful distance I was putting between myself and the IRA on this issue. I was there to support the rights of political prisoners, not armed struggle from Derry to Gaza. I also felt, prophetically as it turned out, that the PLO, which had just come in from the political cold and was keen to get the ear of America, was also keen to put clear blue water between itself and the IRA.

For the sake of the Armagh Women, we agreed to defer the split, and I set off next morning to register as media at the conference centre. So far, so good. Then I registered as a non-governmental organization (UN bureaucracy was lax in 1980) and set up a table in the entrance hall, which resembled a bazaar, as bona fide NGOs set out their stalls and wares. The two women on the neighbouring table represented the Front for the Liberation of Eritrea.

The PLO did not respond to my written request for a meeting, passed in to their headquarters by their security men. The queue to have an audience with the Americans went round the block and extended into next year.

RTÉ radio was there, and reporter Marian Finucane and television researcher Brigid Ruane were professionally obliged to cover

Irish interests, viz.: millions of women in Copenhagen demand equal pay; one Irishwoman demands rights for the Armagh Women.

Next day, Mary Maher arrived in Copenhagen on behalf of the *Irish Times*. On the third day, thanks to the write-up Maher gave me, a delegation of Sinn Féin women arrived, who agreed at once to a split: that is to say, I needed people praising the IRA like I needed a hole in the head, they questioned my right to speak on behalf of republican women, and flounced off to set up their own table, as far away from me as possible. They had books, pamphlets, posters, badges and tapes of rousing republican songs.

They did not have press passes, and they did not know any of the women who represented the Irish government. I did not tell them what I had acquired as a journalist: the timetable showing the slot for the Irish government's speech to the United Nations next morning. That night, I went to their hotel for drinks with the many representatives of women's organizations who had accompanied the government's delegate-in-chief, who was, of course, a man. Back home, Brendan Daly was a junior minister in the Department of Labour, but in Copenhagen he was, as befitted his status, staying in a separate, even more superior hotel.

I had long enjoyed friendships with such women as Sylvia Meehan, chairwoman of the Employment Equality Agency; Monica Barnes, chair of the Council for the Status of Women; and Hilda Tweedy, President of the Irish Housewives' Association. They made me more than welcome and gave me dinner. Sylvia, in particular, was solicitous: did I want to use her bedroom for a shower, her bed for a nap, her phone to ring home?

I told them the plan: I was going to picket Minister Daly on the morrow as he arrived to make his speech at the UN. The women nodded in a noncommittal fashion. I then addressed another Irishwoman at the table, representing the new feminist imprint Attic Press, as if the delegates were not there. Because these women were my friends, I told Róisín Conroy, and because I would die rather than embarrass them, I would arrive with my placard outside the centre at twenty past ten in the morning, ten minutes before Brendan Daly was due to arrive. Wouldn't it be grand, and a fortuitous coincidence, if Sylvia et al. arrived at the centre at 10 a.m., thus sparing themselves the ignominy of being picketed, of breaking a picket, and of seeming to ignore the plight of the Armagh Women? That would indeed be a fortuitous coincidence, agreed Conroy. And would I, she smilingly asked, repeat the time of my scheduled picket, as she was not sure she had heard me properly the first time? I obliged. Then I resumed conversation with the sisterhood, who generously stood me loads of drinks – the price of which was scandalous in Scandinavia.

At the hour of midnight, we heard an American woman singing 'Happy Birthday' in the far, dim corner of the great lounge. A raucous Betty Friedan was serenading a serene Bella Abzug. They made all us Irishwomen welcome, and we sat around the altar of the goddesses. Friedan and Abzug were terrifically accomplished drinkers. I do not remember the conversational exchanges. We eventually went home with a list of all the places and times where Friedan and Abzug intended to speak in Copenhagen during the rest of the week.

Next morning, I picketed the minister – the women had gone in earlier – and my protest was duly reported in the *Irish Times*. Mission accomplished: news coverage back in Ireland was what mattered. I never really expected to win the support of the PLO, the American government or, for that matter, the Eritreans. Nonetheless, I dutifully ploughed on, asking questions at the press conferences given by whatever country: What is the position of your government on the rights of the Armagh Women political prisoners? Friedan and Abzug, at NGO conferences, addressed my questions at increasing length. Minister Daly sportingly invited me to his embassy reception. Ireland is a small, friendly country. And he might have needed numbers to make up a crowd.

Once home, I wrote to the editor of the *Sunday Tribune*, Conor Brady. We had joined the *Irish Times* together. The *Sunday Tribune*, he said, had no vacancies. The earth opened beneath my confidence. I never applied for a job ever again.

I still entertained, though, faint hopes of getting back into the

Irish Times. In the spring of 1980, Mary Maher, wearing her features editor hat, had given me a lifeline by commissioning a weekly opinion column; it was a part-time job, at part-time rates, but it was a foot back on the ladder.

Out of self-interest I avoided writing about the Armagh women. But in August, I could keep silent no longer. I wrote a column suggesting that feminists could not stand aloof from the plight of the republican women prisoners. My opening line was that menstrual blood was being smeared on the walls of Armagh Jail. I made no mention of male prisoners, though clearly such softening of conditions as the women might win would accrue to them, too.

The article attracted attention. The following week, Maher turned a page over to women who argued against me. I did not mind the counter-arguments – some of the feminists were acquaintances with whom I had long campaigned on other issues, and two of them, Maírín de Burca and Nuala Fennell, had been founding members, with myself, of the Irishwomen's Liberation Movement in 1970. What upset me, to put it mildly, was that Maher refused space on the third week to feminists who supported my stance. I argued with her, unsuccessfully, that that amounted to censorship.

In September, I returned to the fray, addressing the arguments of those who opposed me. This time, I suggested that the women seeking political status were pioneering the way forward for all prisoners, whether political or criminal, in that the rights they demanded should be available as a matter of course to anyone in jail – just as, I wrote, benefits flowed from suffragettes to all women voters.

I was feeling very clever, and powerful and salved in conscience. I had never come so close to openly defending the IRA. The defence was tangential, of course, and I was glad of that: I was supporting the neighbour's child, not the actual IRA or its activities. On that political fence, I was still firmly seated.

Then I went to London for an all-women trade union conference on discrimination against women workers. On the plane over, a prominent RTÉ presenter whispered to me: 'Good on ye about the Armagh Women.' I was struck by the fact of her whispering.

The North was dangerously unspeakable. The article I wrote after the conference was a cheerful rant against male-chauvinist union officials. It was based entirely on the facts I had learned in London. I delivered it by hand, on deadline, to Mary Maher's house, which was on the same street as mine. (There were no faxes in 1980, much less e-mail.) There was a furious knocking on my door at midnight. An envelope had been pushed through the letterbox. There was no one outside. My article was inside the envelope, with a hand-written covering note by Maher. She wrote that she would not publish it; she would not suffer such an attack on her male trade union comrades.

I resigned. No clouds of glory or revolutionary thunderclaps attended my resignation. I don't think anybody actually noticed the demise of my column. That winter of 1980, I eked out a living with a weekly radio column on RTÉ radio, sporadic appearances on television, a column for the fortnightly magazine *In Dublin* and contributions to British women's magazines. A small Irish publisher, Ward River Press, commissioned an anthology of my 'In the Eyes of the Law' series, which yielded an advance of a welcome few hundred pounds, and led to peaceful days in the National Library (which boasts the most beautiful toilets in Ireland) reading my own work. Almost simultaneously, another even smaller publisher, the Irish Writers' Co-op, commissioned me to write about the Armagh Women, yielding another few hundred pounds. I was managing.

Chapter Twenty

By a series of astonishing accidents, Kate Millett arrived into our house to stay. The feminist intellectual had been brought to Ireland by the women's branch of the Labour Party, to address a meeting chaired by Senator Mary Robinson. There was a private party afterwards for her in somebody's house, and word of mouth soon spread that no invitations had been issued to women who specifically defined themselves as lesbian. This struck many of us as unfair, given that Millett was an outspoken lesbian, and we arrived at the house, threatening to picket it if we were not let in. We were let in.

The party was lacklustre after the marvellous atmosphere which Millett had wrought earlier in Liberty Hall – she was one of the best, and most gentle, public speakers I had ever heard. Women and men alike were lulled into sympathy as she spoke out against torture worldwide. I was enormously pleased when she matter-of-factly included the plight of the Armagh Women in a litany that linked Chile, Iran and the West, regardless of the systems under which such things happened. 'As a humanist I ask, what about all those prisoners? They're sick. They command our compassion.' American capitalism, Soviet socialism, British imperialism, terrorism, sectarianism and male chauvinism were 'fingers on the souring hands of patriarchy. To stay alive we have to change patriarchal control.'

There was so little fun at the party that we intruders soon left and went dancing in the Hirschfeld Centre, a gay resource centre that David Norris had funded out of his own pocket. Millett had paid generous tribute in her speech to the constitutional action he took in an unsuccessful effort to have homosexuality decriminalized in Ireland. Naturally, I covered his case – and, naturally, coward that I was, I did not stand shoulder to declared shoulder with the brave man who had openly stated his homosexuality. One reason the party was dull was that Millett was closeted in a corner with the women who had come with her from America. None of them, including Millett, showed much interest in anyone, for reasons I understood years later when I had done a few mini tours of my own – if it's Tuesday, it must be . . . wherever.

A few weeks after she left Dublin, word filtered back of the strange and startling things which Millett was doing, and which were being done to her, in the west of Ireland. After speaking in Galway, and touring a little, she had squatted in the toilets at Shannon airport for a couple of days. Then she was taken, forcibly, to a mental home, where, we heard, she was now incarcerated. Sylvia Meehan visited her there. None of this had been mentioned in the media.

The psychiatrist Ivor Browne, partner of June Levine, obtained her release on condition that she had a residence in Ireland. Christina and I agreed to take her in, and I picked her up at Ivor's clinic. She was hungry. She wanted seafood. I took her to the Lord Iveagh, a posh restaurant near Ivor's surgery. The meal cost an arm and a leg – all the money I had on my person – and my heart sank. We apologetically showed Millett the spare bedroom, in which junk was stored, and she said to give her an hour and she'd join us downstairs for cocktails. Cocktails? Yes, at five o'clock, she said – it was a firm ritual with her. She liked gin and ice and olives. And a turf fire in the living room. Christina rushed out and spent money we could not afford on gin and wine and turf briquettes.

At five to five, Millett called us up to her bedroom. The change in it was breathtaking. She had fashioned a snug, elegant boudoir out of bits and pieces, and even set up a writing desk. I had never seen such a transformation. She came downstairs, stood by the fire, and let the flames glint off the cocktail glass. I was enchanted, and crucified with shyness and nerves. I was soon half-cut. American cocktails are dynamite, and I didn't normally drink at that hour – especially after wine at lunch. It did not help that Millett insisted on the curtains being drawn because, she said, the police were probably spying on us. Nothing we said could dissuade her from her belief that Ireland was a police state.

When Christina went to work next morning, I was left alone with the great woman. She was completely and utterly paranoid. I was not to answer the phone – it was tapped. I was not to answer the doorbell – someone was coming to take her away. I was to note the numbers of passing cars – secret agents. I was to photograph the bruises left by injections in her bum, administered in the mental home, as proof of the torture she had been put through: Millett handed me a camera, took down her trousers, lowered her knickers, lay face-down on the floor, and said that I was not to misunderstand the situation. 'Don't make a pass at me, baby dyke,' she said. Me? Dyke? I had never used such a term to describe myself or anyone else, abhorred the self-denigration inherent in it. Such a word had never passed my lips, and now I was being called one. Millett saw my consternation and grinned. 'I'm the big dyke around here, baby dyke.' I sensed affection in her words, but was not mollified. Then I allowed myself an inward smile. If it was good enough for Millett, why not for me? Maybe 'baby dyke' wasn't such a hard term. And could I not be as brave as she?

I could not. We were soon at loggerheads. I wasn't interested in her bloody bum, or her body, or in any way romantically inclined towards her. I was a prisoner in my own house . . . with one of the greatest feminist minds in the world.

This conundrum exercised Christina and me for two exhausting weeks. Millett would not stay in the house alone. She spent a lot of time in her room, reading and writing. Her transatlantic calls to the woman she loved in New York ratcheted up the telephone bill. Soon we were calling the woman ourselves, after Millett went to bed, and to hell with the cost. We got no consolation: New York said that there was no point her coming over until and unless Millett went back on lithium for manic depression. How long might this interlude last? New York said it could take weeks, months . . . Ivor and June and Sylvia Meehan came round often and got nowhere.

The cocktail hour, though, was great.

Eventually, Millett agreed to return to New York, and June, Ivor, Christina and I went by car with her to the airport. When she got there, she wouldn't get out of the car. We repaired to a hotel, where Ivor offered her a tranquillizer. They circled each other round the room. We all drove back to our house.

And then a woman arrived from Amsterdam. I knew her kind at once, having experienced foreigners in Derry and Belfast who flew in to service the revolution, at the level of lackey, if necessary, if it gave them a place among the gods. And was that not exactly what I had done, springing Millett from the asylum, leaping in where others, including Mary Robinson, had failed? The woman had hired a car, and she and Millett were going God knows where. I waved them a heartfelt goodbye.

Millett wrote about the episode in her book *The Loony Bin Trip*, and we got a graceful letter from her. She had blown a remarkable opportunity on her first visit to Ireland, she wrote in her letter, through the 'ill luck of having a nervous breakdown on the spot . . . and I happened to be busy being crazy and alienated and exasperated.' She recalled in the letter the 'fireside at Nell and Christina's, dinner at Sylvia's, the luncheon at June and Ivor's, even the grand hotel, all moments when everything flew asunder because of manic outrage . . . something uneasy, diseased thwarted our interaction . . . my fault . . . to have been crazed – never mind that you're sane and sober remembering it – the remorse is awful.'

The letter had no address other than Provincetown, and we never heard from her again. I will always remember the way she changed the spare bedroom into a soothing sanctuary: Kate Millett, even when crazed, knew what a woman needs.

Shortly after Kate Millett left, I got another call asking if I could help another woman. The caller was a mutual friend of mine and of the academic and TV producer Nuala O'Faolain. Nuala was selling her home and needed a place to stay while purchasing another. Could she have our spare bedroom?

I scarcely knew her, but I agreed at once. That night, when I told Christina the news, she said it was impossible; we had already been through one houseguest trauma and could not face another. Christina had long known and admired Nuala, but she also knew that Nuala was a fragile enough person. She feared that we would have another Millett situation on our hands. Yet again, I felt our relationship creak to snapping point. I wanted to run an open house. I liked not knowing who or what would land in the door, and was eternally curious about difference. Christina wanted order, stability and peace.

On occasion, around the town, Nuala had sought me out, but she was invariably drunk, and conversation was impossible. I presumed that she had a crush on me, like so many other hetero-sexual women who turned to me in despair. Once, at a book launch, she insisted that if we waited until it was over we would be taken to lunch by her father, the dapper society columnist who wrote under the name 'Terry O'Sullivan' using his wife's maiden name, and who, she said, was offered free meals anywhere he went. She introduced me to him. Though the book being launched was a fairly sympathetic tome on the IRA by the *Irish Press* editor Tim Pat Coogan, Terry O'Faolain's boss, Nuala's father had no interest in me whatsoever. I was used to such men: they thought Coogan was all right, but they thought me a rough Northerner. He did not invite us to lunch. I presumed that was because of me, not because his daughter was by then incoherent. I didn't go off to lunch with Nuala anyway, precisely because she was incoherent.

I was aware, nonetheless, that she had a famed intellect. I knew a woman who said that students of English literature in University College Dublin, where Nuala lectured, would literally touch the hem of her academic gown as she walked up the steps of the lecture theatre. Though I had never heard her speak at length, I certainly knew she had to be somebody because the fellow with whom she used to give a dual lecture was Seamus Deane from Derry. Seamus occupied such a rarefied intellectual plane that it was hard to understand him. I had once joked to him that if I could act as his simultaneous translator, using the language of mere mortals, I would make him a star.

There was one other legend about Nuala: she was reportedly considering a marriage of convenience with her great friend, a man who was kept from the pinnacle of his profession by the fact of his homosexuality. I took this to mean that Nuala was not the marrying kind; that she had given up on romantic love.

Christina was adamant that she could not come to our house. I refused to make the call; she picked up the phone, rang Nuala's friend, and withdrew the offer. I had had no right, of course, to make it without consulting her, but I was angry nonetheless.

A month later, I fell completely in love with Nuala O'Faolain, on the basis of an incandescently brilliant speech she made to the annual showcase meeting of the Women's Political Association. It was as simple and instant as that: I love brains. Nuala's language was accessible, intelligible and immediate. Her theme was that 'romance is the worm in the heart of feminism'. A woman would sacrifice independence for the man she loved, and men did not support feminism because it meant giving up male privileges. She put it far more elegantly than that. The timbre of her voice was beautiful. Her theme struck a chord; I had long since come to the conclusion that the heterosexual relationships within hearth and home represented the last great battleground for feminism, which would not be won until men got into that kitchen and rattled those pots and pans.

I went up to her afterwards and asked if she had not considered that lesbian love at least offered an alternative to the wholesale defeat she predicted? The Millett effect was working its demon way: I was fed up with the emphasis on heterosexuality in feminist discourse, and with myself for being shy in the company of intellectuals such as Millett – who came, saw and left without leaving an address. Also I wanted to be near Nuala. She had seemed to be in despair. There was an air of vulnerability about her.

She was shaking at the bar, drink in hand, when Christina and I approached her. She was complaining that she had failed; that the effort wasn't worth the trauma; that no one had caught the meaning of her speech. I was more than miffed at that. Her two female companions consoled her that the women of the WPA were 'bourgeois', 'old fogies' and nobodies. I was astounded. The suggestion about lesbian love was brave, under the unsisterly circumstances. I concluded, though I did not say so, that Nuala should study feminism a little more. The three of them then left the building, which I also did not like – courtesy dictated that Nuala should have returned the compliment of being listened to, by listening to those she had just lectured. She wasn't even curious.

Then I threw courtesy out the window myself and left the building. I knew the bar Nuala frequented in Ranelagh where we both lived. I went into it, and there she was, with a boyfriend and a group of regular drinking companions. Some of them were little legends of their kind – the poets and lawyers who were drinking their talents away. The conversation was boring and laced with tired cynicism. I didn't care. It was enough to be where Nuala was.

Her father died in December. Nuala's sister rang on the night of his burial and said that Nuala wanted to see me. I went round to her house. Nuala was sitting on an armchair in a ramshackle room in a ramshackle house that she had never got round to finishing. I sat opposite her. She was weeping. She shuffled on her knees, across the floor, and put her head in my lap.

A week later, we both attended the first editorial meeting of the women's magazine *Status*, which Vincent Browne was launching as a sister publication to *Magill*. Marian Finucane had left her job in RTÉ to become its editor. Browne had offered me a whopping £1,000 a month to contribute a column and four features a year. Nuala was to be books editor. We went to lunch with two other women, one of whom fancied me. As Nuala became ever more drunk, I decided that I would go to bed with this woman. I did not want to go home to Christina because of the feelings I had for Nuala; I couldn't see myself going to bed with Nuala, despite the fact that she had laid her head in my lap only a week previously. There was no future in it. She had a problem with drink, and she had a boyfriend. The brief physical contact had been like so many others that I had experienced with women: they turned on, then tuned out after a short walk on the wild side.

After the very long, liquid lunch Nuala and I went on to her local, consciously prolonging the moment. The double bed in her home was an amazing contrast to the rest of the house. It was deep and soft and luxuriously dressed in clean linen. Afterwards, I looked out the window at the full moon and told her that I felt like the woman in the movie *Lady Caroline Lamb* who had been driven to insanity by love lost for Lord Byron. 'That was a stupid woman, and it was a stupid film,' Nuala said crisply. I burst out laughing. There would be no sentimentality here.

The house I shared with Christina was a scene of desolation that Christmas season. I had told her about Nuala, and I felt like a murderer. On a Sunday morning Nuala rang. I had not contacted her since the night we spent together. 'How could you?' she said. She was waiting in her car at the foot of the street. I went to her. She drove us to the house of her friend the art critic Máire de Paor and her husband, Liam, the archaeologist. They and their teenage children were having a cooked breakfast. I sat in an armchair with a plate of bacon and eggs and sausages. Nuala sat on the floor, leaning easily back against my legs.

Fifteen years later, when Máire died, and I wrote an article saluting her, Nuala said to me: 'When I told Máire that I was in love with you, she said that of course I would never grace her dining table again.' And indeed Nuala had not, and I had thought that that was because she had swapped the life she professed to hate – eating in society – for the life she enjoyed with me – eating at home.

On Christmas Eve 1980, I took the last bus to Derry, a four-hour journey in the dark. I wept all the way. The young fellow sitting beside me started to cry. 'I don't know what's going on with you,' he said, 'but there's something I have to tell my parents in Derry and it's going to kill them.' I told the youth that his parents would love him, no matter what. We said no more and held hands, silently comforting each other. I was in bits over hurting Christina. I was in bits at the thought of not being able to leave her and go with Nuala. I walked in the door, sat down beside my mother on the sofa, said, 'Mammy, I am a lesbian,' and burst into tears.

Gráinne was sent for. And Carmel. My sister Nuala sat silent and glum in the chair, the peace of her home wrecked once again.

I do not remember the rest of the evening or Christmas Day, except that on Christmas Day I got a phone call from Dublin from a friend of Nuala. He said, 'Nuala asked me to tell you that she's in St Patrick's, the mental home. She's had a nervous breakdown.'

'Over me?' I asked, prone as ever to self-regard.

'No. Over her father,' he said, impatiently.

It was the day after Christmas that I said to my mother, 'Think of me as one of God's freaks.'

'You're no freak,' she said.

I went to see Sister Agatha again. She listened, said nothing, and was afraid for me.

Next afternoon, Christina arrived unexpectedly, to fetch me back to Dublin. At the front door, my mother said, 'Wait a minute,' and ran back into the kitchen. She reappeared with a pair of curtains that she had taken down from the kitchen window. 'This is for your new house,' she said to me and Christina.

I was glad that I had not told her that Christina and I were splitting up. My mother had had enough shocks and confusion. When we got to Dublin, Christina dropped me at the hospital. I sat by Nuala's bed until very late. She was drugged and sad. We held hands.

That New Year's Eve, my sister Carmel told me, she and her two partners from the hairdressing shop called in to see my mother as the clock struck twelve. My sister Nuala and my mother were hunched over the fire. The fire was out.

Chapter Twenty-One

Shortly after I returned to Dublin, I moved out of the home I shared with Christina and into a rented house. I visited Nuala every day, using her car, which was a wreck. She was heavily drugged. I stayed late every night in the psychiatric ward. Once, we sat with the other patients and watched *Porgy and Bess* in black and white. January ended with Nuala's discharge from hospital, the publication of my book on the Armagh Women, and the near-fatal shooting of Bernadette and her husband, Michael McAliskey, by loyalists who broke into their isolated rural home. Michael had placed his body against the door in an effort to keep them out, and been riddled with bullets. They found Bernadette lying across the bed, sheltering her children, and shot her in several places. Bernadette's wounds were life-threatening. I spent some awful nights in Dublin with Mary Holland, who had moved with Eamonn to Ireland, the two of us helpless by the phone, waiting to hear the worst. Not for the first time – indeed it was a pattern by now – happiness in Dublin was offset by misery about the North.

June Levine hired a limousine and escorted me to the launch of *The Armagh Women*. There was not one journalist in the Gresham Hotel room where the book was unveiled, not one photographer – nobody at all, apart from the publisher, June and me. There were good reviews. The book did well for a fortnight, then it was withdrawn because of a threatened libel suit. The small publishing firm the Irish Writers' Co-op had not been able to afford a solicitor to read submitted texts for possible libel.

The alleged libel was that I had written that the (unnamed) husband of one of the (named) women I interviewed was 'on the run' in the Republic and didn't dare return to Belfast. This man wrote, via his solicitor, to my publisher, and to the distributor, Eason, that he was not a fugitive. The only way I could have proved that he was would have been to call the RUC into court to say so. That would have made me an informer and felon-setter. I would not have taken such action, a fact upon which this man relied when he saw an opportunity to win quick, easy damages from the publisher and distributor. His claim was met and paid in full once he had lodged it – an out-of-court settlement of £5,000, a handsome amount of money at the time.

The man was, in strict fact, right. I had been economical with the truth about him – in an effort to save his reputation. The Provisional IRA had expelled him from Belfast, and from the IRA, because he had embezzled money from the organization. I had given him an honourable exit, to spare him and his partner from embarrassment.

It astonished me that neither the publisher nor the distributor contacted me before they withdrew the book and paid damages. Without consulting me, they had capitulated immediately. They got out cheaply – and I paid dearly because, ever after, Eason, by far the biggest bookseller and wholesaler in Ireland, regarded my books askance. Of the seven books I have published to date, Eason only ever again distributed two, both supposedly safe by virtue of the fact that the contents had previously been published in newspapers.

Ignorant of publishing and distribution as I was in 1981, I knew only that the first book I had ever written was successfully sued and pulped. Before it was destroyed, I went to Sinn Féin and to the IRA and asked them to get this man to withdraw his libel suit. I believed the IRA could put pressure on him. Coward and opportunist to the last, I did not say why, or how, I felt that the organization could do this. The IRA responded by saying that I had not praised the Armagh Women for the activities which had left them in prison; that I had supported the women's dirty protest while distancing myself from their activities; that the IRA, and Sinn Féin, had more to do than engage themselves in defending people like me who did not defend and support people like them.

My book had included fierce criticism of male chauvinism within Sinn Féin and the IRA. The women I interviewed pointed out, for instance, that a republican drinking club, named in honour of a woman who was left paralysed after a gunfight with the British army, would not let her into the same club during men-only Sunday sessions. The women also pointed out that republicans had ignored the plight of the Armagh Women until a feminist group, Women against Imperialism, picketed the jail in support of them on International Women's Day 1979. Much of the book, taken out of the mouths of republican women, was an attack on Sinn Féin's reactionary policies, at the time, against basic women's rights such as contraception.

The only satisfaction I derived from the affair was that 2,000 copies of the book were retrieved from the warehouse before they could be destroyed, and illicitly exported to Canada, from where they are still sold; the proceeds are used to support global campaigns for the relief of political prisoners.

At his request, sixteen years later, in 1996 I met the IRA man who sued me. He was in the last stage of a terminal disease. He candidly acknowledged that he had seized the opportunity to make a quick buck and said that he was sorry. He confirmed what I had long known: he had been put up to the scam by ultra-left elements in Irishwomen United.

It seemed that my brilliant career as a book writer had come to a premature end. Before it did, I got a subtle letter from Sister Agatha.

> . . . It must have taken an immense amount of courage to write such a book, laying bare such naked truths. I don't deny, it took me a considerable amount of courage to continue reading the almost unbelievable facts that had to be expressed in such blatant language.
>
> I was very glad to have that talk with you at Christmas. I hope it did you some good. You know, Nell, this 'public life' of yours seems to me just an escape from realities you cannot face, and from the willpower you think you haven't got . . . You have always trusted me and I always trusted you.
>
> . . . Even for my sake, Nell, would you not think of 'going apart'

and looking into your soul. You can still be a tremendous lover of right and truth and one of God's great ones. Nell, I'm not preaching. I'm merely back again in 'the Wee Nuns' and you are seven years old.

My prayer and love,
Your second mother,
Sr Agatha

Nuala was by then in a rented flat, by the sea, facing Dublin Bay, her home having been sold. I moved between my rented house, my home with Christina, with whom I had not made a complete break, and Nuala's flat. I was out of my emotional tree. I could not resist Nuala.

In the early hours of Saturday, 14 February, St Valentine's Day 1981, forty-eight young people died in a fire at the Stardust night-club in Artane, on the north side of Dublin. I had been working on the Friday night, covering the opening of that weekend's Fianna Fáil Ard Fheis, and was at their party afterwards when word of the fire broke. There is no point beating about the bush on the use I made of the tragedy: the disaster was a perfect alibi for not going home. I could claim to have gone to the scene of the fire because I would have to write about it for *Status*. I went to Nuala's flat. She taught me the words of her favourite love song, 'You Are My Heart's Delight'.

On the Sunday, using the *Status* alibi again, we went to the home of Nuala's sister Deirdre, who lived in Artane, near the site of the tragedy. I liked Deirdre, and her husband, Eamon, very much. They reminded me of the Bogside. They lived on Eamon's income as a printer, prized education for their eight children, and made the stranger welcome. They lined their children up on the sofa, and coaxed them into singing 'Lord of the Dance' in tribute to the deaths of the young of their parish. They cooked food for us – Eamon, enchantingly, always cooks the Sunday dinner – were warmly curious about the stranger in their midst, then reverted immediately to priorities: boasting about, and concerned about, their children.

Neither Deirdre nor Eamon had a clue that night about the burgeoning relationship between me and Nuala. Our relationship already had its difficulties. Her idea of a meal was a bag of fish and chips and a six-pack of beer. She would get slightly woozy on the beer, then take a sleeping pill and seek oblivion. I wondered what I was letting myself in for.

One morning she looked at me and said, 'Your hair is the colour of weak tea. You have a heart-shaped face.' I could not get over that – that anybody had taken the trouble to study me so closely and find exactly the right phrase: my hair, when I studied it, was indeed that colour. That was what I had let myself in for: a companion who took that trouble.

She wrote notes to me between classes in college, and during staff meetings, and enclosed erotic doodles. Her heart was 'as full as an egg' with love for me, she wrote. She showed me her contribution to a forthcoming book about Irish women poets and fiction writers: she mentioned Molly Bloom, Maud Gonne and me as exemplars of the 'intractability' of Irish womanhood. I thought she had placed me in just about the right position in the pantheon of exemplars and accepted her adoration.

The best times for us were in the morning, when Nuala was completely sober and somewhat rested. I did not believe her to be the alcoholic she said she was. She never drank more than six beers, and she never, while she was with me, returned to the life of rackety afternoons in pubs with whosoever wanted to get completely drunk.

I loved her mind so much that I learned by heart and savoured observations she made. I called her my central intelligence agency – she was versed in literature, music, history, the meaning of obscure words. The only thing she didn't really grasp, in my opinion, was the North, but then I believed that of practically everybody in the South, and did not hold it against them because no generation since 1921 had really had to deal with unionists, Britain and war. Nuala didn't even read my book.

At the end of March 1981, after my thirty-seventh birthday, Christina and I definitively split. Ivor Browne advised me that I should say goodbye to everything in the house that reminded me of the love that had been there. In her absence, I kissed Christina's shoes – she had twisted her ankle, once, and cried with the pain. And then I went to the tiny furnished house that I had been renting since January. Nuala had by then moved into the terraced house she had bought.

I stayed with her every night. She did not invite me to live with her. That did not unduly upset me. I was emotionally unfit to live with another; the hurt I had visited upon Christina haunted me. I lived the lie that, as long as I didn't formally live with Nuala, I could argue that Christina and I had broken up because our relationship had come to a natural end. I was at the same time angry with Christina, for blaming me: if we were so well together, why did she have affairs? There were two of us in it, as the Gaelic saying has it. As a matter of honour, I continued to pay half the heavy mortgage she had taken on – without a double income, she would never have attempted such debt.

Nuala brought me to England to meet her sisters and brother. I saw London for the first time from the inside. Nuala showed me the street in Oxford where she had lived with her fellow. We stayed in the countryside with two of her friends from her time in the BBC. I was getting a crash course in her past. I noted that her friends in England were all much older than she was. There was little understanding of the North, but much liberal goodwill. I began to understand why she had returned to Ireland.

One morning as we sat outside the front door of Nuala's new home, in the tiny front garden, in the sunlight, eating a breakfast of bacon and eggs and tea and toast, an elderly woman looked over the railings and broke into a smile. It was great to have young blood and life about the street, she said. I was thirty-seven; Nuala was forty-one. We were dead pleased. There was a crew in the street, using jackhammers to dig holes for water pipes. I called one of the men, and he agreed to dig a hole against the front wall, so that we could train greenery up the red bricks. We planted a climbing red rose and clematis. We planted rushing ivy along the fence that separated the garden from the street, to create a private bower. We planted the tiny laurel tree that two gay men, friends of Nuala, presented to us. After the men smoothed fresh concrete over the water pipes directly outside the gate, I inscribed it 'N × N, 1981.'

I took her to Derry that Easter. She linked arms with my mother and her neighbours as they walked through the streets to see the Provisional IRA march out on their Easter Parade, to commemorate the Rising. Then we all drove to Co. Donegal, to the disused fort where Nuala's father had served as an Irish army officer during World War II, where her parents had begun their married life, where Nuala had been a babe in arms. When we returned to Derry that night, it was to riots: two teenage youths had died after being run over by an army Land Rover.

Nuala brought me to a Dublin pub to meet her mother, whose lipstick and powder showed the lineaments of faded glamour. She sat on a high stool at the bar, reading a book, in late afternoon. Her voice was tremulous. Her daughters cajoled her, and were nervous as the effects of alcohol became obvious. Nuala was depressed as we drove home.

In those days, after meeting her mother Nuala would get rapidly drunk. Though she said that it was a comfort to have me there while she drowned her pain, I was helpless. There was nothing I could do to alleviate her nightmare: even as Nuala was making a home, and was in love, her mother was drunk and alone and lonely in a flat on the other side of the city.

Bobby Sands died on 5 May 1981, after a sixty-six-day hunger strike. I was in Derry, sleeping in my mother's house, when the rhythmic banging of metal on a lamppost woke me up around two in the morning. A lonely, breaking, young male voice called out, repeatedly, 'Bobby Sands is dead. Bobby Sands is dead.' My mother and my sister Nuala and I got up, dressed, and, with some of the neighbours, made our way through the dark streets to Free Derry Corner. Thousands of us marched aimlessly, restlessly, speechlessly around the town, the only sound that of our shoes slapping the ground. Other men were on hunger strike – they had joined one by one at weekly intervals. The nationalist North was on a death watch. Margaret Thatcher could not, would not, understand.

I could not comprehend the bravery of these fellows. I knew the wife of one of them. I had taught her in 1968. She used to hang around our street after school, hoping my mother would bring her in for a cup of tea, which my mother did. She had married an orphan, Michael Devine, a republican who lodged with her widowed father, also a republican. He was as young, cheerful and feckless as herself, and they married after she became pregnant by him. Their wedding photo shows him with a bottle of vodka that he had bought on the way to the ceremony. The marriage was a poor one, and they broke up after the birth of their second child. Then he went to jail, for paramilitary activities. She started a relationship with another man. Michael sued for divorce, while in prison, then joined the hunger strike. He would not allow his wife to visit him. As he lay dying, his children were brought to him. Blind by then, he could only feel the outline of their young bodies. The IRA told his wife that he would not be buried, if he died, from her home and that she would not be allowed to attend his funeral. He was buried from his sister's house, his children followed the hearse, and his wife remained invisible. She had three more children by the man she met while her husband was in prison, but she refused to marry him, and all five children carry Michael Devine's surname.

I went to his funeral, as did thousands of other Derry people, most of us attending a paramilitary funeral for the first time. Michael Devine was in the Irish National Liberation Army, an organization that was deeply resented in our area. That was beside the point – he was entitled to political status. I went to the funeral of Patsy O'Hara, also in the INLA. His mother cleaned the public toilets in Derry and was fondly regarded in our area. His paramilitary brother was released from jail for the funeral; his complexion was shocking – sallow and sweaty – and he was a nervous wreck.

Many people were, in that haunting time. The manner of the hunger strikers' deaths was agonizing. A large billboard calendar, erected near Free Derry Corner, numbered the days of their fasting.

The number was changed every day. The higher the number, the closer to death each man came. As in the aftermath of Bloody Sunday, a change was being wrought in the political hearts of Northern Catholics. The prisoners had refused to wear a convict's uniform, and we agreed with them: not one of them had been reared to be a criminal; every one of them would have been a plumber, a carpenter, a doctor, if unionism had not blighted the North and Britain not turned a blind eye. We marched behind the coffins of our own people.

Before he died, Bobby Sands was elected in absentia as Sinn Féin member of the British parliament. 'Put him in, to get him out' was the slogan. The hunger strikes reverberated in the South, too. Before they died, Kieran Doherty and Paddy Agnew were elected to the Dublin parliament, in a general election, and their victory denied Charlie Haughey the majority government he had hoped to form. While the Dáil went through the motions of paying obligatory tribute to the late Kieran Doherty, the TD for Cavan-Monaghan, I sat in the press gallery in the Dáil, wearing a black armband. The chief usher tried and failed to have me thrown out for wearing a political emblem. I said I was mourning my granny.

I think it was the pressure of the hunger strike on politics in the South that led the Taoiseach, Charlie Haughey, and opposition leader, Garret FitzGerald, to agree, one astonishing afternoon, 27 April 1981, to change the Constitution so as to protect what became known as 'the unborn'. An anti-abortion group, set up in the wake of the Pope's visit, had decided that a Constitutional loophole existed which would allow abortion to be legalized. The group called itself the Pro-Life Amendment Campaign (PLAC), and comprised the Catholic elite – leading medics, lawyers, and lay organizations such as the Knights of Columbanus. Overnight, the country was put on red alert and asked to defend zygotes. We hadn't a clue what zygotes were. People were put through a crash course on theology and eclampsia, and were astonished to learn that male ejaculation sent two million sperm up the birth canal, heading for one solitary egg. At first, feminists reacted with mirth. We wanted better odds. None of us, including Haughey and

FitzGerald, realized that by 1983, when the amendment to the Constitution was put to the people, the population would be engaged in a virtual civil war. Households were split; bus conductors were at each other's throats; the Russian Church in Exile split neatly down its tiny congregational middle; grown men, including parliamentarians, wore pins in their lapels to signal their piety – gold-encrusted replications of the tiny feet of the unborn.

The central fact of my political life in 1981, however, was that Sinn Féin, on foot of its success in having Bobby Sands elected, entered the political arena. The optimism engendered by Sinn Féin's espousal of the ballot box – a sign that the war might cease – allowed me to indulge in the luxury of watching Prince Charles marry Diana in July 1981, even as the young men died.

I travelled with Nuala to Co. Clare to watch the televised wedding in the house of her friend. I was the youngest person in the room, in age and attitude and culture, which was to be a recurring theme in my life with Nuala. A group of women gathered in the sitting room, and we had sherry, Windsor soup, smoked salmon sandwiches and wine. The Royal Family is the best soap opera in the world, with the added piquancy that it is not fictional. No amount of money can protect the Windsors from the same family troubles that beset the rest of us, and their troubles were on international display that morning. Diana's parents were divorced, and they turned up with their respective second partners; Charles's great-uncle, the abdicated king, was not invited because Charles's granny would not tolerate the presence of her brother-in-law; Princess Margaret, her rebound marriage now over, sat alone, a reproach to those who would not let her marry her true love, the divorced Peter Townsend. The Queen's mannerly, calm conduct among the shambles over which she presided was an example to us all. Over time, I would realize – and love them for it – that Nuala's family had the same attitude to disaster.

Nuala and I went to Rome that summer. She had booked us into a luxury hotel for the first night, then insisted that we move into an 'authentic' bed-and-breakfast place in the Jewish quarter. It was a big room, hot and airless and authentic as all get out. Travels with Nuala were always going to be authentic. I was so happy that I burst into guilt-soaked tears in a cobbled alleyway, wondering how Christina was getting on. We left Rome and went to an authentic commuter village by the sea. Always eat where the cops eat, Nuala said, and we did and the food was shite – a near-impossible achievement in Italy. From then on I chose the restaurants, just as I chose the hotel where I had overcome all inhibitions and asked for a double bed.

We bought clothes for each other in the market, choosing flounces and silks and white linen. The hit record that summer in Italy was 'By the Rivers of Babylon', and when it boomed out, wherever we were in Sperlonga, I sometimes stood rooted to the spot, thinking 'Nuala, Nuala, Nuala.' I taught her not to be afraid of the sea, and we would rush in between courses during lunch on the esplanade. We found a deserted wooden restaurant at the far end of a beach and rendered ourselves giddy with Amaretto liqueur. Afterwards, stretched out on the sand, when she turned to me, I resisted the embrace, fearful that it would attract unwelcome attention from the families nearby. Nuala paid them no heed at all. I was sorry that I could not behave as naturally as she did.

Taking confidence from her, though, when I got back to Derry I wore the low-cut flouncy dress she had bought me. The neighbours fully approved. At the first night of Brian Friel's play *Translations*, in Derry, the playwright looked approvingly down my cleavage, and Cyril Cusack, a sexy little man, bought me a drink and flirted with me. Nuala was delighted.

She brought me at the end of August to the Merriman Summer School in Co. Clare, to meet the kind of people she admired. Merriman's bawdy poem, 'The Midnight Court', had been written in the eighteenth century as a satirical protest against sexual Puritanism. The Merriman Summer School had been set up in the 1960s to counteract the pessimism still prevailing, and reflect the optimistic belief that the tide had changed: the Vatican, under the laughing Pope John, had advocated relaxation of strict Catholic dogma, and Ireland was stirring.

The school attracted scholars and intellectuals and bohemians, the cream of Ireland's intelligentsia, who wore their learning lightly – often, very lightly, as they spent time between lectures in the pubs, singing the great national songs in both Irish and English, ranging over quarrels both amiable and fierce, scalding each other, mocking each other, then jumping into the sea to cool off. The great issues of the year were formally debated, with guest speakers from home and abroad. Ambassadors came, and diplomats, and government ministers – and the rest of us.

The North provided an undercurrent of tension. I ignored that, though eventually, in the late 1980s, the bile would burst. The school's scholars were debaters, not activists, and you wouldn't find them on a picket line or on demonstrations. Feminism, inasmuch as it penetrated the overwhelmingly male discourse in Merriman, meant livelier women students. Most of the great and good males did not bring their wives to the annual fortnight-long Bacchanalia, but an old Irish saying held true: men would walk over a dozen naked women to get to a pint of stout. A university professor thought it the height of joyful decadence when we persuaded him one starlit night, after drinking ceased, to join a group of women for a naked dip in the sea. He had never swum in the buff before.

With a shrewdness unusual in me, I applied for and was awarded a grant from the Arts Council to subsidize the writing of the great novel. *Status* closed in September, but the grant afforded enough money to get through the winter. My perilous financial situation was further stabilized by the news that Christina was returning to America and renting out her house – no more mortgage.

In the nine months I had been with her, Nuala had not gone out at night in Dublin. She pleaded that it was such a pleasure to have a home life that she wished never to budge. I was, by contrast, bursting for some vestige of social life. I wanted us to go to the theatre, the movies, a restaurant, even the pub she used to frequent – anything to get out of the house. I went to the movies on my own one Saturday night. When Richard Gere, an officer and a gentleman, swept Debra Winger into his arms and walked into the sunset – a great shot for sentimental lovers, that – I was sad. I would have settled for me and Nuala walking out of a Dublin theatre together. I was also worried: no home, no job, one half-finished book, living in a rented room, a tiny grant between me and penury, and Nuala refusing to come out to play.

Then I got a surprise offer of free board and lodging in the newly opened artists' retreat at Annaghmakerrig in Co. Monaghan, which had been bequeathed to the nation by Tyrone Guthrie. Nuala was upset when I told her I was going away. I could not see what else I could do: if I was to earn an income, it would have to be through the great novel, not journalism. I was not going to live off anyone. I was not going to go on the dole.

On the September day I left Dublin, Nuala told me that a true lover had to choose between writing and passion. 'Why not save writing for a resource, for when we fail?' she asked in an anguished tone. I remembered the words of a woman I liked, who said scathingly of the writer she married that reading him was a lot easier than living with him; that writing was a lot easier for him than rearing their children or tending their home. Whatever about writing, rearing children was not going to be an issue for Nuala and me. She had miscarried at three months, just before we met. She was thirty-nine and not even sure who the father might be. She had been told, in her twenties, when she was deeply in love and in a long relationship, that she would have difficulty conceiving and had not sought fertility treatment. And she was with me now, and wanted nothing to distract us from each other. As for myself, I had never, for a second, wanted a baby.

I was lonely on the trip from Dublin to Monaghan, in the company of the centre's director, Bernard Loughlin, and his wife, Mary. They were both from the North, which was a consolation, but I scarcely heard a word they said. I had chosen writing over passion. Then again, Nuala had chosen independence over passion. After they settled me in a lovely room in the great house by the lake, I wrote a long letter to her. So much for the book.

Then I went down to the kitchen for the evening meal, a communal event for the resident artists. There were only two artists in the place. We were the pioneers. The huge room was silent,

353

the long table deserted. Seated at a smaller table by a window overlooking the vegetable garden was a hulk of a man, big of face and hands. Niall Quinn gave me his book *Voyovic and Other Stories* and said that he had cooked himself a pound of prawns in the early hours of the previous night. The fridge-freezer, he said, was of industrial size, packed with the finest food, and we could eat anything we wanted, and as much as we wanted, when we wanted, and besides that, Mary's cooking was delicious. Niall was as broke as myself, and as sure of his talents as I was of mine, and I took to him at once. The fear abated. I wrote to Christina that night, hoping that the news that I was in Monaghan, not Dublin, would ease her pain in America.

There was no television, Niall warned. Next morning, there were no newspapers. Bernard did not believe that artists should be distracted by such frivolities. I set off to the nearest village, two or three miles away, to get the *Irish Times* and post the letters. I never wrote to Christina again, but the short-story-length letters to Nuala were a daily affair.

Pioneering in Annaghmakerrig was difficult. As our numbers rose, so did problems: one writer spent his first night sprawled in a drunken sleep on the great staircase; an artist was drunk most evenings at dinner; a religious maniac insisted on saying grace before meals. Niall and I countered by expressing our own spirituality, dancing and whooping round the table like native Americans. Other women artists arrived, and a stand-off occurred after every dinner, as the females sat resolutely on their seats, waiting for the men to put dirty plates into the dishwasher. I desperately wanted to drink wine with the lovely food, but the others saved their money for the pub afterwards, and my bottle didn't stretch round the table.

One night in November I woke up to find Nuala by my bed. She had found an open window downstairs and climbed in. She was wearing the tailored grey jacket and skirt that I loved. I was by then as much alert to her body as to her mind. She had slender shoulders, neat ankles, a head of thick, dark curls, small pearly teeth and eyelids that I told her were like crushed-velvet curtains when her eyes were bent to a book.

354

She took me in her arms that night and said, 'Let's go home,' and we arrived in Dublin as dawn broke. We lived together from then on. I returned to Annaghmakerrig only to pick up what remained of my things.

That Christmas season, we went shopping for delicacies in Dublin's finest stores, playing a make-believe game that we were about to be locked away for the duration. We met Gay Byrne and his wife, Kathleen Watkins, in the food emporium of Brown Thomas. Hugs and kisses were exchanged. I felt deliciously normal. Nuala's two sisters, married with children and living in Dublin, took us out to dinner. Deirdre made a solemn toast, saying both sisters were happy that we were together; they had never seen Nuala so stable. In all my life, before and since, that was the only toast ever offered to me and a partner.

Nuala's family were the most accepting, nonjudgemental people I have ever met. She and her siblings were, at times, a collective of pain about their parents, and some of them were occasionally inclined to reckless behaviour, but I never ceased to admire their stoicism, tact and acceptance of each other and of whomsoever each introduced into the vast family circle. Nuala could rightly argue that the price of their acquired wisdom was crucifying: I could only reply that the O'Faolains, including Nuala, were an example to us all.

On Christmas Eve 1981 Nuala arrived in the door with gifts for me: a red fox fur coat, and a pair of red silk knickers by Christian Dior. I wore them to bed, and we drank a bottle of Baileys Irish Cream. I wore the coat to mass in the Pro cathedral – I hadn't been to mass on Christmas Day for many years. It was one of the many lost rituals of my youth to which Nuala restored me. Why should we, she asked, let the clerics keep us from communal celebration, and all that beauty of candles, flowers, incense, stained-glass windows and flowers? Why should we be outside the world's rejoicing? That afternoon, she made a turkey dinner. She fell asleep, drunk on the floor, as it burned in the oven, distraught over her mother.

It did not take long to get Nuala to stop the binges. I put a calendar on the wall and, every time she got drunk, I blacked out the day. I blacked out the second day on account of the hangover and the tension between us: every morning after the night before, I insisted that she listen while I described in merciless detail what she was like when drunk. Nuala's mouth went slack when she was drunk. So much for passion, I said, pointing at the black days in any given week. There were more black days than clear ones.

Soon Nuala was off sleeping pills and was a moderate drinker of wine. She ordered a massive double bed from an institution run for blind people. Both sides got their measurements wrong, it could not be taken up the stairs, we had to take out the window to get it in, and there were no sheets big enough (in those restrained times) to cover its six-by-six-foot frame. It was so big you could throw a party in it, and we did, just the two of us.

My novel lay in the drawer. I had taken up a column with the fervently nationalist *Irish Press*. 'It is your natural home,' Tim Pat Coogan sent word to me (as long as I didn't write about abortion: the sole article I wrote about it was given the thumbs down by managing editor Vivion de Valera, son of Eamon de Valera). No matter – the magazine *In Dublin* gave me carte blanche to write anything I wanted on abortion, and I had more freedom in that regard than any journalist in Ireland, which I exploited to the full. The debate was consuming the country. It had been boiled down by the pro-life brigade to simple choice: were we in favour of murdering babies in the womb or were we not?

'The most dangerous place in the world is in a mother's womb,' said Bishop Joseph Cassidy of Clonfert. One of the leading anti-abortion campaigners was Father Michael Cleary, secret father of two, front man for the Pope's visit in 1979, who specialized in bringing disabled children into television studios and stating that abortionists would have them killed in the womb. His sidekick, Bishop Eamon Casey, secret father of one, had already sold a Catholic hospital in his Galway diocese to private health consultants, a condition of sale being that vasectomies and tubal ligation never be practised there. The entrepreneurs gladly assented.

There was fear everywhere. The Council for the Status of

Women declared that it could not take a stand because there was no unanimity among the myriad groups it represented. The Merriman Summer School stayed aloof from the fray. Academics fell over themselves to get in line with doctors and lawyers, and that line was behind the Catholic Church. The Irish Medical Association opened its annual general meeting in Co. Kerry with a mass celebrated by the area's bishop, Kevin McNamara, who gave a sermon against abortion and in support of PLAC. Eighty-four of Kerry's one hundred doctors, and every lawyer in Kerry, signed the PLAC petition. Three of the doctors faxed in their signatures from their holiday havens abroad.

I had my own haven, at home with Nuala, which saved me from the ravages to which the Anti-Amendment Campaign (AAC) was subjected. Mary Holland, the AAC chairwoman, declared that she had had an abortion, and was called a murderer at public meetings. The AAC was hobbled by a refusal to endorse abortion, which forced it into Jesuitical contortions that avoided the core of the PLAC argument: that abortion was murder. The AAC declared itself against the amendment per se, argued that the matter was properly one for legislators, that a foetus could not be given an equal right to life with its mother, and that the proposed amendment, reflecting Catholic theology, was sectarian. (The Protestant churches in the South were tepidly against the amendment.)

For the first time, I did not formally sign up to a campaign I supported. I wanted the selfish luxury of declaring that abortion was necessary, but mainly I wanted to be at home with Nuala. All my adult life I had given more time to politics than to my private life. Public life was a passion, and a deeply pleasing one. So was journalism. I had got great satisfaction, and gratifying feedback, from both. I knew that I was making a difference. Feminism, as Kate Millett said, was great fun, and it made sense. But it never made me as deeply happy as being with Nuala did, and now I was having it both ways: I could go out to speak, come home to love, and didn't have to sacrifice one for the other.

At Christmas 1982, Nuala gave me a note thanking me for 'the two most vivid years of my life . . . enchanted, I am.' Then off we went to Budapest. After a horse-drawn carriage ride through the snow one night, I hummed a tune to the gypsy band in a restaurant, gave them dollars, and glowed with pleasure when they came over to our table and played 'You Are My Heart's Delight'.

I went on the *Late Late Show* for its special Valentine's feature in February 1983, discarded the love song I had previously agreed to sing with Gay Byrne, and sang 'You Are My Heart's Delight'. Nuala, who had asked me to do it, watched from home.

Nuala did not want anyone to come into our house. One Sunday afternoon, after an overnight visit to Sligo by anti-amendment campaigners where we had persuaded the overflow audience at a public meeting on the issue to declare themselves anti-amendment – an achievement which provoked a local priest to denounce me by name from the altar – I brought the other speakers home with me to celebrate. These three women were accomplished public figures: a member of the Dáil, the chairwoman of a state agency, the president of a woman's group. Nuala was visibly re-strained. Her privacy had been violated. She wanted to read her book, drink her wine, and have a Sunday dinner with me. Activism bored her.

Activism also brought fearful consequences. When I responded to a call for help, from a woman whose partner had spent the night beating her, he managed to trap me as I escorted her out. He put his arm across my throat and bent me backwards over the railings on the third storey of the apartment block. I talked my way out of it and testified against him in court. Women's Aid, to which I went, terrified, for advice about what to do when the vengeful man should get out of prison, told me to strengthen locks on doors and windows. Nuala drew the line at barbed wire on the back wall. I had to tell her what I had managed to forget: that a pimp serving a life sentence for the murder of women had sworn vengeance on the feminists who rescued one of the women working for him, and who testified against him. June Levine had given this woman sanctuary in her home and was in real danger, but Marie MacMahon and I had helped her flee from him one night, clambering over backyard walls in the night, laughing as we fled. We were young.

The pimp had not forgotten. He let it be known, when I went into Portlaoise prison to give a lecture on feminism to the IRA prisoners on the upper floor, that I'd have to pass through the ground floor where his cell was located. I assured Nuala that we'd been told by the Department of Justice that this man would serve the full sentence; we needn't worry until well into the second millennium.

I stopped going so often to Derry. I stopped ringing my mother frequently and was aware of tensions in that regard. I wouldn't ring her for a week, feared her reproach, put it off for another week, and had to work up courage to make a call that I knew would be greeted with the words, 'I could have been dead.'

So could I, I would joke, and I was dying to tell her that which I could not: 'Mammy, I'm in love.' The most I could say was that I was happy, an anodyne, inadequate word for the state of delirium in which I lived. I was painting the bedroom one morning when Nuala, on her way to work, said, 'There will be no open relationship here. Fidelity is all.' She may have been thinking of me, lusting in my heart for others as had been my wont until I met her. She was definitely thinking of herself: she had told me how she once went off with a man even when she was engaged to another. I sang in my heart about her commitment to me; there was not the shadow of a doubt that I would love anyone but her.

I was confident of Nuala. I could see that I was giving her strength to cope with the pain of watching her mother drown in drink. If there was one cloud in our lives it was that, and it promised no early end. Nuala's mother was relatively young. I would accompany Nuala on visits, and the more I did that, the more often Nuala went, until it became a weekly thing, on Saturday afternoons. I thought that regular visits would help her to accommodate to the fact that her mother would not change. This succeeded inasmuch as Nuala's desperation after visiting her mother would not endure quite so long. Nuala had something nice to look forward to after the visits – the balm of our home life.

The worst times were when her mother did not answer our knock at the door. We would walk round the back of the apartment block and look in the window: her mother would be lying on the

359

floor, unconscious. On those days I did not soothe Nuala with songs, in the car, on the way home. She might signal that she was coping by rendering a verse of 'I'll Take You Home Again, Kathleen', which her father used to sing to her mother. Decades later, when my own mother fell temporarily into madness, and I could not help her, I drowned my pain in Southern Comfort. In face of what she saw through that window, so often, Nuala was a brave woman. She chose not to escape into a bottle.

On top of her worries about her mother, Nuala was vaguely anxious about my financial situation. The freelance life was a precarious one, she could see. The heart had been put across us both when I left the *Irish Press* for a brief fling with a new tabloid newspaper that had offered me an enormous salary for a weekly column. I persuaded myself that it was time to write for the masses. As far as my own peer group were concerned, I had fallen down a black hole when the *Irish Times* platform was removed. Nobody I knew read the *Irish Press*. So, if I couldn't write about the masses for the liberal few, I'd write about the masses for themselves.

The billboard poster describing me as the 'conscience of Ireland' was cringe-making, but the tabloid promised me free speech and I believed it. I was assigned, for the first edition, to write about the impoverishment caused by increasing marital breakdown in a Dublin suburb, and the still-extant need for abortion. This suited me just fine. Divorce, I argued, would be a help, in that the ex-husband would be forced by law to pay something towards family upkeep, instead of leaving a deserted wife to rely on state welfare. Better yet, as the wages of most working men were insufficient for two households, the deserted wives' allowance should be abolished and a state subsidy paid to full-time mothers.

When I went down to the office to see the first mock edition roll off the press, I did not recognize the articles under my by-line. They had been rewritten by sub-editors in a bowdlerized manner which suggested that – shock, horror – separated working-class couples were relying on welfare payments to put food in the mouths of their children. I resigned forthwith. The editor reinstated my original copy, and I rejoined.

On abortion, I directed readers to the plight of Lucy in *Dallas*, who was considering termination of pregnancy in circumstances which could only elicit sympathy for her plight. The editor, Jim Farrelly, rang me and said, 'Brilliant.' *Dallas* was then at its television zenith in Ireland: if the Constitutional amendment were to be implemented in full, *Dallas* would be banned on the grounds that it gave information on abortion. Nuala herself had been persuaded by me to watch *Dallas* in an enjoyable Saturday-night ritual of spaghetti bolognese, red wine and ignoring the phone.

The newspaper lasted two weeks. I got neither wages nor the expenses for a fancy hotel in Belfast to which I had repaired to write a considered article on the IRA.

I took part in an occupation of the employer's premises. I allowed the proprietor's son to dissuade me from removing an electric typewriter in lieu of wages. Some revolutionary trade unionist I was. Then, when I turned up, newly unemployed, in my red fox fur coat – a redundant woman has to maintain some dignity – to a press conference on abortion, given by beleaguered Taoiseach Charlie Haughey, he sneeringly asked me who I worked for now. He emphasized the 'now'. I named a radical magazine. Charlie declined to answer my full-frontal question on the abortion refer-endum. The rest of the (national) media declined to insist that he do so.

I was not unduly surprised: after leaving the *Irish Times* in 1978, I had joined erstwhile colleagues from all the national papers at the usual media table in the Dáil for lunch, and had been told, in semi-jocular, unmistakably serious tones, that the table was reserved for accredited senior political journalists. Senior? I had been throw-ing petrol bombs when most of them were in nappies. I could not, nevertheless, help but salute the embattled Charlie. I had affronted him in his day, at the meeting where I prevented him hanging a chain of office round a woman's neck.

The day after I had been humiliated by the Taoiseach, I found a note and a cheque for £200, from Nuala, lying on the kitchen table. 'Speak no more of this,' she wrote. I was glad of the money. I repaid her when the *Irish Press* immediately rehired me. I have replicated her splendid gesture many times since with professional women who are going through a bad patch, and have always been repaid.

Still the fact that I was briefly on the breadline put a worm in Nuala's generous, anxious heart from which she never fully recovered. She had grown up in precarious financial family circumstances. Though her first house in Dublin had been gifted to her by a benefactor, who knew it was time for Nuala to leave England, she had incurred debt by moving up to the house we now shared, and by supporting some of her relatives. The letters she had written to me while I stayed rent-free in Annaghmakerrig spoke amiably of that difficulty. I had paid little heed at the time, thinking that she, fully employed, could afford her debts, while I, unemployed, could not afford to undertake any.

Nothing I could say to Nuala would alleviate her anxiety, in 1983, that I was well able to support myself and contribute to our household expenses. She increased her mortgage to pay for renovations to the house. The builders moved in at Easter, and, in the way of things, stayed so long that I asked them what they'd like for Christmas dinner. While Nuala was out at work, I, working at home in what was a building site, oversaw the tedious business of deconstruction, reconstruction, and the shifting of an electrical socket to the place where we actually wanted it.

There was the further anguish caused by a teenage boy who smashed the windows of the bedroom on a regular basis. 'Lezzies,' he used to call. It became a sport with him. It was my worst nightmare come true. Nuala calmly ignored the boy and installed a shatterproof pane of glass. I saw a flash of her mother's queenly indifference to finger pointing, and envied it. Nuala said the boy's hormones would settle, and he would fall in love and forget us. How I wanted him to fall in love.

The harassment added to the despair that I was already feeling about being outside the comfort zone of a staff job and the society of the workplace. The people who derived most benefit from the activities of such as me were the working class, from whose ranks had just come the most overt bigotry. It helped not one whit that

Nuala feared that I would fail in the employment market altogether.

I began to keep a detailed, meticulous record of my earnings, and showed them to her, together with tax records. Nothing prevailed against Nuala's fearful conviction that a freelance like myself was only as good as her last gig. I was actually doing quite well: incomings were twice the amount of outgoings and, although Nuala earned more before tax, there was no great disparity in our net incomes – freelances get generous tax write-offs. Though Nuala paid the mortgage, I paid most of the bills for running the house.

I took to teasing her about the contradiction between her anxiety about money and her espousal of passion:

> Love in a hut, with water and a crust,
> Is – Love, forgive us! – cinders, ashes, dust.

Whatever about Nuala, I didn't believe Keats was right. Besides, the poor fellow was ill, and we were healthy as trouts.

Chapter Twenty-Two

The Pro-Life Amendment was carried by a two to one majority on 7 September 1983. The Constitution now declared that: 'The State acknowledges the right to life of the unborn and, with due regard to the equal right to life of the mother, guarantees in its laws to respect and as far as practicable by its law to defend and vindicate that right.' That meant banning any information regarding abortion. British telephone directories were withdrawn from libraries: they listed the numbers of pregnancy termination clinics in Britain. British magazines were banned. Student organizations were convicted in court for disseminating abortion information. Two women's organizations were shut down for giving counselling about termination. Suggestions that women going to Britain be subject to examination for signs of pregnancy, and examined upon return for signs of termination, were scoffed at, but within a decade a horrible variation on that scenario would bring Ireland to its knees.

Early in 1992 the parents of a pregnant fourteen-year-old who had been raped by a neighbour phoned the guards from England to find out whether a DNA sample from the foetus which it was proposed to abort could be used in evidence against the rapist. The guards informed the Attorney General, who ordered the parents to bring the pregnant child back to Ireland or face prosecution and possible imprisonment upon return if the abortion went ahead. They obeyed. There was public outrage at what was seen as the girl's effective internment in Ireland. The Supreme Court interpreted the amendment to mean that the suicidal girl's life was at risk if pregnancy went ahead, and she was given permission to return to England for a termination. The rapist was subsequently convicted and jailed.

Contentment at home fortified Nuala and me against the anti-woman virus that had poisoned the country. Paradoxically, though organized feminism was under the hammer, and the subject of the North was toxic, my own career flourished, mainly through the launch on RTÉ of the weekly *Women's Programme*, on which I was given a slot, satirically reviewing the print media. Nuala was one of the producers. Though I only turned up for the actual show, while the others collaborated all week, I was in a friendly work environment with Nuala, presenters Marian Finucane and Doireann Ní Bhriain, and chief producer Clare Duignan.

On the first night, I winked at the end of my presentation, and said, 'Good night, sisters.' I remembered Douglas Gageby's reassuring wink when I arrived into work after taking the Contraceptive Train to Belfast. That wink, and that bidding, 'Good night, sisters,' became a code for many a woman who found herself in a position, any position, where she could not speak. On a train journey, when an authoritarian priest stood up and asked commuters in the carriage to say the rosary with him, an elderly lady winked at me, while courteously giving the response to the priest's prayers. 'Good night, sister,' she said, when she arrived at our destination.

Men joined in, asking if I would ever say, 'Good night, brothers.' Sister Agatha sent me a gleeful prayer card, signed by the nuns in her convent 'from all the sisters to another'. I took all these responses to mean that the country was recovering from the Pro-Life Amendment Campaign as one would recover from a hangover, asking what on earth had we done the night before.

Some of my political colleagues had it that I was becoming a clown princess. And if I was, what harm laughter? The sound of that was fading at home. I have often retraced the fall of Nuala and me from grace. There were, she has written in *Are You Somebody?*, 'mutual angers'. She did not specify what hers were. It is a painful fact that she has never retraced, in print or in private, what happened to us.

I know when my angers began. Nuala arranged a surprise weekend in New York that fell between our birthdays in March 1984. I had always told her I wanted to spend the night that began my forties in Berlin – forty was the new twenty-first among feminists, then – but Nuala could not abide Germany, on principle, because of the Holocaust. She had, however, gone there once, to the emotional rescue of her soldier brother (now dead). I think I managed to hide a distinct feeling of ingratitude and arranged to meet the editors of *Ms. Magazine* while in New York – they paid well for articles from me, and I was a contributing editor. Nuala was vexed that I was allowing work to get in the way of passion.

In New York, there was a message at hotel reception. Nuala guessed it was from an old friend, naming a man with whom she'd once had an affair, and whom she had contacted before we arrived. She wanted to show me off to him. In fact, the message was from acquaintances of mine who had heard via *Ms. Magazine* that I was coming. Nuala was vexed again. An unspoken rebellion rose in me.

We had little tugs-of-war on that trip. Nuala said there was no chance of getting tickets for the Metropolitan Opera House; I insisted we should try. We booked seats in the gods, for a modern piece that held out no prospect of pleasure. It was, nonetheless, enough for us both that we should get into the place and see the sights and the people, and, besides, Kiri Te Kanawa was singing.

I left Nuala while I went to visit *Ms. Magazine*. The editors assured me that the taxi they ordered would get me to the opera in time. It did not. The first act had already begun. Nuala was alone in the bar, furious. I pointed out that we had only gone along for the sights. After the interval – what a sight those glossy, groomed Americans presented – we climbed to the rafters. We could barely see or hear Te Kanawa, and what we could hear was dissonance. The opera was a clanger. It was Nuala who decided to leave. She is a woman who cuts her losses. I moped after her to the restaurant she had booked atop a skyscraper for a late supper. The bouncer spotted the trainers I was wearing under the fur coat and refused admission. Oh, lousy night.

Next day, we went to the Oyster Bar. I was subdued. I had not liked the book by Elizabeth Smart, but adored the title: *By Grand Central Station I Sat Down and Wept*. I had not expected to live the title. I had never withdrawn from Nuala before. When we got back to Dublin, early in the morning, and collapsed into bed, Nuala rolled towards me and I turned away.

Neither of us knew, that morning, 6 March 1984, that we would never make love again.

On my actual birthday, at the end of March, we were walking down the street, to a pub, for an unaccustomed drink with friends – 'just a few, and nor for long,' Nuala warned beforehand – when she stopped outside the offices of Cherish, the support organization for unmarried mothers, to deliver a message. I walked in with her, to a surprise gathering she had organized. I was honoured and touched, and wanted to prolong the celebrations beyond the agreed closure of Cherish at 11 p.m. Nuala went on home. I felt like Cinderella, and went on partying – anything, anything, to be abroad beyond midnight.

At the end of summer that year, we went on the annual break to the Merriman Summer School. Nuala rented a house, as always, where her sisters and their partners and their children could join her, in a gallant, heroic ritual of togetherness. It worked, as ever. They were the family they could not be in their childhood. When Merriman ended, we went back to Dublin to get a flight to Portugal. Nuala's brother (now dead), over from London, was staying in our house, coping with a weakness for drugs and drink. He had no money. Nuala would give him none, fearing that he would spend it on self-destruction.

Next morning, I emptied my meagre bank account, and gave money to Nuala's brother. On the way to the airport, Nuala called in on the sister she had just left in Co. Clare; she wanted to savour and relive the success of the family holiday, the sanctuary her now lovely Dublin home afforded her brother, the victory of herself and her siblings over their past, her hopeful life with me.

I hadn't been to Derry that summer. At the airport I cracked. Nuala and her family, I snarled, were all over each other like maggots. It was an ugly remark. I was ashamed of myself. She told me when we finally parted that she never totally trusted me after that. Though we embraced in the sea in Portugal, we had a stiff enough holiday there, unable to breach the gulf I had opened up by judging her family.

Otherwise, 1984 was a very good year. The newly established feminist imprint Attic Press, set up by Róisín Conroy and Mary Paul Keane, published a collection of the articles I had written since leaving the *Irish Times* – it was called *The Best of Nell*. It showed that I wrote very well in the longer format afforded by *Magill*, and *In Dublin* allowed outrageous scope. The *Irish Press* had indeed turned out to be my natural home when it came to writing about the North. The poet Eavan Boland wrote in the introduction that mine was 'the writing of a passionate witness'. Eason agreed to distribute the book, and its sales were very healthy.

Nuala did not read the collection.

Attic Press was interested in my great novel, which I had by then finished, and I showed the manuscript first to Nuala. She literally flung it from her when she came upon a scene that described a woman masturbating. It was disgusting, she said. I was ashamed. I said nothing. I accepted the criticism. (In her novel *My Dream of You*, Nuala wrote about a woman masturbating.) Attic Press told me what I already knew: the great novel, based on the civil rights movement in Derry, was a bore.

Now that I think of it, 1984 was a lousy year.

And still, being at home was a joy compared to being outside. Many of the feminists I knew, then also in their forties, were in the throes of marital breakdown. I heard things that stunned me – when a relationship ends, people speak frankly about their sex lives. A woman spoke of biting the pillow while her man was intimate with her – anything to keep the relationship alive. I could not understand how he hadn't noticed. A man castigated his wife as frigid. I frostily rebuked him that she had not been frigid with me before marriage.

Many people had stayed together, against the odds, because of the children. A woman clutched her stomach in pain, and barely held herself upright against the wall as she told me that the husband, from whom she had long separated, had impregnated his new partner – the wanted baby was proof, beyond mere sexual attraction, of love. I clung to that story. I could not conceive of leaving Nuala because of sex. I couldn't even envisage wanting anybody else. I loved her. Long, long after intimacy stopped, a little girl answered the phone, turned to me with a smile and said, 'Your beloved wants to talk to you.' Nuala was on the other end of the line. I clung to the child's remark – out of the mouths of babes. Children know when something is amiss; this child was happy in our company. An eight-year-old had endorsed my relationship with Nuala, and I took soaring solace from that. Nuala and I were still together and protective of each other – just like any couple who had crossed the bourne. Did any couple make love after a few years? Nuala still called me 'dear'.

Late in 1984 a young unmarried woman in Co. Kerry, Joanne Hayes, who already had a daughter, concealed the birth and immediate death of a baby that she hid on the family farm. Simultaneously, another new-born baby was found stabbed to death on a beach in another part of the county. Members of the Hayes family confessed in detail to this stabbing. Then the body of Joanne's own baby was found.

Blood samples proved that the father of Joanne's daughter, and of her second baby, was not the father of the stabbed baby. Charges were dropped, and a public inquiry was instituted into how it had come about that a family confessed to a murder it could not have committed. The inquiry lasted six months, as the police sought to prove that Joanne had conceived two babies, by two different men, on the same night, and had stabbed the one found on the beach.

A succession of male experts were called to testify on the medical, social and moral fibre of Joanne Hayes. Doctors gave evidence on the dimensions of her vagina during the birth of her first child in hospital. When the inquiry ended, the judge declared, 'There were times when we all believed she had twins.' For me, his declaration encapsulated perfectly the suspicious attitude to Irish women that prevailed in the 1980s.

I had been covering the case for the *Irish Press*. Behind the scenes

I organized a 'yellow flower' protest, asking people to send one daffodil each to Joanne Hayes, to be delivered to the court where she was being crucified. Attic Press coordinated the protest, ringing women's groups everywhere, at home and abroad. The price of one flower was cheap; the publicity enormous: Joanne was wreathed in flowers every day. Thousands of people responded, most of whom had never been in a feminist group. My pride in pulling off the coup did not assuage my shame at sitting silently in court while Joanne testified under sedation. I should have stood up and protested. I was afraid of being jailed for contempt of court.

I left home in the summer of 1985 to write a book about the Kerry Babies case. I lived in a lovely little wooden house on the side of a mountain. Nuala had uncomplainingly given me the car for the duration. Every weekend, she made the five-hour train journey from Dublin to join me. This was love, no? While we were ensconced on the mountainside, Ireland was on the move: thousands flocked like starlings to Blessed Virgin Mary grottoes where, it was believed, the plaster statues could be seen to move. The statues did not all move at the same time, it must be emphasized. The stony-faced Lady in Blue shimmered here a week, shook there for another. Serious newspapers, including the *Irish Times*, printed helpful maps that tracked her movements round the island of Ireland. People stayed up all night, and camped out for days at a time, around the latest reported gig in the grotto, staring, singing and praying.

In the wake of the Kerry Babies Inquiry, I was not dismissive of such mass hysteria. Given what priests, judges, doctors and lawyers were saying about women, it made perfect sense that people preferred to turn their faces to the wall.

On the third night of a lecture tour of Australia that October, I rang Nuala in Dublin. It was six in the morning, Irish time. 'Mammy has died,' she said. Her mother's body had been found slumped on the bathroom floor, blocking the door. Nuala did not want to talk beyond those awful details, which I forced out of her. It was a short conversation.

The organizers offered to fly me back, and pay the lecture fees anyway, but I stayed in Australia for the fortnight. I was afraid of Nuala's grief. I was afraid of being shut out by her. I wanted her to ask me to fly back. I was asking her, without asking her, to define our relationship by asking me to fly back, to be by her side. I defined it myself by not flying back. I defined myself as the passive, self-centred half of the relationship. Another word is selfish. Some partner, I was.

Eason refused to distribute my book on the Kerry Babies case, *A Woman to Blame*, though my lawyers offered to remove anything they considered libellous. Eason did distribute the four other books written on the case. It paid out libels on all four. Nobody sued me. I got great reviews and limited financial reward. Jaysus, but it was difficult writing for a feminist press from a feminist perspective. Nuala did not read the book.

That same year, she did show how to fly under the radar of censorship that fretted over all our days, excelling herself in break-through television documentary, a series called *Plain Tales*, produced and presented by herself, in which she abolished her voice and filmed ordinary women speaking directly to camera about children and abandonment and love and work and poverty and contentment. None of them was famous. The series was an under-stated rebuke of the caricatures conjured up during the amendment years. Nuala won a Jacobs Award, the highest honour that the annual media jury on broadcasting could give. I was her guest on the night. Inasmuch as she went out, I was always with her.

It was a delicate moment for me when Nuala left RTÉ and joined the *Irish Times*, in 1986, at the invitation of editor Conor Brady. The day she stepped out of the house and went off to work with the paper that would not employ me was not without resonance. I don't know what Nuala thought. I got over it by not discussing it. Her opinion column was wonderful, both for her opinions and the quality of her writing. She always gave me her copy to read before submitting it. I devoured the words, memorized them, repeated them to myself, just as I repeated things she said in conversation. As ever, Nuala did not read my columns.

This was the year when the people behind PLAC struck again. Fearing that legislators might actually take the law into their own hands and change the Constitution so as to allow some marriages to be terminated, they persuaded yet another government to hold a referendum to outlaw divorce. The fundamentalists won again, by almost the exact same majority, two to one, this time on the grounds that marital breakdown would mean that the mainly male farming community would have to sell the land to support a divorced spouse.

This further characterization of Ireland as a Catholic state for a Catholic people hindered such hope as there was for coming to an accommodation with the severed Northern part of the island. It helped not at all that Sinn Féin was lukewarm about divorce, though nobody would have heard its mousy squeaks in the debate: by government order, no Sinn Féin spokesperson had been interviewed on RTÉ since 1971, a ban that was gradually adopted by the BBC, which deployed dubbing, using voice-overs by actors, against blacked-out profiles of the republicans. The lip-synch was near perfect; the accents uncannily accurate. As British television was widely obtainable in the South, the situation was surreal. Any song or poem considered rousing was banned from the Irish airwaves, though many RTÉ broadcasters and government politicians could be heard singing the forbidden songs at Merriman.

It became quite the thing for Mary Holland and me to attend Sinn Féin's annual political gathering in Dublin, then repair with the republicans to the late-night party afterwards, in a Dublin pub, where we belted along with protest singers such as Christy Moore, singing 'The Men behind the Wire', 'A Nation Once Again' and 'Kevin Barry'. Mary Holland croaked, rather than sang. She was rather a grand lady, and I never saw her drunk, but she threw her head back in disgraceful fashion, once a year, and outbelted Christy Moore. In those censoring years, Mary Holland, after decades with the *Observer*, was sacked by its newly appointed editor-in-chief, Conor Cruise O'Brien, in 1979. He had not liked a television documentary she made for British television which traced the political journey of Mary Nelis from Housewife of the Year 1967 to blanket woman protesting on behalf of her jailed IRA sons.

The poison infected the trade unions that represented the media. Dedicated anti-republican left-wingers sought out positions of trade union influence from which they could launch offensives against anything that smelled to them of a nationalist agenda. Fair play to them for doing the unpaid job of organizers in local branches – the positions were open to any of us – but bad cess to them for turning every meeting of, say, the Freelance Branch of the National Union of Journalists, into an open-and-shut discussion of the North. The meeting would open with an emergency resolution condemning whatever the IRA had just done, a counter resolution was proposed against all forms of violence, including that of the British army, a filibuster ensued on both sides, then the meeting was closed before we could get on to any other business – such as wages and working conditions.

Nuala had often come home from trade union meetings intimidated and horrified. The Workers' Party had, perfectly legitimately, set up a branch in RTÉ, and its members formed a fierce, brilliant caucus. The Workers' Party mainly comprised disaffected Republicans who had split from Sinn Féin in the 1970s, and it had a militantly anti-nationalist agenda. Within RTÉ, Eoghan Harris was its guru. He scorned the 'hush puppies' who did not totally condemn Sinn Féin and/or the IRA. In fact, most people were against the Provos, but were trying to fulfil the station's commitment to objectivity in political reportage. There was a great deal of fearful self-censorship in RTÉ. Northerners who worked there were guilty by association with the place of their birth. Mary McAleese, then a current affairs reporter, felt the cold: she could be seen eating alone in the canteen, conspicuously shunned by her colleagues seated nearby. In her childhood, McAleese had carried a hurley on the way to school, through the killing fields of North Belfast. Loyalists had bombed her family home and blown up the family's pub.

The morning that the result of the divorce referendum came out – defeated yet again – I met the indomitably cheerful Noreen Greene, a leading trade unionist, on a street corner, and we smoked cigarettes and devised a daring plan for a whole new life, should we survive into old age. We would rob a bank. If we were caught, the judge would give us a suspended sentence on the grounds that we were so old. If we did not get caught, we'd have a fortune, some of which we would piously give to the women's movement in Ireland.

We would use the expertise of the Provisional IRA, in the person of Rita O'Hare. Rita had told me once of a bank robbery gone wrong in Belfast. The robber who had gone to the counter was too short to climb over it and get to the safe. The bank gave the gang bags and bags of heavy cash, and as they dragged the booty to the getaway car, the bags burst open. They were filled with coins that had been taken out of circulation following the introduction of a new currency. Not a great CV for a bank-robbery team, but better than our own. Standing on the street corner that day, we had to refuse applications from many feminist passers-by who wanted to rob a bank in old age. With such idle fantasies did we console ourselves during the anti-feminist, anti-nationalist 1980s.

When I told Rita of the hopes that Noreen and I had invested in her, she roared with laughter. She was recovering from a near-death experience in a Dublin hospital after undergoing a hysterectomy. She had been too shy to tell the surgeon beforehand that there was shrapnel in her body, and after he opened her up he had been obliged to use a great deal more anaesthetic than he was comfortable with. Rita was by then Sinn Féin's press officer. In the history of the world, there cannot have been a press officer who was so shy.

I was fond of Rita O'Hare, which was politically incorrect in the 1980s. She belonged to that segment of the 1968 civil rights generation which had then joined the IRA and now found itself in jail North and South, or on the run in the Republic. She had begun her prison career on foot of a sentence imposed for carrying a hurley. When I met her, in Dublin, she was in permanent exile from her beloved Belfast. You could not have a conversation about politics with Rita unless you were prepared to spend the first twenty minutes looking at photographs of her parents and of her children, and listening to family news. Free as I was to roam, I knew more about the physical layout of her hometown than she now did; I could visit my family any time.

The longing for home felt by IRA people on the run was exemplified by a man in his twenties who asked me to help him get away to America. He needed an excuse not to report daily at a garda station in Dublin while on bail awaiting trial. I rang a nurse, who supplied a pharmaceutical recipe that would render the fellow so ill that the doctor would confine him to bed, and the guards would excuse him. He gathered the necessary drugs, was heartily ill – then decided to stay in Ireland. He preferred the expected ten-year jail sentence (which he duly got) to permanent exile under another name.

Practically every time I went on radio or television, I was invited to condemn the Provisional IRA. This was a favourite tactic of Conor Cruise O'Brien, who wanted to flush out the 'hush puppies'. Conor would begin every discussion by asking other panellists if they supported the IRA. This was invariably met by a formulaic response: 'I do not support the IRA, but I understand why it is engaging in armed struggle and, if we do not show understanding of that, we cannot hope to achieve a political solution.'

The same formula had been employed during the tumult over abortion: 'Nobody would support abortion, as such, but I understand why women feel driven to it and condemning them does not advance understanding of the solution, which is to ensure safe, responsible, protected sex, using contraception . . .'

My thinking on the IRA was even more convoluted. The left-wing response in the early days of the war was one of 'critical support' to armed struggle, meaning that the killing of soldiers was necessary, the killing of civilians was not. I did not agree with that left-wing response. My reasoning was simple enough: if you put a gun or a bomb into the hands of an IRA volunteer, you had to accept that noncombatants would die. It happened in any war. They would die because the volunteer was inexperienced, or frightened, or was sectarian, or did not give a damn. 'Critical support' was quietly dropped as war deepened and casualties mounted; nobody had expected such a long struggle. Personally, though I did not support the IRA, I would not condemn the neighbour's child.

But – was I not supporting the IRA when I walked behind the coffins of the hunger strikers in 1981? Worse, was I not supporting the INLA, which I despised? And was I not supporting all nationalist paramilitary groups by refusing to use the confidential telephone number advertised by the RUC and British army? They guaranteed anonymity to whoever called. The calls were free of charge. No nationalist, not even the most vocal, sincere opponents of the IRA, ever publicly advocated ringing that number – not John Hume, not a Catholic Bishop, nobody – though most people had a fairly informed clue about its membership, especially those involved behind the scenes.

I knew that my silence protected IRA volunteers as they went forth. I never ate the face off the ones I personally knew. They were the neighbours' children. They were, increasingly, my relatives.

The world outside the front door seemed ever more unremittingly hostile. In the North, death rained down; in the South, contumely was visited upon women. Attic Press brought out another collection of my journalism, entitled *Good Night Sisters*. I wrote in the preface that: 'the 1980s will go down in history as a lousy decade for women. During what have become known as "the amendment years", Church and State fought for control of our bodies and our destiny. The 1980s were as shocking as they were ineffably sad. The feminist vision was reduced to survival.'

Nuala did not read the collection, which came out in August 1987.

The death toll from the Troubles had reached 2,282 by 7 November 1987, when I was invited on to a current affairs radio programme to mark the birthday of Conor Cruise O'Brien, and assess his contribution to politics. Conor went round the panel, as usual, getting ritual answers to his ritual question.

I was the last one to whom he posed it: 'Do you support the IRA?'

I said, 'Yes, I do.' There was a moment of total silence. You could feel the air being sucked out of the studio.

Startled, at a loss for words, Conor paused, then said, 'Your honesty is refreshing.'

The interviewer immediately moved the topic along. Nobody asked me why I supported the IRA. Nobody wanted to talk about it. I believe that I was the first person ever – outside of the republican movement – to make such a declaration. One of my employers, *Irish Press* editor Tim Pat Coogan, who was on the panel with me, did not probe because he was well aware of the precarious position in which I had placed myself: I was now wholly beyond the Dublin political pale.

The panel did not repair, as was usual after discussion on Saturday, to the nearest hostelry. There were no birthday drinks for Conor. I went home. Nuala was abroad on assignment.

Next day, at 11 a.m., the IRA blew up eleven Protestants in Enniskillen. I sat there, covered metaphorically in blood. Mary Holland rang to check that we would go to a fundraiser for the Rape Crisis Centre that afternoon. I pointed out that the centre would hardly benefit from my presence. She hesitated, then agreed. I was well ahead of her about the coming fall-out.

On Monday, RTÉ announced that I was banned from the airwaves.

It was the least of my problems. I had spent the weekend listening to survivors of the bomb speak on radio and television. Protestants had gathered on Sunday morning, at the war memorial in Enniskillen, for the annual commemoration of the dead of both world wars. 'At the eleventh minute of the eleventh hour of the eleventh day . . . we will remember them.' They had actually gathered on the eighth day of the eleventh month, the nearest Sunday to 11 November. The IRA's bomb was supposed to explode when police and British soldiers arrived at the memorial in advance of the Remembrance Day ceremony, but when it did not go off the IRA walked away, knowing what would happen. There was no excuse whatsoever for the IRA's action.

Bad timing, some said, referring to the Protestants, and to my declaration of support for the IRA the day before the bomb. I was used to savage jokes, to the black humour used to keep pain at bay.

377

I had repeated many myself, in my day. When anyone murmured 'Bad timing' to me after the IRA bomb killed eleven Protestants in Enniskillen, I did not shrug and take my oil. I used these rare moments to gabble frantically about how bad I felt. I gabbled a lot with so very few: hardly anybody in media circles talked to me. I did not need to be shunned in order to understand the enormity of what had happened. The IRA's action was morally criminal. They had left the Protestants to die. I spent days alone, at home, by the radio and television, reading newspapers. A member of the Protestant male-voice church choir in Enniskillen said that he would sing at his father's funeral. 'I never sang for my father before,' he said. There was a man in a coma – from which he would never recover, from which he would die years later.

It would have been cowardly to recant. I was stuck with my own morality: that once you put a gun in their hands, you accept responsibility for their actions. All the papers and magazines and radio stations other than RTÉ, for which I worked, asked me to write about how I felt now. I wrote and I broadcast that I would seek redemption – the arrogance of that, redemption – by handing in my Irish passport and taking up a British one. That would prove to Northern Protestants, I hoped, that I did not want a united Ireland without their agreement. I did not want to force my politics down anybody's throat at the point of a gun. At the same time, I would not be forced into anything by a British gun.

After I said that on BBC radio, I got a call from my mother. I was too upset to pick up the phone. I listened to her voice on the answering machine. 'Nell,' she said, 'Nell, pick up the phone. I love you, daughter. Pick up the phone, daughter.'

I was satirized, wonderfully, on BBC Radio Ulster by a Derryman who composed a ditty about my proposed British citizenship, 'Lady Nell, from Brandywell'. I got a call from Brian Friel offering me refuge in his holiday home in Donegal, if I needed to get away. I got a lovely note from Tim Pat Coogan, wishing me well: my job was not in danger. A teenage boy in Derry stopped me in the dark street and said, 'Thanks for what you said about us in the IRA.'

At the British Embassy, the porter gave me an application form for British citizenship, to which I was entitled by virtue of being born in the North. He stood under a portrait of the Queen. My Queen? I needed a sponsor for my application: I got a sombre letter from the great Irish parliamentarian John Kelly, of Fine Gael, implacable opponent of the IRA, in which he declined to sponsor me. It was not that I was untouchable. He could not, would not, ask anyone to give up Irish citizenship. My union sent a formal letter of protest about the ban to RTÉ, then shut completely up.

Nuala was magnificent. She came home, said nothing, and brought me as her lunch companion to the annual print media awards a fortnight after the bomb, where she was named Journalist of the Year. There was a frisson as we entered the room. Journalists with whom I had worked for seventeen years did not talk to me. There were journalists there who had been glad of my company in the North, as I steered them clear of danger of which they were blithely ignorant; who had partaken of my mother's hospitality; who had shared amiable nights with off-duty Provos; who had supported my feminist activities; who turned conspicuously away, or made their way to our table, congratulated Nuala, and had not a word of greeting for me.

Nuala chatted steadfastly to me, and did not mention the war or the shunning. Under her calm influence, I did not have recourse to alcohol, which was freely flowing. I did not mistake her companionship for endorsement of my politics. Christ, was I glad this woman loved me.

I disappeared from public view, but, paradoxically, invitations flowed in to speak at universities and civic groups and women's groups. Though they didn't agree with me, people wanted to hear what it was that the government and public broadcasting service did not want them to hear. The Section 31 broadcasting ban, which kept the Provos off the airwaves, did not end until 1994, but in the years leading up to that there was plenty of discussion about them, and with them, among political insiders. An under-secretary from the British Embassy took me to dinner regularly. (I informed Sinn Féin of the relationship, lest they mistake me for an informer.)

Ambassador Jean Kennedy Smith had me to dinner at the American Embassy. I became a member of the Northern Star Lunch Club, which had been set up in 1979 by journalist Andy Pollak of the *Irish Times*, and which held private weekly meetings in Dublin with Northern guests such as Peter Robinson, deputy leader of Ian Paisley's party; David Ervine, leader of a loyalist paramilitary group; Harvey Bicker, deputy commander of the Ulster Defence Regiment which had replaced the B Specials; and Gerry Adams and Martin McGuinness. Our membership included TDs David Andrews, of Fianna Fáil, and Ruairi Quinn of Labour. Nobody minded listening to me behind closed doors.

When my mother had a stroke in late 1987 I rushed to Derry. I was in the kitchen when the second stroke hit her. Her mouth was pulled down, her features were contorted, her words came out mangled. She knew what was happening. I could see the fear in her. I knelt beside her and started saying the Act of Contrition. I felt her kick me and heard her say, clear as a bell, 'It's a doctor I want, not a priest.'

The young priest arrived after the doctor recommended bed rest. He gave my mother the last rites in the sitting room and heard her confession and was gone in minutes. She was not as joyful as I fondly imagined a Catholic on her deathbed who had just made peace with her God should be. 'He said I would have no sins to confess, at my age. He was a boy. I want a man.' I ran over to the cathedral and left a note for Bishop Daly. He came immediately. The confession lasted well over an hour. The Bishop's married brother had just attracted publicity for running away with another woman. I asked the Bishop who had been confessing to whom in the sitting room. He smiled and ignored me. My mother looked like one redeemed seventy-seven-year-old sinner.

I arranged with Carmel that I would spend every second week in Derry. She, too, would take every second week off her job. I did not discuss this with Nuala; I told her. Some lover I was; some priority I gave to my own home life. My mother had actually only asked me to do one thing for her. 'You haven't spent Christmas in

Derry for years. It's time you came back to me.' I agreed at once. I had spent years swinging from seasonal chandeliers with Nuala, from Budapest to the west of Ireland. I told Nuala – told her! – that I was spending Christmas in Derry. She came up and cooked the turkey for my mother and sister and me and herself. The only photograph of me and Nuala, the only photograph I have of our fifteen years together, is the one taken of the two of us, bent to our domestic tasks, in the scullery in Derry, that Christmas morning of 1987. We are both dressed to the nines, in our frocks and aprons. Nuala's bum looks just lovely.

Then Peggy Deery died. Her IRA son had been killed by his own bomb months before. She had reared fourteen children, been shot and maimed on Bloody Sunday, and remained indomitable. Her funeral was a small, unregarded affair, on a cold, wet day in January 1988. Still banned by RTÉ, unable to get my books distributed, I decided at her graveside to write a book about Peggy that might explain who we were in Derry, what we believed in, why we had turned out as we had.

The *Irish Press* gave me unpaid leave. Attic Press gave an advance that would cover the lost wages. The other work – writing opinion columns, and broadcasting opinions for the BBC – could be done from Derry. I told Nuala what I was doing. I would still see her every weekend. She let me keep our car in Derry, to help me run around and interview Peggy's large and scattered family, in the afternoons, when I had cooked dinner and my mother was resting in bed.

I crept back on to RTÉ, thanks to Betty Purcell. Though the ban only applied to live broadcasts, I had effectively dropped off the air altogether since the Enniskillen bomb, as inviting me to contribute on anything left the programme producer open to 'hush puppy' suspicions. Betty arranged for me to do a pre-recorded interview with Marian Finucane on the subject of Mother's Day cards. We did not discuss in advance what I would say from the Derry studio. I resisted the temptation – it was easy, my livelihood depended on it – to remark that I knew that Martin McGuinness always sent his mother a card and that my mother had complained to Peggy McGuinness that I never, ever, sent her one. Betty and Marian behaved as if it were the most natural thing in the world for me to be on air. By September, I was back on air live with my weekly radio column on Marian Finucane's *Liveline*. The ban was never formally lifted. It was deemed to have lapsed with the retirement of the person who had issued it.

The book came out in August and was sold on to Virago, the British feminist imprint. I was proud of *Peggy Deery: A Derry Family at War*. Eason refused to distribute it. Britain was not interested. Nuala did not read it. In September the BBC, under pressure, quietly dropped my radio column. Still, I was back on RTÉ with my weekly slot.

By the start of 1989 my mother was back on her feet, minding the grandchildren, and I was back in Dublin. I kept my promise to my mother, though – spending every subsequent Christmas with her, always with Nuala along. Nuala did not like it and saw no contradiction in the three-line whip she had imposed, since we first met, on us always turning up to her family's post-New Year gathering. Her logic was forceful: her family met after the holidays; mine was now meeting during them. I weakly argued that we left my family on Stephen's Day and went to foreign climes. And I argued, 'Welcome to the club. Family, family, family, there's just too much family. We're part of the human race.' Returning to my section of the human race was a source of contention until we split.

We were in desperate straits. It was Nuala who suggested that we move to a bigger house: 'Such a little house this is, for two such big egos.' I was forty-six, and had never owned a home. It created an involuntary imbalance of power between us. If we bought together, we would be casting our lot together. We agreed to apply for a joint mortgage. Nuala's bank manager would have none of it. The life of a freelance journalist did not appear to him a stable one.

I proposed buying Nuala's house from her and renting it out at a rate that would cover the mortgage, thus leaving me free to contribute to the mortgage of her new home. Nuala was dismissive.

No bank manager would give me the money. I did not earn enough. My earnings were not guaranteed. Again, I hauled out my bank statements and income tax certificates. She would not yield. I could see that she was worried about taking on a bigger mortgage that would leave her reliant on someone as unreliable as me. Yet she was willing to do this thing to save our relationship.

I decided to buy the house from Nuala. A number of my employers cheerfully inflated my earnings for the benefit of the mortgage society to which I applied. Christina, flourishing in her business, gave me back the money I had paid towards her mortgage. A friend of both Nuala's and mine offered to make up whatever shortfall was necessary for the deposit: I could see the tactful warning in that. She was aware of the strains between us. She said simply, 'Every woman should have a house of her own.'

In the event, I didn't have to avail of her offer. The building society gave me the loan. I bought Nuala's house at market price, less the percentage she would have had to pay an auctioneer. It was the most decisive action I had ever taken on my own behalf, and well beyond time. Now Nuala and I were on a completely equal footing. We were full of hope. We told each other that when Nuala retired at sixty, in the year 2000, I would retire early at fifty-six, sell my house, and use the money to supplement our pensions and finance our world travel. There was a certain amount of desperate truth in that dream. There was another truth we did not voice: that if the dream should go up in smoke, and the relationship end, I would have a house of my own to go to.

And if my freelance life should collapse, as Nuala continually predicted, sure, I would cash in on my fame and write the great autobiography – as soon as my mother was dead, which would be any day now. I would have to await her death before I could write openly about being gay. Nuala was horrified. An autobiography would be an invasion of our privacy. Passion came before writing. It would be vulgar to let the world into our love affair. I was simultaneously delighted and saddened. She loved me; I could never make the last great revolutionary leap towards feminist freedom. But she loved me, she loved me, and nothing could compare

383

to that. There were enough other gay women about to make the revolution.

I went to Italy to report for RTÉ radio on Ireland's progress in the World Cup in the summer of 1990. I knew little about football, but I knew how to party, and I was in the company of several thousand Irishmen who were intent on that. The growing success of the Irish football team, under the Englishman Jack Charlton, had gone to the collective head of the nation. There was a war in the North, the economy had tanked in the South, but, hey, look at us – the more the English acted like football hooligans, the more elaborately mannered the singing, drinking, peaceful Irish became, as ambassadors of the nation worldwide. Some brought their grannies and wives and children along. John Egan, with whom I was doing a two-handed report, brought me along, coaxing me out of fountains in Genoa as dawn broke, feeding me black coffee and Coca-Cola during the broadcast, talking football after I had talked of the parties. I got a Jacobs broadcasting award that year, the first and only one of my life. For football. For celebrating Irish men. The clown princess. In my acceptance speech, I looked forward to an end to the broadcasting ban which kept Sinn Féin off the airwaves. It was clear to me, in 1990, that the Provos were going to end the war. With the supposed cream of Ireland's media in the ballroom, and the speech going out live to the nation, I was not going to be just a pretty laughing face. I did not get a standing ovation. Which was a bit of a waste of the designer frock I had worn.

I decided to learn how to cook properly that winter, to show Nuala that I was home for good. I enrolled in a cordon bleu course with a male friend who was already an enthusiastic man in the kitchen. He was a shining exception in my experience of men in 1990. He seldom let his wife cook. He loved standing over a hot stove. Once in a rare while, a man gives a woman confidence, and this guy convinced me that I should start at the top. It was lovely at night school, as lovely as it had been when I was learning to be a car mechanic. I brought a three-course meal home once a week.

Nuala never ate one of them. It was 9.30 p.m., sometimes ten, well past her dinner time, and she would not wait.

Margaret Thatcher resigned in November, and we watched the television broadcast of her last Prime Minister's question time from the Dispatch Box in the House of Commons. She put one arm on the box, looked around her and went to bat with a grin on her face. 'Go on, I'm enjoying this,' she said defiantly to her tormentors, knocking their questions back into their teeth. She was magnificent. I remarked to Nuala that I looked forward to writing about the contradiction: the woman who had done so little for women was an example to us all. Something like that.

'We can't both write about it,' said Nuala.

'Why not?' I asked. 'It's common for journalists to cover the same topic.'

'We can't both write about the same thing,' said Nuala, 'and this is important, and I write for the *Irish Times*.'

I am ashamed to say that I did not write about Margaret Thatcher.

We went to Derry for my mother's surprise eightieth birthday, also in November. My sister Nuala, Darby to my mother's Joan, had arranged mass and a dance and a buffet in a parish hall. It was splendid and moving. My mother, in common with the Pope, has a habit of greeting people by placing her hands on either side of their faces. The video of that night shows the smile that lit up her face as she greeted grandchildren and nieces and nephews and neighbours and pals. The eighty-year-olds had made it through from the hungry 1930s. The women of that generation were the last of the full-time mothers. They all owned their own fully furnished houses and had enough in the Credit Union to pay for their own funerals and more. They had seen young relatives jailed and killed. There were ex-prisoners at the party. Nuala knew hardly anybody. She went home early.

Late in the year, I had to get glasses for reading. Tears sprang into my eyes. The consultant could not understand why I should cry about putting furniture on my face. 'I've got Elizabeth Taylor eyes,' I said. 'Mine are even more beautiful.' There are things men don't understand. It did not help that my Afro curls had wilted almost overnight and my hair now had, as Nuala sweetly said, 'silver threads among the weak tea'.

The first book I read with my glasses on was the *Field Day Anthology*, a massive compendium of Irish writing and oral history from the beginning of time right up to the present day, edited by Seamus Deane. I went straight to the index to look up my name: examination of the women's movement in Ireland would be incomplete without my name. I hadn't got a mention. The women's movement had not got a mention.

Mary Robinson was inaugurated as President of Ireland on 3 December 1990. During her campaign for the Presidency, Robinson had declared that she practised her Catholic religion, and now that she was elected other feminists came out of the closet and acknowledged that they had been quietly having their children baptized. It was sensational. During the two decades we spent fighting them, we had yearned to belong to the institutions of Church and State.

My cup overflowed when I watched a televised event where President Robinson sat on a chair on an altar and accepted, as head of state, the obeisance of the head of the Irish Catholic Church, Cardinal Cahal Daly. He did not, of course, mention the contraceptive bill she had introduced, and he had opposed, all those decades ago. I did, chanting at the TV set.

Behaviour such as that goes a long way to explaining why the women's movement, in all its myriad manifestations, did not feature too prominently in Robinson's campaign. She had called us to a meeting in her home to discuss how best we might contribute to it. Given her own strict separation of public and private life, this was quite a gesture. Few of us had ever been inside her house before. There were about thirty of us, including Mary Holland, Sylvia Meehan, Mary Maher, Máirín de Burca and Anne O'Donnell – a veritable roll call of the way we were. We had not one single practical idea between us, but we knew her lacklustre campaign needed an injection of *joie de vivre* – she was being controlled by the men in suits.

On the way home, there was enthusiastic endorsement of Mary Maher's suggestion that Robinson should appoint Anne O'Donnell as her public relations officer. Anne was the bright-eyed, laughing feminist, all dangly earrings and colourful clothes, who had shown a backbone of steel as director of the Rape Crisis Centre. She was prominently identified with resisting all the efforts of the fundamentalist brigade to slam shut the door on abortion and divorce. The appointment of someone like her would be a subtle signal that Robinson did not object to attempts to prise that door open.

Robinson agreed, and offered Anne the post. Within forty-eight hours the offer was withdrawn. The men, we assumed, had blown their tops. We feminists went into a huff with the nameless men. Worse, we were on the horns of an awful dilemma: principle dictated that we stand by Anne and sever links with Robinson. It was a rotten situation. A round robin of phone calls led to a painful consensus: we would quietly fade away and hope that nobody would notice that we were not by Robinson's side.

I got a phone call from Mary Robinson. She was humble. She was ringing all of us individually, she said, to say she was sorry for hurting us. She accepted full responsibility for the mess. And by the way, she said, it was not men who had advised her to withdraw the offer to Anne O'Donnell, it was her spokeswoman Bride Rosney, in whose judgement she had total trust.

Her courage was disarming. I said I wouldn't say in public what had happened and wished her well. I thought about it afterwards and remembered the meeting that she, Seán MacBride and I had addressed, in 1971, where I advocated confrontation and barricades, and the two lawyers counselled patience and constitutional struggle. Without ever declaring her hand on abortion, Robinson had kept students and women's groups out of prison when they fought to distribute abortion information. Rosney was right. Robinson didn't need a Trojan horse. Robinson was the Trojan horse. She wouldn't win the election, of course, but damned if I was going to stand idly by while she lost it. I went down to her campaign headquarters and signed on as a volunteer. As I left the room with an armful of leaflets, Robinson said wryly, 'Don't make promises I can't keep.'

Rosney asked me to take part in a photo opportunity in Dublin with actors and writers who had declared support for Robinson. I spoke at a rally for her the night before, in Galway, and got up early next morning to find my car trapped in the hotel yard by another car, the driver of which released me after he got up for his leisurely breakfast. I missed the photo call in Dublin, a lovely one, which showed Robinson high-stepping, arm in arm, with such characters as world-famous actor Niall Toibin; of course, had I been in that photo, there would have been no need for people to bite their nails right up to the moment the election result was announced. Bride Rosney knows her stuff.

The morning of Mary Robinson's inauguration I sat in the house, watching her on television, keeping her all to myself. 'Mna na hÉireann,' she addressed us – 'Women of Ireland.' In that instant, I became slightly law-abiding.

Chapter Twenty-Three

In 1991 Nuala and I settled into the house she had bought. It was a beautiful, spacious home with a garden front and back. I dug and replanted the lawn; Nuala planted huge red poppies; I espaliered pyracantha; Nuala planted a grove of silver birch; I liberated yellow bricks from a skip to raise the wall and found a discarded marble step that would take us elegantly up from the pink tiled patio on to the green green grass of our own little lawn.

We were hardly in the house before the interest rate on mortgages doubled. I was paying out more than I was getting in rent, but – what the hell – the two award-winning journalists were earning more than enough.

Marie came over from Sweden. I said to her, proudly, 'Nuala is not a lesbian.'

Marie gazed at me: 'And you boast about that?'

Nuala loved, regardless of gender, I said; it was the future, I said. We were living the future.

'And does your future allow you to boast of being lesbian?' Marie asked.

As soon as my mother was dead, I said, lying about the privacy pact I had struck with Nuala.

We went to spend a night in the house which Carmel and her husband had rented in Co. Sligo for themselves, their three young children, my mother and sister Nuala, and Kevin's parents. It was crowded and cheerful. The talk was of the North. This drove Nuala to drink. She threw down the gauntlet, announcing that the Provos were 'murderers'. There have been better starts to family holidays. The gauntlet was not picked up.

The following year, Carmel and her husband and their three young children came to stay with us for a week. It was their first time in Dublin as a family. I wanted to show them that antagonism to Northerners was much eased. There were only two bedrooms in the house, but one was massive and they would fit in easily.

Nuala moved out for the week. There was not enough room, she said.

I stood in the kitchen that year, 1992, and said, 'Nuala, do you want me to stay, or go?'

She was sitting by the window reading, and sipping a glass of wine.

She said softly, without looking up, 'Don't go.'

That was a major declaration of love. I seized it and cherished it. I had not wanted to go.

Nuala's sister from London stayed regularly with us, but always came alone. Her brother sometimes came, alone. We still spent the Merriman week with the growing, rambunctious O'Faolain clan.

In 1993, our third year in the new home, Nuala was white with tension at the imminent arrival of my family. I vomited into a hedge outside the house. I had pains in my arm – arthritis, old before my time, Jesus help me – and went to an acupuncturist. Nuala left the house again, but arranged to take the children out to a glamorous fast-food joint. She can be terrific with children.

We came back half an hour late from a jaunt in the Wicklow mountains. Nuala was waiting. 'You're late,' she said to me. At least she didn't say it in front of my family.

The acupuncturist said to me, 'I do therapy, too.' I burst into tears, and the whole sorry tale of Nuala and me came tumbling out. The acupuncturist suggested that we set aside a half-hour a day to talk. One of us would speak, uninterrupted, for that time, and the following day the other would respond for an uninterrupted half an hour. Jesus, Jesus, but we tried, Nuala and I, to save ourselves.

She accepted an invitation to talk about political prisoners at a meeting in Derry, in 1994, to be chaired by me. Bernadette was the other speaker. Nuala spoke critically, and rightly, about the unsung sacrifices women made to keep home fires burning while the men were in prison. As she spoke Bernadette tore up paper, rolled it into little balls, and flicked it around the floor. Many in the audience applauded this horrible pantomime.

Increasingly, while Nuala was out at work, I spent the day looking out the window at the garden. I can spend whole hours doing nothing. There are birds to look at, and clouds, and such friends as still persisted in breaching the gilded tower preferred to call when Nuala was not there. Before she came home at six in the evening, I would go into the study and write for one of the many publications for which I was churning out work. Yes, churning. I was sometimes too affectedly busy to greet her with a kiss as she came in the door. I know now, from reading what she wrote of us, that she was abjectly lonely, too. 'Dead sea fruit, we are,' I said to her during a sorrowful quarrel. 'Lovely on the outside, empty inside, touch and it crumbles into dust.' I worked all evening in the study; Nuala sat in the kitchen, reading and sipping wine and listening to opera.

When she went abroad on work, we wrote to each other almost daily. 'Don't be lonely. Take what comfort is offered to you,' I wrote to her. 'Fucking on the road doesn't count,' I despairingly quoted the old story about actors who worked away from home. Ah, but we got on well when one of us was abroad and felt lonely and needed support from the home base. We were happy as sandpipers on holiday together.

I will not go unkissed to my death, I raged at her when we returned home, where we desperately, consolingly, sexlessly, clung to each other in the double bed. We always embraced, always held each other in bed. During those years without sexual intimacy, we were heroic with each other. I never told her – and did not know until I read her book that she was doing it also – that I winced as I looked out the window of railway trains on foreign platforms at the sight of entwined lovers.

In 1993, my mother fell seriously ill again. I started the one week on, one week off again. A great dream of Nuala's came true: we had enough between us to pay a deposit on a cottage in Co. Clare. On her birthday, I presented her with a blown-up ordnance survey map that pinpointed the little hamlet where the cottage was situated on half an acre. Us! Landowners! Goodbye, Cromwell and famine. The West's awake.

The deeds were signed on International Women's Day. Nuala rang me at the town where I was giving a talk, and I announced the fact to the women's group as proudly as if I were announcing the birth of a child. They applauded my good fortune.

I started going round Ireland in circles. I had bought a second vehicle, having finally appreciated how wrong it was to expect Nuala to live without the one we owned. I'm a slow but steady learner, me. I drove south from Derry to Dublin on a Friday night, Nuala drove us west to Clare on Saturday mornings and back to Dublin on Monday nights, and I drove north to Derry. Sometimes I drove from Derry direct to Clare.

I kissed an Englishwoman who had lusted after me in my youth, who called me when she returned once more to Dublin. It was no more than that, one kiss, in the street, as we said good night, but I hadn't been deeply kissed since 1984, nine long years. Next morning, I was terrified that the woman would turn up on the doorstep. I felt sexually rejected when she did not. I spent the day both terrified and rejected. That night I confessed the infidelity to Nuala. She smiled, wanly, and said nothing. She was immersed with her own ghosts, in the therapy course she was undergoing, talking, she said, about her family.

I spent the weekends homesteading at the cottage. I knocked down a dividing wall with a sledgehammer, painted and papered and plastered, cut hedges with a machete. My brother Hugh rewired the house. Carmel contributed carpet. Nuala's sister Deirdre and her husband, Eamon, painted the spouting, and turned the outhouse into a workshed, built a garden bench, planted seeds. Nuala and I agreed that family members should each have a week in the cottage, free, every year. My mother recovered and was brought triumphantly to the little old house in the West. She loved the haybarn. She snipped wild roses and chose where they should be planted.

It was lovely of Nuala to ensure that the great and the good of her acquaintance came to the opening night of the one-woman play I had written, *Worm in the Heart*, my first work for the stage. I had defined the relationship between children and mothers, not romance with men, as the worm. I waited behind the curtain for the cries of 'Author, author' which did not come. Nuala went home early from the after-play party, which was more in the nature of a wake. The play transferred to London, where Nuala happened to be giving a lecture. For the only time in our life together, I put my little foot down and insisted she attend the opening night with me, instead of the opera to which she proposed going. Afterwards, she said in surprised tones that the play had better things in it than she remembered from the Dublin opening. That she had noticed was to me like rainfall in drought.

In 1994, my mother fell ill again. I resumed the week-on, week-off routine.

Nuala told me that she had made her will. She had left the house in which we lived and all her money to her family. We were both self-sufficient and well off, she said, and her family had grown up in poverty. I was somewhat stunned. Should I outlive her, I asked, was it reasonable to expect me, in great old age, to leave the home we were building together and return to the house I had bought and rented out? I could see the dismay on her face, and knew she was desolate at the thought of not leaving money to her family.

I suggested that we agree that, upon her death, I would sell my house and divide the proceeds between both our families, and that she give me, in return, life tenancy in our home, while assigning ownership to her family. That would take care of the disparity in value between our two houses. She told me some days later that she had changed her will. I made mine accordingly. The morbid mood in our home had nothing to do with physical health.

Weeks later, in the spring of 1994, another play of mine opened. Nuala did not come to the opening. Before the curtain rose, as I stood alone in the foyer, a woman introduced herself and offered me a glass of wine. I felt a tingling in my skin that I had not felt since the day I fell in love with Nuala. I flirted with the woman. When I finally got home, drunk, the phone was ringing. I heard the woman leave her ex-directory number. The call ended before I could lift the receiver. I pressed the wrong button and erased the message. Had I got the number, I would have gone round to the woman at once.

For my fiftieth birthday that year, Nuala gifted us with tickets to Timbuktu. I had never been to Africa before. This would be the best journey ever. The trip would not take place until September, when it was cooler, Nuala said. We would discuss and arrange the orderly ending of our relationship when we got there, she said.

She said it out of the blue. It did not sound so strange. It felt right. Two friends who had persisted in keeping contact down all the years of our relationship joined us in the Shelbourne for an afternoon birthday-party tea. It was a muted affair. Our friends, Marian Finucane and Evelyn Conlon, were as alert as hares and did not probe. We told them about Timbuktu, nothing else. It was a lonely afternoon. When I got home, I threw into the wastepaper basket the hundreds of printed business cards that announced that 'Nell McCafferty has moved to . . .', the house where Nuala and I resided. Jaysus, but I was moving up in the world with those cards, and the cordon bleu cookery course and the espaliered pyracantha. It was over now. We had moved the telephone number with us when we changed address after ten years. The number was fourteen years old. I was fifty. Ten, fourteen, fifty. I multiplied the figures, divided them, played arithmetic in my head as my father had taught me. Doing sums fills the blank spaces in your head.

That summer Nuala announced that she was going to London to see the only man she had ever truly loved, 'while I still have teeth in my head'. I understood perfectly. When I lost my first adult tooth, shortly after I met Nuala, it was to Marie in Sweden that I immediately turned; Marie had known me in the full of my youth. Marian and Evelyn, as it happens, were there also, that day Nuala announced she was going to England. Maybe they were keeping a death watch. They allowed themselves raised eyebrows.

Nuala came back from England, stoic and soft. He had a wife and a boy child and a big dining table and a future. It was not the first time Nuala got a relationship absolutely wrong: he and his wife parted shortly afterwards. He still had a drink problem; his wife loved someone else.

For the first time at Merriman, we stayed apart, travelling separately from our cottage to Ballyvaughan. We even went on separate days. I sought out, and spent a whole afternoon in conversation with, a man whom Nuala had mentioned. She'd had a lovely conversation with him, she said. I listened slavishly, feeding the man compliments to keep him going. I was trying to find out what men had, conversationally, that I might not have. The idiot didn't have the wit to recall the things Nuala said to him. He had not learned a single one of her remarks off by heart. That night, I bought a small bottle of whiskey. I drove to Doolin pier, a large, stony expanse, and listened to the sea. I drank myself drunk, all on my lonesome. Next morning, Nuala, disgusted, pointed to the bits of hedgerow stuck in the wheels of the car.

She was in the cottage and it was my turn at Merriman the day in 1994 that the Provisional IRA declared a ceasefire. The 800-year war was over. Oh, day of joyful days. Not everybody was as generous – why praise the IRA for stopping its murderous campaign? (At a previous Merriman, in 1988, Professor John A. Murphy, who had sometimes been a houseguest of Patsy Murphy's when I lived in her house, had sent me a note across a hotel room, written in black marker and block capitals: 'IN CASE YOU'RE DEAF – NO PROVO-LOVERS WANTED HERE – JOHN A. MURPHY') The TV presenter Prionnsias Mac Aonghusa, socialist, Irish-language enthusiast, and husband of one of my favourite judges, Catherine McGuinness, hugged me. His companion, the aloof, erudite Tomás de Bhaldraithe, author of the English-Irish dictionary, to whom I had never dared address a sentence, smiled wordlessly, warmly, and shook my hand.

After Merriman, we flew to Africa. The first night there, Nuala shut the window panes, closed the shutters, drew the curtains, lit an anti-mosquito ring, sprayed the room with insect repellent, covered her body with anti-mosquito cream and attempted to erect over our bed the netting she had brought from Ireland.

Terrific – my first night in Africa and I was going to suffocate in her arms. Well, it was one solution to our heartbreak, but my body fought for life – amazing, that, matter over mind – and I persuaded her to open the curtains, then the shutters, and we breathed again. How on earth was this woman going to travel without me?

The thing nobody says about Timbuktu is that within the great mud-walled city in the desert there are no public toilets. No hidden nooks either, in the alleyways, where a woman might use her plastic chamber pot – a *de rigueur* accessory in Africa. We went through the city like, well, shite through a duck. Another thing nobody tells you about Timbuktu is that the only tree – a bush, really – behind which a woman can do what a woman has to do is in the middle of the airport runway, in a direct line of sight from the viewing station. Maybe we were there in the dry season when other trees didn't grow. Anyway, who gives a shit about accurate travelogues? Stanley and Livingstone, Nuala and I were not.

We hired a wooden boat, with an awning and outdoor motor, and were steered down a river by two gorgeous youths. The trip took three dreamy days. I saw a French doctor use a battery-operated laptop one night, to send e-mails, my first sight of the coming technological revolution. We fetched up in a wooden house on the beach, in Senegal, and sat down finally to discuss the end of our relationship. Mostly, I spent the night alone, on the porch steps, in the pitch dark, looking at the sea and the stars. Huge crabs came up out of the sand with the rising of the moon, wave after wave of the creatures, intent on getting into the house, their claws clicking loudly, incessantly, on the wood as they dragged themselves up the steps of the porch. I fended them off with the chair. I erected a palisade of chairs. I defended my woman. The crabs withdrew as the sun came up.

Round and round the relationship Nuala and I went by day, in ever-narrowing circles, always ending at the same central place, which was nowhere at all, a black hole in each of our lives, in the life we lived together.

We ended the African journey in Isle de Gorey, the island off the coast from which people were shipped as slaves. They were chained in a dungeon, then offloaded through its tall cut-granite mouth straight on to the narrow stone pier that sloped down into the salty sea. Time dragged for us there as we waited for the day the plane would fly us home.

Shortly after our return I was rushed to hospital and put on ice. I had contracted the kind of malaria that kills you, but I was caught in time. 'I'll choose where we go for my sixtieth birthday,' I croaked to Nuala as they put me into the ambulance. It was the most romantic thing I'd said to her in a long while. She visited me every day for six weeks. After I got out, a stone lighter and fetchingly pale, we decided to stay together.

I wrote to a psychologist of considerable standing, asking if she would give us counselling. She responded as quickly as the Bishop did to my mother. God bless the women's movement.

Sometimes we'd leave the weekly consultation high with hopes; sometimes we'd leave in tatters. These were the longest personal conversations we'd had in years, and we were mannerly in the presence of the therapist. I hardly remember any of it, now. Nuala protested that we slept together like sisters – but sisters don't sleep together naked, arms entwined. I protested that I had to look after my mother – but you don't look after your mother without so much as a consultation with your partner.

In the spring of 1995, I set off to Derry to see my mother, who wasn't even ill. Nuala went to Clare for the weekend. Halfway on the long road north, the penny dropped and I turned off the main road and headed west. Nuala was sitting alone, by the turf fire, reading and drinking her wine. She looked up and gave me such a surprised smile, an open smile that showed her lovely even teeth. I have divorced my mother, I said.

We walked down to the seashore and along the headland and sat down on a sheltered ledge we knew, where the moss retained the heat of the sun. I dared to stretch out and lay my head on Nuala's lap. I could feel the breath rise and fall in her body. We had not been so nakedly intimate since 1984. Next day we took the boat to the nearest of the Aran Islands and walked between the little stone walls and watched a man spade seaweed over his potato drills. We spent the night on the island.

397

As the boat approached the coast of Clare next morning we recited, like twins, John Locke's 'The Exile's Return', the poem we always quoted in spring:

O Ireland, isn't it grand, you look
Like a bride in her rich adornin'?
With all the pent up love of my heart
I bid you top of the mornin'.

I came back from Derry late one night in April to find a wailing puppy in the hall. I did not understand: we had discussed getting a dog and decided against it because the care of it would interfere with our wanderlust. I fed the little thing, and brought it to the bedroom. Nuala woke up. 'I wanted something to love,' she said. I understood and did not care to explore the understanding. Molly – what a lovely name, chosen by Nuala – looked smashing, so she did, a black-and-white streak of pure freedom when she raced across the green fields beside our cottage. Go, Molly, go.

Within weeks of Molly coming into Nuala's life, I was out of it.

I was due to go to Scotland, to a feminist conference on racism and sectarianism. Nuala mentioned it to one of the rare visitors to our house and was dismissive. 'The things Nell has to do to get her fare paid for a trip out of the country,' she said. I responded by naming a noted English writer and socialist, Beatrice Campbell, who was going. I was reduced to defending myself and feminism? Offended to the core I roared at Nuala when our visitor left. 'Hush.' She put her hands affectedly to her ears. 'The neighbours will hear.' I would not be quiet.

That night, I went into the other bedroom. At six in the morning I got up, slipped into bed beside her, put my arm around her.

'It's over,' she said.

'I know,' I said.

She turned on her side and I spooned up to her, as usual.

She got up at half past eight, packed a bag, went downstairs and rang a couple we knew, both separated, in an Ireland where divorce was still illegal, and I heard her say, 'Nell and I can't be your bridesmaids in New York. We have split up.' There was a short response. 'Goodbye,' Nuala said, her soft, breaking voice under tight control. I heard her put down the phone. I heard her footsteps go down the hall. I heard the front door slam closed. An awful sound is that, a door slamming closed on a life.

There followed what I called 'The Reader's Digest Year'. A month before Nuala and I split up, the *Irish Press* collapsed, owing me eight weeks' wages. It scarcely mattered, I was earning so much money. One column was syndicated in several provincial newspapers, and I had taken to doubling the fee offered when anybody commissioned something. It always worked. The money made up for lack of job satisfaction. I went everywhere, would write on any topic, and by night I turned my face to the wall and drank Southern Comfort. I ordered records from the Reader's Digest, which I never played, books and atlases I never looked at, videos on wildlife that I never watched.

The only thing going for me was the house I had bought from Nuala in 1990. The house seemed very small and dark when I returned there. The tenants had not been kind to it. Christina helped me pack to move back. Though Eamonn McCann sent me flowers – 'to the irresistible Nell' – when I told him that Nuala and I had parted, I had cut off contact with anyone I knew in Dublin, except for Christina, and, though I was glad of her help, I told her candidly that I was accepting it as a form of expiation – as she had been heartbroken by me, now she could see me heartbroken in turn.

The *Sunday Tribune* asked me to write about the siege of Sarajevo. Christina woke me from a drunken sleep to get me on the plane. I went into that besieged city in a British army tank. The tank was hot and noisy and confined, and bullets pinged off its skin. The tank commander dropped me off at Snipers' Alley, told me I'd have to make a run across the road through gunfire to reach the hotel, and said, 'You'll know what else we had to go through in the Bogside.' As if I cared about bullets. I woke up one morning in Bosnia calling Nuala's name, tears streaming down my face. She picked me up at the airport upon my return.

When I returned to Dublin, Nuala called me regularly at home, crying. She asked me, and I agreed, to go on holiday with her, but we had to cancel after I was brought by ambulance from a hotel in Waterford to the local hospital: my back had frozen, and the room-service waiter found me on the floor, so paralysed with pain that I could not reach up to the telephone. Nuala came to the hospital and wrote in longhand the article I had been due to file from the hotel.

I was shifted to Dublin and given loads of morphine and Valium, and the hospital, one of the few not controlled by the Catholic Church, allowed me wine with my meals as I recovered movement. God bless the Protestant ethos. (The hospital has since closed.) The woman who had made my skin tingle the year before Nuala and I split turned up with a carton of cigarettes, which I was allowed to smoke in my private room.

I was frightened when I went home alone from hospital. What if my back should seize as I was getting into the bath? I was fortuitously rescued by two women from the Chernobyl Children's Project, which had been sending convoys of medicine to Belarus, which had been devastated by an accident in a nuclear reactor. They invited me to accompany them. Adi Roche and Ali Hewson assured me that the ambulance in which I would travel was stocked with painkilling drugs. They did not know that I would have welcomed death by radiation. A chain-link fence separated the population from the still-leaking reactor. Hundreds of people stood by the roadside, in the dark, wherever we went, begging for aspirin from Ireland. They needed morphine. I forgot about my back.

I began a relationship in 1996 with the woman who had brought me cigarettes in hospital. Among other considerable things, it was sexually joyful. Nuala suggested that we form a threesome – the woman would be my consort and Nuala would be my travelling companion. The woman rightly scorned the very notion. Nuala suggested a trip to Albania. Albania! I had, for decades, stood on Greek shores and looked across the narrow water to the forbidden place of shimmering green fields, the last Communist country in the world to keep out visitors. Hoxha had fallen, Nuala was calling, so off we went. If Nuala had called me to go to a corner shop with her, I would have gone.

Albania was more than authentic. There were concrete pill-boxes every hundred yards, in country and city, erected by Hoxha in the event of invasion. There was an unchanged wooden hotel, where the stables still stood that had housed camels travelling the Silk Road. Nuala told me casually that her memoir *Are You Somebody?* would be published in October. She had previously shown me the first page of the chapter she was writing on me. But, I protested, what about my mother? The revelations about our relationship would frighten her. It was time my mother was stood up to, Nuala said. Had she dropped the line that I was a slave to my family? I asked. She had, Nuala said. And had she dropped the term 'lesbian', applied to me but not to herself? She had, Nuala said. I could injunct her book, I threatened. Remember *The Armagh Women*, Nuala said. Even as I protested, I was thinking that, if I had to come out with somebody, it was better to come out in style with the great Nuala; no better woman than Nuala to write sensitively about love and passion between women, without frightening the horses.

I got off one great line as we parted at the border, she to continue her travels in Greece, me to go back to Dublin. 'We'll always have Albania,' I said. When I got home, Nuala rang often, leaving messages on the answering machine, but I was not there as falsely promised. I was away trying, unsuccessfully, to mend the relationship with the woman I had left behind. The woman who had brought me back to life never forgot Albania.

I made one last attempt at reconciliation with Nuala. The memory of it makes me blush. I booked a window table in the Shelbourne Hotel. I wore the matching top and skirt we had chosen in a boutique in Paris and put on earrings. I had done one more list of our finances that showed how close we were to having it all – a home in Dublin, a cottage in the west, enough money from the sale of my house to finance world travel. Nuala was an icy stranger. I would have to sell my half of the cottage, I threatened, hoping that would force her to sell her half also. She could not possibly afford yet another full mortgage. I was determined to have some sort of retribution. (Good for Nuala, she later bought me out and held on to her dream.) I watched her walk away from the table, through the crowded dining room, then past the window, off into the rain and the night. She looks lovely, womanly, mature, when she dresses up. I ordered a brandy and considered my doom.

Her book *Are You Somebody?* did not mention the passion between us. She did not mention that I worked as a journalist or wrote books.

Over the next two years, I spent £30,000 rebuilding my house so that it was flooded with light on golden wood floors. I was offered an honorary doctorate by Staffordshire University, though for what exactly I was unable to tell Nuala. 'Probably a general doctorate, for people qualified in no specific field,' she said. The university later specified that I would be a Doctor of Letters, for my writing about feminism and the North. 'It's a red-brick university,' Nuala pointed out. She said she would like to come with me for the ceremony. Grand, I said, I'll book two rooms. Ah no, she said, she would just fly in and out for the actual conferring in the morning. Sure, didn't I know that she did not like socializing? No thank you, I said, and I became a Doctor of Letters all on my own. I was dead proud. Other honorary doctors include Mo Mowlam, the English minister who brokered a peace deal in the North. God bless the English.

Nuala rang me one Friday night in 1999 to say that, on foot of the success of *Are You Somebody?* in America, she had been given a million-dollar advance to write a novel. She wanted to share her success with me, more than with anybody, she said. Would I be her guest for a fortnight in that Tuscan villa to which we had always dreamt of retiring? I would, I said. I continued writing my weekly article. I stopped writing the article. I rang Nuala back and said that now she was rich and could afford it, I would prefer, instead of a fortnight in Tuscany, some financial recompense for the contributions I had made over fifteen years to her various homes and to the cottage.

She was livid. 'Join the queue. How much do you want of my

fortune?' There was pain and anger and disappointment in her screeching voice. Twenty-five thousand pounds, I said, which worked out at £1,500 a year, or £30 a week, which was not much, I said, given that the value of her house and cottage had gone through the roof in the last half of the booming 1990s. She hung up. I sent her a written account of all that I had contributed, including such details as the fact that I had always been the named driver on our car insurance and had to start from scratch, with no discount bonuses or anything, when we split. A penny-pinching accountant could not have done better.

We met, once, briefly, to discuss it. 'I owe you nothing,' she said. 'You were my lodger.' So much for love, I arched an eyebrow, looking down on her at last from the high moral ground. She recaptured it months later with a hand-delivered envelope containing a cheque for £25,000. There was no note. I found the envelope lying on the hall floor. I cashed the cheque and bought shares to the value of £10,000 in the privatized former state telephone company, Eircom. They were cheaply priced, the government said, and we could sell them later at a profit, which was the government's way of letting taxpayers retrieve some of the money they had contributed to the state. A Marxist magazine in England had already declared that buying shares was an acceptable practice for the workers, in that it allowed them to get some of the wealth they had created, so I was not selling out socialism when I bought into Eircom. Had any of us workers understood the stock market, we would have sold our shares the first week Eircom was launched. We didn't, and we lost one-third of our investment when the shares sank, never to rise again. However, I got lucky. Newly rich, thanks to Nuala's cheque, I also put £10,000 into a telecommunications company called Esat, on the advice of a woman who had heard that it might be taken over at double its value. It was indeed taken over, and I made £10,000 profit. It was all accidental – the stock-market fever of the Celtic Tiger had replaced football fever in Ireland. And I am my gambling father's daughter. I reinvested my profits in dotcom stocks and watched my profits climb to £40,000.

I was in Newfoundland in March 2000, giving a lecture, when

the dotcom revolution collapsed. My profits disappeared in the fortnight I was away. I still invest, though. So far, since 1999, I have made about 10,000 euros. Euros, dollars, sterling: we workers have made the language of capitalism our own.

And doing numbers in my head eased the heartbreak.

Nuala, a full-time fiction writer now, and attempting love again, would appear to have resolved the problem that dogged her days: that the engagement of writing diminishes the lover's passion for another human being. She left a copy of her first novel outside my front door and e-mailed me angrily weeks later, demanding 'the common courtesy' of a response. 'I'm in a terrible state wondering how it is likely to be received . . . to not even acknowledge receipt of two years' work of mine is beyond insensitive . . .'

The thing is, I did not like her work of fiction, and had been using the time to gather compliments for her from people who liked the book better than I did. I thought the populist novel she had written did not reflect her huge talent. I sent selective praise to her as soon as the others had reported back to me, and asked her, given her anguish at waiting, if she would explain to me now why she had never read my books.

She e-mailed back: 'I've thought about that very often – and I've tried to interrogate my near-unbelievable insensitivity – my reluctance to engage with you as a thinker and writer. I see it different ways – as a power ploy, as self-protective, as a testing you to make sure you were strong enough not to need me (i.e. make demands on me) . . . the loss was mine, not to join in your work . . .'

That peaceful interlude between us did not last long.

I knew I would write this book when an American magazine sent me an interview it had done with Nuala, which focused on the mildly graphic heterosexual love scenes in her novel *My Dream of You*. The interviewer asked her to reconcile the focus on heterosexuality with her relationship with me. The magazine asked if I would care to comment on her response.

Nuala said to the interviewer:

Luckily, Nell had a big crush on me and I was so derelict I didn't see or care what happened. It was one of the great strokes of my life [meeting Nell], and I did love her. I got better through her and through having a home for the first time . . . I never thought of Nell as a woman, and when I woke up with Nell it didn't seem remarkable to me at all. God knows I'd woken up in bed with other people. And God knows she was much nicer and more honourable and more loving. It was much more healthy and life-giving than any relationship with a man. But I would still walk across fifty-nine women to get to one man if I was attracted to him . . . Nell is very bitter. She says this book is a disgrace.

I was undone when I read that. I was not a woman? I was not to be called a woman? All I was was a lesbian? I thought heterosexual love disgraceful?

I sent her a short e-mail when I read the interview.

It said, 'Shame on you.'

Nuala wrote back that this was the moment she had dreaded: that I would one day see the interview (which attracted no public mention in Ireland). She said that I should always remember that she and I had loved each other well enough, that nothing could distort that, and that I was not to do so. She closed the missive: 'However, I am not open to discuss this or any other matter with you.'

I could have played the victim, and flaunted the interview as an example of how this woman had betrayed and exploited me. Upon sore reflection, I realized that adopting such a pose, especially to myself, would do me no good at all. In playing the victim, I would be declaring myself a fool for having loved her, and been duped by her. And anyway, there was a time, however brief, I still believed, when Nuala did love me.

I came to the conclusion that Nuala just could not deal with anyone thinking of her as a 'lesbian'. And if she feared the label 'lesbian' – she for whom the lesbian phase was but a fifteen-year moment, and who could still retreat, hand on heart, to the blissfully safe, socially sanctioned, God-blessed sanctuary of heterosexuality – then what was it like for me who had no such bolt hole, who could not truthfully say other than that I am lesbian? The night I read the interview in which Nuala O'Faolain denied and derided me was the loneliest of my life. I was not to consider that I was once beloved. And she would not talk to me about it.

At the end of that awful week, I had to appear on the *Late Late Show*. The young fellow who was on before me was a rising film star. I paid him no attention at all. When I had finished talking about feminism, and returned to the hospitality suite, this fellow knelt in front of me and promised to love me all night long. I explained why this would not work. He grinned, asked if he could pretend anyway, flipped up the long tunic top I was wearing, put his head under it and simulated cunnilingus. The room froze. I was delighted with his gesture, and sorry that I had not the strength to go drinking with him, at least, in Dublin's clubs. I will not have a word said against Colin Farrell. His unbridled enthusiasm for women made me feel just great – just like a woman.

I knew I was over Nuala O'Faolain when I realized, several weeks after her sixty-second birthday, in 2002, that I had forgotten to send her a card. So it would not have mattered to me – though once it would have brought me to my knees – that Nuala had, that very year, met a man in New York with whom she was going to live there. The man had a little daughter, who stayed with himself and Nuala for half of every week.

When she wrote in her second memoir *Almost There* that she was jealous of the sweet child, I understood exactly what she meant and defended her against pious expressions of outrage. For Nuala, passion was all. Simultaneously, I allowed myself a wonderful bout of *schadenfreude*. I had had a short relationship, in the first year of the millennium, when I was fifty-six, with a woman who had children. *Snow White and the Seven Dwarfs* loses its appeal on the ninety-ninth showing. Truly, parents are heroes. Now Nuala was up to her eyes in *Beauty and the Beast*?

There is one sentence from that memoir that leaps out: 'Of all things I would ask of life now, the thing I want most to learn is ordinary, daily love.' My mother told me she always knew, when her children were walking out the door, which of their marriages would fail.

'What did you think of Nuala coming in the door?' I asked.

'She was too old for you,' my mother said gently. 'She'd already lived her life.'

Chapter Twenty-Four

To celebrate my mother's ninetieth birthday, in November 2000, the retired Bishop Edward Daly said mass in her kitchen. Mickey Quigley, the best man at her wedding, sat beside her on the sofa of the crowded room. As the Bishop approached them with the communion wafers, my mother held Mickey's glass of whiskey while he took the communion in his hand. The Bishop waited until the glass was handed back, before giving my mother her communion. My mother then took ill, colour draining from her face, vomiting gently into the towel Carmel held to her mouth, and the Bishop waited until she waved a hand at him, giving him permission to finish the mass. Mickey sipped contentedly at his whiskey through the service. He looked smashing in his cravat. My mother, a teetotaller, sipped water. She looked smashing with her full head of silver curly hair.

I knelt before the Bishop, accidentally cast as altar girl. That was all right: Bishop Edward Daly was the priest who waved the white hankie at the British soldiers on Bloody Sunday 1972, as he carried a dying boy through the gunfire. This birthday mass was a grand way to end the first year of the millennium. There were neighbours and relatives in all the rooms, out in the street, out in the back yard, joining in the prayers and hymns as the sacred words and tunes filtered back, wave after wave. There were feminists, and atheists, and IRA volunteers and party politicians.

Eamonn McCann has said of the changes in the tiny area of the Bogside in which we live – 100 square metres – that it is easier to get hold of an elected representative than it is to get a plumber. Those eight streets have produced, since the civil rights uprising of 1968: John Hume; Martin McGuinness; Mitchell McLaughlin, chairman of Sinn Féin; Mary Nelis, now a Sinn Féin member of the Stormont Assembly; Seamus Deane; Eamonn McCann himself; Paddy

Doherty, chair of the Inner City Trust, which has retrieved and restored historic buildings within the walled city; and Brendan Duddy, my old friend with the café who went on to become a millionaire and one of the three secret mediators who brought about the IRA ceasefire in 1994, at considerable risk to his personal safety.

There is a book called *Lost Lives* which gives the names of everyone who died until a power-sharing agreement and government was formed in Northern Ireland in 1998. By then, thirty years after the Northern Ireland Civil Rights Association had been established, 3,630 people out of a population of one and a half million people had been killed. That is less than 0.25 per cent of the population. It feels like an awful lot more. The book is like a sombre walk through a familiar graveyard. Each death gets a tombstone: a paragraph that tells that there she died, and how, and why, and by whom, she was killed, or by the hand of which organization; there he died, how and why.

I read it sometimes, still, looking back over the years of war, now that we have peace to look back, and I am aghast. Some pages, relating to just one day, run on and on and on because, on some days, people died by the dozen and more. There are whole swathes of the book which force me to acknowledge that I didn't know anybody had died on a particular day, or how many. Death rained down through those three decades. Often, it didn't make the front page of the newspapers. Often, you'd read the little headline on a middle page, in a sidebar, and not read the small print underneath. Often, if you hadn't read the paper, or listened to the news on radio or television that day, or had been out of the country on holiday, you wouldn't even know that people had died.

The book holds, in parts, the fascination of a gruesome jigsaw: there are cross-references which show that years after X killed Y, X was shot by A, who was a relative of Y; that some families lost B, C and D, though the relatives were years and miles apart. It is probably only because the North is such a tiny place, with such a small population, that such a complete, detailed book of our troubles was possible.

Lost Lives is a complete account of death in war. It is a relentless, kindly, respectful tolling of death, but it pulls no punches. Some details, of many of the deaths, are horrifying. I am glad I will not again have to read such a book about the place of my birth and rearing. *Lost Lives* is the print equivalent of Picasso's *Guernica*.

Thirty years after I smoked cigarettes with Senator Paddy Wilson, on the day he was killed in 1973, I sat in the loyalist headquarters of the man who had admitted stabbing him and who had served fourteen years in prison, where he took an Open University degree in social science and criminology. John White, aged twenty-two when he killed Wilson, was by then the wealthy political adviser to Johnny Adair, the notorious Shankill paramilitary leader, and had been to Downing Street for discussions with Prime Minister John Major. Now he and Adair and their gang were engaged in a turf war with other loyalists. The three of us ate a Chinese takeaway together, around midnight, and he nodded when I reminded him of Paddy Wilson. I got on grand with John White, but it was on the basis, which I outlined before we started talking, that we would not discuss the source of his wealth. I was no fool, I told him, and wasn't interested in the feud. I just wanted to know what it was like being with a loyalist. Neither White nor Adair was remotely interested in my own background.

It was a relief to finally meet the kind of people who killed Catholics. I did not get the impression that White wanted to return to those days. Adair was just interested in turf war, per se, with Catholic, Protestant or dissenter. There was no traction in the conversation I had with him. A few days after that night, Adair, who was on probation, was returned to prison, and the other loyalists forced White to go on the run on the continent.

That interview with Johnny Adair and his supporters was one of my last assignments in journalism. It is odd that I do not miss it at all since I left the *Sunday Tribune*, where I worked for fifteen years, in February 2003. That might be because my experience there, under former editor Matt Cooper, was the most miserable of my thirty-three years in a profession about which I was so passionate.

After he took over as editor, we began well enough: I told him that I hadn't had a rise in years, nor holiday pay, and he promptly gave me both. The relationship deteriorated almost immediately when he stood over a misleading headline on an article I wrote about President Mary McAleese's first six months in office. I wrote, mildly enough, that the diary of Mary Robinson's successor was not completely full. The *Tribune* headlined the article 'The New Paddy Hillery', comparing her to a previous incumbent of the residence, Patrick Hillery, who had spent a very low-profile fourteen years as president – until Mary Robinson transformed it, the presidency was almost invisible. Nothing in my article had suggested, hinted or implied that McAleese's presidency was comparable in any way to Hillery's.

The headline caused a furore. McAleese was furious and called a meeting of the editors of the daily papers to protest. She criticized misleading journalism. Cooper, when I reproached him, appeared unconcerned about the headline. I wrote a strongly worded letter – effing and blinding, actually – to the president, pointing out that she, as a former journalist, should know the difference between a sub-editor's headline and a journalist's text. She replied, disarmingly, that she still had on her mantelpiece a photograph of me and her favourite priest, taken at her inauguration (at which I represented the National Union of Journalists), and that the invitation to bring my mother to meet her still stood.

One of my last altercations with the *Tribune* concerned abortion. Yet another PLAC-inspired amendment to the Constitution was proposed in 2002, and it was clear that journalists were weary of covering the matter yet again. Twenty years down the line, they asked no hard questions and reported by rote such little debate as there was. I suggested to the *Tribune* that I be assigned to cover a press conference given by the masters of the three national maternity hospitals, in which the masters proposed to declare support for the new amendment, which would have constitutionally sealed the limit on such severely restricted abortion practice as was legal in Ireland. *Tribune* news editor Martin Wall refused, saying that with mid-week news our Sunday paper followed through on the dailies.

I responded with the mantra I had tried to drum into the *Tribune*, 'Nothing is covered properly until the *Tribune* covers it,' and said that I was going to go along anyway. Wall forbade me to represent the *Tribune* if I did.

I signed in to the press conference under the name of one of the provincial papers I wrote for and proceeded to do a two-hander with Emily O'Reilly, of the *Sunday Times*, a veteran who had written a book exposing the machinations of PLAC. Between us, we asked the right questions, and the three young masters – who had never faced a press conference before – agreed that the amendment, if passed, would prevent them from offering best medical practice of abortion to women whose babies were incapable of surviving outside the womb. They said they would have preferred to see such practice legalized in Ireland, but feared that politicians would refuse to legislate for it. They reiterated, though now with marked reluctance, support for an amendment which would protect doctors and let women down. The news made radio, television and national headlines. The reporter whom the *Tribune* belatedly sent along, who arrived just before the conference ended, couldn't write about it. The *Tribune* would not let me write about it. The amendment was roundly defeated because of the declared ambivalence by the three masters.

For all that I do not miss being a journalist, I am thankful beyond words to the profession. The reports of a journalist in the New York *Daily News* in December 1935 have led me to hire an American lawyer and start proceedings to clear the name of my Uncle Brian, the man who allegedly killed a prostitute. The reports show inconsistencies in the search for the killer of Loretta Peabody on Christmas Eve that year. Brian and she were seen drinking together all that day. They were finally thrown out of a bar. Brian acknowledged that he subsequently paid her for sex in a derelict building. Then he returned to the bar alone. Her body, when found, had been mutilated. The barman saw no blood on Brian or on his clothing. The police found no incriminating evidence when they picked Brian up from his apartment on Christmas Day. He was never tried, convicted or jailed. He was adjudged, on the grounds of insanity, unfit to plead, and spent twenty years in a penal institution for the insane. There is reason to believe that Loretta Peabody, who worked independently of the brothels and pimps, was killed by the Mafia, which controlled prostitution in New York and had police and judges on their payroll. I have applied, under the American Freedom of Information Act, for the file on my uncle Brian Duffy.

Chapter Twenty-Five

I have a picture in my mind's eye of my mother. She stands in the doorway between the scullery, where she cooks, and the kitchen, where we eat. She wears an apron. Leaning on the doorjamb, one foot crooked behind the other, she is chuckling about the latest thought in her head. She holds a wooden spoon aloft, which she will use to conduct the rhythm of the telling of this thought – after she has stopped laughing.

Sometimes, these days, I give her the wooden spoon, and she tries to lift it up and down above her head, which is difficult, after all the strokes. I make her repeat the word exercises that Kirk Douglas used in the film where he portrayed a man who has lost speech. 'Ba-la, ba-ma, ba-la.' My sister Nuala will coax her to go further with 'Peter Piper picked a peck . . .' and my mother will stumble, burst out laughing and say – fluently – 'Ah, go take a big shite.'

An impending stroke drove her temporarily out of her mind a month after I forgot Nuala O'Faolain's birthday. She heaved herself out of the bed, pushed my sister Nuala aside, and made her way to the front door. She did not know what to do there or where to go. It was after midnight. Nuala woke the neighbours, and they coaxed her back into the house. She made Nuala lie beside her in the bed all through the night while she fought off the strange men who were coming at her through the wallpaper. My sister, then aged sixty-one, was herself suffering the aftermath of a stroke that limited her strength and movements.

I went to Derry next day and promised my sister that she would never again have to cope alone. I slept on the floor, wrapped in a duvet, beside my mother's bed. She had caught a bug which caused her to vomit and evacuate her bowels. I was vomiting, too, and it made more sense to stay in my mother's downstairs bedroom, using the commode and basins and the downstairs bathroom. I changed my mother's bed linen three times that night. I wondered how on earth she had coped during the years of my father's illness. When I had changed the sheets for what we hoped was the last time, and laid myself down on the floor, exhausted, I heard her voice in the dark.

'Thank you, Nell.'

She spoke so humbly. She had never soiled herself before; I had never washed my mammy's bum before. I still sleep beside her on the floor. It's good for my back.

She ain't heavy, my mother, so it meant nothing, and everything, when I told Nuala that I would henceforth always be at home when my mother was at home, which is every weekend now, from Friday morning until Monday night, when she returns to the Nazareth House nursing home where she stays midweek.

After the brief madness of 2002, she was restored to sanity in the mental home, and, after the stroke that hit her in the asylum, she was sent to recover in the hospital. In April, there was a family conference with staff about where she should go next. Nuala certainly couldn't manage my mother on her own, at home. I couldn't give up my job in Dublin. The staff formally asked my mother what she intended to do, affording her the illusory dignity of making an independent decision. My mother swung her near-blind head around the room, unable to see where any of her adult children were, and asked, 'What will I do, Nell?'

I told her that she would have to go into a nursing home and promised that I would come up from Dublin to bring her home every weekend, and that our Muireanna, Nuala and Carmel would stay with her all day, every day, in the nursing home – which we had agreed beforehand, before I swung the verbal axe down on my mother's hope of returning full-time to the house where she had reared us.

Carmel, who has three children, is the last to leave my mother at night in the nursing home. She knows how I quail from the cruel fact of saying good night to my gallant mother in her bed there, and she takes over before I leave for Dublin; we work seamlessly together. My friend Gráinne asked me, when I was feeling murderously weary and angry, what she could do to help, and, though she had just then retired from a strenuous job as school principal, she cooks and freezes four meals a week for my mother, Nuala and me, and brings lavish fresh puddings, and stands in on nights when Carmel is onstage in the theatre.

The Nazareth House nursing home was an inspired choice after I had done the rounds of others more modern and luxurious. The Nazareth, once a convent and orphanage, is on the edge of the Bogside. It has a hometown Catholic ethos. Sister Muradech, from Mayo, pours whiskey and sherry on birthdays and anniversaries, during football matches, at Easter and Christmas, during concerts and seasonal festivities. When they didn't know I was in the vicinity, I have seen staff caress my mother's head, and lie on her bed during breaks swapping gossip. My mother knows the seed, breed and generation of most of them and, on the rare occasion when she does not, she loves to hear their family stories. My student niece works there during college breaks. Carmel stands in for the hair-dresser during holidays. People read the death columns of the *Derry Journal*, scanning for vacancies for their relatives in Nazareth.

Being back in Derry suited me very well. There was purpose to it, and I was mentally and emotionally ready after the seven months in therapy which saw the end of my weekend drinking. The doctor had recommended therapy after I asked him for an antidepressant course to supplement the sleeping pills and Xanax which sup-plemented the booze. I no longer cared about revealing the truth behind my famous self to a stranger. Desperation brings humility. The therapist asked me straight away if it was my intention to avoid truth-telling by trying to seduce her, and we were away on a hack. When my mother fell grievously ill, I abandoned the therapist – sooner than I would have liked – and the drink and the antidepress-ants and sleeping pills and Xanax; though I am not above taking one of the Valium tablets which lie in a bottle by my mother's bedside, when it is clear that she is facing into a night of pain. It is my normal wont to turn my face away from my mother's physical suffering, but I can't always be rousing Carmel to come and deal with it.

We have a lovely ritual in my mother's house on a Saturday night. The neighbours come in after mass and I give them tea, buns, scones and whatever concoctions Gráinne has made. The conversation goes on until after eleven sometimes. I have noticed that my mother recovers full power of speech when the gossip is red-hot. It is usually sparked off by a review of the death notices of the past week in the *Derry Journal*, or news of who won how much in the parish raffle. The women know all there is to know about the dead, given their great ages – my mother will be ninety-four in November 2004, Eileen is ninety, Tessie is eighty-five and young Bridget is in her seventies. They supplement gaps in each other's memories – or tell things the others did not know, which makes everybody else sit up straight, astonished that they had missed something all those decades ago, affronted that it had escaped their emotional radar, delighted to hear news, still, about the dead, even more delighted if it is about the living.

I have envied these women the pithiness of their phrasing, the beauty of their speech.

'Sure, who did she ever harm but herself? That drink's a curse. It's wild hard to get off it once it gets you.'

'She's nothing to make answer for. God, but she was born ugly, and, all her life, blood came out of her face, imagine that, your period coming out of your face.'

'He poured tea leaves over her scone bread, the cruel git.'

'He put up wallpaper and broke all the plates in one week, and she saw evil ahead of her, but she was wrong. The poor man was just doing his best to fix their house.'

My mother's house is seldom empty for long. Tessie brings the breakfast porridge over every morning that my mother is at home because I cannot make it without lumps. Jean brings a home-baked scone. Ronnie comes through to bring the wheelie bin down to the end of the lane for collection. Peggy brings over soup on Friday afternoons. Bridget sends down home-made fish and chips. Jackie picks Nuala up, in his car, for mass. Frankie helps me get my mother and her wheelchair over the doorstep when we come back from Sunday-afternoon gallivanting. On the many occasions when there have been false alarms about my mother's impending death from the latest setback, Mary has kept vigil by her bedside.

If my mother and I are still asleep after a very late night visit from the doctor, neighbours let themselves in next morning by the key in the door, peep into the bedroom, say nothing, and later mock us both about the 'cut of the two of ye, sleeping the day away'.

Before I lift her, my mother stands like a little soldier by the bed – she is smaller than me now – waving me away, determined to do it by herself. When she fails, and I catch her, I hold her just that little bit longer in my arms, nuzzling her. It is a ballet sequence now. My heart catches when she wakes in the night, calls for an audience, grins, starts to tell her thought, then falters because the words in her brain do not always come to her mouth. 'Och, I dunno . . .' she trails into frustrated silence. Some nights when she wakes up and turns on the radio, I roar at her to, for God's sake, let me sleep; other nights I give in and we sing along to the music, turning off the radio if the music is not suitable, when we will sing our own tunes. My mother gives a particularly ironic rendition of 'Darling, I am growing old', giggling at the 'silver threads among the gold' because her hair is thicker by far than mine.

She is vain. She changes her frock every day. She wants the frock and cardigan to be colour coordinated, though she is hardly in a position to tell – as I remind her, when I am exasperated with tiredness. The odd thing is that she can sometimes tell, as she can sometimes see a piece of paper on the floor, as she can always see a person's teeth.

Watching soap opera on television is difficult because all she sees is the dark shape of a face and you often have to explain who's just said what. When she puts a face, from memory, to the voice she's just heard, her search for confirmation is a soap opera in itself. 'Is that the one with no chin? . . . Is that the one that smokes all the time, with the wrinkles? Nell, are you going to stop smoking? . . . Is that the one that left yer wan and went off with the wee girl, the dirty oul' man, he should catch himself on . . . dear God, does anybody marry anyone before they live together, these days?'

There are long days, when it rains and we can't go out in the car, and time hangs heavy in the silence as we sit side by bored side in the kitchen. She scolds me when I come to bed late, and I lose my temper, pointing out that the only time I get to read newspapers or books is after she's gone to bed herself. I swell with pride that she has the confidence to take out her teeth and, without apologizing, hand them to me to steep. She cannot see, and does not know of, the day's detritus that is trapped in the gum shield: her parents died with all their own teeth, as did my father, because they died young, so she does not know of this thing.

More and more often now, I let her sleep the whole day away, the whole weekend away – apart from Saturday nights when the neighbours restore her to normality. She says it is a welcome relief to close her eyes to a world she cannot order, in which she cannot take part, where she cannot escape into the written word of the books she once read avidly. I say she's right to enjoy her sleep, and I seize the chance to read or nod off myself.

There are nights when she calls out to me and I ignore her, praying to myself, 'Please, baby Jesus, let her go back to sleep,' then I snap ashamedly awake to her urgent humble plea: 'I want to go to the toilet.' She sounds like a helpless child when she is forced to do that. I am learning to forgive myself my weaknesses, but that plea, to which I have so often reduced this helpless adult, my mother, is a killer. 'Please, baby Jesus' is the nearest I have come to asking anything of God, if there is one. I have no hesitation in praying to my mother's God, on her behalf.

When Sister Agatha died, she left instructions that I was to carry the ciborium to the altar during her funeral mass. The ciborium contains communion wafers, which Catholics hold to be the body of Christ. It is the highest honour that the Holy Men allow women. After the mass, my mother and I took our seats at the funeral feast among the nuns and bishops. My mother was pleased to be with this particular daughter in a gathering of the elite of the faith she practised. I wore the designer black frock I had bought for my mother's funeral. My mother laughed when I poured myself a glass of white wine that turned out to be apple juice. There would have been wine at a Holy Man's funeral feast, I said.

I thought, in the beginning, of killing my mother with an overdose of pills, then I worked out that, if I did, it would be more for my sake than hers because I could not cope with putting her into a nursing home. I did not want to face the fact that I was choosing my happiness over hers; my survival over hers. The decision not to kill her was the first truly grown-up choice I have ever made.

I do not expect, or want, to have romantic love again. It was powerful while it lasted, and I am glad that I knew it with as splendid a woman as Nuala sometimes was. It was impossible, I see now, to try to love anyone else so soon after breaking with her – culturally impossible, among other things, to find myself attempting and failing to say to another what I had said so recently to her. You cannot change religion overnight, unless you were mistaken from the beginning. I am no St Paul on the road to Damascus, and that story owes more to myth than fact.

Nonetheless, I could easily make the case for having two serious loves in the long lives that most of us now live. There will come a day when people will turn to each other and say, 'Thank you, darling, that was wonderful, but we are different people now to what we were and I must go and find another who suits my changed persona.'

It happens all the time.

I would not relish it happening to me. I like the life I lead now – one way or another I will write until I die – and would not welcome disturbance of precious routines and rhythms. I run an open house; I never know, when I return from Derry, what friend will be ensconced in the spare bedroom, but I know there will be no jealousies, or competition, or need for compromise. My friends fill the fridge and cook meals in an easy balance of power where I pay the mortgage and they have their own homes to go to, should there be a row. They oil the social wheels, an art in which I continue to be alarmingly deficient, and we go out of the house in enthusiastic search of ordinary pleasures. My family come and go as they please, though three days of the young sprawled with their

420

friends before the television set is the limit. They have talked me through Eminem and *Sex and the City*. I am free to look after my mother and rediscover Derry in the talk of the neighbours – a return to that beloved home place which has imprinted all my days.

It would seem that all my battles, in love and war, are now over. The menopause has gone, for which, much thanks. Never again will I wake up in the morning to plot, before I get out of bed, whom I will attack that day. The hormones, too, have gone into abeyance, for which I am grateful, but that relief has brought other problems: when food poisoning struck me recently, and I was alone and frightened in the middle of the night, I did not much value the solitude. I turned sixty on 28 March 2004, and I am just about able to cope with that. I have been called many things in my life, but nobody has ever called me sixty. I hate that moment where an acquaintance fondly rubs the speck of dirt off my face and I have to point out the speck is an age freckle, one of millions which disfigure my gorgeous face and hands.

When Mary Holland, the journalist of our times, fell gravely ill, I took up swimming. She died on 7 June 2004, at the young age of sixty-eight. I have lost a stone and eat fruit and green vegetables every day. I am determined to be fit for the future: I have to go to Argentina to learn the tango and go to a Dublin dance studio first to learn how to throw a few shapes (just enough to cause an initial sensation when I hit the floor in nightclubs – first impressions are so important). I will buy a jukebox and have rock and roll at the push of a button. I am ready now to play all those operas and classical music records that I got from Reader's Digest. I will have three days a week to read books. I will sit out in the front yard, which I share with my neighbour Gregg – whose parents bought him a brand-new cooker for his birthday. Gregg can cook. I can bang on his front door in the wee small hours if I need a drink from his well-stocked shelves – alas, I am still at the stage where I finish any bottle I open, so I seldom keep bottles in my own house.

Romance would intrude on all that. As the English officer said of World War II: 'The noise, my dear, the confusion.'

I think now, looking back, that Nuala and I outstayed our

welcome to each other because we both feared a return to the separate worlds we had so gladly abandoned. She feared loneliness and that worm in the heart of feminism which she called loving a man. I feared a return to the lesbian ghetto, and the social exclusion that came from engaging as a Northerner with the South in which I lived.

This book might take the fear of that word 'lesbian' out of me. It might undo my mother. It might undo me. It might undo such social and professional standing as I have, given its demand that I am embraced for all that I am. I will soon know from readers how I am doing with them. I will know how I am doing with myself when I go out to talk about it. I am free now, perhaps free-falling.

I am, anyway, in the eyes of the state, already a threat. The government, citing objections by the Department of Defence, has refused to release the files it has kept on me all these years. Actually, there are only four files, short reports compiled in April 1971, the month when the Irishwomen's Liberation Movement took the Contraceptive Train to Belfast. Release of the files would compromise the defence, security and safety of the State, the government says. Me? A threat – still – to the bond between Catholic Church and State that once defined and stifled this country? How right they are: we're all feminists now.

Mary Maher told me recently that during a consciousness-raising session in that same year, 1971, each woman was asked to say what she liked about herself, and that I said, 'I can always make myself laugh.' I was delighted to be reminded. If I was born lesbian, I was also born optimistic. The Catholic Church has said of people like me that we are 'intrinsically disordered'. I think that is just about right. I find the social order under which people live globally to be intrinsically out of true, still, in all regards, but, exhilaratingly, I have found that it has changed, slowly, for the better, in my adult lifetime. The best is yet to come. While we await that glorious day, the sensible response is to laugh and be a disorderly woman.

Index

NM stands for Nell McCafferty throughout. Subheadings are in chronological order, with some in alphabetical order where appropriate. Entry for Nell McCafferty is also arranged in subject paragraphs.

McAuley, Róisín 79

McBrearty family 17–18

MacBride, Seán 231

McCafferty, Carmel: childhood 6, 72; visit to Queen's University 75–6; lending NM clothes 131–2; meets Vincent Hanna 149; during Battle of the Bogside 165, 172; British army interested in 243; on Bloody Sunday 259, 262, 263; staying in Dublin 280; hairdressing business 293–4; and NM's sexuality 304–5; wedding 309; death of father 315; visits to NM 389–90; and mother in nursing home 415

McCafferty, Gráinne 143, 155, 227, 241, 262, 263, 304, 415–16

McCafferty, Hugh (NM's brother): childhood 6, 42; work 72; married 95, 113, 114–15, 134, 140–41; family row 315

McCafferty, Hugh (NM's father): courtship and marriage to Lily 8, 47, 48–9; during NM's childhood 14, 14–15, 15, 29, 31–2, 35–6, 36, 40, 42; erects a clothesline 39–40; and money 40–41; work 17, 40, 42–3; workshop 42; and death of John Duffy 63; and daughters going to dances 64–6; and NM's sexuality 1, 64; and NM at university 77, 79; and NM's move to London 117; strokes 135–6; during Battle of the Bogside 166, 172; trips in NM's car 291–2; sore thumb 308–9; and Carmel's wedding 309; death 314–15

McCafferty, Joe 23

McCafferty, Lily (NM's mother) 414; childhood 45, 46; as surrogate mother 4, 46–7, 114; courtships and marriage 47–9; miscarriage 5;

at weekly gatherings 26, 27, 28; spending 41; new kitchen 41–2; and older brother Brian 5–6, 8; and death of nephew John 62; and NM's friends 69; and NM at university 77, 79–80; and NM's pupils 94, 114; and NM during Six Day War 108; visits Bishop Farren about job for NM 113–14; marching 135; and children's marriages 406–7; member of LLP 136, 141–2; during Battle of the Bogside 165, 172; and Bernadette Devlin 194, 232, 233–4, 238; counselling 204–6; letters to NM 212, 213, 218, 227–8, 232–4, 317; on Bloody Sunday 262–3; and army raids on house 286–7, 288; worried for NM 304, 305; and death of husband 315, 316; discovers pleasures of reading 316; vanity 316–17; and Pope's visit to Dublin 322, 323; and NM's sexuality 1, 8–9, 339, 340; rings NM after Enniskillen 378; stroke 380–81; eightieth birthday 384–5; at NM's cottage 392; ninetieth birthday 408; illness 3–4, 9, 391, 393, 414–15; in a nursing home 415–16; NM living with 416, 416–20

McCafferty, Mary 22

McCafferty, Michael 142–3, 155, 227, 262, 263, 304

McCafferty, Muireanna see Friel, Muireanna

McCafferty, Nell:
childhood 10–15; bicycle 43; Christmas crossword 37; Christmas pantomime 19–20; cowboy outfit 24; day trips to the seaside 28–30; friends 20–21,

release of Bernadette 207–212; visits to Derry 234, 235–6; introduction of internment 239; shooting of William McGreanery 242; approached by Goulding 251, 252; Bloody Sunday 257, 260–66; invited to America 270–71, 272; reaction to killing of Ranger Best 274–5; fear of being killed 282–3; raids by British army 285–8; prisoners in Northern jails 324–5; supporting women in Armagh Prison 326–9, 330, 341–3; death of hunger strikers 347–8; on the IRA 374–6, 376; Enniskillen bombing and after 377–9; Provisional IRA declare ceasefire 395; talking to loyalists 410

and the women's movement 133, 422; founding of Irishwomen's Liberation Movement 201–2, 220; on the *Late Late Show* 217; 'Contraceptive Train' demonstration 221–2, 223–7; picketing the Dáil 228; social work in Ballymun 229; engages in consciousness raising 232, 422; WMLI 246; speaking on women's issues 246, 247, 248, 293; helping others 296–7; Irishwomen United 293, 295, 298, 300, 301, 343; actions for women's rights 299–300; helping Mary 310–313; Reclaim the Night march 318–20; abortion issue 357, 358; dangers of activism 358–9; Kerry Babies case 369–370; Mary Robinson's presidential campaign 386–8

McCafferty, Nuala 6, 95; working 72; has cancer 89; LLP member and voluntary work 127, 141–2; missing 149; during Battle of the Bogside 165, 172; on Bloody Sunday 262; during strikes 290; death of father 315; and Pope's visit to Dublin 322; and NM's sexuality 339, 340; caring for mother 385, 414

McCafferty, Paddy 6, 72, 81, 241, 315

McCallion, Carmel *see* McCafferty, Carmel

McCann, Eamonn: NM first notices 68; at Queen's University 74, 77–8, 80–81; leaves for England 81; and CAC 125–6; and LLP 115, 127, 141, 161, 162; and NM 130, 143, 163; and Mary Holland 132, 143, 170, 178–9, 197; and Belfast to Derry march 1969 142, 149, 152; Radio Free Derry 151; 1969 general election 154, 155; during Battle of the Bogside 163, 165, 169, 174; and CDA 175, 176, 177, 179; training in warfare 179–80; mission to Omagh 188–9; candidate in UK general election 194; and release of Bernadette Devlin from prison 207, 208–9, 210–211; and satirical revue by Mac Anna 249–50; reaction to Bloody Sunday 264; sends NM flowers 399

McCartan, Pat 311

McClenaghan, Dermie 116, 126, 149, 152, 168–9, 176–7

McCloskey, Frank 161

McCool, Thomas 195

McCutcheon, Mary 203

McDaid, Michael 263, 264, 266

McDevitt, Miss 57

MacEntee, Paddy 311